'The scope of economic crimes are unparalleled in modern times, particularly with the rise of the Internet and online financial services. This work provides an excellent approach to understand these offenses, and the individuals responsible. It is essential reading for professionals and the academy'.

Thomas Holt, School of Criminal Justice at
Michigan State University, USA

'This volume makes a convincing case for an offense-based approach to the category of economic crimes, ranging from corporate cartels and money laundering, to counterfeiting, industrial espionage and intellectual property crime. It provides an encompassing overview of these crimes as well as a highly up-to-date and integrated discussion of national, transnational and private policing of economic crimes. An accessible and well-written introduction that is useful to anyone interested in understanding the character and harmfulness of crimes in the context of global business, as well as in the design of smart prevention strategies'.

Judith van Erp, Professor of Regulatory Governance,
Utrecht University, The Netherlands

'This is a very helpful compendium to guide private and public sector practitioners and scholars through a rapidly evolving field of theory and action, and a clarion call for more serious evidence-based resourcing and policy attention to a range of economic crimes'.

Michael Levi, Professor of Criminology, Cardiff University

'This book delivers on the case for economic criminology! In an engaging and accessible style, it walks the reader through the complexity of the types, causes and consequences of economic crimes. Effectively balancing theory and practice, and not shying away from critical definitional issues, it is chock full of illustrative and provocative examples. Button, Hock and Shepherd have created a strong foundation for students, scholars, policy makers and practitioners to further advance this critical yet understudied area of criminology'.

Jeremy M. Wilson, Professor, School of Criminal Justice,
Michigan State University, US

'This is a go-to text for understanding the latest patterns in the fast-evolving area of economic crime. The authors combine analytical clarity with an entertaining readable style, providing fascinating insights into an area that is under-researched despite being an increasingly present part of our lives'.

Elizabeth Dávid-Barrett, Professor of Governance and
Integrity, University of Sussex

Economic Crime

This book is the first attempt to establish 'economic crime' as a new sub-discipline within criminology. Fraud, corruption, bribery, money laundering, price-fixing cartels and intellectual property crimes pursued typically for financial and professional gain, have devastating consequences for the prosperity of economic life. While most police forces in the UK and the USA have an 'economic crime' department, and many European bodies such as Europol use the term and develop strategies and structures to deal with it, it is yet to gain traction as a widely used term in the academic community. *Economic Crime: From Conception to Response* aims to change that and covers:

- definitions of the key premises of economic crime as the academic sub-discipline within criminology;
- an overview of the key research on each of the crimes associated with economic crime;
- public, private and global responses to economic crime across its different forms and sectors of the economy, both within the UK and globally.

This book is an essential resource for students, academics and practitioners engaged with aspects of economic crime, as well as the related areas of financial crime, white-collar crime and crimes of the powerful.

Mark Button is Professor of Criminology and Director of the Centre for Counter Fraud Studies at the University of Portsmouth, UK.

Branislav Hock is a senior lecturer in Economic Crime at the School of Criminology and Criminal Justice, University of Portsmouth, UK.

David Shepherd is a senior lecturer in Economic Crime at the School of Criminology and Criminal Justice, University of Portsmouth, UK.

Global Issues in Crime and Justice

For more information about this series, please visit: https://www.routledge.com/
Global-Issues-in-Crime-and-Justice/book-series/GICJ

Economic Crime

From Conception to Response

Mark Button, Branislav Hock and David Shepherd

Routledge
Taylor & Francis Group

LONDON AND NEW YORK

Cover image: © Yulia Reznikov / Getty Images

First published 2022
by Routledge
4 Park Square, Milton Park, Abingdon, Oxon OX14 4RN

and by Routledge
605 Third Avenue, New York, NY 10158

Routledge is an imprint of the Taylor & Francis Group, an informa business

British Library Cataloguing-in-Publication Data
A catalogue record for this book is available from the British Library

Library of Congress Cataloging-in-Publication Data
Names: Button, Mark, author. | Hock, Branislav, author. |
Shepherd, David (David William James), author.
Title: Economic crime : from conception to response / Mark Button,
Branislav Hock and David Shepherd.
Description: Abingdon, Oxon ; New York, NY : Routledge, 2022. |
Series: Global issues in crime and justice |
Includes bibliographical references and index. |
Identifiers: LCCN 2021052831 | ISBN 9780367533861 (hardback) |
ISBN 9780367533878 (paperback) | ISBN 9781003081753 (ebook)
Subjects: LCSH: Commercial crimes. | White collar crimes. |
Crime–Economic aspects.
Classification: LCC HV6768 .B87 2022 | DDC 364.16/8–dc23/eng/20220106
LC record available at https://lccn.loc.gov/2021052831

ISBN: 978-0-367-53386-1 (hbk)
ISBN: 978-0-367-53387-8 (pbk)
ISBN: 978-1-003-08175-3 (ebk)

DOI: 10.4324/9781003081753

Typeset in Times New Roman
by Newgen Publishing UK

Contents

Figures

Tables

About the authors

Mark Button, Director of the Centre for Counter Fraud Studies, University of Portsmouth, has written extensively on counter fraud, cyber-fraud and private policing issues, publishing many articles, chapters and completing ten books, including his two latest: *Private Policing* and *Cyber Frauds, Scams and their Victims*, both published by Routledge. Some of the most significant research projects include a Home Office-funded study on victims of computer misuse, leading the research on behalf of the National Fraud Authority and ACPO on fraud victims. Mark has also worked on four Government's Annual Cyber Security Breaches Survey.

Branislav Hock, a senior lecturer in Economic Crime, University of Portsmouth, has been involved in a broad range of research, teaching and consultancy activities, many of which have been related to money laundering, anti-corruption, tax evasion and compliance. He is an author of *Extraterritoriality and International Bribery: A Collective Action Perspective*, Routledge 2020. Hock supervises doctoral and master projects in the areas of international corruption and money laundering. Branislav is the founding member of the European Compliance Center.

David Shepherd, is a senior lecturer in Economic Crime, University of Portsmouth. Following a career in product and process engineering, David moved into research, focusing on white-collar crime, fraud and corruption. Using quantitative and qualitative methods, David's research encompasses organisational characteristics and compliance, offender behaviour, security and justice. David is also a co-author of *Commercial Fraud and Cyber Fraud: A Legal Guide to Justice for Businesses*, published by Bloomsbury.

Acknowledgements

A book such as this involving three authors is built upon many years of research and numerous previous outputs. Many of those journal articles, chapters and books involved other authors, not involved in this book. It is therefore important to acknowledge these, who over many years have helped not only in the completion of research projects but also in helping to develop and test ideas; some of which have found their way into this book. The list of fellow authors includes Dean Blackbourn, Graham Brooks, Jim Gee, Paul Gilmour, Richard Kapend, Chris Lewis, Peter Stiernstedt, Lisa Sugiura, Jacki Tapley, Alison Wakefield and Victoria Wang.

The research this book is built upon could not have happened without the participation of victims, enforcement agencies, policy makers and members of the public. Many have given up valuable time and shared sometimes painful accounts. There are far too many to name, but all those who have helped must be thanked.

Many of these projects required funding and it is important to thank some of the principal funders of some of our work: Crowe, EPSRC, Home Office, Intellectual Property Office, Ipsos/MORI, and Nuffield Foundation to name some.

The team from Taylor and Francis who first accepted the idea for this book and then helped in the completion of this project must also be thanked, particularly Thomas Sutton and Jessica Phillips, as well as the anonymous reviewers.

A project such as this also takes up much time, many hours beyond the contracted working week, and for this reason, families must be thanked for the patience and support they have shown while we have worked on this project.

Abbreviations

ABC	anti-bribery compliance programmes
ACC	Australian Competition & Consumer Commission
ACFE	Association of Certified Fraud Examiners
AML	anti-money laundering
BHRA	British Horse Racing Authority
BTP	British Transport Police
CDSC	Company Development and Selection Committee
CFCD	Counter Fraud, Compliance and Debt
CMA	Competition and Markets Authority
CPS	Crown Prosecution Service
CRO	Civil Recovery Orders
CSEW	Crime Survey for England and Wales
DCPCU	Dedicated Card and Payment Crime Unit
DDoS	distributed denial of service attacks
DMCA	Digital Millennium Copyright Act
DOJ	Department of Justice
DPA	deferred prosecution agreement
DWP	Department for Work and Pensions
EPPO	European Public Prosecutor's Office
EU	European Union
EUIPO	European Union Intellectual Property Office
FACT	Federation Against Copyright Theft
FATF	Financial Action Task Force
FBI	Federal Bureau of Investigations
FCA	Financial Conduct Authority
FCPA	Foreign Corrupt Practices Act
FCTC	Framework Convention on Tobacco Control
FIFA	Fédération Internationale de Football Association
FSA	Food Standards Agency
FTC	Federal Trade Commission
GDPR	General Data Protection Regulation

GI	geographical indications
GRECO	Group of States Against Corruption
GTRI	General Trade-Related Index of Counterfeiting
HMG	Her Majesty's Government
HMICFRS	Her Majesty's Inspectorate of Constabulary, Fire and Rescue Services
HMRC	Her Majesty's Revenue and Customs
IACC	International Anti-Corruption Coordination Centre
ICC	International Chamber of Commerce
ICCACU	International Cricket Council Anti-Corruption Unit
ICT	information communication technology
ICU	International Corruption Unit
IFED	Insurance Fraud Enforcement Department
IP	Intellectual Property
IPO	Intellectual Property Office
IRS	Internal Revenue Service
JMLIT	Joint Money Laundering Intelligence Taskforce
MDP	Ministry of Defence Police
MLR	Money Laundering Regulations
MPS	Metropolitan Police Service
MTIC	Missing Trader Intra-Community Fraud
NAEA	National Association of Estate Agents
NCA	National Crime Agency
NCCT	Non-Cooperative Countries and Territories
NECC	National Economic Crime Centre
NFIB	National Fraud Intelligence Bureau
NGO	Non-Governmental Organisation
NHS	National Health Service
NPA	non-prosecution agreement
NPCC	National Police Chiefs' Council
OCG	Organised Crime Group
OECD	Organisation for Economic Co-operation and Development
OLAF	European Anti-Fraud Office
ONS	Office for National Statistics
OPBAS	Office of Professional Body Anti-Money Laundering Supervision
PIC	Private International Cartel
PIPCU	Police Intellectual Property Crime Unit
POCA	Proceeds of Crime Act
ROCU	Regional Organised Crime Units
RRD	Rolls Royce Deutschland
SAR	suspicious activity report
SEC	Securities and Exchange Commission

SFO	Serious Fraud Office
SME	small and medium-sized enterprises
SRA	Solicitors Regulation Authority
TECAS	Tackling Economic Crime Awards
TFEU	Treaty on the Functioning of the European Union
TIU	Tennis Integrity Unit
TRIPS	Trade-Related Aspects of Intellectual Property Rights
UKFIU	UK Financial Intelligence Unit
UNCAC	United Nations Convention Against Corruption
UNTOC	United Nations Convention Against Transnational Organized Crime
UWO	Unexplained Wealth Orders
WCO	World Customs Organization
WHO	World Health Organization
WIPO	World Intellectual Property Organization
WTO	World Trade Organization

Chapter 1

Economic crime and economic criminology

Introduction

In the midst of the summer of 2021, Boris Johnson's government in the UK published a crime plan (Home Office, 2021). A few days earlier the Office for National Statistics (ONS) had released the latest crime statistics from the Crime Survey for England and Wales (CSEW). This had shown a 36% increase in fraud and computer misuse offences, which now accounted for the clear majority of crimes – 6.3 million of the 11.1 million estimated crimes (ONS, 2021). One would have expected a flourish of media interest and comment on the plan, particularly as it contained a whole chapter on fraud and online offences, on what the impact on fraud might be. The media, however, were much more interested in other aspects of the plan:

> "Boris Johnson pledges to target crime and anti-social behaviour" – *BBC News*

> "Freed burglars to wear 24-hour tags under Prime Minister's Crime Crackdown" – *Telegraph*

> "Thieves tagged 24-hours a day and crooks forced to clean streets in crime crackdown" – *Express*

Typical of much of the commentary was the focus on aspects of the plan dedicated to traditional crime problems. Given the plan included replacing Action Fraud (with a new reporting system) – an organisation steeped in controversy in the UK, this might seem doubly surprising.[1] This typifies the media's attitude to economic crime: apathy unless a story contains sensationalist infotainment value (Levi, 2006; van Erp, 2013).

Apathy is not restricted to just journalists: economic crime has attracted little serious attention in academia and policing practice. While the study of traditional volume crimes such as robbery, burglary and theft have received a great deal of attention by criminologists, economic crimes such as fraud and bribery have largely been ignored (Brooks, 2016; Levi, 2008a; Rider, 2015a). Be it the

DOI: 10.4324/9781003081753-1

complexity of these crimes or an erroneous perception that economic crimes are victimless crimes, academics and practitioners have not paid sufficient attention to the unique practical and theoretical problems of economic crimes. *Economic Crime: From Conception to Response* fills this gap by introducing the origins and development of economic crime as a subject of social science research.

This chapter explores the term 'white-collar crime', the traditional home for the study of most economic crimes, and the term 'corruption', and illustrates their strengths and theoretical and practical limitations for the study of contemporary economic crime problems. The chapter then builds the case for the concept of economic crime, constructing its key components, definition and offering insights into the origin of the crime. The link to corruption – which has attracted more interest amongst scholars and practitioners – is also explored. The chapter will then argue that economic crime deserves far more attention, setting out the case for what the authors call 'economic criminology', a new paradigm within criminological research, study and practice. The chapter will end by outlining the rest of the book.

White-collar crime and corruption

White-collar crime

White-collar crime has become the 'lingua franca' for encapsulating many of the economic crimes that will be considered in this book. It is not a legal term for a specific offence: a person cannot be charged with white-collar crime. Rather, it is a social science concept originally coined by Edwin Sutherland, a prominent American criminologist:

> White-collar crime may be defined approximately as a crime committed by a person of respectability and high social status in the course of his occupation.
>
> (Sutherland, 1949, p. 9)

Sutherland (1940) devised the phrase to represent a group, or typology, of offending behaviours that share common offender and contextual characteristics:

- White-collar criminals are respectable offenders.
- Their offences involve an abuse of trust.
- Their criminal activities are integrated into their professional work routines.

Sutherland sought to bring attention to the hidden financial crimes and immoral practices of corporations and the professional elite, including fraud, bribery, false advertising, price-fixing and intellectual property crime. In doing so, he exposed the stark contrast in attitudes towards white-collar crimes and the physical 'street' crimes of violence, vandalism and theft. He noticed how policymakers, criminal enforcement agencies and academics paid scant regard to the very substantial crimes of the wealthy, preferring to focus their efforts on the far more modest crimes of the disadvantaged. He argued with some passion that the immunity of white-collar criminals to prosecution is due to class bias in the courts and the power of the privileged class to influence the administration of the law (Sutherland, 1940). This led to his central conclusion that the propensity to commit crime is essentially the same in the upper and lower classes, but the types of crimes differ due to opportunity.

Edwin Sutherland's original concept was not just concerned with financial crimes. It also encompassed financially motivated physical crimes, such as labour abuses, health and safety violations, environmental harms and even financially motivated war crimes (Friedrichs, 2002, 2010; Sutherland, 1945, 1983). Sutherland used the crime label loosely so as to include non-criminal wrongdoing, which was typically handled by regulatory authorities or litigated through the civil courts, but which he believed should be regarded as criminal and prosecuted as crimes.

Debates about the definition and scope of white-collar crime have continued since Sutherland coined the term (Geis, 2016). Arguments and definitions have emerged that either narrow or expand its typological scope. Some maintain a purely legalistic view, that the term white-collar crime should only be applied to acts which have been prosecuted and proven in criminal courts (Tappan, 1947). Others have a completely contrary view, claiming that the acts are matters for regulators, not the criminal courts (Dinitz, 1977). Shapiro (1990) argues that the concept's narrow focus on the *offender*, the respectable professional, hinders our understanding of the *offence*. Shapiro called for the concept to be liberated from the constraints of the offender's characteristics in order to focus research attention on the deviant behaviour. She maintained that the defining characteristic of white-collar crime is the abuse of trust element of Sutherland's concept (ibid.).

Later academics followed Shapiro's call to focus on the offence and expanded the scope of white-collar crime to include 'blue collar' and non-occupational offenders who commit fraud (Weisburd et al., 1994, 2001). From a feminist criminology perspective, Daly (1989) argued that Sutherland's definition is gender biased because corporate white-collar workers are predominantly men. Daly broadened the concept to include anyone, including blue-collar workers and unemployed persons, who violate trust or commit fraud. Some commentators have criticised this downward trajectory that trivialises white-collar crime and ignores the importance of power that is integral and central to the concept (Pontell, 2016). It is also somewhat absurd to, in effect, excise the 'white-collar' part of the concept so that all we are left with is 'crime'.

A key problem that Pontell (2016) alludes to is that many academics have struggled to find a conceptual home for their research into the non-physical, financially motivated criminality of offenders who are not 'white collar'. As a consequence, instead of developing an appropriate framework, they have followed Shapiro's lead and corrupted the white-collar concept to conveniently squeeze their work into the white-collar scholarship.

In an attempt to develop a unified meaning, the White Collar Crime Center in the USA commissioned a group of academics to develop a definition. Their formulation describes the offence as criminal or unethical (i.e. non-criminal) and a violation of trust, the offender as an organisation or a high-status individual and the context as occupational (Cliff & Desilets, 2014, p. 487):

> Illegal or unethical acts that violate fiduciary responsibility of public trust, committed by an individual or organization, usually during the course of legitimate occupational activity, by persons of high or respectable social status for personal or organizational gain.

However, illustrating how readily people abandon the definition, Cliff and Desilets (2014) immediately introduced terrorism and romance fraud as examples of white-collar crime, yet neither crime exhibits fiduciary responsibility, public trust, legitimate occupational activity or respectable persons.

Corruption

Compared to white-collar crime, corruption is an even more slippery concept to define. There is, as Gorta (2006) points out, no universally accepted definition of corruption. A major problem with the concept is that it means very different things to different people in different contexts. Some see 'corruption' as a form of large social inequality, and when politics and law-making produce unfair and ineffective laws (see Chapter 3). Others view corruption as a fluid concept because it is highly dependent on local cultural norms and laws (Brooks, 2016; Eicher, 2012; Fletcher & Herrmann, 2012; Hough, 2013). For example, Guanxi is a central cultural idea in China that refers to the networks of personal relationships that enable members to support each other (Zhoa & Ha-Brookshire, 2018). It allows members of a social network to expect assistance of favours from other members. This expectation to provide mutual assistance permeates Chinese society and is an inherent component of commerce in China (Zhuang et al., 2010). From a Western ethical perspective, Guanxi bears the hallmarks of corruption, but such an accusation might be rejected by Chinese people as it is so rooted in their culture (Graycar & Prenzler, 2013).

Corruption is frequently used synonymously with bribery, mainly because bribery is the most recognisable, and probably the most frequent, species of corruption. However, as Chapter 3 explains, corruption is a typological collection of crimes, and bribery is just one of them. The typology varies widely in the literature, variously including bribery, conflict of interest, clientelism, cronyism, extortion, favouritism, fraud, nepotism, political lobbying, state capture, theft, trading in influence, vote rigging and others (Graycar & Smith, 2011; Langseth, 2006; OECD, 2014; Transparency International, 2011). This list of offences illustrates a perceptual problem with the definition of corruption. It encompasses such a broad range of offences that it is difficult to identify the core concepts or characteristics that coherently link them: how is physical theft associated with nepotism and vote rigging?

The features that unify 'corruption offences' are the characteristics of the offender and the underlying behaviour of the offender. Transparency International (n.d.) defines corruption as 'the abuse of entrusted power for private gain'. There are variations on the TI definition, for example, the OECD (2014) defines it as the 'abuse of public or private office for personal gain'. These definitions reveal the three key attributes of corruption:

- At least one offender in any corrupt event holds a position of power and trust.
- Their offences involve an abuse of that entrusted power.
- Their criminal activities are integrated into their occupational work routines.

Applying this conceptual construction to theft, we see that not all theft is corruption. Theft is only a type of corruption when, for example, the offender is a rogue politician who steals state assets. The core attributes of corruption suggest it is very close to Sutherland's white-collar crime concept. However, there are important conceptual differences, which in turn lead to a different, though overlapping typology. Firstly, whereas white-collar crime predominantly focuses on the private sector, corruption includes the illicit activities of those entrusted with power in both the private and public sectors. Secondly, whereas the dominant underlying motivation in white collar is financial, corruption is also concerned with political power. The study of corruption is particularly interested in the grand and political corruption of the ruling elites who use corruption as a tool to achieve and maintain their political power as well as their wealth (Fletcher & Hermann, 2012; see Chapter 3). Thirdly, corruption encompasses lower status public officials in positions of relatively modest power such as corrupt police officers and customs officers who abuse their occupational positions of public trust.

Financial crime

'Financial crime' is another common term which has grown in use to describe white-collar and economic type crimes. It has tended to be used to cover fraud and money-laundering offences and has gradually been expanding in scope to cover acts such as bribery (Levi, 2015). There are clear overlaps with economic crime, but the term's weakness for the authors is that 'financial' could clearly imply all acquisitive crime that leads to a financial benefit. It is too broad. As this chapter will shortly illustrate, the benefit of 'economic' over financial is that it limits the scope of activities, more clearly excluding crimes such as burglary, which are based upon force.

Economic crime and deviance

Economic crime, white-collar crime and corruption

All the above discussion illustrates the lack of consensus around the definition of white-collar crime and corruption, the limitations of these concepts and their elasticity. Our conception of economic crime respects and builds upon the discussion of white-collar crime and corruption. The power of Sutherland's formulation in bringing attention to the criminality of respectable professionals during the course of their work should be respected. By creating a conceptual framework under the banner 'economic crime', this book respects Sutherland's formulation whilst avoiding its constraints. Taking the cue from Daly (1989) and Shapiro (1990), economic crime is conceptualised around the core characteristics of the offence rather than the attributes of the offenders. More specifically, it focuses on the group of offences which share characteristics under the 'economic crime' umbrella irrespective of the status of the offender or the occupational context of the crimes. The core characteristics common to all economic crimes are financial motivation and secretive deception.

Turning to the influence of corruption, from one perspective, the concept provides a means to address broad questions of fairness, morality and legitimacy of existing societal systems and institutions. From another perspective, corruption is a broad typology of offences and wrongs involving the abuse of entrusted power for private gain (see Chapter 3). The latter, more conventional understanding of the term 'corruption' informs the discussion about economic crime in that many, but not all, economic crimes do exhibit abuse of trust, just as some corruption and white-collar crime offences involve deception.

Like white-collar crime, a key issue with the economic crime label is that it is not a specified offence in law; rather it is a social science concept and a typology of offences that exhibit the financial motivation and deception characteristics. Furthermore, the 'crime' label does not reflect the many deviant acts which are often classified as civil torts or regulatory breaches instead of crimes. However, as Sutherland (1949) argued in relation to white-collar crime, the importance is not the judicial process or outcome, but whether such behaviours should be regarded as crimes and subject to criminal laws.

The 'crime' label has also become increasingly nebulous in the international context because jurisdictions differ significantly in the treatment of prohibited behaviours (see Chapter 11). Consider, for example, the transborder cartel activity whereby corporations illegally conspire to fix product prices. In this area, the EU, its Member States and the UK enforce antitrust rules by imposing non-criminal, administrative sanctions on corporations based on Article 101 of the Treaty on the Functioning of the European Union (TFEU). On the other hand, national criminal enforcement is used against individuals who break the antitrust laws (Whelan, 2012). This is very different from the US antitrust enforcement regime: the Sherman Act (1890) gives the Department of Justice (DOJ) the authority to bring criminal charges against both corporations and individuals (see Chapter 4). To overcome these definitional problems, this book deliberately follows Sutherland's practice in applying 'crime' to deviant behaviour as well as acts specified as criminal in law.

As Tappan (1947) explicated, a final issue associated with the economic crime term, and indeed with all types of crime, arises from the rule of law (see Chapter 10). Justice systems demand that egregious acts are independently examined by authorised bodies before they can be labelled crimes, regulatory breaches or civil wrongs. The courts and the regulators ultimately decide whether a wrongdoing has occurred and whether a defendant is a wrongdoer. In addition, independent police services identify and record all incidents which they believe qualify as crimes (Maguire & McVie, 2017). However, as only a tiny fraction of economic crime incidents catch the attention of the authorities, applying these legal constraints would severely restrict the study of economic crime because it would appear to be a minor crime problem and unworthy of attention. To overcome this problem, practitioners and academics alike have to make conceptual adjustments in order to accommodate all events where there would be a prima facie case for criminal, civil or regulatory justice if they were detected and presented to the authorities.

To summarise this section, by avoiding the constraints of occupational position, social status, abuse of trust and proven criminality as defining characteristics, and by focusing on financially motivated deceptive behaviour, economic crime has a distinct conceptual role with significant advantages in enabling broad lines of coherent sociological enquiry into behaviour, social structures, institutions, prevention and enforcement practices.

Ubiquity of 'economic crime'

In recognising the case for 'economic crime', it is also important to acknowledge the growing ubiquity of the term. 'Economic crime' has become more common in the lexicon of policymakers, law enforcement and academics in the UK and beyond. The premier conference in this field in the world organised by Professor Barry Rider, 'The Cambridge International Symposium on Economic Crime', has run since 1982 using 'economic crime' as the central banner. The UK government has an economic crime plan (Home Office, 2019). Furthermore, the National Crime Agency hosts the National Economic Crime Centre (NECC), the Crown Prosecution Service has an economic crime strategy (see HM Treasury & Home Office, 2021). Economic crime has become one of the most common terms used to describe specialist police units that focus on fraud, money laundering and cyber-enabled offences in the UK. Button et al. (2015) found that 41 out of 48 police forces in the UK had some form of specialist unit dealing with economic crimes, and of these 29 at the time had economic crime in the title. At a global level, the United Nations Office on Drugs and Crime (UNODC) has a 'Corruption and Economic Crime Branch', the Council of Europe has an 'Economic Crime and Co-operation Division' and Europol has a 'European Financial and Economic Crime Centre'. Several other countries also use the term, such as Sweden's 'Economic Crime Authority' and Nigeria's 'Economic and Financial Crimes Commission' to name some.

Economic crime and the economy

The term 'economic', which is the social science term concerned with the production, distribution and consumption of goods and services, provides the foundations for considering the crimes and wrongs in this book. Most frauds occur within the supply and consumption of goods and services; corruption is often associated with purchasing; money-laundering lurks in the shadows of the financial outputs from the production, distribution and consumption of goods and services; intellectual property crime is associated with the production, distribution and consumption of goods and services; and market manipulation is a form of economic market failure. Most, but not all, the crimes and wrongs considered in this book largely occur *through* the production, distribution and consumption of goods and services, whereas most, but not all, traditional volume crimes are physical crimes that occur through normal social life. Table 1.1 provides examples that illustrate the distinction.

There are of course traditional volume crimes that also link to the economy, shoplifting is a prime example. However, physical acquisitive crimes are excluded from our conceptualisation of deceptive economic crime. The essence of the crimes and wrongs that will be considered in this book is that they are anchored within the economic system, the operation of the market and the financial systems. These economic features provide the foundation for the development of our definition of economic crime in the next section. Some crimes, such as corporate cartel offences, sit at the heart of the market economy. Others are more peripheral, for example, person-to-person identity fraud, but they are nevertheless included because many of their forms are financially motivated crimes of deception that exploit the financial systems.

Table 1.1 The context of volume crimes

Crime	Conduct	Context
Burglary	Homeowner returns from holiday to discover house has been burgled	Social, physical
Robbery	Teenager with expensive mobile phone mugged by gang who steal it	Social, physical
Car theft	Car parked in street stolen by gang of car thieves	Social, physical
Fraud	Family purchase holiday online and later discover the website is fake Mobile phone shop experiences customers with false identity purchase phones who then disappear never to pay again	Economic supply and consumption
Bribery	Buyer in company seeking to secure a supply of fleet of vehicles takes bribe to favour one car dealership	Economic supply and consumption
Cartel price-fixing	Three manufacturers with very large market share agree to increase prices of their products	Economic production
Money laundering	A drug cartel uses a professional enabler to hide the true nature of crime proceeds and purchase with them legitimate assets	Economic supply and consumption

Economic crime and existing definitions

Whilst white-collar crime can be traced back to the USA and Sutherland's works of the 1940s, the notion of 'economic crime' has its origins in Europe where economic or business crimes are distinguished from other crime types because they are subject to separate legal treatment in law (Leigh, 1980, p. ix; Levi, 2015). The common law systems of the Anglo-Saxon world are less familiar with this compartmentalised approach. However, despite the strong legal origins of the term, Leigh (1980) offered no definition of economic crime. Indeed, searching academic outputs that have explored economic crime very few have provided coherent definitions that distinguish it from white-collar crime. For example, Dinitz (1977) set out to provide a detailed definition of economic crime based on deception, concealment and secrecy. Although these characteristics are apposite for economic crime, Dinitz's definition is unhelpful as it is grounded in Edelhertz's (1970) earlier definition of white-collar crime. Furthermore, in direct opposition to Sutherland, Dinitz (1977) argued that deviant business behaviour is not a crime problem, rather it is a matter of appropriate regulation.

Perhaps the first significant attempt at a definition can be traced back to the 8th Conference of European Ministers of Justice held in Stockholm in 1973, which discussed economic crime and led to the 12th Conference of Directors of Criminological Research to discuss the 'criminological aspects of economic crime'. Their work focused on the crimes of business, which impacted on the efficiency of the European economy. It culminated in Recommendation R(81)12, a list of powerful policy recommendations to protect the economy and consumers from business malpractice (Council of Europe, 1981). It also provided the following typological definition of economic crime.

Owing to the generally recognised difficulty of giving an exact definition of economic crime, it was found necessary to delimit the concept by means of a list of offences:

1 cartel offences;
2 fraudulent practices and abuse of economic situation by multinational companies;
3 fraudulent procurement or abuse of state or international organisations' grants;
4 computer crime (e.g. theft of data, violation of secrets, manipulation of computerised data);
5 bogus firms;
6 faking of company balance sheets and book-keeping offences;
7 fraud concerning economic situation and corporate capital of companies;
8 violation by a company of standards of security and health concerning employees;
9 fraud to the detriment of creditors (e.g. bankruptcy, violation of intellectual and industrial property rights);
10 consumer fraud (in particular falsification of and misleading statements on goods, offences against public health, abuse of consumers' weakness or inexperience);
11 unfair competition (including bribery of an employee of a competing company) and misleading advertising;
12 fiscal offences and evasion of social costs by enterprises;
13 customs offences (e.g. evasion of customs duties, breach of quota restrictions);
14 offences concerning money and currency regulations;
15 stock exchange and bank offences (e.g. fraudulent stock exchange manipulation and abuse of the public's inexperience);
16 offences against the environment (Council of Europe Committee of Ministers, 1981).

The difficulty with the Committee's offence typology is that it is, again, essentially a restatement of white-collar crime. It focuses on high-status corporate crimes and includes health, safety and environmental offences but excludes offenders and offences outside of the occupational context. The 'loose' use of the term as noted by Tupman (2015) illustrates the need to try and draw clearer boundaries to it.

Table 1.2 sets out and compares a range of alternative typological definitions created by various organisations and academics. It clearly illustrates the lack of consensus as to which offences fall under the economic crime banner. The types of offences most commonly recognised are fraud, bribery and corruption and money laundering followed by intellectual property crime, which includes counterfeiting and industrial espionage, terrorist financing, market manipulation, sanctions evasion and cyber-dependent financially motivated crime. Most of the organisations in Table 1.2 use the phrase '*bribery and corruption*' due to their uncertainty about the meaning of corruption. This is unhelpful because, as previously explained, corruption is a wide typology of crimes that includes bribery as well as offences like nepotism and vote rigging.

Attempts to construct conceptual definitions are often supplemented by a short offence typology and are usually both conceptually and typologically flawed. For example, Europol (n.d.) use both a conceptual definition and a short list of offences:

> Economic crime, also known as financial crime, refers to illegal acts committed by an individual or a group of individuals to obtain a financial or professional advantage. The principal motive in such crimes is economic gain. Economic crime areas of specific interest to Europol joint investigation teams include:
>
> - MTIC (Missing Trader Intra-Community Fraud) fraud, which involves the criminal exploitation of value-added-tax (VAT) rules in the EU, resulting in lost revenue running into the billions of euro for Member States;
> - excise fraud, which refers to the smuggling of highly taxed commodities such as tobacco, alcohol and fuel;
> - money laundering, the process of making the proceeds of criminal activity appear legal.

It is reasonable for Europol to associate economic crime with financial crime and to include individuals and groups of individuals as offenders, but it omits corporate entities. The reference to financial or professional advantage is so vague that it could encompass almost any crime, including drug dealing, burglary, modern slavery and even falsifying qualifications. It then lists a very narrow range of offences covering just tax evasion and money laundering whilst implying just one type of victim, government victims of lost tax revenue.

Table 1.2 Typologies of economic crime offences

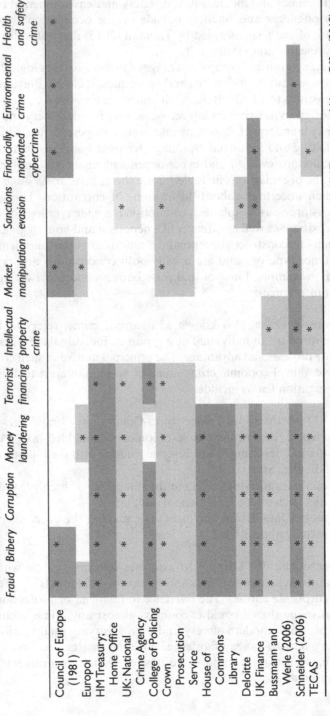

	Fraud	Bribery	Corruption	Money laundering	Terrorist financing	Intellectual property crime	Market manipulation	Sanctions evasion	Financially motivated cybercrime	Environmental crime	Health and safety crime
Council of Europe (1981)	*	*					*		*	*	*
Europol	*			*			*				
HM Treasury; Home Office	*	*	*	*	*						
UK: National Crime Agency	*	*	*	*	*						
College of Policing	*	*	*	*	*			*			
Crown Prosecution Service	*	*	*	*	*		*				
House of Commons Library	*	*	*	*		*					
Deloitte	*	*	*	*		*		*	*		
UK Finance	*	*	*	*				*		*	
Bussmann and Werle (2006)	*	*	*	*		*					
Schneider (2006)	*	*	*	*		*	*		*	*	*
TECAS	*	*	*	*							

Sources: Council of Europe Committee of Ministers (1981), Crown Prosecution Service (2021), Europol (n.d.), HM Treasury and Home Office (2019), College of Policing (n.d.), House of Commons Library (2020), UK Finance (n.d.), Deloitte (2020), Bussmann and Werle (2006), Schneider (2006), TECAS.

Willott et al. (2001, p. 443) offer an unusually wide definition that unhelpfully includes burglary:

> We will use the term "economic crime" to indicate a range of financially motivated offenses, including offenses such as residential burglary, that are typically thought of as "blue collar" and offenses such as embezzlement and fraud, that are associated more with "white collar".

Although burglary is financially motivated, it is a physically intrusive crime rather than based on secretive deception. An improved conceptual and typological definition is offered by Schneider (2006, p. 308), who defines economic crime as:

> [...] a wide variety of nonviolent illegal acts of deception for financial gains that are committed by an individual, or an informal or formal organization that may take place both within and outside legitimate commerce. The most common economic crime offences include: credit card fraud, phone/ telemarketing fraud, computer/internet fraud, bankruptcy fraud, healthcare fraud, environmental law violations, insurance fraud, mail fraud, government fraud, tax evasion, financial fraud, securities fraud, insider trading, bribery, kickbacks, counterfeiting, public corruption, money laundering, embezzlement, economic espionage and antitrust violations.

Schneider's definition is reasonable in embracing individual and organisational offenders, and the typology is very helpful. However, it is difficult to reconcile the conflict between economic crime and legitimate commerce: commerce must be illegitimate if it involves crime. Furthermore, the inclusion of environmental crimes is problematic as they are not always reliant on deception.

Constructing a coherent definition of economic crime

Drawing upon the positive aspects of previous attempts at defining economic crime, this book sets out the following conceptual and typological definition. The conceptual component of the definition focuses on the dominant characteristics common to economic crimes – financial motivation, deception, secrecy, absence of physical force and the intention to make a gain or cause a loss:

> Economic crime is a typology of financially motivated crimes and deviant acts perpetrated by corporations, groups or individuals, which take place predominantly by deception, without threat of or actual physical force, against any person or entity, with the intention of making a

gain or causing a loss, and where there is a prima facie case for criminal, regulatory or civil justice. It commonly includes crimes predominantly linked to the production, distribution and consumption of goods and services, such as fraud, bribery, money laundering and terrorist financing, intellectual property crime, industrial (and economic) espionage, market manipulation, tax evasion, and financially motivated cybercrime.

Financial motivation driven by need, greed or lure provides the impetus for economic crime (Karstedt, 2016). Financial motivation refers to the desire to make an economic gain, or to cause a loss, which is usually monetary, but often involves assets or economic opportunities with financial value. The absence of physical force clearly differentiates economic crime from physical, acquisitive crimes. All the crimes involve deception and secrecy to some extent in their planning and execution, though it is important to note the targets of the deception varies between the offence types. Fraud schemes secretly deceive the targeted victims. Bribery schemes secretly deceive parties not involved in the schemes: for example, a buyer who secretly demands a kickback to award a supply contract deceives his employer and deceives the supplier's competitors. Price-fixing cartels secretly deceive the markets and the consumers. Money-laundering schemes secretly deceive unwitting participants, such as banks and estate agents. Counterfeit products are designed to deceive consumers by pretending they are genuine items, and they deceive governments through tax evasion. Industrial espionage involves secretly deceiving the targets of illicit information gathering.

Dishonesty is the very human attribute which enables the deception (Ariely, 2012) and takes two forms in economic crimes. The law recognises two forms of dishonesty (see the Fraud Act 2006). The most recognisable form is the intentional false statement or claim, but equally important is the silent dishonesty whereby a person deliberately conceals important information to deceive a victim. The level of secrecy required to successfully execute economic crimes depends on the type of offence. Most high volume, low value scams and identity frauds require the falsehood and the intent to remain obscured until completion, at which point they are often detected but the fraudsters will have disappeared into the electronic ether. Similarly, money-laundering schemes only need to be disguised until the crime proceeds have been sufficiently integrated into the economy.

However, those committing sustained, complex offences rely on continued secrecy to maintain their schemes and avoid detection. Price-fixing cartels and corporate bribery schemes have to operate deep in the shadows and can do so for many years (Andresen & Button, 2019; Oindrila De, 2010). ACFE (2020) found that occupation fraud schemes last for an average of 14 months. Even major investment frauds like Madoff's Ponzi scheme and corporate mis-selling schemes, such as the payment protection insurance (PPI) scandal in the UK, can continue operating in plain sight because the offenders' dishonesty and intent is kept secret (Quisenberry, 2017; Tombs, 2013). Deception, dishonesty and secrecy are the attributes that make most economic crimes hard to detect, disrupt and bring to justice (van de Bunt, 2010). Unlike violence or burglary, economic crimes are not loudly declared by blood or broken windows (Pontell, 2016).

As with all concepts and typologies, there are ambiguities, limitations and inevitable murky boundaries. In particular, some behaviours captured by the typology do not exhibit all the characteristics of economic crime. Cultural and legal variations mean that a criminal act in one place is legal and acceptable in others (Fletcher & Herrmann, 2012). America is an illuminating example, where some forms of bribery within the private sector are legal in some states and illegal in others (Rohlfsen, 2012). Counterfeiting and piracy present a particular conceptual problem as they are high volume crimes that cause significant economic harm and deceive governments by way of tax evasion, but they are mostly conducted in plain sight without deceiving most consumers who knowingly acquire the products (Chapter 6; OECD and EUIPO, 2019). The solution to these issues is not a futile search for the perfect concept or definition, but to identify and explain discrepancies when they are encountered.

Justification for more interest in economic crime

The most powerful justifications for engaging in a topic are quantitative: the size of the problem or the size of the benefit. A small problem or a small benefit justifies less attention and resources than a big problem or a big benefit. An essential paradox at the heart of economic crime is that it is a huge problem, but, reflecting the observations of Sutherland (1940), it attracts little attention from scholars, politicians, law enforcement, commerce and the public. The problem is not just the number and value of offences, it is also the consequential personal, social and economic impacts: financial crashes due to fraud and the failure of regulation, market failures due to cartel price-fixing, deaths from counterfeit products, mass deaths from terrorist financing and poverty driven by corruption.

The true scale of the problem is not known, but data is available that illustrates it is a far bigger problem than traditional volume crimes. This section examines available data. First, however, it introduces a theory that explains why it is important to measure the extent of economic crime, and some of the obstinate challenges in doing so.

Deviancy attenuation and differential rationalisation

There is an old saying, 'what gets measured gets done'. The essence of this is that things, particularly problems such as crimes, need to be measured in order to stimulate action to reduce them (Button & Gee, 2013). Without adequate measurement, there would be no evidence of a problem and no need to stimulate action. Most economic crimes have not been measured accurately and regularly in the UK and other countries. The exception is fraud and computer misuse against individuals in England and Wales, which in 2016 was added to the CSEW, resulting in a doubling of annual crime rates (see Chapter 2).

The lack of regular and accurate measurement creates the conditions for what Button and Tunley (2015) have described as the circle of 'deviancy attenuation'. At the top of the circle of attenuation, decision makers do not regard an issue as a problem, therefore resources are not allocated to accurately measure it; there is therefore no evidence of a problem; therefore, it is not a priority; action and resources to tackle the problem are not required because there is no problem; leading to further evidence it is not a problem as there are fewer cases of detection and successful enforcement; completing the circle, there is no evidence there is a problem, therefore decision makers do not regard it as a problem. This, Button and Tunley (2015) argued, leads to immoral phlegmatism, the antithesis of a moral panic. The latter occurs whenever a social problem is exaggerated out of proportion, leading to excessive, disproportionate action (Cohen, 1972).

Immoral phlegmatism describes the opposite circumstance to a moral panic, where there is a large problem but the response is so disproportionately low that it can be considered immoral (Button & Tunley, 2015). Improved accuracy in the measurement of fraud and computer misuse in England and Wales since 2016 has arguably stimulated some action in the UK to tackle these problems (see Chapter 2 and Home Office, 2021). However, economic crime encompasses more than just fraud and computer misuse, and accurate and regular measurement of these wider problems remains lacking both in the UK and other countries.

Another important theory that contributes to the measurement problem is differential rationalisation. If an organisation discovers it is a victim of economic crime, it would be natural to assume that management would want to investigate the crime, deal with the offender and resolve related issues. However, Shepherd and Button (2019) argue many organisations are reluctant to engage with the problem for a variety of reasons, such as to protect:

- the interests of the organisation and to avoid bad publicity;
- the interests of a social group, such as those from the same class;
- the career of the person responsible who may suffer should the problem be exposed.

These avoidant rationalisations constructed by organisations add to the veil of secrecy and silence (van de Blunt, 2010), which reassures and emboldens offenders. The importance of this contribution to the measurement problem is that it is wrong to assume that organisations want to detect incidents or uncover the scale of a problem.

Indeed in the summer of 2021 discussions with an expert close to the politicians in the UK responsible for public finances revealed that they (the politicians) were reluctant to discover the true scale of fraud in the large funds created to support individuals and businesses during the Covid-19 pandemic. In areas of expenditure where accurate measurement is already established, such as in fraud in the payment of social security benefits, there was evidence of a significant rise during the pandemic to an all-time high of 14.5% for universal credit compared with just over 9% in the previous year (Department for Work and Pensions, 2020; House of Commons Public Accounts Committee, 2021). With likely evidence of possibly higher rates of fraud in the crisis expenditure, taxpayers would be perplexed to discover a lack of enthusiasm for uncovering the scale of the problem and taking action to deal with it.

So, to go back to the old saying, 'what gets measured gets done' at the start of this section, economic crime must be measured accurately and regularly in order to do something about it. Using a variety of data sources of varying quality for individual and organisational victims, Table 1.3 illustrates the scale of economic crime in the UK compared to traditional crime. The table includes the official recorded crime figures (mainly police recorded crime), estimates of actual victimisation from surveys and cost data. It shows, just as Sutherland did 80 years ago, that economic crime dwarfs all other crimes with respect to frequency and financial impact.

First and foremost, there are many caveats to the data. In particular, there are gaps in the coverage of the data, and not all economic crimes are covered. For incidents, only the shaded data in Table 1.3 can be relied upon with confidence as they are based upon specific high-quality victimisations surveys (CSEW and cyber security breaches survey). Some data only covers England and Wales, some based upon estimates and data of varying quality applied to size of the UK. It is nevertheless our best attempt at gauging the scale of the problem. The table highlights:

- at least 10.7 million individual victims of economic crime versus 5.8 million of traditional crime;
- just over 3 million organisational victims of economic crime;
- a total cost of economic crime to the UK of around £350 billion, 23 times greater than the £15 billion for traditional crime. Even removing the £100 billion estimate for money laundering, which potentially double counts economic crime because it is driven by predicate traditional and economic crimes, the total harm amounts to £250 billion, around 16 times greater than traditional crimes.

Economic crime is, in terms of the number of offences, victims and costs, a much bigger problem than traditional crime. Furthermore, the number of offences that come to the attention of the authorities is the tip of the iceberg, just a fraction of the true level of criminality, which remains hidden in the

Table 1.3 The scale of economic crime in the UK

	Estimated victims		Recorded crime	Estimated cost
	Individuals	Organisations		
Fraud	3,710,000	413,000	739,131	£190,000,000,000
Computer misuse	915,000	1,888,000	23,135	£27,000,000,000
Bribery	48,717	177,000	115	
IP crimes	6,031,941	No data	424	£16,200,000,000
Cartel crimes	N/A	No data	>1	£16,000,000,000
Money laundering	N/A	573,085	>2,000	£100,000,000,000
Total economic crime	**10,705,658**	**3,051,085**	**762,805**	**£349,200,000,000**
Traditional crime	5,821,000	No data	5,013,284	£14,623,707,700

Notes and sources:

1 CSEW data is used for individual victims for fraud, computer misuse and individual victims (ONS, 2019c).
2 For bribery, survey data from 1996, 2000 and 2005 on the experience of street-level corruption in the UK is used, with the median of 0.1% applied to the adult population of the UK (van Dyjk et al., 2007).
3 For IP crime, survey data from the EU of 9% who bought counterfeit products after being misled is applied to the adult population (EUIPO, 2017).
4 For organisational victims, the findings from the Home Office (not yet published) economic crime survey of 7% victims of fraud and 3% corruption are applied to the UK business population (5.9 million businesses).
5 For cybercrime against organisations, the percentage experiencing cybersecurity breaches (32%) according to the government's annual survey is applied to the UK business population (Finnerty et al., 2019).
6 For money laundering, SARs statistics are used (NCA, 2020).
7 For recorded incidents, ONS data on recorded crime is used for fraud, computer misuse and traditional crime. For bribery, IP crime, market abuse and money laundering, the number proceeded against is applied (Intellectual Property Office, 2020).
8 For costs, the best available estimates were used for each crime type (Cabinet Office, 2011; Centre for Counter Fraud Studies, 2017; NCA, 2019; OECD, 2019). For cartels, based on analysis by Connor (2016) and Boyer and Kotchoni (2015). Bribery costs are excluded as likely to overlap with cartel costs. The annual cost of international cartels to the UK economy is £16–62 billion. The cost of domestic-only cartels is unknown.
9 For traditional crime, the costs were calculated using the government's estimate of costs of crime, focusing upon value lost (Home Office, 2018).
10 Some data applies to England and Wales (such as CSEW) other data is UK wide.

secret shadows (Button et al., 2018). The realisation of the scale and nature of the problem led one eminent think tank to describe just the threat from fraud alone as a 'national security concern' and that the 'lack of prominence' is 'hard to justify' (Wood et al., 2021, p. 43).

Not victimless crimes

Economic crime does not just cause financial losses. In the following chapters, some of the impacts of the different economic crimes will be considered. It will show how some individuals experience disruption to their lives, psychological and emotional harms, damage to reputation and physical and mental health problems. Some even commit suicide as a result of economic crime victimisation. It will show how some economic crimes such as counterfeiting can cause health problems and even deaths (Button & Cross, 2017; Button et al., 2014). It will show how corruption can undermine the institutions and infrastructure of a country. It enables organised crime and even terrorist groups to flourish. Describing economic crime as victimless hugely underestimates the significant harm it causes.

All sections of society do it

Conventional criminology has largely focused on the typical profile of criminals involved in traditional, high volume crimes: young, males, poorly educated and relatively deprived. For example, in England and Wales, the profile of a burglar is:

- 84% male
- 53% majority aged 25–39 (ONS, 2019a)

The profile for criminal damage offenders is:

- 76% male
- 52% majority aged under 25 (ONS, 2019b)

Furthermore, the majority of traditional crime offenders do not specialise in one type of crime but are versatile in committing several types (Simon, 1997), the average reoffending rate is 47% for adults released from prison (ONS, 2020), and they tend to be of lower education and socio-economic status (Stadler et al., 2013).

However, as the following chapters will reveal, economic crime attracts a much greater diversity of offenders. These include the young, middle aged and old, the rich and the poor, organisations and states. The book will show that ordinary, generally law-abiding members of the public are willing to perpetrate economic crime. Despite the diversity in the demographics of offenders, and despite the huge scale of the problem, economic crime is an under-researched topic that has attracted relatively little attention from conventional criminologists. It needs to break the restraining shackles of conventional criminology in order to attract funding, research focus and further understanding of the most prevalent of all crime types. The next section sets out the case for 'economic criminology'.

The case for 'economic criminology'

Criminologists have a tendency, as do many academic disciplines, to divide themselves into schools dedicated to certain perspectives or orientations, for example, 'radical criminologists', 'cultural criminologists', 'feminist criminologists' and 'green criminologists' to name some. There are many differences between these groups of criminologists, but they all stem from a common sociological core with, therefore, similar interests in the human behaviours and interactions that shape and structure society. The dominant concerns of these sociological crime scholars have always been and are still the traditional volume acquisitive and physical crimes against individuals. Smaller groups congregate around specific topics, such as criminal psychology, criminal justice, restorative justice, policing, rehabilitation and cyber-crime. Just a small minority of fringe criminologists specialise in the study of economic crime. The collective attitudes towards economic crime, within traditional criminology, can be broadly divided into three categories: the crimeblind, the radicals and the economic criminologists.

The crimeblind: This is the dominant perspective in criminology, the criminologists who are oblivious to the importance and social relevance of economic crime. Most criminologists are steadfast in their adherence to traditional crimes; researching the causes of these crimes; inquiring into the purpose, effectiveness and justness of law enforcement; examining the treatment of victims and offenders; and exploring the utility of theoretical concepts. These self-imposed constraints of the scholarship are illustrated by one of the premier publications of criminology, the *Oxford Handbook of Criminology*: just one of its 43 chapters is concerned with 'white collar and corporate crime' (Liebling et al., 2017). This is typical of criminology textbooks and academic journals. There are some signs of change with more interest in frauds against individuals and the exciting technological intersection with cybercrime (see, for example, McGuire & Holt, 2017), but in general, most criminologists can be considered 'crimeblind' when it comes to economic crime, thus leaving the topic largely on the fringes.

The radicals: This group of criminologists do take an interest in economic crime, but within the bounds of white-collar crime and from a radical perspective that is highly critical of the social structures and institutions within elitist, capitalist society. This group of scholars are focused on the social causes of economic crime, particularly the criminogenic nature of corporations as offenders, the powerful elite, and the problems they see arising from the capitalist framework (Tombs & Whyte, 2015). They generally have no interest in corporations or other organisations as victims and little interest in individual economic crime victims. Their focus is the offending of corporations and the senior people that run them.

The economic criminologists: This is a very small group of scholars who recognise the scale of the harm arising from economic crime, are interested in both organisations and individuals as offenders and victims. Most importantly, in the tradition of 'administrative criminology', they are interested in pragmatic approaches to research that informs policies and methods to reduce the harms of crime (Mayhew, 2016). We locate ourselves within this space. There is a cohort of academics who have contributed to this space, without claiming to be 'economic criminologists', such as Michael Benson, Michael Levi, David Weisburd, Barry Rider, Martin Gill, Kristy Holtfreter, Cassandra Cross, Petter Gottschalk and Nicholas Lord, to name a few (see, for example, Benson, 1985; Benson & Simpson, 2014; Cross, 2016; Gill, 2014; Gottschalk, 2020; Gottschalk & Benson, 2020; Holtfreter et al., 2008; Levi, 2008b; Lord, 2014; Rider, 2015b; Weisburd et al., 1991). It is also important to note that some criminologists who focus on cybercrime also contribute to this area, such as David Wall, Thomas Holt and Eric Rutger Leukfeldt, to name a few (Leukfeldt & Holt, 2019; Wall, 2007). The economic crime perspective of these scholars is not devoid of interest in the abuse of corporate leaders and the power relationships in society associated with the radical criminologists, but it does embrace a much broader range of sociological, behavioural, legal and technological issues.

We believe that 'economic criminology' ought to be recognised as a scholarly perspective and orientation within criminology in its own right, similar to other schools such as 'green criminology'.

Theoretical foundations of economic criminology

Economic criminology builds upon five key vectors of study. Firstly, there are the early white-collar scholars such as Edwin Sutherland and Donald Cressey, who were concerned with the crimes committed by corporations and corporate managers (Cressey, 1953; Sutherland, 1949). This branch of criminology is dominated by radical, conceptual studies into the criminogenic nature of corporations and the failure of the authorities to tackle their elite crimes. Prominent scholars include Michael Benson, John Braithwaite, John Coleman, Gilbert Geiss, Michael Levi and Weisburd (see, as examples, Benson, 1985; Braithwaite, 2013; Coleman, 1992; Geiss, 2016; Levi, 2008b; Weisburd et al., 2001).

Secondly, a contrasting vector into economic criminology is the body of work concerned with crimes against organisations, particularly businesses. Organisational victimology encompasses a broader range of crimes against businesses than just 'economic crimes', for example, burglary, theft, shoplifting and vandalism, and often focuses on specific sectors such as retail. It is dominated by administrative criminology with the aim of identifying vulnerabilities and improving prevention, security, policing and enforcement. Some of the prominent writers here include Joshua Bamfield, Mark Button, John Clark, Martin Gill, Read Hayes and Richard Hollinger (see, as examples, Bamfield, 2004; Button, 2019; Gill, 1994; Hayes, 2007; Hollinger & Clark, 1983). Linked to this is a body of work preoccupied with regulatory governance aimed at maximising compliance of organisations through prevention and appropriate levels of enforcement. The scope of this literature is much broader than economic crime, but such crimes have been important in many of these studies and central in some (see Ayers & Braithwaite, 1992).

Thirdly, practitioners represent an important vector into economic criminology, which is firmly grounded in the administrative criminology of organisational victims. Joseph Wells was a prominent scholar, who founded the Association of Certified Fraud Examiners (ACFE) in 1988. Coming from an accountancy background via the FBI as a special agent, Wells wrote dozens of publications addressing the financial damage caused by occupational fraud and effective means to tackle the problem. His writing includes seminal practitioner guides, such as 'Principles of Fraud Examination' and 'Corporate Fraud Handbook: Prevention and Detection' (Wells, 2014, 2017). Others have followed Wells' administrative criminology route into economic criminology, producing best-practice guides to tackling the problem, for example, Brytting et al. (2011), Button and Gee (2013), Comer (2003), Iyer and Samociuk (2006), Tickner (2012), Young (2013).

The final vector into economic criminology is the wide body of work beyond traditional criminology that is also orientated towards finding ways to combat economic crimes. This practical vein of economic criminology draws on work from computer science, business and management, accounting, economics, and engineering. The combined efforts of these scholarly silos are generating a substantial body of work. For example, a Scopus search (carried out in April 2021) for 'fraud prevention' reveals 501 publications in the following disciplines:

  computer science 22%;
  social science (including criminology) 16%;
  business and management 12%;
  engineering 12%;
  economics 11%.

The database search shows that sociology/criminology has a surprisingly minor role in the study of fraud prevention. Most of the scholars are based in other disciplines, including computer science, business and management, engineering, economics and law. Many of these academics may not recognise themselves as such, but we define them all as economic criminologists because they study economic crime. Unlike traditional criminology's obsession with the social aetiology and experiences of crime, these disciplines are far more focused on finding pragmatic solutions. For example, one of the highest cited papers concerned with fraud in Scopus (1,698 citations) is a paper by Beasley (1996) regarding the composition of boards of directors and levels of fraud. It is published in *The Accounting Review*.

Economic criminology at its simplest is therefore the study of the financially motivated economic crimes and deviant acts perpetrated by individuals or organisations against individuals or organisations. It is orientated to generating knowledge with the aim of reducing the harms of these crimes and deviant acts, improving the response to them as well as wider questions concerning power relations and the application of relevant theory. It draws upon a wide base of interdisciplinary scholars, who are not just located in traditional schools of criminology. Some might argue that economic criminology is nothing more than a branch of administrative criminology that is focused on reducing economic criminality. This would be wrong as economic criminology must embrace the radical criminology espoused by white-collar scholars and others, whilst drawing on every specialist discipline that contributes to the understanding of economic crime, including economics, computer science, security, accountancy, business management, psychology, rehabilitation, policing and all forms of justice.

Outline of book

This book will commence by considering in depth some of the most significant economic crimes chapter by chapter. These chapters will include fraud, bribery and corruption, cartel and antitrust offences, economic cybercrime, intellectual property crime and illicit trade, industrial and economic espionage and ending with money laundering. Each of these chapters will explore what the crimes involve, define them, examine some of the legal context, quantify the crimes, explore their social impacts and introduce the evidence describing who the offenders are.

A chapter seeking to explain why people commit economic crimes will then be considered and the book will then move on to explore the regulation and policing of economic crime in three chapters. The first of these three chapters will consider the importance of regulation of economic crimes based upon both the law and self-regulation. The next chapter reviews the state or public bodies dedicated to economic crime; it reveals a much greater plurality in

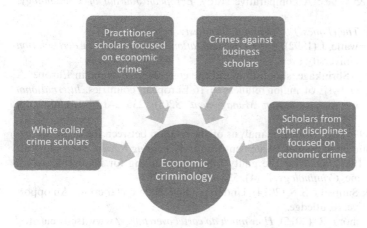

Figure 1.1 The contributions to economic criminology.

comparison to traditional acquisitive crimes. This is followed by a chapter investigating the very large and important contribution of the private sector in countering economic crimes, ranging from commercial to voluntary initiatives. The book ends with a concluding chapter that sets out an agenda for researching and combatting economic crime.

Conclusion

This chapter has introduced the case for economic crime and the study of it through economic criminology. It began by exploring the problems of white-collar crime as a home for the crimes considered in this book. The origins, scope and definition of economic crime were then presented, along with an exploration of the link to corruption. The case for more study and interest in economic crime was then presented, which linked to the broader case the authors advocate for the development of a new paradigm of 'economic criminology'. The chapter ended by outlining the structure of the book.

Note

1 Some media outlets did pick up on this a few days later but focused on the 'scrapping' of Action Fraud, which *The Times* linked with an expose of the agency it had undertaken in the previous year. The omission of economic crimes like fraud from serious attention is not just restricted to journalists.

References

ACFE. (2020). *Report to the nations*. www.acfe.com/report-to-the-nations/2020/
Andresen, M. S., & Button, M. (2019). The profile and detection of bribery in Norway and England & Wales: A comparative study. *European Journal of Criminology, 16*(1), 18–40.
Ariely, D. (2012). *The (honest) truth about dishonesty*. Harper Collins.
Ayres, I., & Braithwaite, J. (1992). *Responsive regulation: Transcending the deregulation debate*. Oxford University Press.
Bamield, J. (2004). Shrinkage, shoplifting and the cost of retail crime in Europe: A cross-sectional analysis of major retailers in 16 European countries. *International Journal of Retail & Distribution Management, 32*(5), 235–241. https://doi.org/10.1108/09590550410699233
Beasley, M. S. (1996). An empirical analysis of the relation between the board of director composition and financial statement fraud. *Accounting Review, 7*(4), 443–465.
Benson, M. L. (1985). Denying the guilty mind: Accounting for involvement in a white-collar crime. *Criminology, 23*(4), 583–607.
Benson, M. L., & Simpson, S. S. (2014). *Understanding white-collar crime: An opportunity perspective*. Routledge.
Boyer, M., & Kotchoni, R. (2015). *How much do cartel overcharge?* www.tse-fr.eu/sites/default/files/TSE/documents/doc/wp/2015/cartel_overcharges.pdf

Braithwaite, J. (2013). *Corporate crime in the pharmaceutical industry*. Routledge.

Brooks, G. (2016). *Criminology of corruption: Theoretical approaches*. Springer.

Brytting, T., Minogue, R., & Morino, V. (2011). *The anatomy of fraud and corruption: Organizational causes and remedies*. Gower.

Bussmann, K. D., & Werle, M. M. (2006). Addressing crime in companies: First findings from a global survey of economic crime. *British Journal of Criminology, 46*(6), 1128–1144.

Button, M. (2019). *Private policing* (2nd ed.). Routledge.

Button, M., Blackbourn, D., & Tunley, M. (2015). 'The not so thin blue line after all?' Investigative resources dedicated to fighting fraud/economic crime in the United Kingdom. *Policing: A Journal of Policy and Practice, 9*(2), 129–142.

Button, M., & Cross, C. (2017). *Cyber frauds, scams and their victims*. Taylor & Francis.

Button, M., & Gee, J. (2013). *Countering fraud for competitive advantage*. Wiley.

Button, M., Lewis, C., & Tapley, J. (2014). Not a victimless crime: The impact of fraud on individual victims and their families. *Security Journal, 27*(1), 36–54.

Button, M., Shepherd, D., & Blackbourn, D. (2018). 'The iceberg beneath the sea', fraudsters and their punishment through non-criminal justice in the 'Fraud Justice Network' in England and Wales. *International Journal of Law, Crime and Justice, 53*, 56–66. https://doi.org/10.1016/j.ijlcj.2018.03.001.

Button, M., & Tunley, M. (2015). Explaining fraud deviancy attenuation in the United Kingdom. *Crime, Law and Social Change, 63*(1–2), 49–64.

Cabinet Office. (2011). *The cost of cybercrime*. https://assets.publishing.service.gov.uk/government/uploads/system/uploads/attachment_data/file/60943/the-cost-of-cyber-crime-full-report.pdf

Centre for Counter Fraud Studies. (2017). *Annual fraud indicator 2017*. www.experian.co.uk/assets/identity-and-fraud/annual-fraud-indicator-report-2017.pdf

Cliff, G., & Desilets, C. (2014). White collar crime: What it is and where it's going. *Notre Dame Journal of Law Ethics and Public Policy, 28*, 481–523.

Cohen, S. (1972). *Folk devils and moral panics: The creation of the mods and rockers*. MacGibbon and Kee.

Coleman, J. (1992). The theory of white-collar crime: From Sutherland to the 1990s. In K. Schlegel & D. Weisburd (Eds.), *White-collar crime reconsidered* (pp. 53–77). Northeastern University Press.

College of Policing. (n.d.). *Economic crime investigator*. Retrieved from https://profdev.college.police.uk/professional-profile/economic-crime-investigator/

Comer, M. J. (2003). *Investigating corporate fraud*. Gower Publishing.

Connor, J. (2016). *International cartel stats: A look at the last 26 Years*. www.researchgate.net/profile/John-Connor-12/publication/309995039_International_Cartel_Stats_A_Look_at_the_Last_26_Years/links/59e8ecd3458515c3632b38a3/International-Cartel-Stats-A-Look-at-the-Last-26-Years.pdf

Council of Europe. (1981). *Recommendation no. R (81) 12 of the Committee of Ministers to Member States on Economic Crime*. https://rm.coe.int/CoERMPubli cCommonSearchServices/DisplayDCTMContent?documentId=09000016806cb4f0

Cressey, D. (1953). *Other people's money*. Wadsworth Publishing.

Cross, C. (2016). Using financial intelligence to target online fraud victimisation: Applying a tertiary prevention perspective. *Criminal Justice Studies, 29*(2), 125–142.

Crown Prosecution Service. (2021). *Economic crime strategy 2025.* www.cps.gov.uk/ publication/economic-crime-strategy-2025

Daly, K. (1989). Gender and varieties of white-collar crime. *Criminology, 27*(4), 769–793.

De, O. (2010). Analysis of cartel duration: Evidence from EC prosecuted cartels. *International Journal of the Economics of Business, 17*(1), 33–65. https://doi.org/ 10.1080/13571510903516946

Deloitte. (2020). *Protect, monitor, respond.* www2.deloitte.com/uk/en/pages/financial-services/articles/economic-crime.html

Department for Work and Pensions. (2020). *Fraud and error in the benefit system 2019 to 2020.* www.gov.uk/government/statistics/fraud-and-error-in-the-benefit-system-financial-year-2019-to-2020-estimates/fraud-and-error-in-the-benefit-system-2019-to-2020

Dinitz, S. (1977). Economic crime. In S. F. Landau & L. Sebba-See (Eds.), *Criminology in perspective: Essays in honor of Israel Drapkin.* Lexington Books.

Edelhertz, H. (1970). *The nature, impact, and prosecution of white-collar crime* (Vol. 2). National Institute of Law Enforcement and Criminal Justice.

Eicher, S. (Ed.) (2012). *Corruption in international business: The challenge of cultural and legal diversity.* Ashgate.

EUIPO. (2017). *European citizens and intellectual property: Perception, awareness and behaviour.* https://euipo.europa.eu/tunnel-web/secure/webdav/guest/document_library/observatory/documents/IPContributionStudy/2017/european_public_opinion_study_web.pdf

Europol. (n.d.). *Economic crime.* www.europol.europa.eu/crime-areas-and-trends/ crime-areas/economic-crime

Finnerty, K., Fullick, S., Motha, H., Navin, J., Button, M. & Wang, V. (2019). *Cyber security breaches survey 2019.* Ipsos/MORI.

Fletcher, C., & Herrmann, D. (2012). *The internationalisation of corruption: Scale, impact and countermeasures.* Gower.

Friedrichs, D. (2002). Occupational crime, occupational deviance and workplace crime: Sorting out the difference. *Criminal Justice, 2*(2), 243–256.

Friedrichs, D. (2010). *Trusted criminals: White collar crime in contemporary society* (4th ed.). Wadworths.

Geis, G. (2016). The roots and variant definitions of the concept of "white-collar crime". In S. Van Slyke, M. Benson, & F. Cullen (Eds.), *The Oxford handbook of white-collar crime.* Oxford University Press.

Gill, M. L. (Ed.) (1994). *Crime at work.* Perpetuity Press.

Gill, M. L. (Ed.) (2014). *The handbook of security.* Palgrave Macmillan.

Gorta, A. (2006). Corruption risk areas and corruption resistance. In C. Sampford, A. Shacklock, C. Connors, & F. Galtung (Eds.), *Measuring corruption.* Routledge.

Gottschalk, P. (2020). Determinants of fraud examination performance: An empirical study of internal investigation reports. *Journal of Investigative Psychology and Offender Profiling, 16*(1), 59–72.

Gottschalk, P., & Benson, M. L. (2020). The evolution of corporate accounts of scandals from exposure to investigation. *British Journal of Criminology, 60*(4), 949–969.

Graycar, A., & Prenzler, T. (2013). *Understanding and preventing corruption.* Palgrave MacMillan.

Graycar, A., & Smith, R. (2011). *Research and practice in corruption: An introduction. Handbook of global research and practice in corruption*. Edward Elgar.

Hayes, R. (2007). *Retail security and loss prevention*. Springer.

HM Treasury & Home Office. (2019). *Economic crime plan, 2019 to 2022*. www.gov.uk/government/publications/economic-crime-plan-2019-to-2022/economic-crime-plan-2019-to-2022-accessible-version

Hollinger, R. C., & Clark, J. P. (1983). Deterrence in the workplace: Perceived certainty, perceived severity, and employee theft. *Social Forces, 62*(2), 398–418.

Holtfreter, K., Reisig, M. D., & Pratt, T. C. (2008). Low self-control, routine activities, and fraud victimization. *Criminology, 46*(1), 189–220.

Home Office. (2018). *The economic and social costs of crime* (2nd ed.). https://assets. publishing.service.gov.uk/government/uploads/system/uploads/attachment_data/file/954485/the-economic-and-social-costs-of-crime-horr99.pdf

Home Office. (2019). *Economic crime plan 2019–2022*. www.gov.uk/government/publications/economic-crime-plan-2019-to-2022/economic-crime-plan-2019-to-2022-accessible-version

Home Office. (2021). *Beating crime plan*. https://assets.publishing.service.gov.uk/government/uploads/system/uploads/attachment_data/file/1006825/Crime-Plan-accessible-version_2.pdf

Hough, D. (2013). *Corruption, anti-corruption and governance*. Springer.

House of Commons Library. (2020). *Economic crime in the UK: A multi-billion pound problem*. https://commonslibrary.parliament.uk/research-briefings/cbp-9013/

House of Commons Public Accounts Committee. (2021). *Fraud and error. Ninth report of session 2020-21*. https://committees.parliament.uk/publications/6469/documents/70574/default/

Intellectual Property Office. (2020). *IP crime enforcement report*. https://assets. publishing.service.gov.uk/government/uploads/system/uploads/attachment_data/file/913644/ip-crime-report-2019-20.pdf

Iyer, N. K., & Samociuk, M. (2006). *Fraud and corruption: Prevention and detection*. Gower.

Karstedt, S. (2016). Middle-class crime: Moral economies between crime in the streets and crime in the suites. In S. Van Slyke, M. Benson, & F. Cullen (Eds.), *The Oxford handbook of white-collar crime*. Oxford University Press.

Langseth, P. (2006). Measuring corruption. In C. Sampford, A. Shacklock, C. Connors, & F. Galtung (Eds.), *Measuring corruption*. Routledge.

Leigh, L. (1980). Introduction. In L. Leigh (Ed.), *Economic crime in Europe*. MacMillan.

Leukfeldt, R., & Holt, T. J. (Eds.) (2019). *The human factor of cybercrime*. Routledge.

Levi, M. (2006). The media construction of financial white-collar crimes. *British Journal of Criminology, 46*(6), 1037–1057.

Levi, M. (2008a). Organized fraud and organizing frauds: Unpacking research on networks and organization. *Criminology & Criminal Justice, 8*(4), 389–419.

Levi, M. (2008b). *The phantom capitalists: The organization and control of long-firm fraud*. Ashgate Publishing.

Levi, M. (2015). Foreword: Some reflections on the evolution of economic and financial crimes. In B. Rider (Ed.), *Research handbook on international financial crime*. Edward Elgar Publishing.

Liebling, A., Maruna, S., & McAra, L. (Eds.) (2017). *The Oxford handbook of criminology*. Oxford University Press.

Lord, N. J. (2014). Responding to transnational corporate bribery using international frameworks for enforcement: Anti-bribery and corruption in the UK and Germany. *Criminology & Criminal Justice, 14*(1), 100–120.

Maguire, M., & McVie, S. (2017). *Crime data and criminal statistics: A critical reflection* (Vol. 1, pp. 163–189). Oxford University Press.

Mayhew, P. (2016). In defence of administrative criminology. *Crime Science, 5*(1), 1–10.

McGuire, M. R., & Holt, T. J. (Eds.) (2017). *The Routledge handbook of technology, crime and justice*. Taylor & Francis.

NCA. (2019). *National Economic Crime Centre leads push to identify money laundering activity*. www.nationalcrimeagency.gov.uk/news/national-economic-crime-centre-leads-push-to-identify-money-laundering-activity

NCA. (2020). *UK Financial Intelligence Unit suspicious activity reports annual report 2020*. www.nationalcrimeagency.gov.uk/who-we-are/publications/480-sars-annual-report-2020/file

OECD. (2014). *The rationale for fighting corruption*. www.oecd.org/cleangovbiz/49693613.pdf

OECD & IPO. (2019). *Trade in counterfeit Products and the UK economy – 2019 update*. www.oecd.org/gov/risk/trade-in-counterfeit-products-and-the-uk-economy-2019.htm

ONS. (2019a). *Nature of crime: Burglary. Year ending March 2018*. www.ons.gov.uk/peoplepopulationandcommunity/crimeandjustice/datasets/natureofcrimeburglary

ONS. (2019b). *Nature of crime: Criminal damage. Year ending March 2018*. www.ons.gov.uk/peoplepopulationandcommunity/crimeandjustice/datasets/natureofcrimecriminaldamage

ONS. (2019c). *Crime in England and Wales: Year ending December 2020 appendix tables*. www.ons.gov.uk/peoplepopulationandcommunity/crimeandjustice/datasets/crimeinenglandandwalesappendixtables

ONS. (2020). *Proven reoffending statistics quarterly bulletin, England and Wales, January 2018 to March 2018*. www.gov.uk/government/statistics/proven-reoffending-statistics-january-to-march-2018

ONS. (2021). *Crime in England and Wales: Year ending March 2021*. www.ons.gov.uk/peoplepopulationandcommunity/crimeandjustice/bulletins/crimeinenglandandwales/yearendingmarch2021#computer-misuse

Pontell, H. N. (2016). Theoretical, empirical, and policy implications of alternative definitions of "white-collar crime". In S. Van Slyke, M. Benson, & F. Cullen (Eds.), *The Oxford handbook of white-collar crime*. Oxford University Press.

Quisenberry, W. L. (2017). Ponzi of all Ponzis: Critical analysis of the Bernie Madoff scheme. *International Journal of Econometrics and Financial Management, 5*(1), 1–6.

Rider, B. (2015a). Introduction. In B. Rider (Ed.), *Research handbook on international financial crime*. Edward Elgar Publishing.

Rider, B. (Ed.) (2015b). *Research handbook on international financial crime*. Edward Elgar Publishing.

Rohlfsen, R. (2012). Recent developments in foreign and domestic criminal commercial bribery laws. *University of Chicago Legal Forum, 2012*(1), 151–193.

Schneider, S. (2006). Privatizing economic crime enforcement: Exploring the role of private sector investigative agencies in combating money laundering. *Policing & Society*, *16*(3), 285–312. https://doi.org/10.1080/10439460600812065

Shapiro, S. P. (1990). Collaring the crime, not the criminal: Reconsidering the concept of white-collar crime. *American Sociological Review*, *55*, 346 365.

Shepherd, D., & Button, M. (2019). Organizational inhibitions to addressing occupational fraud: A theory of differential rationalization. *Deviant Behavior*, *40*(8), 971–991.

Simon, L. (1997). Do criminal offenders specialize in crime types? *Applied and Preventative Psychology*, *6*(1), 35–53.https://doi.org/10.1016/S0962-1849(05)80064-2

Stadler, W., Benson, M., & Cullen, F. (2013). Revisiting the special sensitivity hypothesis: The prison experience of white-collar inmates. *Justice Quarterly*, *30*(6), 1090–1114. https://doi.org/10.1080/07418825.2011.649296

Sutherland, E. (1940). White-collar criminality. *American Sociological Review*, *5*(1), 1–12.

Sutherland, E. (1945). Is "white collar crime" crime? *American Sociological Review*, *10*(2), 132–139.

Sutherland, E. (1949). *White collar crime*. Dryden.

Sutherland, E. (1983). *White collar crime: The uncut version*. Yale University Press.

Tappan, P. (1947). Who is the criminal? *American Sociological Review*, *12*, 96–102.

Tickner, P. (2012). *How to be a successful frauditor: A practical guide to investigating fraud in the workplace for internal auditors and managers*. John Wiley & Sons.

Tombs, S. (2013). Corporate theft and fraud: Business as usual: Steve Tombs discusses the latest chapter in a long history of financial services frauds. *Criminal Justice Matters*, *94*(1), 14–15.

Tombs, S., & Whyte, D. (2015). *The corporate criminal: Why corporations must be abolished*. Routledge.

Transparency International. (2011). *Corruption in the UK: Overview and policy recommendations*. www.transparency.org.uk/publications/corruption-in-the-uk-overview-policy-recommendations/

Transparency International. (n.d.). *What is corruption?* www.transparency.org/en/what-is-corruption

Tupman, W. (2015). The characteristics of economic crime and criminals. In B. Rider (Ed.), *Research handbook on international financial crime*. Edward Elgar Publishing.

UK Finance. (n.d.). *Economic crime*. www.ukfinance.org.uk/arca-of-expertise/economic-crime

van de Bunt, H. (2010). Walls of secrecy and silence: The Madoff case and cartels in the construction industry. *Criminology & Public Policy*, *9*(3), 435–453.

van Dyjk, J., van Kesteren, J., & Smit, P. (2007). *Criminal victimisation in international perspective key findings from the 2004-2005 ICVS and EU ICS*. Retrieved from www.unicri.eu/services/library_documentation/publications/icvs/publications/ICVS2004_05report.pdf

van Erp, J. (2013). Messy business: Media representations of administrative sanctions for corporate offenders. *Law & Policy*, *35*(1–2), 109–139.

Wall, D. (2007). *Cybercrime: The transformation of crime in the information age* (Vol. 4). Polity.

Weisburd, D., Waring, E., & Chayet, E. F. (2001). *White-collar crime and criminal careers.* Cambridge University Press.

Weisburd, D., Wheeler, S., Waring, E., & Bode, N. (1991). *Crimes of the middle classes: White-collar offenders in the federal courts.* Yale University Press.

Weisburd, D., Wheeler, S., Waring, E., & Bode, N. (1994). *Crimes of the middle classes: White-collar offenders in the federal courts.* Yale University Press.

Wells, J. T. (2014). *Principles of fraud examination.* John Wiley & Sons.

Wells, J. T. (2017). *Corporate fraud handbook: Prevention and detection.* John Wiley & Sons.

Whelan, P. (2012) Legal certainty and cartel criminalisation within the EU member states. *Cambridge Law Journal, 71*(3), 677–702.

Willott, S., Griffin, C., & Torrance, M. (2001). Snakes and ladders: Upper-middle class male offenders talk about economic crime. *Criminology,* 39(2), 441–466.

Wood, H., Keatinge, T., Ditcham, K., & Janjeva, A. (2021). *The silent threat: The impact of fraud on UK national security.* www.tomkeatinge.net/uploads/1/7/8/4/17845871/the_silent_threat_web_version.pdf

Young, M. R. (2013). *Financial fraud prevention and detection: Governance and effective practices.* John Wiley & Sons.

Zhao, L., & Ha-Brookshire, J. (2018). Importance of Guanxi in Chinese apparel new venture success: A mixed-method approach. *Journal of Global Entrepreneurship Research, 8*(1), 1–19.

Zhuang, G., Xi, Y., & Tsang, A. S. (2010). Power, conflict, and cooperation: The impact of Guanxi in Chinese marketing channels. *Industrial Marketing Management, 39*(1), 137–149.

Chapter 2

Fraud

Introduction

In the summer of 2021 while writing this chapter, one of the authors received the following text message, 'Your parcel has a £1.09 unpaid fee. Visit …'. At the time, the author was waiting for a parcel and initially, this seemed a plausible message. Further investigation, however, revealed it was a fraud designed not only to secure the small amount of money, but also to harvest banking details. Thousands of people fell for this scam and even more fall for similar frauds every day. It is an illustration of how most people through everyday normal activities are targeted with frauds on a regular basis through SMS messages, emails, telephone calls and the websites they visit. In England and Wales, the most common crime is fraud. It encompasses a much wider range of schemes than the scams most people are targeted with every week. It ranges from simple scams involving using another person's credit card without their permission to complex investment schemes (Levi, 2008).

This chapter will explore the diversity of this crime. The chapter will start by exploring what fraud is by examining both legal and academic definitions. The chapter will then move on to further explain the nature of fraud by providing examples of frauds using a typology developed for this book. Evidence of the extent and trends in fraud will then be provided, illustrating the high volume of incidents and expanding numbers over the last 50 years. Finally, this chapter will explore some of the literature on the fraudsters themselves, exploring everyday fraudsters through to organised criminals.

What is fraud?

'Fraud' is a very commonly used term that has meaning in both social language, to describe someone or an incident that involves some element of deception, and in law, to describe an actual offence. It is therefore a much more flexible term than the labels used to describe many other deviant behaviours. For example, it is rare to describe a person as a thief, robber or burglar without proof of the crimes, whereas fraudster is applied much more loosely to

DOI: 10.4324/9781003081753-2

politicians, salesmen, election results when there is just a suggestion of deception. In defining fraud, it is therefore important to understand that fraud has meaning both legally and more widely in language to describe certain deceptive behaviours. It would be useful to start the discussion with a dictionary definition. The *Collins English Dictionary* defines fraud in four key ways:

- deliberate deception, trickery or cheating intended to gain an advantage;
- an act or instance of such deception;
- something false or spurious: his explanation was a fraud;
- informal a person who acts in a false or deceitful way.

Indeed if the man or woman on the street was asked to define fraud, it would be highly likely deception and gain would be found in the words they use. However, any attempt at definition opens up a variety of questions and consequences. The dictionary entry above, for example, does not use the word crime. Does this mean fraud does not need to be a criminal offence? Deception and trickery to cause a gain are also commonly used in politics, advertising, many other areas of business and personal relationships. For example, if a politician stands for election on a platform of a specific policy, then, when in office does the opposite, is that fraud? One might argue the reality of governing caused the politician to change her mind, but if evidence emerged that the politician knew such a policy was unsustainable, does that overt deceit constitute fraud? Is it a fraud when a businessman makes a false claim about his business to secure a contract that saves his business and secures the jobs of his employees? The dictionary definition *prima facie* might seem to capture fraud, but for the rigours of academic and legal definitions – to which we shall soon come – they are not adequate.

The academic debates over what constitutes fraud have been fairly limited. Wells (2017, p. 2) defines fraud as, 'any crime which uses deception as its principal modus operandi'. This definition is important because Joseph Wells founded the Association of Certified Fraud Examiners (ACFE), which is the world's largest association for anti-fraud professionals, and it continues to use this definition. Crucially Wells' definition differs from the dictionary because it introduces 'crime' as an aspect of the definition. Levi (2012) similarly describes fraud as simply a way of making money illegally by deception. However, Levi (2003) also notes that a key challenge is defining the boundary between sharp practice and illegal fraud.

Button and Cross (2017) explore this boundary by distinguishing between scams that are not technically illegal and clearly criminal frauds. They argue 'scam' is a much wider term to describe deceptive activities for securing a gain, including activities which are legal but clearly unethical. On the other hand, they suggest that fraud is more clearly linked to intentional deceptions which break the law. They use the example of scams surrounding the European Union Healthcare Card (Button & Cross, 2017). These were free to UK citizens (when the UK was a member of the EU), but some alternative websites offered them for a fee, which was not an offence because the small print on the websites informed the applicants they could get the cards free from a government website. Though legal, this is an example of arguably unethical practice, and anyone who paid for a card and then discovered they are available at no cost would no doubt feel deceived.

To help distinguish between unethical practices and illegal fraud, we need to examine the essential components of fraud: the intention to make a gain and/or cause a loss to a victim by the use of deception. Imagine a person, let us call him Mr Space, sets up a website, Asteroid.com, to promote claims, which he knows to be untrue, that a massive asteroid is on a collision course with the Earth and that the authorities have conspired to cover up the impending disaster. The website receives huge interest and publicity making Mr Space a celebrity, but he makes no direct monetary gain from this venture. Mr Space's dishonesty and deception amount to fraud according to the dictionary definition, but the absence of intention to make a gain or cause a loss means it is not a fraud. However, Mr Space then decides to exploit his celebrity and offer a fee paying subscription service, which will alert subscribers to the imminent impact. The ingredients for fraud have now formed: he is now dishonestly perpetrating a deception with the intention of making a financial gain and causing loss to the subscribers.

It is important to explore what is meant by gain and loss in fraud schemes. The Asteroid.com scenario is typical of most frauds: the purpose of the fraud scheme is for the offender to make a monetary gain by causing a loss to the victim. However, this is not always the case. In many cases, the offenders do not directly benefit from the frauds: employees defraud customers for the benefit of their employers; a solicitor may deceive a client in a land transaction so that his builder friend can acquire it at a lower price. This example illustrates that the gain often involves an economic asset, such as a house, car or company shares rather than money.

A frequent objective is to avoid spending money rather than acquiring money, for example, dishonest insurance applications enable the offenders to save money at the expense of the insurers (CPS, n.d.). Many frauds provide the fraudsters with an economic gain, but they do not cause a direct loss to the victim. Curriculum Vitae fraud (CV fraud), for example, is very common and its purpose is to secure a job and a salary, but it usually does not cause a direct loss to the deceived employer (Cifas, 2019). Similarly, application frauds for driving licences or passports permit the offenders to enjoy the economic advantages of identity documents, driving and travel, but cause no loss to the issuers provided the fees are paid. These examples illustrate three important features of fraud:

- Fraud yields some kind of financial or economic gain to someone.
- Fraud does not always cause a financial or economic loss to someone.
- The financial or economic gain does not always benefit the fraudster.

A key question is whether fraud has to be a crime, that is, an action that contravenes the criminal law specified by lawmakers. The authors of this book argue that fraud has a broader meaning than the criminal specification. However, the term would become meaningless if it were to encompass all instances of human lying, cheating and deception. It therefore needs to be constrained by a recognisable legal framework. As this book will show, acts of fraud and many other economic crimes are dealt with by other means, including by civil and regulatory laws. If our Mr Space were to add a small-print disclaimer on the Asteroid.com website that describes the doom claims as obviously false, he would be unlikely to face criminal prosecution. However, he could be liable to civil claims by fooled subscribers and regulatory action for mis-selling. Indeed, these justice alternatives are often favoured even when there is justification for criminal prosecution (Button et al., 2018). This is because the police do not prioritise fraud, and because the criminal standard of proof, 'beyond reasonable doubt', is much higher than the 'balance of probabilities' standard in civil and regulatory cases. Based on these considerations, the authors restrict the term 'fraud' to instances where there is a *prima facie case for criminal, civil or regulatory justice*.

The authors therefore set out the following definition of fraud which combines the key elements of dishonesty, intentional deception, gain or loss and the alternative justice routes, the authors set out the following definition of fraud:

> Fraud is the intention to dishonestly deceive a person or legal entity in order to make a financial or economic gain for the offender or another, or to cause a financial or economic loss to the person or legal entity, such that there is a prima facie case for criminal, civil or regulatory justice.

This definition is thus clearly grounded in the legal framework of criminal, civil and regulatory law. It is illustrated as two components of the fraud continuum in Figure 2.1 as regulatory and civil fraud, and criminal fraud. Unethical but lawful scams which cause gain and/or loss are represented at the left of the continuum.

Figure 2.1 The fraud continuum.

Fraud in law

Criminal law in England and Wales

This section considers some of the legal definitions of fraud. In England and Wales, the criminal definition of fraud was codified with the passage of the Fraud Act 2006 (Farrell et al., 2007). Despite the extensive provisions of this legislation, many other statutes remain in force that cover specific types of fraud, for example, in social security, tax, accounting and trading. However, the legal definitions underlying all these statutes are conveniently described by the Fraud Act 2006 under three principal offences. All three offences emphasise the intention of the offender rather than the actual outcome of their actions: proven offenders are guilty even if they do not actually make a gain or cause a loss.

Section 2: Fraud by false representation

A person commits fraud if he dishonestly makes a false representation with the intention of making a gain for himself or another, or to cause loss to another. This section reflects the definition of fraud previously set out in this chapter. It covers the most common types of fraud, for example, application fraud, identity fraud, sales invoice fraud and false overtime claims.

Section 3: Fraud by failing to disclose information

A person dishonestly fails to disclose to another person information which he is under a legal duty to disclose in order to make a gain or cause loss. This is a particular type of false representation, or silent fraud, in which a person intentionally avoids disclosing important, relevant matters when they have a legal duty to do so. A key element of this offence is the relationship which gives rise to the duty. For example, a solicitor handling the purchase of a property for a client deliberately fails to inform the client about known property damage in order to maximise the price of the property for the seller.

Section 4: Fraud by abuse of position

A person dishonestly abuses his position of trust with the intention of making a gain or causing loss. This is an occupational offence that focuses on the person's professional role and their duty to protect the interests of others, such as their employer or their clients. Although these acts would usually involve deception, the offence is cast widely so that it does not require deception. For example, a purchasing manager dishonestly and intentionally abuses the company's purchasing system to grant inflated contracts or discounts to friends, relatives and associates.

The innocent until proven guilty doctrine within criminal law places the burden of proof on the prosecutor to prove the case, not on the defendant to prove her innocence (Farrell et al., 2007). The combination of the high criminal standard of proof, beyond reasonable doubt, and non-expert juries makes the burden very challenging in fraud cases (Smith & Shepherd, 2019).

Moreover, until *Ivey v Genting Casinos* this task was further complicated by the need to demonstrate dishonesty in the mind of the defendant.[1] Under English law, the criminal courts apply a dishonesty test. Historically, the long-standing test as set out in *R v Ghosh* required that defendants must subject-ively view their actions as dishonest.[2] *Ivey v Genting Casinos* and its latest incarnations have made this task easier.[3] The test now comprises two stages which must be passed to find a defendant guilty (CPS, 2020a):

1   What was the defendant's actual (subjective) state of knowledge or belief as to the facts (and whether such belief is genuinely held); and
2   Was the defendant's conduct dishonest as determined by objective standards of ordinary decent people?

The second stage of the test is a more traditional jury question, whether ordinary people would objectively regard the conduct as dishonest. The first stage of the test relates to the defendant's knowledge and belief associated with the facts of the case. In determining whether the defendant acted dishon-estly, the court must first ascertain their actual state of mind as to the facts in which they acted. For example, in order to decide whether a person travelling in a bus without a ticket acts dishonestly, it is also required to establish their own actual state of knowledge of how public transport works. If a person comes from a country where public transport is free and they genuinely believe that public transport is free in the UK too, there is nothing objectively dishonest about them not paying on the bus.[4]

Unlike the long-standing test as set out in *R v Ghosh*, however, the prosecutors do not have to prove that the defendant knew they were acting dishonestly. According to the Supreme Court:

> Truthfulness is indeed one characteristic of honesty, and untruthfulness is often a powerful indicator of dishonesty, but a dishonest person may sometimes be truthful about his dishonest opinions [...]. For the same reasons which show that Mr Ivey's conduct was, contrary to his own opinion, cheating, the better view would be, if the question arose, that his conduct was, contrary to his own opinion, also dishonest.[5]

This overrules the long-standing *Ghosh* test that maintained that the defendant must view their actions as dishonest. The standard of dishonesty is now based on the objective standard of ordinary decent people, and not whether defendants knew they were acting dishonestly.

Civil law in England and Wales

Civil courts are very different from criminal courts in that they provide a means to resolve private disputes between parties. Although it is very expensive, some fraud victims prefer civil litigation over criminal prosecution, even when fraudsters have committed egregious crimes, because they want their money or assets returned, the standard of proof is lower and cases are heard by a single judge with no jury (Smith & Shepherd, 2019). The tort of deceit is the closest civil tort, or wrongdoing, under English civil law to Section 2 of the Fraud Act 2006. The elements of a deceit claim are (McGrath, 2008):

1   the defendant (fraudster) makes a dishonest representation;
2   with the intention that the claimant (victim) relies on the representation;
3   the claimant does act in reliance on the representation; and
4   the claimant suffers actual damage as a result of reliance on the representation.

In plain English, deceit is a dishonest misrepresentation that intentionally causes unlawful loss to a victim. Like the criminal law, claimants have to prove the dishonesty of the fraudster using the two-stage dishonesty test, which can be very challenging. Unlike the criminal law, claims can only be brought if the victim has actually suffered loss. Other civil claims are available to victims, depending on the specific circumstances of their cases. For example, breach of fiduciary duty, which is the nearest equivalent to Sections 3 and 4 of the Fraud Act 2006, unjust enrichment and breach of contract (McGrath, 2008). These kinds of claims are often preferred because they do not rely on proving dishonesty (Smith & Shepherd, 2018).

Comparative examples

USA

The USA is a federal state and there are fraud-related criminal offences at both the state and federal levels. With 50 states, it would not be possible (or desirable) in the space available in this book to consider the state-level offences. However, at a federal level, two offences are very commonly used to deal with the frauds that cross state or international boundaries:

- United States Code: 1341: Mail fraud
- United States Code: 1343: Wire, radio television fraud

Thus, if a fraudster entices a person into a fraud by sending letters that go across a state border, they breach 1341 or if they use telephone or emails it would be 1343. These federal laws capture many of the frauds enabled by modern electronic communications. For both, the maximum sentence is 20 years for most cases with 30 for some specified cases (Gov.info, n.d. a,b).

Continental legal systems

Crimes, including the offence of fraud, are approached differently in continental or civil law systems, such as the Austrian, French, German, and the Czech systems. This is associated with more general differences between the Anglo-American legal tradition and the Roman law tradition (see Glenn, 2014). Austria, France, Germany, the Czech Republic, and other legal systems based on the civil law tradition place greater emphasis on well-structured and coherent legal codes and detailed written law. The fact that juries are rare and judges do not make law influences also how fraud and other crimes are investigated, prosecuted, and what is the function of trial (see Jackson & Summers, 2012).

The Criminal Code of the Czech Republic, for example, includes the general definition of fraud (Section 209) and a number of specific fraud offences, including insurance fraud (Section 2010), credit fraud (Section 2011) and subvention fraud (Section 2012). Under Section 209 of the Criminal Code of the Czech Republic, fraud is committed by:

> Whoever enriches him-/herself or another by inducing error in someone, by using someone's error, or by concealing material facts and thus causing damage not insignificant to property of another [...]
>
> (for translation see ejtn, n.d.)

Unlike in the UK law, however, there is no standard of dishonesty and standards of ordinary decent people to be tested. The key issue under the Czech criminal law is the culpability of the defendant, including its two elements – knowledge and intent. The prosecution is often in a difficult position to prove the culpability because it is not only required to prove that the defendant intentionally enriched themselves, or attempted to do so, but also that they sought to cause harm or that they were aware that such harm may occur. The need to prove that a person intended to harm someone else limits the application of criminal law in fraud cases (see Heranová, 2012, pp. 55–58).

Fraud: a heterogeneous crime

Fraud has a diversity that is so mixed it often makes generalisation difficult. Some frauds are very simple and low value, for example, the dishonest use of a stolen credit card. At the other extreme, some frauds are very complex and high value, for example, investment frauds involving multiple legal entities and structures in multiple jurisdictions, which even experienced investigators, accountants and lawyers struggle to comprehend.

Offenders are equally as varied. Some are ordinary people who exploit the vulnerabilities of their employers; others are conventional criminals who are attracted to the lower risks and higher rewards of fraud compared to burglary or shoplifting; and there are the respected businessmen who turn to white-collar fraud. The level of organisation also varies considerably, from lone fraudsters to conspiratorial groups and criminal enterprises. Finally, similar frauds are treated as a crime resulting in lengthy prison sentences or dealt with through regulatory or civil means.

Although the heterogeneity of fraud makes it very difficult to list a definitive and comprehensive typology, the fraud types in Table 2.1 assists our understanding of the contextual relationships between perpetrators and victims. Further examples are introduced below the table, organised by victim. Table 2.1 sets out the main categories of offenders: individual, lone fraudsters, organised crime groups, employee fraudsters and companies. For present purposes, companies include both businesses and charities. The categories of victims in the figure partly mirror the perpetrators with individual victims, companies and governments and other public bodies. The matrix serves to illustrate that all areas of society perpetrate fraud against all areas of society. It also shows that the types of fraud accessible to offenders is dependent on their opportunity context. Employees

Table 2.1 A typology of fraud

Perpetrator types	Victim types		
	Individuals	Companies	Governments/public bodies
Individuals	Identity frauds Mass-marketing frauds	Insurance frauds Banking frauds Procurement frauds	Tax frauds Social security frauds
Organised crime groups	Identity frauds Mass-marketing frauds	Insurance frauds Banking frauds Procurement frauds Chief executive frauds	Tax frauds Social security frauds Procurement frauds
Employees	Identity frauds Sales frauds	Expenses frauds Procurement frauds Payroll frauds	Expenses frauds Procurement frauds Payroll frauds
Companies	Investment frauds Consumer frauds	Insurance frauds Banking frauds Investment frauds Procurement frauds	Tax frauds Grant frauds

have a different range of opportunities compared to individuals outside of the employment context. Companies are presented with a different range of opportunities compared to organised crime groups operating in the shadows.

There is a vast array of frauds targeting individuals which, as Table 2.1 illustrates, emanates from all types of perpetrators. One of the most common 'family' of frauds are those that have commonly become known as mass-marketing frauds, which Beals et al. (2015, p. 11) divide into seven categories. The common feature of these frauds is the marketing of an expected benefit:

- Consumer investment fraud: the expected benefit is investment returns and includes fake shares, Ponzi schemes, film frauds.
- Consumer products and services fraud: the expected benefit is the product or service and this includes fake tickets, bogus holidays, dietary pills that don't work, products that don't arrive.
- Employment frauds: the expected benefit is employment and these include fake opportunities for jobs such as work at home scams, model agency work.
- Prize and grant fraud: the expected benefit is winning a prize or other windfall and this includes fake lotteries and 419 scams.
- Phantom debt collection fraud: the expected benefit is avoiding the consequences of failing to pay creditors, including bogus payment demands for debt and taxes.
- Charity fraud: the expected benefit is contributing to a charity, but the reality is that the victim is contributing to the fraudsters, not a legitimate cause.
- Relationship and trust fraud: the expected benefit is a relationship, but the reality is usually a fake identity aimed at securing money from the victim (Beals et al., 2015, pp. 11–12).

Button and Cross (2017) also argue identity fraud should be added as an eighth category when it involves marketing a benefit to victims in order to obtain their identity credentials. Phishing scams offering tax refunds or warning of imminent arrest for tax fraud are increasingly commonplace in the UK (HMRC, n.d.). These eight categories of fraud are largely undertaken by organised criminal groups, but also individuals. Advances in information communication technology (ICT), social networking and low-cost communication across large distances have amplified the extent of this type of fraud. Some examples will now be presented to illustrate such frauds.

Plastic card fraud against individuals is a very common type of identity fraud whereby the fraudster impersonates the legitimate cardholder. At its simplest, a pickpocket might steal a credit card to purchase goods and services online or over the phone or by forging the signature in person. The advent of the dark web has enabled some criminals to sell credit card data harvested in data breaches. This means some fraudsters simply go on the dark web to purchase card details. The individual victim then experiences unauthorised transactions on their statement. Other identity frauds involve the use of personal data to take out credit cards, loans and even mortgages in the name of the individual. Although these types of identity frauds target individuals, the victim – unless clearly negligent – usually gets their money back from their bank. Therefore, although the individuals are the primary victims, often it is the bank in these cases that becomes the victim in terms of loss.

However, research has shown that financial loss is only one component of the impact on victims, and refunded victims can still experience significant psychological, health and social impacts (Button et al., 2014). An example to illustrate this type of fraud comes from the USA, where a former IT professional had used his position to steal the credentials of thousands of customers from the company he was working for. He then set up eight computers running a programme automatically to apply for credit products 24 hours a day. Over 8,000 victims had been hit with losses amounting to US$3.5 million. The culprit pleaded guilty to wire fraud among others (FBI, 2018).

Mass-marketing frauds cover a wide range of different types of frauds. Common types of fraud within this category are lottery frauds and advanced fee frauds. For example, many people receive an email or text to state they have won a prize, but they have to pay an administrative fee to secure access to it. Another common type of fraud in this category are websites offering products and services which do not exist. Often this is a clone or close copy of a real website. Victims purchase products and services in good faith, only to find that it is a fake and that they have lost their money. This occurs for consumer products, holidays, tickets and investments. Bogus websites selling tickets have been a particular issue. In one case from Ireland a man set up web adverts selling tickets for Adele, Justin Bieber and Electric Picnic and netted over €7,000 before being caught (Irish Times, 2017).

Investment-related fraud is also a common type of mass-marketing fraud that can lead to victims losing life-changing sums of money. The bogus investments are frequently sold via pressured telephone sales through what is known as 'boiler rooms'. For example, in 2019, four men were convicted in the UK of a boiler room scam selling bogus land investments in which they used high-pressure cold calling to trick largely elderly pensioners. They had secured over £7.5 million from 193 victims (Money Marketing, 2016).

Another common type of fraud in this category is romance fraud (see Cross & Holt, 2021; Sorell & Whitty, 2019). Romance fraud usually occurs online and commences with the fraudster courting the target victim online using a fake profile. The emotional grooming leads to the victim falling for the fabricated person, at which point the fraudster uses emotional manipulation to persuade the victim to hand over money. The financial and emotional harms in these cases can be considerable. In one US case, a man based in San Francisco defrauded six women of around US$550,000. He developed a relationship with each of the women and then convinced them to invest in his company. He was convicted of wire fraud and sentenced to three and a half years in prison (US Department of Justice, 2020).

Most of the frauds described above are perpetrated by either organised crime groups or lone fraudsters. Some are perpetrated by corrupt employees, such as a call centre operative stealing personal information for the purposes of fraud. However, individuals can also be defrauded by legitimate corporations. For example, there have been numerous examples of companies defrauding pensioners by illegally raiding pension schemes, such as the famous case in the UK where prominent businessman Robert Maxwell did this (Spalek, 1999). Numerous corporations have been found to be built on endemic fraud, deceiving investors and resulting in losses to investors, with the Enron scandal the most high profile (Li, 2010).

At a more mundane level, some generally respected companies have been implicated in fraudulent scams. For example, a British television company was fined after it was found to run telephone prize competitions which viewers paid to participate, but did not enter large numbers of paying participants into the draw (Guardian, 2007). Such regulatory approaches to corporate wrongs, which have many of the hallmarks of fraud, are quite common. In the UK, there have been a series of scandals involving the mis-selling of financial products. During the 1980s, around 2.4 million people were sold high-risk private pensions to replace their occupational pensions, over 5 million were mis-sold endowment mortgages and a similar number were sold worthless payment protection insurance (Tombs, 2013). These mis-selling scandals were based on misrepresenting the value and utility of the products resulted – at least initially – in millions of victims losing money. Rather than criminal prosecution of organisations or their staff, the enforcement approach in these kinds of cases is dominated by regulatory and civil responses involving financial penalties and restitution to the victims (Tombs, 2013).

Frauds against companies

Companies (and charities) are also commonly victims of frauds. They face many of the same frauds individuals experience from external criminals, although they are usually more tailored to the corporate environment. Procurement frauds are very common (National Fraud Authority, 2011). Fraudsters try to change the payment details of legitimate invoices or simply send false invoices to an organisation. For example, in 2019, a Lithuanian man pleaded guilty to sending fake invoices to Google and Facebook purporting to be from the firm Quanta. Between 2013 and 2015, he had secured over US$100 million (Independent, 2019). 'Chief executive scams' have become common where fraudsters impersonate the officer online or via telephone and create a fake scenario where urgent funds need to be sent to an organisation. In one example reported in the media, a UK energy company was reported to have been defrauded of US$243,000 when the Chief Executive thought he was talking to his boss from the parent company and was asked to transfer the money to what he thought was a Hungarian supplier. The fraudster had used AI voice technology to impersonate the boss (Forbes, 2019).

Employees and contractors are also significant sources of frauds for organisations (ACFE, 2020). There are numerous ways this occurs, but some of the common include staff exaggerating expenses or abusing corporate credit cards. Procurement processes are also vulnerable to fraud, for example, corrupt employees divert payments, set up fake supplier companies, conspire with suppliers to falsify purchase invoices or add additional items to orders for their own benefit (Shepherd & Button, 2019). In one infamous case, an accountant for the company Toys R Us set up a fictitious toy manufacturer supplier and proceeded to make payments of over £3.6 million, which he used to fund his liking for high-class prostitutes (Mailonline, 2010).

Customers are also the source of fraud in a number of sectors. Insurers face a significant risk of their customers exaggerating or inventing claims. In the banking sector, many customers exaggerate earnings to secure additional credit or build up debts they have no intention to pay back. Some claim their cards were lost or stolen to try and avoid spending liabilities. In 2017, a man was convicted of fraud after he was found to have exaggerated an insurance claim for a burglary by £40,000 by adding gold jewellery and Apple products (You Talk Insurance, 2017).

Companies often defraud each other, frequently leading to civil litigation. For example, in one high-profile case, British Sky Broadcasting sued the company electronic data systems (EDS) for fraud relating to a contract to build a customer relationship management system they had been awarded. EDS were unable to deliver and Sky ended building the system itself and alleged EDS had lied about the project and timescale. The High Court upheld one of the claims and EDS settled by agreeing to pay £318 million (Pinsent Masons, 2010).

Frauds against the public sector

Just like companies, public sector organisations also face a wide variety of fraud risks from clients, employees, contractors, organised criminals and companies. There are many tax frauds where individuals seek to avoid liability for the tax they owe by illegal means. At its simplest, unrecorded cash transactions enable small businesses to evade tax. Governments hand out lots of money through social security benefits and grants and many applicants use false information to receive money they are not entitled to. Governments

Table 2.2 Examples of frauds against the public sector

Tax fraud

In 2020, a UK company director was convicted of tax fraud after deliberately under-declaring turnover to reduce his liability for value-added tax by £100,000 (CPS, 2020b).

In 2019, a UK builder was convicted of tax fraud after failing to declare income from over £250,000 from projects resulting in a fraud loss of over £100,000 in missed tax and national insurance payments (Accountancy Daily, 2019).

Benefits fraud

A UK woman was jailed for falsely claiming disability benefits claiming she was blind and needed a wheelchair. Surveillance showed her driving, walking and reading a newspaper. She had been using two identities and had been claiming for over 15 years, amounting to just over £1 million (Guardian, 2020a).

A Welshman was convicted of benefits fraud after claiming £17,000 in unemployment benefits while actually working as a self-employed driver for Deliveroo (Walesonline, 2021).

Employee frauds

There are thousands of examples of employee frauds conducted against the public sector that can be found in the media, but probably one of the most infamous was the case of Rita Crundwell who, as the comptroller of the city of Dixon, Illinois in the USA, stole over US$53 million from the authority. The case culminated in a documentary on Netflix called *All the Queen's Horses*, showing how she diverted funds to pay for her lavish lifestyle and horse farming business (US Department of Justice, 2013).

Contract frauds

In the UK, G4S the security company became implicated in a fraud relating to overcharging the Government for services provided related to tagging contracts. It reached a settlement with the government worth £121 million and then to avoid prosecution by the Serious Fraud Office entered into a non-prosecution agreement which incurred another £44 million fine (Guardian, 2020b).

NHS fraud

In the UK, the National Health Service (NHS) is a frequent victim of fraud. The NHS Counter Fraud Authority estimates that the NHS is vulnerable to £1.14 billion worth of fraud each year (NHS, 2021). The so-called NHS fraud takes many forms including, for example, general practice fraud, dental contractor fraud, pharmaceutical contractor fraud and procurement fraud.

In 2021, Essex IT manager at Mid Essex Hospital Services NHS Trust was sentenced to 5 years and 4 months' imprisonment for defrauding the NHS and HMRC of over £800,000. The manager was the director of two companies that had received a large amount of money because the manager was submitting and settling the invoices. No products or services invoiced for by the companies were ever provided to the NHS. The manager also was fraudulently charged for the VAT (NHS, 2021).

Covid relief-related frauds

Governments around the world have set up unprecedented schemes to support businesses during the pandemic. In one case in the UK, two people were convicted of using false identities to claim almost £500,000 in government-backed 'bounce back' loans (Metropolitan Police, 2021).

In the USA, a man was convicted of falsely claiming over US$1 million from the Paycheck Protection Program by submitting claims with false information on the payroll of the company (US Department of Justice, 2021).

also face frauds perpetrated by employees and contractors in similar ways to corporations. The following figure provides a variety of cases of frauds against the public sector from the UK and USA.

Cyber-enabled frauds

It is important to stress the importance of communication technology in the growth and facilitation of fraud. There are two key categories of cyber-crime (Furnell, 2002). Cyber-dependent crimes are the new, technology era crimes that can only be committed via computer technology; Chapter 5 addresses cyber-dependent economic crimes. Cyber-enabled crimes are pre-digital era crimes that are assisted by ICT. Fraud is not a new crime, but ICT has facilitated the huge growth in the crime, and introduced new variants (Amasiatu & Shah, 2014; Button & Cross, 2017; ONS, 2021). Many of the frauds previously discussed in this chapter are not new, such as the mass marketing, identity, romance, credit card and banking frauds, but they have become prominent social problems because of ICT. The expansion of readily accessible new forms of communication enabled by the Internet and low-cost telephony has facilitated the following processes in facilitating fraud:

> *Scaling up*: ICT has enabled more victims to be accessed at lower cost through email, websites, SMS, and social media, typically by way of phishing attacks for ID fraud purposes. Compared to traditional mail and telecommunications, frauds can be industrialised by sending large volumes of correspondence at very low costs.
>
> (Button & Cross, 2017)

> *At a distance communication*: through the growth of social media, email, and SMS, ICT has enabled fraudsters to communicate with potential victims at a distance cheaply and easily. A fraudster in London can easily target victims in Edinburgh, New York and Sydney as easily as someone in the same city. At a distance communication is also more palatable for many offenders as they do not have to meet with or speak with the victim directly.
>
> (Button & Cross, 2017; Duffield & Grabosky, 2001)

> *New opportunities*: ICT has facilitated new ways of doing things which have gradually become exploited by fraudsters, including online banking, shopping and romance frauds.
>
> (Button & Cross, 2017)

> *Technological tools*: tools are now easily available to help facilitate fraud, from mainstream tools such as Photoshop to create false documents to

software that spoofs telephone numbers or fakes the voice of the fraud-ster. The dark web also provides resources to conduct frauds such as compromised bank account details and official documents.

(Gee et al., 2018; Whitty, 2019)

Digital interfaces: many services are now undertaken with no human interaction and providing false information to a 'computer screen' is much easier than via telephone or in person.

(Button & Cross, 2017)

Learning: digital advances and the dark web have made it easier for criminals to share knowledge on how to conduct frauds.

(Gee et al., 2018)

All of the above features of the cyber world have made fraud easier to commit, thus contributing to growth in the extent of the problem.

The extent and impact of fraud

There are a number of indicators which illustrate fraud is one of the most common crimes. In England and Wales, the Crime Survey for England and Wales (CSEW) is unique (in the international context) in regularly asking questions about fraud victimisation. Crime surveys are the gold standard when it comes to gauging victimisation. They seek information from samples of a population which, because of the quality of the methodology, can be extrapolated to the whole population. Originally, the CSEW did not ask about fraud victimisation, but this was reformed in 2016 and the first publication of

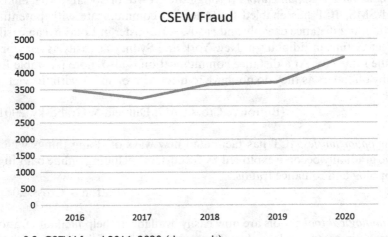

Figure 2.2 CSEW fraud 2016–2020 (thousands).

the experimental statistics for fraud and computer misuse under the CSEW added 5.2 million crimes (3.4 million fraud and 1.8 million computer misuse) to the 5.9 traditional crimes experienced by individuals in the year ending March 2017 (ONS, 2017). The levels of fraud have continued to account for a significant proportion of all crimes against individuals. The pandemic has changed the methodology of the CSEW from face-to-face interviews to telephone, making ONS more cautious of comparison. However, the graph below illustrates the trends in CSEW fraud since it was added in 2016. It shows an upward trend from around 3.5 million incidents in 2016 to around 4.5 million in 2020.

In 2020, of all CSEW crimes the most common was fraud, accounting for 37% of all CSEW crime, and when computer misuse is added, they account for over half. The CSEW, however, does not cover organisational victims and there is no equivalent survey of businesses.[6] Recorded crime statistics, which are less accurate because of non-reporting and other issues, do cover organisational victims. For the year ending December 2020 and 2019, Table 2.3 provides the number of recorded frauds by Action Fraud, Cifas and UK Finance. It shows fraud (and computer misuse) only accounts for 16% of recorded crime. However, many victims do not report frauds and the CSEW should be taken as a better indicator of the extent of the crime (ONS, 2021).

Recorded fraud might not be the most accurate measure of the problem, but it has at least been used as a measure for a much longer period of time to enable trends over time to be illustrated. Figure 2.3 provides the police recorded fraud statistics from 1948 to 2020, so the more recent stats where Cifas and UK Finance data are excluded. It shows a long-term trend of increasing fraud, with a dip in the mid-noughties, which can be partly explained by the move from police receiving reports to the Action Fraud call centre.

Fraud also has many impacts. Top of the list is the financial impact as victims lose money in most cases. Indeed, as was shown in Chapter 1 fraud

Table 2.3 Recorded frauds in England and Wales for 2019–2020

	2019	2020
Action Fraud	337,983	377,756
Cifas	334,413	299,786
UK Finance	94,119	106,701
Total fraud	766,515	784,243
Total recorded crime (excluding fraud and computer misuse)	5,325,884	4,801,109

Note: Action Fraud figures include computer misuse offences of 23,135 and 29,651, respectively.

Source: ONS (2021).

Recorded Fraud 1948-2020

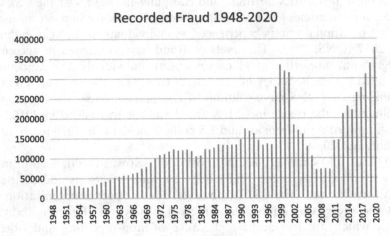

Figure 2.3 Police recorded fraud in England and Wales 1948–2020.

is one of the most expensive crimes: the Annual Fraud Indicator in the UK in 2017 estimated fraud losses at £190 billion (Centre for Counter Fraud Studies, 2017). Those areas of expenditure which are subjected to the highest quality measurement using random sampling show significant losses to fraud and error with the average loss ranging from 4% to 9% in the years Gee and Button have been monitoring such exercises (see Gee & Button, 2021). Behind these figures are some companies and individuals with losses which are life-changing (Button & Cross, 2017; Button et al., 2014). These include:

> *Disruption*: frauds for both organisations and individuals can be disruptive, from the initial investigation, identification of what happened, and rectifying the situation. The costs of dealing with the aftermath in organisations can be very high.
>
> (Button et al., 2015)

> *Psychological and emotional*: a wide range of psychological impacts on individual victims have been noted, including anxiety, stress, and embarrassment.
>
> (Button & Cross, 2017)

> *Health*: the stress and impact of fraud can lead to physical health and mental health problems. Some fraud victims have even committed suicide as a result of the incident.
>
> (Button & Cross, 2017)

Secondary impacts: for both organisations and individuals, frauds can lead to secondary impacts such as damage to reputation, and it can often lead to changes in behaviour, such as not going online or avoiding e-banking if that is where the fraud occurred.

(Button et al., 2015)

Fraud is very clearly not a victimless crime and the financial cost is just one component of harm. It would now seem timely to consider some of the different types of fraudsters that engage in this negative behaviour.

Fraudsters

This chapter has already alluded to the diversity of fraudsters in Figure 2.1, including lone fraudsters, organised groups operating in conspiracies of varying size and sophistication, employees and organisations. This section introduces some of the findings from research into the most prominent types of fraudster.

Everyday fraudsters

It is important not to think of fraud as some special kind of behaviour only a select few are capable of. There is a broad array of low-level frauds that many people are willing to engage in. Karstedt and Farrall (2007) found that 61% of people in the UK have at some time committed at least one minor crime, such as stealing something from work, falsely claiming refunds or padding an insurance claim. They further found that a large portion of the populations in the UK and Germany would consider committing the following fraud crimes (Karstedt & Farrall, 2006):

- paying cash in hand to avoid taxation – 46% in England and Wales and 68% in Western Germany;
- padding an insurance claim to make money – 22% in England and Wales and 40% in Western Germany;
- claiming for refunds they knew they weren't entitled to – 10% in England and Wales and 23% in Western Germany.

The regular reports by the Institute of Business Ethics (2021) provide a variety of evidence on a range of issues across the EU on attitudes to petty misconduct. For example, 9% thought minor exaggeration of travel expenses to be acceptable. There are many other surveys that illustrate how so-called crimes of everyday life are considered relatively normal. A recent study in the USA by the National Retail Federation (2021) found that fraudulent merchandise returns to merchants amounted to $25 billion in 2020.

There have also been some studies that have looked at everyday fraudsters in more depth such as the research by Button et al. (2016) on household insurance fraudsters, showing how ordinary people seize on the opportunity a household insurance policy provides to make additional money with fraudulent claims. There are many examples to be found that illustrate this attitude in the public to low-level frauds. One case that epitomises 'everyday fraudsters' was the case of a priest convicted of fraudulently using one of his dead parishioners 'blue badge' (a car parking pass in the UK for the disabled that enables the holder to park in restricted zones) (Bexhill-on-Sea Observer, 2017). This type of parking fraud has become a particular problem in the UK. These low-level frauds that significant sections of the population are willing to do stand in contrast to how many would consider committing crimes, conventional theft, drug peddling and burglary crimes. A feature, which distinguishes many frauds from other volume crimes, is that they are easy to rationalise, an issue which will be returned to in Chapter 9. The essential point to take away is that most fraudsters are ordinary, respectable people who silently commit fraud as part of their everyday lives. They do not carry the hallmarks of the archetypal wicked, antisocial criminal.

Employee fraudsters

Many fraudsters use their working position to conduct fraud. Employee fraudsters, also known as internal or insider fraudsters, are one of the most commonly researched of all fraudsters (for example, Cressey, 1965, 1986; Ditton, 1977; Holtfreter, 2005; Mars, 1982; Nettler, 1974; Shepherd & Button, 2019). The Toys R Us accountant and Dixon comptroller frauds, discussed earlier, are sensational examples of a very common occurrence. In an extensive study involving 9,175 employees of 45 organisations, Hollinger and Clark (1983) found that one-third of employees offend at least once per year. This result again indicates that fraud is committed by ordinary people as they go about their daily lives. Their data suggests that most employee fraudsters are occasional offenders, but a small minority of around 7% are habitual offenders who perpetrate 68% of the frauds.

There have been multiple studies which seek to profile those engaged in fraud and other white-collar crimes based upon those who have been caught. The regular ACFE (2020) Report to the Nations provides a wealth of data on occupational fraud cases, including the profile of perpetrators. KPMG (2016) have published research on the profile of employee fraudsters as have Bussmann and Werle (2006). There are some common traits, such as the dominance of men: the data suggests that around three quarters of fraudsters are male. Across all three studies, the middle aged are dominant, as are managers and senior executives. Given these demographic characteristics, it is also not surprising that the level of education is also high, with ACFE (2020)

Table 2.4 The profile of occupational fraudsters

	ACFE (2020)	Bussmann and Werle (2006)	KPMG (2016)
Gender	72% – male	87% – male	79% – male
Age	53% – 41–55	71% – 31–50	68% – 36–55
Employment			52% – 4 years plus service
Status in organisation	20% – owner/executive, 35% manager	18% – top management	58% – executive to top management
Education	64% – at least graduates		
Other traits	4% – had prior related fraud conviction		38% – respected, 10% low repute

noting 64% of perpetrators had at least a degree. The ACFE data also shows that only 4% of occupational offenders had prior convictions for fraud. The ACFE is an underestimate because employers typically prefer to just dismiss fraudsters rather than seek prosecution (Shepherd & Button, 2019).

The demographic profile suggests that many detected fraudsters are respected male employees in senior positions who engage in fraud for the first time. Indeed, the theory most often cited as the explanation for employee fraud, Donald Cressey's fraud triangle, was based on research into respectable, professional, male employees (Cressey, 1953). The theory stipulates that three conditions need to be present for employee fraud to occur: an employee under personal financial pressure with the opportunity to commit the fraud, and rationalisations to justify the fraud. The theory is discussed further in Chapter 9. For present purposes, it is important to note the relevance of opportunity to the typical profile of occupational fraudsters: males dominate the professional roles which provide the opportunities for employee fraud.

Professional fraudsters

There are also fraudsters who develop into highly professional fraudsters who conduct frauds to make a living, often a very good living. One of the most famous examples is the US financer Bernie Madoff. He set up an investment business that attracted the rich and famous. It was in reality a giant Ponzi scam, whereby investments from new members pay the 'interest' to the existing members. He was found guilty and sentenced to 150 years in jail for running a US$65 billion Ponzi scheme involving over 37,000 victims in 136 countries (CNBC, 2021). Frank Abagnale is another example, whose early fraud and forgery crimes are the subject of the Hollywood movie, 'Catch Me If You Can'. Abagnale later switched sides to become a counter-fraud consultant and author (Abagnale, 2019).

Organised fraudsters

Fraud is a low risk, high-value revenue stream for organised fraudsters (May & Bhardwa, 2017). Research by Perpetuity Research and Police Foundation (2016) concluded that between 31% and 45% of reported frauds are perpetrated by organised crime groups. They are involved in 'cash-for-crash' insurance scams (Button et al., 2017), mass-marketing frauds including 'boiler room' frauds and identity fraud (Perpetuity Research and Police Foundation, 2016; Shover et al., 2004). These crime groups typically operate globally from a variety of countries and regions, such as Nigeria, Cameroon, India and Eastern Europe (see Levi, 2008; Smith, 2010; Whittaker & Button, 2020).

In 2019, a gang of fraudsters were jailed for their part in a sophisticated fraud, which involved the use of malware to catch the email login details of individuals and businesses. They then used the access credentials to monitor email traffic and identify high-value transactions, which were then diverted to 165 mule accounts. Ten members of the gang were jailed for a total of 44 years for the 228 frauds totalling over £10 million (Action Fraud, 2019).

Corporate fraudsters

Ultimately, it is only people who can conduct acts which are frauds, but sometimes an organisation (or part of it) becomes so permeated with fraud and conducts itself in such a way that it is liable for staff actions. In these cases, the corporation is itself considered the offender, that is, classic white-collar crime. One of the most significant examples in terms of impact was the subprime mortgage scandal in the USA in 2008. This scandal was the result of a variety of fraud-related problems, from mortgage applicants fabricating false information, brokers exaggerating their clients' prospects, to the construction of securities to sell packaged mortgages based upon inadequate credit ratings (Financial Crisis Inquiry Commission, 2011). The consequences of these frauds led to one of the worst recessions since the Second World War, costing the USA alone by 2016 15% of GDP and US$4.6 trillion (Mukunda, 2018).

The global meltdown from the subprime mortgage scandal is particularly remarkable because it followed a very similar pattern of greed and weak regulation in America in the 1980s. The so-called savings-and-loans scandal involved widespread fraud within the US mortgage industry. It led to the conviction of over 800 white-collar criminals and cost the US taxpayer about $1 trillion (Calavita & Pontell, 1994). Enron is another example of a major corporate scandal which involved numerous staff in an American energy company engaged in the exploitation of accounting loopholes and misrepresentations to build one of the biggest corporate frauds in history in which the US$60 billion company collapsed leaving very little for its investor (Healy & Palepu, 2003). Indeed, the predisposition of corporations to offend (not just for fraud) led Tombs and Whyte (2015) to call for their abolition. As corporations and any other type of organisation are essentially collections of people, it is no surprise that corporations offend, so expecting any type of organisation to never offend is naïve.

Conclusion

This chapter has explored the highest profile and probably most ubiquitous economic crimes: fraud. It began by exploring the core elements of what fraud is before moving on to examine some of the legal definitions. The chapter then illustrated the huge diversity of fraud with respect to the types of fraud, the type of offenders and the range of victims. The analysis shows that fraud permeates all areas of society. There are many offenders in all sections of society and all areas of society are vulnerable. Fraud is an everyday feature of life perpetrated by ordinary people during their everyday routines, as well as by determined criminals and corporate white-collar criminals. Consequently, the extent of the crime and its impact is huge.

Notes

1 Ivey v Genting Casinos (UK) Ltd t/a Crockford [2017] UKSC 67.
2 R v Ghosh [1982] 3 WLR 110.
3 See also R. v Barton and Booth [2020] EWCA Crim 575.
4 Ivey v Genting Casinos (UK) Ltd t/a Crockford [2017] UKSC 67, para 60.
5 *Ibid.*
6 The Home Office commissioned a survey of economic crime and in the sectors covered (only part of the private sector) 7% had been victims of fraud and 3% victims of corruption in the previous year.

References

Abagnale, F. W. (2019). *Scam me if you can: Simple strategies to outsmart today's rip-off artists*. Portfolio.

Accountancy Daily. (2019). *Builder jailed for £110k tax fraud*. www.accountancydaily.co/builder-jailed-ps110k-tax-fraud

ACFE. (2020). *Report to the nations*. www.acfe.com/report-to-the-nations/2020/

Action Fraud. (2019). *Gang of fraudsters jailed for 43 years by the Metropolitan Police after reports to Action Fraud*. www.actionfraud.police.uk/news/gang-of-fraudsters-jailed-for-43-years-by-the-metropolitan-police-after-reports-to-action-fraud

Amasiatu, C. V., & Shah, M. H. (2014). First party fraud: A review of the forms and motives of fraudulent consumer behaviours in e-tailing. *International Journal of Retail & Distribution Management, 42*(9), 805–817. https://doi.org/10.1108/IJRDM-05-2013-0112

Beals, M., DeLiema, M., & Deevy, M. (2015). *Framework for a taxonomy of fraud.* Financial Fraud Research Center. http://162.144.124.243/~longevl0/wp-content/uploads/2016/03/Full-Taxonomy-report.pdf

Bexhill-on-Sea Observer. (2017). *A priest who was caught fraudulently using a dead parishioner's Blue Badge has been fined and ordered to carry out 200 hours of unpaid work.* Bexhill-on-Sea Observer. www.bexhillobserver.net/news/bexhill-priest-sentenced-blue-badge-fraud-2073127

Bussman, K., & Werle, M. (2006). Addressing crime in companies: First findings from a global survey of economic crime. *British Journal of Criminology, 46*(6), 1128–1144.

Button, M., Blackbourn, D., Lewis, C., & Shepherd, D. (2015). Uncovering the hidden cost of staff fraud: An assessment of 45 cases in the UK. *Journal of Financial Crime, 22*(2), 170–183. https://doi.org/10.1108/JFC-11-2013-0070

Button, M., Brooks, G., Lewis, C., & Aleem, A. (2017). Just about everybody doing the business? Explaining 'cash-for-crash' insurance fraud in the United Kingdom. *Australian and New Zealand Journal of Criminology, 50*(2), 176–194. https://doi:10.1177/0004865816638910

Button, M., & Cross, C. (2017). *Cyber frauds, scams and their victims.* Taylor & Francis.

Button, M., Lewis, C. & Tapley, J. (2014). Not a victimless crime: The impact of fraud on individual victims and their families. *Security Journal, 27*(1), 36–54.

Button, M., Pakes, F., & Blackbourn, D. (2016). 'All walks of life': A profile of household insurance fraudsters in the United Kingdom. *Security Journal, 29*(3), 501–519.

Button, M., Shepherd, D., & Blackbourn, D. (2018). 'The iceberg beneath the sea', fraudsters and their punishment through non-criminal justice in the 'Fraud Justice Network' in England and Wales. *International Journal of Law, Crime and Justice, 53*(1), 56–66. https://doi.org/10.1016/j.ijlcj.2018.03.001.

Calavita, K., & Pontell, H. (1994). The state and white-collar crime: Saving the savings and loans. *Law Society and Review, 28*(2), 297–166.

Centre for Counter Fraud Studies. (2017). *Annual Fraud Indicator 2017.* www.crowe.com/uk/croweuk/-/media/Crowe/Firms/Europe/uk/CroweUK/PDF-publications/Annual-Fraud-Indicator-report-2017

Cifas. (2019). *Cifas research reveals sharp rise in employment application fraud by middle-aged job seekers.* www.cifas.org.uk/newsroom/application-fraud-by-middle-aged-job-seekers

CNBC. (2021). *Bernie Madoff, mastermind of the nation's biggest investment fraud, dies at 82.* www.cnbc.com/2021/04/14/bernie-madoff-dies-mastermind-of-the-nations-biggest-investment-fraud-was-82.html

CPS. (2020a). *Company director jailed for tax fraud.* www.cps.gov.uk/mersey-cheshire/news/company-director-jailed-tax-fraud

CPS. (2020b). *The Fraud Act 2006.* www.cps.gov.uk/legal-guidance/fraud-act-2006

CPS. (n.d.). *Car insurance fraud penalties.* www.cps.gov.uk/sites/default/files/documents/publications/disclosure_10.pdf

Cressey, D. (1953). *Other people's money.* Wadsworth Publishing.

Cressey, D. (1965). The respectable criminal. *Criminologica, 3*(1), 13–16.

Cressey, D. (1986). Why managers commit fraud. *Australian and New Zealand Journal of Criminology, 19*(4), 195–209.

Cross, C., & Holt, T. J. (2021). The use of military profiles in romance fraud schemes. *Victims and Offenders, 16*(3), 385–406. https://doi:10.1080/15564886.2020.1850582

Ditton, J. (1977). *Part-time crime: An ethnography of fiddling and pilferage.* MacMillan Press.

Duffield, G., & Grabosky, P. (2001). *The psychology of fraud: Trends and issues in crime and criminal justice no. 199.* Australian Institute of Criminology. www.aic.gov.au/publications/tandi/tandi199

ejtn (n.d.). *Criminal Code of the Czech Republic* (English translation). www.ejtn.eu/PageFiles/6533/Criminal%20Code%20of%20the%20Czech%20Republic.pdf

Farrell, G., & Pease, K. (2007). The sting in the tail of the British Crime Survey: Multiple victimisations. In M. Hough & M. Maxfield (Eds.), *Crime prevention studies volume 22: Surveying crime in the 21st century.* Willan Publishing.

FBI. (2018). *Identity thief sentenced Nevada man stole multiple identities, millions of dollars.* www.fbi.gov/news/stories/nevada-identity-thief-sentenced-091818

Financial Crisis Inquiry Commission. (2011). *The financial crisis inquiry report: The final report of the National Commission on the causes of the financial and economic crisis in the United States including dissenting views.* www.govinfo.gov/content/pkg/GPO-FCIC/pdf/GPO-FCIC.pdf

Forbes. (2019). *A voice deepfake was used to scam a CEO out of $243,000.* www.forbes.com/sites/jessedamiani/2019/09/03/a-voice-deepfake-was-used-to-scam-a-ceo-out-of-243000/

Fraud Act. (2006). *c. 35.* www.legislation.gov.uk/ukpga/2006/35/contents

Furnell, S. (2002). *Cybercrime: Vandalizing the information society.* Addison-Wesley.

Gee, J., & Button, M. (2021). *The financial cost of fraud 2021.* Crowe. www.crowe.com/uk/insights/financial-cost-of-fraud-2021

Gee, J., Hall, L., Wang, V., Button, M., & Joseph, E. (2018). *The dark web-bad for business.* Crowe. www.crowe.com/uk/croweuk/-/media/Crowe/Firms/Europe/uk/CroweUK/PDF-publications/Dark-Web-Report.ashx?la=en-GB&hash=BFCB10939528D385EE7E3AD763EC329BB46EAD90&hash=BFCB10939528D385EE7E3AD763EC329BB46EAD90

Glenn, H. P. (2014). *Legal traditions of the world: Sustainable diversity in law* (5th ed.). Oxford University Press.

Gov.info. (n.d. a). *Content details.* www.govinfo.gov/app/details/USCODE-2019-title18/USCODE-2019-title18-partI-chap63-sec1341

Gov.info. (n.d. b). *Content details.* www.govinfo.gov/app/details/USCODE-2011-title18/USCODE-2011-title18-partI-chap63-sec1343

Guardian. (2007). *GMTV phone-in scandal: The biggest fraud in UK TV history?* www.theguardian.com/media/organgrinder/2007/sep/26/gmtvphoneinscandalthebigge

Guardian. (2020a). *Woman who falsely claimed more than £1m in benefits is jailed.* www.theguardian.com/uk-news/2020/jun/08/christina-pomfrey-falsely-claimed-1m-pounds-benefits-jailed-manchester

Guardian. (2020b). *G4S fined £44m by Serious Fraud Office over electronic tagging.* www.theguardian.com/business/2020/jul/10/g4s-fined-44m-by-serious-office-over-electronic-tagging

Healy, P. M., & Palepu, K. G. (2003). The fall of Enron. *Journal of Economic Perspectives, 17*(2), 3–26.

Heranová, S. (2012). *Trestněprávní postih podvodných jednání proti majetku. Disertační práce.* https://dspace.cuni.cz/bitstream/handle/20.500.11956/41605/140020121.pdf?sequence=1&isAllowed=y

HMRC. (n.d.). *Phishing emails and bogus contact: HM Revenue and Customs examples.* https://assets.publishing.service.gov.uk/government/uploads/system/uploads/attachment_data/file/515727/Phishing_emails_and_bogus_contact_Apr_16.pdf

Hollinger, R., & Clark, J. (1983). Deterrence in the workplace: Perceived certainty, perceived severity and employee theft. *Social Forces, 62,* 398–418.

Holtfreter, K. (2005). Is occupational fraud "typical" white-collar crime? A comparison of individual and organizational characteristics. *Journal of Criminal Justice, 33*(4), 153–165.

Independent. (2019). *Man pleads guilty to stealing $100m from Google and Facebook by sending fake invoices.* www.independent.co.uk/news/world/americas/google-facebook-scam-fake-invoice-wire-fraud-guilty-a8840071.html

Institute of Business Ethics. (2021). *Ethics at work: 2021 International survey of employees.* www.ibe.org.uk/uploads/assets/9f4fba9a-d466-4cb3-80c8dbd529dedbe8/7786cb1f-f7f2-4ba1-b0e88221821ac24b/IBE-EaW2021.pdf

Irish Times. (2017). *Man jailed over selling fake tickets to Adele and Justin Bieber concerts.* www.irishtimes.com/news/ireland/irish-news/man-jailed-over-selling-fake-tickets-to-adele-and-justin-bieber-concerts-1.2966465

Jackson, J. D., & Summers, S. J. (2012). *The internationalisation of criminal evidence: Beyond the common law and civil law traditions.* Cambridge University Press.

Karstedt, S., & Farrall, S. (2006). The moral economy of everyday crime: Markets, consumers and citizens. *British Journal of Criminology, 46*(6), 1011–1036.

Karstedt, S., & Farrall, S. (2007). *Law abiding majority? The everyday crimes of the middle classes, Briefing 3, June 2007.* Centre for Crime and Justice Studies. www.crimeandjustice.org.uk/opus45/Law_abiding_Majority_FINAL_VERSION.pd

KPMG. (2016). *Global profile of fraudsters.* https://assets.kpmg/content/dam/kpmg/ca/pdf/2016/09/ca-kpmg-global-profiles-of-the-fraudster.pdf

Levi, M. (2003). The Roskill fraud commission revisited. *Journal of Financial Crime, 11*(1), 38–44. https://doi.org/10.1108/13590790410809022

Levi, M. (2008). Organized fraud and organizing frauds: Unpacking research on networks and organization. *Criminology and Criminal Justice, 8*(4), 389–419. https://doi.org/10.1177%2F1748895808096470

Levi, M. (2012). Trends and costs of fraud. In A. Doig (Ed.), *Fraud: The counter fraud practitioner's handbook.* Gower.

Li, Y. (2010). The case analysis of the scandal of Enron. *International Journal of Business & Management, 5*(10), 37–41.

Mailonline. (2010). *Sex-mad Toys R Us boss stole millions from company to pay for call girls and sports cars.* www.dailymail.co.uk/news/article-1290821/Sex-mad-Toys-R-Us-boss-Paul-Hopes-stole-millions-pay-girls-sports-cars.html

Mars, G. (1982). *Cheats at work: An anthropology of workplace crime.* Allen and Unwin.

May, T., & Bhardwa, B. (2017). *Organised crime groups involved in fraud.* Springer.

McGrath, P. (2008). *Commercial fraud in civil practice.* Oxford University Press.

Metropolitan Police. (2021). *Two jailed for fraudulently claiming Covid Bounce Back loans.* https://news.met.police.uk/news/two-jailed-for-fraudulently-claiming-covid-bounce-back-loans-423511

Money Marketing. (2016). *Boiler room gang jailed over £7.5m landbanking fraud.* www.moneymarketing.co.uk/news/boiler-room-gang-jailed-7-5m-landbanking-fraud/

Mukunda, G. (2018). The social and political costs of the financial crisis, 10 years later. *Harvard Business Review.* https://hbr.org/2018/09/the-social-and-political-costs-of-the-financial-crisis-10-years-later

National Fraud Authority. (2011). *Procurement fraud in the public sector.* https://assets. publishing.service.gov.uk/government/uploads/system/uploads/attachment_data/ file/118460/procurement-fraud-public-sector.pdf

National Retail Federation. (2021). *$428 billion in merchandise returned in 2020.* https://nrf.com/media-center/press-releases/428-billion-merchandise-returned-2020

Nettler, G. (1974). Embezzlement without problems. *British Journal of Criminology, 14*(1), 70–77.

NHS. (2021). *Senior IT manager sentenced for £800,000 fraud against NHS and HMRC.* https://cfa.nhs.uk/about-nhscfa/latest-news/senior-IT-manager-sentenced-for-fraud-against-NHS-and-HMRC

ONS. (2017). *Crime in England and Wales: Year ending March 2017.* www. ons.gov.uk/peoplepopulationandcommunity/crimeandjustice/bulletins/ crimeinenglandandwales/yearendingmar2017

ONS. (2021). *Crime in England and Wales: Year ending December 2020 Appendix Tables.* www.ons.gov.uk/peoplepopulationandcommunity/crimeandjustice/datasets/ crimeinenglandandwalesappendixtables

Perpetuity Research and Police Foundation. (2016). *Organised fraud in local communities.* Police Foundation. https://perpetuityresearch.com/wp-content/uploads/2016/ 08/org_fraud_in_local_communities_final.pdf

Pinsent Masons. (2010). *BSkyB and EDS settle IT dispute for £318 million.* www. pinsentmasons.com/out-law/news/bskyb-and-eds-settle-it-dispute-for-318-million

Shepherd, D., & Button, M. (2019). Organizational inhibitions to addressing occupational fraud: A theory of differential rationalization. *Deviant Behavior, 40*(8), 971–991.

Shover, N., Coffey, G. S., & Sanders, C. R. (2004). Dialling for dollars: Opportunities, justifications, and telemarketing fraud. *Qualitative Sociology, 27*(1), 59–75.

Smith, D. J. (2010). *A culture of corruption.* Princeton University Press.

Smith, I., & Shepherd, D. (2019). *Commercial fraud and cyber fraud: A legal guide to justice for businesses.* Bloomsbury.

Sorell, T., & Whitty, M. (2019). Online romance scams and victimhood. *Security Journal, 32*(3), 342–361.

Spalek, B. (1999). Exploring the impact of financial crime: A study looking into the effects of the Maxwell scandal upon the Maxwell pensioners. *International Review of Victimology, 6*(3), 213–230.

Tombs, S. (2013). Working for the 'Free' Market: State complicity in routine corporate harm in the United Kingdom. *Revista Crítica Penal y Poder, 5,* 291–313.

Tombs, S., & Whyte, D. (2015). *The corporate criminal: Why corporations must be abolished.* Routledge.

US Department of Justice. (2013). *Former Dixon comptroller Rita Crundwell sentenced to nearly 20 Years in Federal prison for $53.7 million theft from city.* www.justice.gov/ usao-ndil/pr/former-dixon-comptroller-rita-crundwell-sentenced-nearly-20-years-federal-prison-537

US Department of Justice. (2020). *Fraudster sentenced to three-and-a-half years in prison for romance scam.* www.justice.gov/usao-ndca/pr/fraudster-sentenced-three-and-half-years-prison-romance-scam

US Department of Justice. (2021). *Man sentenced for his role in directing COVID-19 relief fraud scheme.* www.justice.gov/opa/pr/man-sentenced-his-role-directing-covid-19-relief-fraud-scheme

Walesonline. (2021). *Convicted burglar worked for Deliveroo while claiming £17,000 in benefits*. www.walesonline.co.uk/news/wales-news/deliveroo-driver-benefit-fraud-burglar-19567682

Wells, J. (2017). *Corporate fraud handbook: Prevention and detection* (5th ed.). Wiley.

Whittaker, J. M., & Button, M. (2020). Understanding pet scams: A case study of advance fee and non-delivery fraud using victims' accounts. *Australian and New Zealand Journal of Criminology, 53*(4), 497–514.

Whitty, M. T. (2019). Predicting susceptibility to cyber-fraud victimhood. *Journal of Financial Crime, 26*(1), 277–292. https://doi.org/10.1108/JFC-10-2017-0095

You Talk Insurance. (2017). *Man sentenced for false insurance claims worth over £40,000*. https://youtalk-insurance.com/broker-news/man-sentenced-for-false-insurance-claims-worth-over-%C2%A340000

Chapter 3

Bribery and corruption

Introduction

The UK and other countries, which have historically failed to prosecute corporations and their managers for complex economic crimes, have adapted their approaches to increase their enforcement activities. Especially the increased enforcement of foreign anti-corruption laws has made the culpability of corporations and their directors a practical problem. For many corporations, bribery and corruption are no longer the cost of doing business in developing countries – corporations and their managers around the world must now proactively prevent and detect bribery and corruption in order to avoid liability based on national and international legislative standards.

This chapter focuses on key issues associated with bribery and corruption. The 'Essentials of corruption' section explores what corruption is by examining its legal and academic definitions and key classifications such as grand corruption, petty corruption, foreign corruption and domestic corruption. The section analyses consequences of corruption and the extent of the problem. The 'The problem of international bribery' section provides an analysis of the problem of international bribery including laws that regulate it and the complexity of international bribery cases. The 'Preventing corporate bribery – compliance' section focuses on the prevention of corporate bribery and anti-bribery and corruption compliance. We will see how enforcement authorities place great importance on anti-bribery compliance programmes (ABC programmes), why organisations invest significant resources in creating and implementing them and what the features of an adequate ABC compliance programme are.

Essentials of corruption

This section guides the reader through key perspectives that will support their independent thinking about the nature of corruption and an appropriate anti-corruption response.[1] It starts by discussing the concept of corruption

DOI: 10.4324/9781003081753-3

and its consequences. It will then consider key issues associated with measuring corruption.

Concept of corruption

Corruption is a cross-cutting issue for which there is no universal definition (Hough, 2017; Lambsdorff, 2006). The Transparency International definition, 'the abuse of entrusted power for private gain', is often used to support analyses and referred to in many studies (for example, Sullivan, 2009, p. 6). Although this definition is helpful in focusing attention on the crimes of the powerful, it does not adequately capture all the characteristics of corrupt exchanges. It is clearly relevant to public officials and corporate executives who abuse their positions. Yet it excludes situations in which the powerless are compelled to comply with the demands of the powerful in a fleeting or enduring corrupt relationship (Button et al., 2019). Moreover, it overlooks a systemic character of corruption as a form of large social inequality (Johnston, 2010), and when politics and law-making produce unfair, ineffective and inefficacious laws (Pasculli, 2019; Pasculli & Ryder, 2019).

One way to deal with the complexity of corruption is to simply view it as the taxonomic name for a group of economic crimes. The United Nations Convention Against Corruption (UNCAC), for example, is the most wide-reaching and comprehensive international treaty against corruption signed by 187 countries, yet it avoids defining the term 'corruption', preferring instead to rely on a set of specific types of corruption (for an analysis, see Zagaris, 2015, pp. 137–138):

- Article 15 – Bribery of national public officials
- Article 16 – Bribery of foreign public officials and officials of public international organisations
- Article 17 – Embezzlement, misappropriation or other diversion of property by a public official
- Article 18 – Trading in influence
- Article 19 – Abuse of functions
- Article 20 – Illicit enrichment
- Article 21 – Bribery in the private sector
- Article 22 – Embezzlement of property in the private sector
- Article 23 – Laundering of proceeds of crime

Although corruption is often used as a synonym for bribery, the UNCAC framework clearly illustrates that bribery is just one of a range of corrupt acts. The UNCAC also includes occupational fraud (embezzlement), theft (misappropriation) and money laundering as well as the broadly framed offences of trading in influence and abuse of functions. Except for money laundering (Article 23 of the UNCAC; see also Chapter 8), an explicit and important feature of all the crimes in the UNCAC approach is that at least one party perpetrates the corrupt act during the course of their occupation.

The literature offers alternative ways to classify corruption and provides various descriptive typologies (see generally Fletcher & Hermann, 2012). The most important are set out below:

- **Grand corruption**: it is associated with high level, high value exchanges between political elites, corporations and powerful interest groups. Political elites abuse their position to distribute a variety of resources in exchange for political support (Philp & Dávid-Barrett, 2015). For example, in economies with large state ownership, they often privatise state ownership in a way to enrich themselves and those that support them (Dávid-Barrett & Fazekas, 2020).
- **Petty corruption**: as opposed to high-level corruption, petty corruption involves low value exchanges, usually associated with lower ranked government officials and others that can misuse their position for their own benefit. For example, a citizen who has a right to be issued with a public document, such as a marriage license or a birth certificate, might in some countries be required to pay an unofficial fee. Many forms of petty corruption are the so-called facilitation payments, or speed payments, that might be required by certain administrators in order to act in a timely manner, for example, to speed up a business-related licencing process.
- **Active vs passive corruption**: these terms are used to distinguish between the actions of those that are seeking to corruptly influence another to obtain a favourable outcome (active corruption) and those that require or receive an improper advantage (passive corruption). They are sometimes referred to as the supply side and demand side of corruption. For example, active bribery relates to the supplier who pays a bribe to win a contract, and passive bribery relates to the customer who takes a bribe to place the contract.
- **Domestic and foreign corruption**: domestic corruption refers to corrupt exchanges which take place within a country. International or foreign corruption refers to corrupt exchanges that cross international borders.

The distinction between domestic and foreign corruption is particularly important as it represents a legal dichotomy for law enforcement. This dichotomy is central to the Organisation for Economic Cooperation and Development's (OECD) Convention on Combating Bribery of Foreign Public Officials in International Business Transactions (OECD Anti-Bribery Convention), which was adopted in 1997 to solely address active bribery of foreign public officials. The OECD Anti-Bribery Convention follows America's 1977 Foreign Corrupt Practices Act (FCPA) criminalising the bribe payer in corrupt exchanges with foreign officials and not addressing the passive bribery of the official.

Moreover, the domestic and foreign bribery dichotomy is explicitly recognised in the UNCAC. Whilst Article 15 of the UNCAC requires signatories to criminalise both active and passive bribery involving domestic public officials, Article 16 of the UNCAC mirrors the OECD Anti-Bribery Convention by only requiring nations to make illegal active bribery of foreign public officials. The logic here is that the foreign country's own justice system is best placed to prosecute its own public officials under domestic legislation.

Although the structural logic and flexibility built into international conventions such as the UNCAC and the OECD Anti-Bribery Convention are pragmatic in seeking to positively influence domestic legal orders, they have limitations. Corruption is not just a simple, unitary concept involving an improper economic exchange (Johnston, 2010). The complexity of the corruption problem can be framed in terms of the rule of law, morality, economic development, poverty, social equality, trust, competition and tradition. The values and meanings attached to these concepts are neither universal nor static. This is why the notion of what constitutes corruption is subject to the dynamics of cultural influences, societal values, accepted beliefs and political tensions (Johnston, 2010; Lambsdorff, 2006). This conceptual discussion on corruption is closely related to the discussion about the consequences of corruption.

Consequences of corruption

Economic exchanges are variously regarded as criminal, unethical or legitimate practice depending on local cultural norms and their expression in national laws. Early commentators advocated that corruption is in some instances an efficient phenomenon that serves to insert 'grease in the wheels' of commerce and overcome the dysfunctional inefficiencies of bad administrations (Huntington, 1968). However, this is primarily a utilitarian perspective from the supply side that sees corruption as a tool to get things done. It ignores the huge, long-term harm caused on the demand side, especially in developing nations. Corruption might indeed overcome a government's administrative failings in the short term, but in the long term, it amplifies systemic inefficiencies (Bardha, 1997; Hock, 2020a, pp. 22–23). It becomes a corrosive problem that pervades public administration and commerce (Fletcher & Hermann, 2012).

Corruption contributes to poverty, inequality, social divisions, political instability, lowers rates of economic growth, lowers incentives to invest and diverts public funds to useless vanity projects (Rose-Ackerman, 1999; Vishny & Shleifer, 1993). It is a deadly problem worldwide: over $500 billion in lost health resources and 140,000 childhood deaths are attributable to corruption each year (Bruckner, 2019; Hanf et al., 2011). According to the Stanford Law School (n.d.), the healthcare industry is second only to the oil and gas industry in the number of actions brought under the FCPA for foreign bribery, accounting for 12% of all such actions, and just ahead of the aero-space industry.

From a policy perspective, both the UNCAC and the OECD Anti-Bribery Convention make clear moral statements that corruption is unacceptable. The conventions represent collective agreements on how corruption should be tackled and why it should be tackled. The introduction to the UNCAC describes corruption as an 'insidious plague' and an 'evil phenomenon' that threatens 'the stability and security of societies, undermining the institutions and values of democracy, ethical values and justice and jeopardizing sustain-able development and the rule of law' (UNCAC: 2). The Preamble of the OECD Anti-Bribery Convention describes bribery as a widespread phenom-enon 'which raises serious moral and political concerns, undermines good governance and economic development, and distorts international competi-tive conditions'. These are fine words, but policy makers worldwide need hard evidence to turn the sentiments into action (see Hough, 2013). The justifica-tion for building sufficient capacity to tackle corruption mainly rests in quan-tifying the aggregated harmful consequences and costs of the phenomenon, that is, measuring the extent of the problem.

Extent of corruption

Measuring the extent of corruption is fraught with challenges (Sampford et al., 2006). The basic measures of crime, such as police recorded crime statistics, are largely useless when applied to corruption. In part, this is because the secrecy of corruption means that the large majority of cases remain hidden. Those that are discovered are often not reported to the authorities, and many that are reported are not investigated. Investigations then often fail to deter-mine whether a crime has actually occurred. Unlike burglary, where there is usually clear evidence of a crime, such as a broken window and missing prop-erty, corruption often involves just suspicion and little actionable evidence.

Another important issue is that the broad concept of corruption is not always coterminous with specific pieces of legislation. In the UK, acts of corruption could, for example, fall under the UK Bribery Act 2010, Misconduct in Public Office (common law offence), the Fraud Act 2006, the Theft Act 1968 and the Competition Act 1998. Identifying which specific cases prosecuted under these laws involved corruption is very difficult. Misconduct in Public Office is itself a broadly framed offence that encompasses, for example, the wilful neglect of a person in police custody to intentional acts of fraud, theft and bribery perpetrated by public officials (Andresen & Button, 2019; Crown Prosecution Service [CPS], 2018). Consequently, official statistics relating to corruption cases represent the tip of the iceberg. Based on the Bribery Act 2010 and the assumption that all Misconduct in Public Office offences involve corruption, Table 3.1 sets out the number of corruption offences recorded in the UK between 2017 and 2020 (Office for National Statistics [ONS], 2020).

Table 3.1 Recorded corruption offences in the UK

	2017–2018	2018–2019	2019–2020
Offering bribes	7	12	8
Accepting bribes	6	3	2
Corporation – failure to prevent bribery	0	1	0
Misconduct in a public office	92	127	118
Total corruption offences	**105**	**143**	**128**

Source: ONS (2020).

At less than 150 cases per year, the data erroneously suggests corruption is a very small problem.

However, a variety of other methods have been developed to improve estimates. Surveys of the general population, business leaders and procurement specialists are used to quantify the perception of the extent of corruption. The European Commission (2017) survey found that 68% of the public across Europe believed corruption was widespread. The results varied widely from 21% in Finland to 96% in Greece. 55% of UK respondents thought it was widespread, a figure which stands in stark contrast to the small number of recorded cases.

Perception, however, is not the reality and some of the most influential surveys such as the Transparency International's Corruption Perception Index have been heavily criticised (Andresson & Heywood, 2009). An alternative approach is to conduct an experience survey. In addition to capturing perceptions, the European Commission (2017) survey asked respondents whether they had been victims of corruption in the prior year. The results were much lower than the perception figures. Overall, 7% had been victims of corruption, 10% in Greece, 2% in Finland and 2% in the UK. The findings indicate that perceptions substantially exaggerate the scale of the problem. Nevertheless, the UK finding suggests that the authorities are scratching at the surface of the problem in delivering less than 150 justice outcomes per year.

As an alternative, some studies used econometrics and big data to estimate the extent of corruption (see Fazekas et al., 2013). Many of these approaches relate to corruption in public procurement. The European Commission (2013) report, for example, indicates that direct costs of corruption in public procurement are between 2% and 10% of the overall value of procurement depending on the industry sector. When applied to the €2 trillion annual procurement budget of public authorities in the EU, the lower 2% figure is equivalent to €40 billion per year.

The problem of international bribery

In the search for profit, and under pressure from their competitors, organisations sometimes engage in paying bribes to secure business. Bribes are often disguised as commissions, facilitation fees, presents and donations. It is well documented how large businesses in many sectors understood bribery as a 'way of doing business', especially in developing markets. Historically, as businesses failed to establish effective anti-bribery control procedures, states had to regulate them.[2]

In this section, we discuss how Western governments have developed legislation and practice to counter international bribery. This started with the US FCPA in 1977, followed by the adoption of multilateral treaties in the late 1990s and moved on to the adoption of the 2010 Bribery Act and similar foreign anti-bribery statutes across the world.

International anti-bribery laws

In the 1970s, the USA faced a series of corruption scandals associated with the US aircraft manufacturer Lockheed and the so-called Watergate scandal (see Spalding, 2010, pp. 357–360). Lockheed paid bribes to foreign public officials between the 1950s and 1970s in order to secure military contracts. Watergate was a major political scandal related to the Nixon administration. These scandals triggered subsequent investigations by the US Securities and Exchange Commission (SEC), which discovered that hundreds of US organisations admitted making questionable or illegal payments to foreign public officials. As a result, in order to restore public confidence in the integrity of the US business, the FCPA was passed in 1977, which introduced sanctions against US businesses associated with bribery of foreign public officials in international business transactions.

The rationale of the FCPA is illustrated by an extract from the US Senate debate on the Act:

> Corporate bribery is bad business. In our free market system it is basic that the sale of products should take place on the basis of price, quality and service. Corporate bribery is fundamentally destructive of this basic tenet. Corporate bribery of foreign officials takes place primarily to assist corporations in getting business. This foreign corporate bribery affects the very stability of overseas business. Foreign corporate bribes also affect our domestic competitive climate when domestic firms engage in such practices as a substitute for healthy competition for foreign business.
>
> (US Senate, 1977)

Academics have long discussed what is, and should be, the leading rationale of the FCPA, identifying a set of moral and efficiency rationales (Hock, 2014).

The FCPA has been continually developing and, especially since 1998, the FCPA has been expanded so as to allow enforcement authorities to prosecute non-US corporations and nationals (see Hock, 2020a, 2021). The US

Department of Justice (DOJ) and the SEC have also produced several guidance documents, including the Resource Guide (DOJ & SEC, 2020) released in 2012 and updated in July 2020. The Resource Guide provides information to all levels of enterprise, which includes who and what is covered by the FCPA's anti-bribery and accounting provisions; what constitutes proper and improper gifts, travel and entertainment expenses; the nature of facilitating payments; how successor's liability is determined in the mergers and acquisitions context; the hallmarks of an effective corporate compliance programme; and the different types of civil and criminal resolutions available.

International bribery overlaps with other types of economic crimes such as tax fraud, money laundering and accountancy fraud. Consequently, defendants in international bribery are often charged with alternative charges. The FCPA itself includes two types of provisions: anti-bribery provisions and accounting provisions. Moreover, the accounting provisions include two types of charges – books and records as well as internal control charges. Table 3.2 provides the most important features of these provisions.

While the FCPA was adopted in 1977, the first international attempt to counter international bribery and corruption took place only in 1997 with the OECD Anti-Bribery Convention. Paradoxically, it was the US business lobby that facilitated the adoption of the OECD Anti-Bribery Convention. The US businesses wanted non-American businesses to comply with standards equivalent to the FCPA standard (Rose, 2015, p. 1). They were successful: up to August 2021, the 37 OECD members and seven non-members – Argentina, Brazil, Bulgaria, Costa Rica, Peru, Russia and South Africa – had adopted the OECD Convention.

The UK adopted a special foreign anti-bribery statute too. Following a series of high-profile cases such as the BAE Systems, the UK was harshly criticised by the OECD for its ineffectiveness and the lack of compliance with the OECD Anti-Bribery Convention. In response, the UK adopted the

Table 3.2 Charges under the FCPA

FCPA	
Anti-bribery charges §78dd-1,2 or 3	FCPA prohibits the offer of a payment, a promise to pay or an authorisation of payment of money or anything of value knowing that this would induce a foreign official to do or omit to do an act in violation of their lawful duty, or to secure an important advantage.
Books and records charges §78m(b) (2)(A)	FCPA requires companies to meet its accounting standards, especially maintaining books and records that accurately and fairly reflect their transactions.
Internal controls charges §78m(b) (2)(B)	FCPA requires companies to devise and maintain an adequate system of internal controls.

Bribery Act in 2010. The Bribery Act has radically changed the law relating to bribery extending the reach of the law beyond the borders of the UK to many individuals and organisations with a connection to the UK (Hock, 2020a, pp. 54–55). The legislation sets out the following key offences:

Section 1: Bribing Another Person
This offence relates to the briber, rather than the recipient. It essentially relates to a person offering some form of advantage (frequently, but not always financial) to another person in return for some form of improper performance.

Section 2: Offences Related to Being Bribed
The second offence relates to the recipient. A person is guilty of an offence if they request, receive or agree to some financial advantage in return for improper performance.

Section 6: Offences of Bribing Foreign Public Officials
This section extends the reach of the law beyond the UK borders making it an offence to bribe a foreign public official.

Section 7: Failure of a Commercial Organisation to Prevent Bribery
Section 7 makes it an offence for a commercial organisation to fail to prevent bribery. However, there is a defence of having adequate procedures in place, which incentivises organisations to implement adequate compliance programmes.

The UK Bribery Act is generally considered as one of the most comprehensive anti-bribery laws as it covers not only active and passive bribery on a public level but also business-to-business bribery. In addition, Section 7 of the Bribery Act introduces the failure to prevent bribery offence, which provides for wide extraterritorial jurisdictions.

Law enforcement and complexity of international bribery cases

International bribery remains under-researched by criminologists (Lord, 2014a,b). Historically, policing of international bribery was limited to individuals and corporations under the jurisdiction of the FCPA, which was enacted in 1977 to prohibit the active bribery of foreign public officials. This statute has far-reaching jurisdiction and is backed by well-resourced enforcement authorities – the DOJ and the SEC (see Hock, 2017).

The vast majority of cases are resolved out of the court through administrative sanctions and negotiated settlements involving deferred prosecution agreements (DPAs) or non-prosecution agreements (NPAs). Between 2010 and 2019, corporations paid penalties of $19.1 billion and individuals paid $1.3 billion in cases brought by the DOJ and the SEC (Stanford Law School, n.d.). These settlement agreements very often include binding undertakings for the corporations to introduce robust ethics and compliance programmes. The prosecutors sometimes agree with corporations to appoint external monitors to ensure the compliance programmes are adequately implemented (Ford & Hess, 2008).

International bribery has recently become an enforcement priority in a number of countries, including the UK, France, Brazil, Singapore and Canada. An increase in enforcement activity is evidenced by the emergence of the so-called global enforcement bundles whereby an offending corporation agrees to settle a package of charges out of court with prosecutors in multiple jurisdictions (Hock, 2021). The emergence of these bundles is associated with globalisation of business, the global nature of international bribery and overlapping jurisdictional claims of states that started policing international bribery (Gutterman, 2019a,b).

The largest global settlement bundles involving the UK enforcement authorities are Rolls Royce, Airbus and Amec Foster Wheeler Energy (Table 3.3).[3]

The emergence of global anti-bribery bundles presents the key development in this area, as international anti-bribery laws were previously only sporadically enforced. It was only in the late 2000s when the US enforcement authorities started sanctioning the US corporations as well as non-US corporations for their bribes in far-away jurisdictions. Hock (2020a) argues that the focus of US anti-bribery enforcement on Swiss, Dutch, Brazilian, French and other non-US corporations incentivised national enforcement authorities of these countries to improve their legal frameworks and become more active in their own enforcement. The emergence of global enforcement bundles in this area is an alternative to uncoordinated multilateral enforcement, US unilateral enforcement and, most importantly, to markets in which large organisations are free to bribe (see Hock, 2020a; King & Lord, 2018).

The complexities of international bribery schemes, global policing and the limitations of international enforcement are illustrated by all global settlement bundles discussed in Table 3.3 where *Rolls Royce*, *Airbus* and *Amec* cases share a number of common characteristics. Bribers in these cases are large, complex, publicly listed corporations with multiple subsidiaries, divisions and offices across the world; they operate in the aerospace industry and oil and gas sector selling low volume, high value products and services so every contract is important to their financial health. In addition, the official prosecution documents in all three cases (SFO v. Airbus SE; SFO v. Rolls-Royce plc; SFO v. Amec Foster Wheeler Energy Limited) identify a number of common, pathological features which contributed to the aetiology of the crimes. Consider some of these features identified in the court papers associated with Rolls Royce and Airbus (Figure 3.1).

The court documents indicate that the dominant feature in both schemes is the relationship with two executives of AirAsia. In the Airbus case, the executives demanded $50 million in stages to favour Airbus in a high value

Table 3.3 Global settlement bundles with the UK presence

Corporation	Sanctions and enforcers	Facts
Rolls Royce (17/01/2017)	$800 million global settlement: UK £497 million; Brazil $25.6 million; US $170 million	Rolls Royce, a UK aeroengine manufacturer, admitted to paying substantial bribes to corporate executives and public officials between 1989 and 2013 in several countries, including Brazil, China, India, Malaysia, Russia and Thailand. Rolls Royce settled the allegations to avoid prosecution in 2017 by way of DPAs with the Brazilian, US and UK authorities and over $800 million in penalties (SFO, 2017).
Airbus (21/01/2020)	$3.9 billion global settlement: France $2.29 billion; UK $1.09 billion; US $527 million	Airbus, an aerospace corporation registered in the Netherlands and with operational headquarters in France, settled allegations of international bribery by concluding a $3.9 billion global settlement involving DPAs with the French, UK and US authorities (SFO, 2020a). Airbus also admitted to systematic bribery in multiple jurisdictions to win aircraft orders in China, Ghana, Indonesia, Malaysia, Sri Lanka and Taiwan.
Amec Foster Wheeler Energy Limited (01/07/2021)	$177 million global settlement: UK £103; USA and Brazil	Amec Foster Wheeler Energy Limited (Amec), a subsidiary of John Wood Group, a UK-based global engineering company, settled allegations of international bribery by concluding a $177 million global settlement involving DPAs with the UK and US authorities, and facing a parallel proceeding in Federal Court Brazil (as of July 2021). The US and Brazilian parts of the bundle focus mainly on the scheme to pay bribes to officials in Brazil in exchange for an approximately $190 million contract to design a gas-to-chemicals complex. The UK part of the bundle focuses on systematic bribery in multiple jurisdictions in the oil and gas sector from 1996 to 2014 in Nigeria, Saudi Arabia, Malaysia, India and Brazil (SFO, 2021).

contract involving the purchase of 180 aircraft (SFO v. Airbus SE). The $50 million was paid to a sports team, Caterham F1, as sponsorship. The team was owned by the AirAsia executives (Das & Lee, 2020) and turned out to be a short-lived vanity project (Benson, 2014). The corrupt relationship

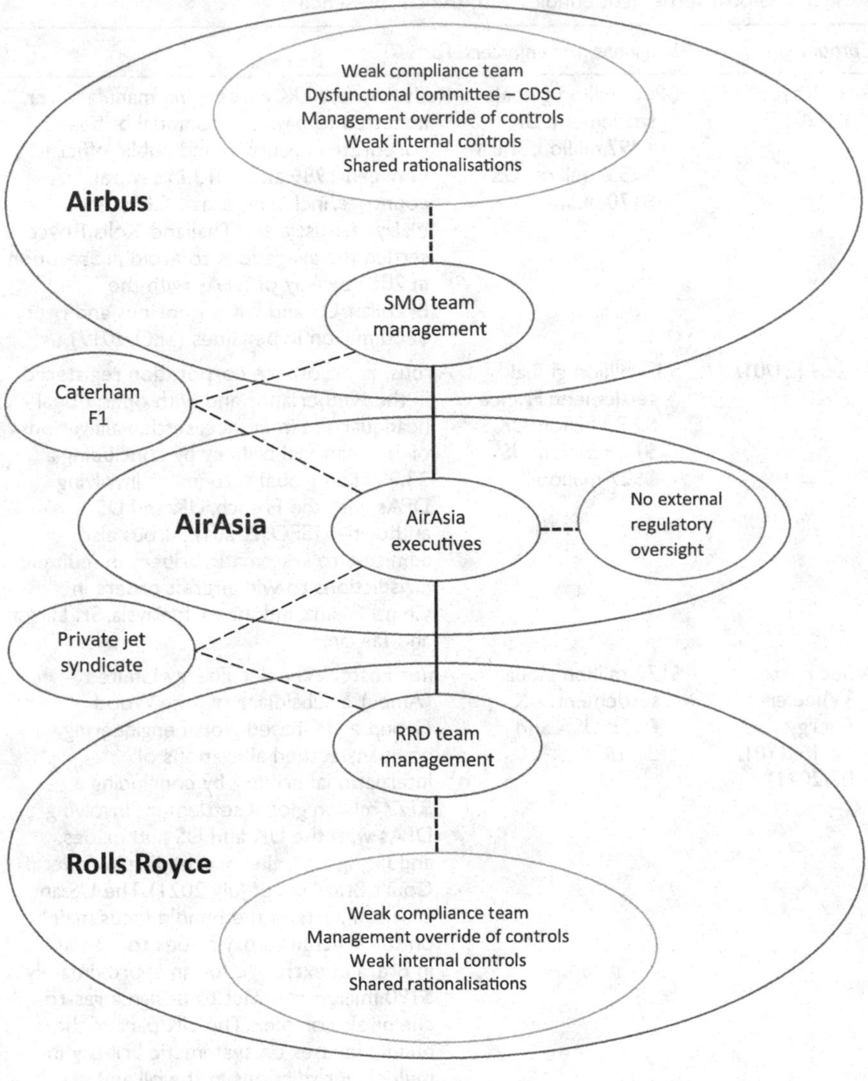

Figure 3.1 The complexity of airbus scheme and Rolls Royce scheme.

was managed by the Strategy and Marketing Organisation (SMO), a department within a French subsidiary of Airbus. The SMO sought and obtained approval for the arrangement from a dysfunctional senior management group, the Company Development and Selection Committee (CDSC). Knowing that the payment was improper, the CDSC in turn sought advice from a compliance team, whose primary role in the affair was to 'engineer' a solution so that the scheme could be rationalised as legitimate sponsorship. The compliance team was particularly concerned that the AirAsia executives were abusing their positions so recommended greater transparency to the board and shareholders of AirAsia:

> The purpose is to mitigate the risk of being accused of conspiracy on transfer value from the airline to the majority shareholder private interests.
>
> (Regina v Airbus SE, p. 18)

The SFO v Rolls Royce court documents reveal a similar pattern. The AirAsia executives demanded a significant discount on a maintenance programme for a private jet, or the cash equivalent, in return for substantial maintenance contracts for the commercial fleet. The private jet was owned by a syndicate including the executives and others. The relationship was managed by Rolls Royce Deutschland (RRD), a German subsidiary. RRD sought approval from the compliance department which advised that the arrangement would breach the FCPA and the Bribery Act, and should be made transparent to the board and shareholders of AirAsia.

Like Airbus, Rolls Royce's managers sought a solution to the problem involving a structure and language that would navigate a way round the laws. Frustrated by progress, the AirAsia executives linked the bribe to the payment of outstanding debts to Rolls Royce, demanded cash instead of a discount and demanded the removal of the Rolls Royce account manager by email: 'I will not meet with liars next week'. The parties eventually settled on a credit arrangement that gifted the private syndicate $3.2 million worth of maintenance.

The court papers in both these schemes portray the AirAsia executives as the aggressive, corruptors and Airbus and Rolls Royce management as submissive actors. Despite having anti-bribery policies and structures in place which raised warnings, senior managers in both companies acquiesced to the corrupt demands to win very substantial contracts. In both cases, management did not possess sufficient moral integrity to countenance the risk of losing the substantial commercial opportunities. Whilst higher loyalty rationalisations were undoubtedly an important factor (Sykes & Matza, 1957), they also negotiated internally over the construction of specific rationalisations to assuage any moral dissonance and deflect regulatory scrutiny: Airbus managers characterised their bribe as sponsorship, Rolls Royce managers characterised their bribe as commercial credit. Dysfunctional committees and senior managers then accepted these rationalisations and their purpose in overriding management controls. Crucially, the compliance functions lacked the power and independence to reject the rationalisations.

Following detection and investigation by the SFO and other enforcement authorities, Rolls Royce and Airbus agreed, among others, to be charged with failing to prevent bribery under Section 7 of the Bribery Act 2010. However, the absence of equivalent domestic oversight in Malaysia, and perhaps also the lack of interest of UK, US and other enforcement authorities to apply their laws extraterritorially, meant that neither AirAsia nor its executives faced justice or any kind of regulatory intervention. Indeed, a committee formed by AirAsia to review the Airbus case with the assistance of accountancy firm, BDO, concluded after just one month that the executives had acted properly (AirAsia, 2020).

The cases such as Airbus and Rolls Royce show how corporations rely on extensive networks of groups and individuals within organisations and between organisations. Clearly, our analysis shows that this complexity might be difficult to be dealt with by underlying laws and regulations. For example, laws should be enforced equitably to both sides of the corrupt exchange and enforcement should prioritise the human corruptors. Currently, international enforcement usually fails in both regards because its primary strategic focus is the supply side where an out of court settlement with a corporation is conveniently feasible.

On the other hand, and as has been the case in other areas of economic crime such as money laundering, foreign anti-bribery laws have been increasingly enforced in recent years.[4] The foreign anti-bribery enforcement incentivised the proliferation of compliance programmes, which are discussed in the following section.

Preventing corporate bribery – compliance

The foreign anti-bribery enforcement incentivised the proliferation of compliance programmes that corporations must implement to prevent bribery and corruption as well as to signal that they are a company of good character (see section above). Bribery is also open to a wide range of preventative actions which can be targeted at it (Brooks et al., 2013; Stiernstedt & Button, 2018). The Rolls Royce and Airbus examples, however, demonstrate that espoused compliance and ethics policies are mere window dressing if they are not backed up with meaningful intent and action. Without meaningful intent, ordinary people can easily be drawn into corrupt relationships, especially when the corporation operates in a vulnerable industry and in regions where the corruption is high. Yet, many European and US corporations paid billions to resolve their failures to comply with foreign anti-bribery laws. Turning a blind eye on suspicious activities, and the lack of willingness to prevent international bribery have become more costly worldwide.

Anti-bribery and corruption compliance

The US, UK and other enforcement authorities place great importance on ABC programmes, and it became worthwhile for organisations to invest significant resources in creating and implementing them, so as to reduce their risk and establish an affirmative defence if their managers, employees or intermediaries were found to have violated anti-bribery laws. Consider, for example, Chapter 8 of the US Federal Sentencing Guidelines that provides mathematical formulae for calculating sanctions, which allow for consider-able discounts in the event of self-disclosure, cooperation and remediation. For example, companies that voluntarily self-disclose misconduct, fully cooperated, and remediated in a timely and appropriate manner can receive a declination, or a 50% reduction from the bottom of the penalty range (US Department of Justice, 2017). In the UK, the level of discount is also based in large part on the company's cooperation with the SFO's investigation, and the court has approved terms permitting discounts of 50% in recognition of the levels of cooperation (SFO, 2020b).

In this field, unlike in some other areas such as cybercrime, industrial espionage and fraud, economic crime prevention and internal prevention programmes are mainly the matter of legislative obligation. In other words, while there are many strategic, cultural and economic reasons for corporations to prevent bribery and corruption, it was state regulation and enforcement that incentivised businesses to undertake efforts internally to prevent and detect violations of foreign anti-bribery laws (Carr & Lewis, 2010; Griffith, 2016; Hock & Karpacheva, forthcoming; McAllister, 2017).

In the UK, DPAs must be concluded under the supervision of a judge. Unlike US law, UK law provides that the UK judge must assess whether an agreement is likely to be in the interests of justice, and whether the proposed terms of the DPA are fair, reasonable and proportionate (see Grasso, 2016).

In the first instance, a prosecution must apply a two-stage test: the eviden-tial test and public interest test. The former requires the existence of sufficient evidence providing a realistic prospect of conviction and a reasonable sus-picion upon some admissible evidence that the company has committed an offence. The latter includes a balancing exercise of public interest factors that tend to support prosecution and those that do not. SFO (2020b) indicates that these public interest factors include, for example:

- A history of similar conduct/lack of history of similar conduct;
- Bribery was the established business practice/the existence of a proactive corporate compliance programme;
- Failure to self-report;
- A conviction is likely to have collateral consequences.

The public interest factors, and other factors such as the level of cooper-ation during negotiations, will be considered by the judge. In the Airbus case, for example, the judge indicated that:

> Whether a DPA is likely to be or is in the interests of justice and whether its terms are likely to be or are fair, reasonable and proportionate are

In the UK, DPAs must be concluded under the supervision of a judge. Unlike US law, UK law provides that the UK judge must assess whether an agreement is likely to be in the interests of justice, and whether the proposed terms of the DPA are fair, reasonable, and proportionate (see Grasso, 2016).

In the first instance, a prosecution must apply a two-stage test: the evidential test and public interest test. The former requires the existence of sufficient evidence providing a realistic prospect of conviction and a reasonable suspicion upon some admissible evidence that the company has committed an offense. The latter includes a balancing exercise of public interest factors that tend to support prosecution and those that do not. SFO (2020b) indicates that these public interest factors include, for example:

- A history of similar conduct/lack of history of similar conduct
- Bribery was the established business practice/the existence of a proactive corporate compliance programme
- Failure to self-report
- A conviction is likely to have collateral consequences

The public interest factors, and other factors such as the level of cooperation during negotiations, will be considered by the judge. In the Airbus case, for example, the judge indicated that:

> "Whether a DPA is likely to be or is in the interests of justice and whether its terms are likely to be or are fair, reasonable and proportionate are questions to be determined by reference to all of the relevant facts and circumstances of a particular case." (SFO v Airbus SE, para 10).

Moreover, the supervision of a judge also takes into account corporate cooperation (that under UK law can lead to significant reduction from the penalty charge). In Airbus, the judge appreciated that Airbus have cooperated with the prosecuting authorities conducting the investigations, to the fullest extent possible (SFO v Airbus SE, para 69).

Indeed, despite a "slow start" Airbus opened a kimono and worked hard to identify a comprehensive compilation of red flag cases. Moreover, Airbus also presented "all" suspicious business partner relationships, got access to 30.7 million documents, and even helped with designing technology to assist in the prioritization and identification of relevant documents (see Hock, 2020c).

Importantly, while we have seen some discussion whether the lack of self-disclosure could prevent reaching a DPA in the UK, the recent case-law suggests that it is not the case. Consider, for example, the view of judge in the Amec Foster case:

> A culture of self-reporting of such conduct is of very substantial benefit to the interests of justice in that it should bring criminal behaviour to light which might otherwise go entirely undiscovered [...] An example of the culture which should be discouraged is the "cleansing process" of 2007-2009 in this case. The whole outcome of the case would have been far better if FWEL had self-reported in 2007, although given the fact that corruption appears to have been endemic then and at a very high level, it may be doubted that this would ever have happened. [...] (SFO v Amec Foster Wheeler Energy Limited, para 36).

Figure 3.2 DPAs in the UK.

questions to be determined by reference to all of the relevant facts and circumstances of a particular case.

(SFO v Airbus SE, para 10)

Moreover, the supervision of a judge also takes into account corporate cooperation (that under UK law can lead to significant reduction from the penalty charge). In Airbus, the judge appreciated that Airbus has cooperated with the prosecuting authorities conducting the investigations, to the fullest extent possible (SFO v Airbus SE, para 69).

Indeed, despite a 'slow start' Airbus opened a kimono and worked hard to identify a comprehensive compilation of red flag cases. Moreover, Airbus also presented 'all' suspicious business partner relationships, got access to 30.7 million documents and even helped with designing technology to assist in the prioritisation and identification of relevant documents (see Hock, 2020b).

Importantly, while we have seen some discussion whether the lack of self-disclosure could prevent reaching a DPA in the UK, the recent case law suggests that it is not the case. Consider, for example, the view of judge in the Amec Foster case:

A culture of self-reporting of such conduct is of very substantial benefit to the interests of justice in that it should bring criminal behaviour to light which might otherwise go entirely undiscovered [...] An example of the culture which should be discouraged is the "cleansing process" of 2007-2009 in this case. The whole outcome of the case would have been far better if FWEL had self-reported in 2007, although given the fact that corruption appears to have been endemic then and at a very high level, it may be doubted that this would ever have happened. [...]

(SFO v Amec Foster Wheeler Energy Limited, para 36)

Risk assessment and ABC

Before crafting ABC programmes, organisations must undertake a thorough risk assessment. Organisations need to identify, assess and understand their corruption and bribery risks. For example, a corporation that only sells goods and services locally to small businesses will have a very different risk profile from a multinational energy corporation that conducts business with multiple governments around the world. There are multiple helpful resources that assist practitioners in setting up a solid risk assessment (see Global Compact, 2013; Home Office, 2016). The summary of key stages of the risk assessment process is provided in Table 3.4.

The FCPA, UK Bribery Act and other foreign anti-bribery laws are not fully prescriptive. Similarly, to other areas of economic crime such as money laundering, the company is best placed to understand its own business from a commercial perspective, and to identify, assess and define its risk profile.[5]

Table 3.4 ABC risk assessment

Risk Assessment	
Establishing the process	Compliance or internal audit departments should involve key stakeholders in the process. A risk-assessment workshop focusing on planning, setting objectives, resources and establishing risk tolerance is an important part of the process. The use of risk registers to document individual risk factors is a common practice.
Identify the risk	This stage is associated with the identification of reasons why corruption and bribery may occur within an organisation. There are multiple economic crime-related theories, such as routine activity theory, the fraud triangle and control theory, that explain this (see Chapter 10).
Rate inherent risk	The level of risk prior to the imposition of a control is called inherent risk.
Identify and rate mitigating controls	The imposition of an effective control reduces the likelihood of a risk occurring and, in some cases, the impact of that risk should it crystallise.
Calculate residual risk	It is often not possible to completely eliminate risk through the application of controls. The risk remaining after the application of controls is called residual risk.
Develop action plan and risk management	Having identified a risk and estimated its occurrence and the consequences, there needs to be an evaluation made as to whether the risk is tolerable to the organisation, or whether there needs to be action taken to reduce or control it. The response plan is largely based on the level of risk tolerance/risk appetite of the corporations.
	When deciding on whether mitigating actions are needed, and if so which type of action, the 4Ts analysis can be particularly useful. There are four options under this analysis: **TOLERATE, TREAT, TRANSFER OR TERMINATE** (Giles, 2012). The application of the 4Ts can be explained by reference to car ownership.
	• An infrequent rattle coming from the glove box – it might be that something negative occurring in the engine, but the car is working fine. **TOLERATE** the risk.
	• The car might breakdown due to parts failure – **TREAT** the risk by having the car serviced in accordance with the manufacturer's recommendations.
	• The car may be involved in an accident and lead to significant expense – **TRANSFER** the risk through insurance.
	• A driver has recently contracted epilepsy – this may lead to an accident and thus the risk would be **TERMINATED** by the driver deciding not to drive at all.

What makes risk assessment appropriate is the ability to document the way how risk methodology and data inform a risk-tailored and proportionate allocation of compliance resources. Moreover, it is also the ability to tailor the risk and revise a compliance programme in light of lessons learned from previous failures. In this context, the understanding of risk assessment is the starting point for a prosecutor's evaluation of whether a company has a well-designed compliance programme (US Department of Justice, 2019).

ABC compliance programme

While the question of what constitutes an effective programme has been subject to significant ambiguity, various enforcement authorities have started releasing guidance documents to clarify how they plan to assess the effectiveness of these compliance programmes (Vozza, 2022). The most authoritative is the US DOJ Criminal Division Evaluation of Corporate Compliance Programs (US Department of Justice, 2019), which impacts corporations globally. According to the DOJ guidance, effective compliance programs are tailored to the company's specific business and to the risks associated with that business. The summary of key elements of the corporate compliance programme based on the DOJ's guidance (US Department of Justice, 2019) is provided in Table 3.5.

The Evaluation of Corporate Compliance Programs guidance is meant to assist prosecutors in making informed decisions about the corporation's compliance programme (US Department of Justice, 2019). Nevertheless, knowing what considerations stand behind an investigation and the evaluations of compliance programmes serves as an informal guide to corporations themselves. This general guidance is further specified by foreign bribery-specific enforcement policy, namely the FCPA Corporate Enforcement Policy (US Department of Justice, 2017), which provides an incentive framework for self-disclosure of corporate bribery, cooperation during investigations of potential misconduct and effective ABC compliance programmes. Again, this policy only confirms that the leading driver in this area is the threat of enforcement. Many other areas of economic crime, such as insurance fraud, are also subject to risk assessment and internal controls. The incentive not to be defrauded by corporate clients, however, is a sufficient incentive for fraud prevention, and the government does not lead this area through the threat of corporate criminal liability should a corporation fail to prevent fraud.

Conclusion

This chapter has explored the problem of bribery and corruption. It began by exploring the core elements of what corruption is, its consequences and extent, before moving on to examine its specific manifestation: international

Table 3.5 Effective compliance programme

Key hallmarks of effective compliance programme	
Policies and procedures	Policies and procedures should provide both content and effect to ethical norms and should build upon the risk assessment process. The commitment to the culture of compliance set out in a code of conduct must be incorporated into the day-top-day operations.
Training and communications	Effective guidance relating to compliance policies, communications to employees about potential misconduct, appropriately tailored training.
Confidential reporting structure and investigation process	The most common way that integrity issues are brought to light is through whistleblowing by a disaffected employee or former employee. Such disclosures have long been regarded as malicious and an act of betrayal, prompting no further action. However, confidential reporting mechanisms, such as confidential reporting and compliance hotlines for employees to report corruption, bribery and other criminal conduct, are generally considered as a key hallmark of effective compliance programme. In addition, an organisation should ensure responsiveness, including further investigation and accountability for the response and outcome.
Third party management	Risk-based due diligence to third-party relationship. Establishing clear business rationale for having the third party in the transaction and associated risk posed by that party. The third parties also involve consultants and distributors that are commonly used to conceal illicit transactions.
Adequate resources and empowerment	The involvement and leadership of top management such as the board of directors and executives is crucial for the success of a compliance programme. Company leadership is crucial for the creation and support of appropriate incentives structure based on the culture of ethics and compliance. While a programme may be well designed, it is only a 'paper programme' without sufficient resources invested to implement it in practice, in terms of competent staff, and autonomy from management (see also Miller, 2015).
Continuous improvement, periodic testing, and review	It is important that the compliance programme has a capacity to improve and evolve. The actual implementation of controls in practice will necessarily reveal areas of risk and potential adjustment. As business context changes over time, so will the corruption and bribery risk. Organisations need to be able to continuously re-assess the risk they face and review the adequacy of their controls.

bribery. The chapter then analyses international bribery laws and cases to illustrate the complexity of this problem.

Presently, the international anti-bribery enforcement regime focuses primarily on the supply side of bribery where prosecution is considered feasible. DPAs and NPAs are in effect regulatory regimes that avoid criminal prosecution (Hock, 2021). They impose fines, relieve the corporations of their illegal benefits and force managers to develop compliance programmes. Very few individuals, however, are prosecuted either because effective laws are absent, or because criminal justice systems cannot cope with corrupt conspiracies.

Airbus, Rolls-Royce, Amec and other cases of international bribery illustrate that employees need the constraints of robust ethical governance in order to protect the integrity and interests of the corporate entity. The corporation should not have to rely on external, regulatory intervention. It is the responsibility of management to provide the corporation with a resilient ethics function that is capable of identifying and mitigating risk of corruption and bribery. Shall they fail to do so, both their organisation and themselves can be held criminally liable for failing to prevent bribery.

As the representation of the organisation's conscience, the compliance and ethics function should be independent of the operations and sufficiently remote from everyday routines so as not to be caught up in the strains, toxic associations, opportunities and constructed justifications for corruption and bribery. It should be invested with the authority to intervene at the nascence of corrupt deals and with the integrity to report corrupt events to the authorities when controls do fail. To achieve its aims, an effective compliance programme should be empowered to reject all 'engineered solutions' that are really rationalisations constructed in support of corrupt relationships and to reject all rationalised excuses for turning a blind eye to corruption (see Shepherd & Button, 2018).

Note

This chapter draws on parts of Hock, Shepherd, D. and Button, M. (Forthcoming).

Legislation, international treaties and judgements

Bribery Act 2010, c. 23.

Foreign Corrupt Practices Act of 1977, 15 U.S.C. s 78dd-1 ff.

Fraud Act 2006, c. 35.

OECD Convention on Combating Bribery of Foreign Public Officials in International Business Transactions, 17 December 1997, www.oecd.org/daf/anti-bribery/ConvCombatBribery_ENG.pdf

Regina v Airbus SE, Statement of Facts [2020] www.sfo.gov.uk/download/
airbus-se-deferred-prosecution-agreement-statement-of-facts/
SFO v. Airbus SE [2020] www.sfo.gov.uk/cases/airbus-group/
SFO v. Amec Foster Wheeler Energy Limited [2021] www.sfo.gov.uk/cases/
amec-foster-wheeler-plc/
SFO v ROLLS-ROYCE PLC Respondents ROLLS-ROYCE ENERGY
SYSTEMS INC [2017] www.sfo.gov.uk/cases/rolls-royce-plc/
United Nations Convention against Corruption, 31 October 2003, www.
unodc.org/documents/brussels/UN_Convention_Against_Corruption.pdf
US Federal Sentencing Guidelines 2018, c. 8 www.ussc.gov/guidelines/2018-
guidelines-manual/2018-chapter-8

Notes

1 This section and the *Law enforcement and complexity of international bribery cases*
subsection are based on Hock, B., Button M., & Shepherd, D. (2022). Corruption,
bribery, and corporate crime: Victims and perpetrators. In M. Gill (Ed.), *The handbook of security*. Palgrave Macmillan (forthcoming).
2 For example, Carr and Outhwaite (2011) argue that those hoping to see corruption
addressed by a wave of CSR activity are likely to be disappointed. But consider,
for example, how voluntary standards systems help regulate the behaviour of
governments and companies (Dávid-Barrett & Okamura, 2016).
3 Note that Amex is a coordinated global settlement between UK, US, and
Brazilian authorities. The US authorities imposed approximately $41 million
($18.375 million to resolve the DOJ's criminal charges and $22.76 million for the
SEC's disgorgement and prejudgment interest). The US charges are subject to
offset up to the agreed value paid to the Brazilian authorities and UK authorities
(see SEC, 2021).
4 See Chapter 8, section 'Policing money laundering'.
5 See Chapter 8, section 'The effectiveness of AML compliance'.

References

AirAsia. (2020). *AirAsia report on the findings of the independent internal inquiry
conducted by BDO Governance Advisory Sdn. Bhd.* https://newsroom.airasia.
com/news/2020/3/20/airasia-report-on-the-findings-of-the-independent-internal-
inquiry-conducted-by-bdo-governance-advisory-sdn-bhd
Andersson, S., & Heywood, P. M. (2009). The politics of perception: Use and abuse of
transparency international's approach to measuring corruption. *Political Studies,
57*(4), 746–767.
Andresen, M. S., & Button, M. (2019). The profile and detection of bribery in Norway
and England & Wales: A comparative study. *European Journal of Criminology,
16*(1), 18–40.
Bardhan, P. (1997). Corruption and development: A review of issues. *Journal of
Economic Literature, 35*(3), 1320–1346.
Benson, A. (2014). *F1: Caterham team is sold by Tony Fernandes to a consortium.* BBC.
www.bbc.co.uk/sport/formula1/28129627

Brooks, G., Walsh, D., Lewis, C., & Kim, H. (2013). *Preventing corruption: Investigation, enforcement and governance.* Springer.

Bruckner, T. (2019). *The ignored pandemic: How corruption in healthcare service delivery threatens Universal Health Coverage.* Transparency International. http://ti-health.org/content/the-ignored-pandemic/

Button, M., Shepherd, D., & Blackbourn, D. (2019). Explaining the causes of bribery from an offender perspective. In N. Ryder & L. Pasculli (Eds.), *Corruption in the global era: Causes, sources and forms of manifestation* (pp. 140–162). Routledge.

Carr, I., & Lewis, D. (2010). Combating corruption through employment law and whistleblower protection. *Industrial Law Journal London, 39*(1), 52–81.

Carr, I., & Outhwaite, O. (2011). Controlling corruption through corporate social responsibility and corporate governance: Theory and practice. *Journal of Corporate Law Studies, 11*(2), 299–342.

CPS. (2018). *Misconduct in public office.* www.cps.gov.uk/legal-guidance/misconduct-public-office

Das, K., & Lee, L. (2020). *Malaysia probes allegations that Airbus bribed AirAsia bosses.* Reuters. https://uk.reuters.com/article/us-airbus-probe-airasia/malaysia-probes-allegations-that-airbus-bribed-airasia-bosses-idUKKBN1ZV3LV

Dávid-Barrett, E., & Fazekas, M. (2020). Grand corruption and government change: An analysis of partisan favoritism in public procurement. *European Journal of Criminal Policy Research, 26*, 411–430.

Dávid-Barrett, E., & Okamura, K. (2016). Norm diffusion and reputation: The rise of the extractive industries transparency initiative. *Governance, 29*(2), 227–246.

DOJ & SEC. (2020). *A resource guide to the U.S. Foreign Corrupt Practices Act.* www.justice.gov/criminal-fraud/fcpa-resource-guide

European Commission. (2013). *Identifying and reducing corruption in public procurement in the EU.* https://ec.europa.eu/anti-fraud/sites/antifraud/files/docs/body/identifying_reducing_corruption_in_public_procurement_en.pdf

European Commission. (2017). *Special Eurobarometer 470, Corruption.* https://ec.europa.eu/commfrontoffice/publicopinion/index.cfm/ResultDoc/download/DocumentKy/81007

Fazekas, M., Tóth, I. J., & King, L. P. (2013). *Anatomy of grand corruption: A composite corruption risk index based on objective data.* Corruption Research Center Budapest. Working Paper Series: CRC-WP/2013:02.

Fletcher, C., & Herrmann, D. (2012). *The internationalisation of corruption: Scale, impact and countermeasures.* Routledge.

Ford, C., & Hess, D. (2008). Can corporate monitorship improve corporate compliance? *Journal of Corporation Law, 34*(3), 679–738.

Giles, S. (2012). *Managing fraud risk: A practical guide for directors and managers.* Wiley.

Global Compact. (2013). *A guide for anti-corruption risk assessment* https://d306pr3pise04h.cloudfront.net/docs/issues_doc%2FAnti-Corruption%2FRiskAssessmentGuide.pdf

Grasso, C. (2016). Peaks and troughs of the English deferred prosecution agreement: The lesson learned from the DPA between the SFO and ICBC SB Plc. *The Journal of Business Law, 2016*(5), 388–408.

Griffith, S. J. (2016). Corporate governance in an era of compliance. *William & Mary Law Review, 57*, 2075–2140.

Gutterman, E. (2019a). Banning Bribes Abroad: US Enforcement of the Foreign Corrupt Practices Act and Its Impact on the Global Governance of Corruption. *European Political Science, 8*, 205-216.

Gutterman, E. (2019b). Extraterritoriality as an Analytic Lens: Examining the Global Governance of Transnational Bribery and Corruption. In D. S. Margolies, U. Özsu, M. Pal, & N. Tzouvala (Eds.), *The Extraterritoriality of Law: History, Theory, Politics* (pp. 183-199). Routledge.

Hanf, M., Van-Melle, A., Fraisse, F., Roger, A., Carme, B., & Nacher, M. (2011). *Corruption kills: Estimating the global impact of corruption on children deaths.* PLoS One, *6*(11), e26990.

Hock, B. (2014). *Intimations of global anti-bribery regime and the effectiveness of extra-territorial enforcement: From free-riders to protectionism?* TILEC Discussion Paper, 2014-009.

Hock, B. (2017). Transnational bribery: When is extraterritoriality appropriate. *Charleston Law Review, 11*(2), 305–352.

Hock, B. (2020a). *Extraterritoriality and international bribery: A collective action perspective.* Routledge.

Hock, B. (2020b). *Airbus – How the UK and France learned to investigate and sanction international corruption.* European Compliance Center. https://complianter.eu/airbus-international-corruption/

Hock, B. (2021). Policing corporate bribery: Negotiated settlements and bundling, *Policing and Society, 31*(8), 950–966.

Hock, B., Karpacheva, E. (Forthcoming). An insider from abroad: the impact of US whistleblowing laws on anti-corruption regulation in Europe. In C. Grasso (Ed.), *Whistleblowers: Voices of justice.* Springer.

Hock, B., Shepherd, D., & Button, M. (Forthcoming). Bribery. In M. Gill (Ed.), *Handbook of security* (3rd ed.). Palgrave.

Home Office. (2016). *Bribery and corruption assessment template.* www.gov.uk/government/publications/bribery-and-corruption-assessment-template

Hough, D. (2013). *Corruption, anti-corruption and governance.* Palgrave Macmillan.

Hough, D. (2017). *Analysing corruption.* Agenda Publishing Limited.

Huntington, S. P. (1968). *Political order in changing societies.* Yale University Press.

Johnston, M. (2010). *Syndromes of corruption: Wealth, power, and democracy.* Cambridge University Press.

King, C., & Lord, N. (2018). *Negotiated justice and corporate crime: The legitimacy of civil recovery orders and deferred prosecution agreements.* Palgrave Pivot.

Lambsdorff, J. G. (2006). Causes and consequences of corruption: What do we know from a cross-section of countries. In S. Rose-Ackerman (Ed.), *International handbook on the economics of corruption* (pp. 3–51). Edward Elgar.

Lord, N. (2014a). *Regulating corporate bribery in international business: Anti-corruption in the UK and Germany.* Ashgate Publishing.

Lord, N. (2014b). Responding to transnational corporate bribery using international frameworks for enforcement: Anti-bribery and corruption in the UK and Germany. *Criminology & Criminal Justice, 14*(1), 100–120.

McAllister, B. (2017). The impact of the Dodd-Frank whistleblower provisions on FCPA enforcement and modern corporate compliance programs. *Berkeley Business Law Journal, 14*(1), 45–86.

Miller, G. P. (2015). The compliance function: An overview. In J. N. Gordon & W. G. Ringe (Eds.), *The Oxford handbook of corporate law and governance* (pp. 981–1002). Oxford University Press.

ONS. (2020). *Crime in England and Wales: Other related tables.* www.ons.gov.uk/peoplepopulationandcommunity/crimeandjustice/datasets/crimeinenglandandwale sotherrelatedtables

Pasculli, L. (2019). Seeds of systemic corruption in the post-Brexit UK. *Journal of Financial Crime, 26*(3), 705–718.

Pasculli, L., & Ryder, N. (2019). Corruption and globalisation: Towards an interdisciplinary understanding of corruption as a global crime. In N. Ryder & L. Pasculli (Eds.), *Corruption in the global era: Causes, sources and forms of manifestation* (pp. 3–23). Routledge.

Philp, M., & Dávid-Barrett, E. (2015). Realism about political corruption. *Annual Review of Political Science, 18*(1), 387–402.

Rose, C. (2015). *International anti-corruption norms: Their creation and influence on domestic legal systems.* Oxford University Press.

Rose-Ackerman, S. (1999). *Corruption and government: Causes, consequences, and reform.* Cambridge University Press.

Sampford, C., Shacklock, A., Connors, C., & Galtung, F. (Eds.) (2006). *Measuring corruption.* Ashgate Publishing.

SEC. (2021). *SEC charges Amec Foster Wheeler Limited with FCPA Violations related to Brazilian bribery scheme.* www.sec.gov/news/press-release/2021-112

SFO. (2017). *SFO completes £497.25m Deferred Prosecution Agreement with Rolls-Royce PLC.* www.sfo.gov.uk/2017/01/17/sfo-completes-497-25m-deferred-prosecution-agreement-rolls-royce-plc/

SFO. (2020a). *Deferred prosecution agreement.* SFO v. Airbus. www.sfo.gov.uk/download/airbus-se-deferred-prosecution-agreement-statement-of-facts/#

SFO. (2020b). *Deferred prosecution agreements (guidance for corporates).* www.sfo.gov.uk/publications/guidance-policy-and-protocols/guidance-for-corporates/deferred-prosecution-agreements-2/

SFO. (2021). *SFO enters into £103 DPA with Amec Foster Wheeler Energy Limited.* www.sfo.gov.uk/2021/07/02/sfo-enters-into-103m-dpa-with-amec-foster-wheeler-energy-limited-as-part-of-global-resolution-with-us-and-brazilian-authorities/

Shepherd, D., & Button, M. (2018). Organizational inhibitions to addressing occupational fraud: A theory of differential rationalisation. *Deviant Behavior, 40*(8), 971–991.

Spalding, A. B. (2010). Unwitting sanctions: Understanding anti-bribery legislation as economic sanctions against emerging markets. *Florida Law Review, 62*(2), 351–428.

Stanford Law School. (n.d.). *Foreign and Corrupt Practices Act Clearinghouse.* http://fcpa.stanford.edu/index.html

Stiernstedt, P., & Button, M. (2018). A case study of an EU procurement process in an African country. In I. Kubbe & A. Engelbert (Eds.), *Corruption and norms – Why informal rules matter* (pp. 347–366). Palgrave.

Sullivan, J. (2009). *The moral compass of companies: Business ethics and corporate governance as anti-corruption tools* (Working Paper). International Finance Corporation. https://openknowledge.worldbank.org/handle/10986/23980

Sykes, G., & Matza, D. (1957). Techniques of neutralization: A theory of delinquency. *American Sociological Review, 22*(6), 664–670.

US Department of Justice. (2017). *FCPA Corporate Enforcement Policy (USAM 9-47.120)*. www.justice.gov/jm/jm-9-47000-foreign-corrupt-practices-act-1977

US Department of Justice. (2019). *Evaluation of corporate compliance programs*. www.justice.gov/criminal-fraud/page/file/937501/download

US Senate. (1977). *Report of the Committee on Banking, Housing, and Urban Affairs, United States Senate, No 95-114*. www.justice.gov/sites/default/files/criminal-fraud/legacy/2010/04/11/senaterpt-95-114.pdf

Vishny, A., & Shleifer, R. (1993). Corruption. *Quarterly Journal of Economics, 108*(3), 599–617.

Vozza, D. (2022). Exploring voluntary and mandatory compliance programmes in the field of anti-corruption. In S. Manacorda, F. Centonze (Eds.), Corporate compliance on a global scale (pp. 313–339). Springer.

Zagaris, B. (2015). *International white collar crimes: Cases and materials*. Cambridge University Press.

Chapter 4

Cartel and antitrust offences

Introduction

Sutherland (1949) considered antitrust violations to be a form of white-collar crime, devoting a whole chapter to the 'restraint of trade'. In his analysis of court records in the USA, Sutherland observed five types of practices: business consolidations, price fixing, price discrimination, limiting supply and patent pooling. All these practices are perfectly legal business strategies. Businesses merge to form larger corporations with higher efficiency, greater investment potential and lower prices. They set prices that are similar to competitors. Prices are differentiated between markets and are discounted for high-volume customers. Capacity is deliberately limited to sustain higher prices, especially when businesses are uncertain of customer demand during the early phases of marketing a new product. Corporations share their patented technologies so that complex products such as smartphones can be brought to the market-place efficiently, without unnecessary conflict and litigation over patent rights (Kinsbury & Gammann, 2013).

All these practices are recognised as reasonable and legitimate until they are exploited for the purposes of dominating a market and eliminating fair competition. Business strategies based on engineering market dominance are entirely rational as they create economic efficiencies and high profits for the companies that effectively control the market (Connor & Lande, 2012). However, such unrestrained dominance is an anathema to the free market ideals of capitalism, which relies on competition as a mechanism for setting fair market prices and rewarding firms that innovate and deliver the best value for money (Australian Competition & Consumer Commission [ACCC], 2019). The consequence of dominance is market failure, which leads to restricted choices for both business customers and consumers, high prices, lower quality and stifled innovation (London Economics, 2011).

US legislatures were at the forefront in recognising that regulation was required to prevent this kind of systematic market failure with the introduction of the Sherman Antitrust Act in 1890, which criminalised cartel activity.

DOI: 10.4324/9781003081753-4

The word 'trust' in the Act's title refers to groups of businesses that either collude in informal cartels or formally merge in order to create a monopoly that dominates a market. In contrast, the rest of the world, including European nations, had a more ambivalent attitude to business collusion (Harding, 2006). Cartels were tolerated or even encouraged as an expedient means of dealing with the harm resulting from periods of chaos, such as war or economic crisis (Levenstein & Suslow, 2008). English law, for example, regarded collective monopolies or cartels as reasonable practice until the introduction of the Monopolies and Restrictive Practices (Inquiry and Control) Act 1948 (Roth, 2019).

Signalling an increased international intolerance of cartel practices, the nascent European Union introduced collective competition laws in 1957 with the Treaty on the Functioning of the European Union (TFEU). The regulatory approach under the TFEU remains at the core of the EU's legislative framework, prohibiting the anti-competitive practice of collusive cartels (Article 101) and the abuse of dominant market positions (Article 102). The UK has adopted and followed the EU regulations since the introduction of the Competition Act 1998. The Organization for Economic Co-operation and Development (OECD, 2021) has drawn on both the American criminal approach and the European regulatory system to develop a benchmark framework for international adoption.

This chapter is grounded by the principles underpinning these legal frameworks to provide an overview of the organised criminality associated with cartel crimes. It uses the word crime broadly to encompass criminalised activities and regulatory infringements, with a primary focus on the 'trust' offences encapsulated in the Sherman Act and in Article 101 of the TFEU. The chapter's main concern is therefore the secretive activities of business cartels that illegally collude to engineer collective market dominance and market failure. It will illustrate that the essential purpose of the laws is deterrence in adjusting the strategic calculations of business executives so that they rationally choose to avoid conspiring in corrupt cartels.

The chapter draws on two illustrative cases. The estate agency case refers to a domestic cartel based in Wokingham, a small town in England, wherein four estate agents colluded to fix minimum agency fees for residential conveyancing (Competition and Markets Authority [CMA], 2019). The cartel lasted for seven years until one of its members self-reported to the CMA. The bearings case refers to an international cartel of large corporations that manufacture bearings. The cartel also endured for seven years until it was exposed in 2013 when one of its members self-reported to the Japan Fair Trade Commission (JFTC, 2013) and the case was subsequently adopted by the European Commission (EC, 2014). The chapter begins with the requisite discussion of what constitutes an illicit cartel.

From cooperation to collusion

In a Chatham House address, Mond (1927) argued that cartels produce a common social good: a mechanism for cooperation, rather than destructive competition, that enables economic stability and efficiency, lowers prices, raises output and increases employment. Mond (1927) further held merged international conglomerates as the most effective form of cartel. Others at the same venue argued that cartels are an abuse of power that serve only the interests of business owners. In their view, the objective of cartels is to maximise profits by agreeing high fixed prices at the expense of the consumer and to the detriment of the public good.

Mond's paper illustrates the tension in the debate between cooperation and competition. Cooperation is generally regarded as a good thing and always preferable to conflict. There is, for example, broad approval for trade associations that set minimum standards of quality, service and behaviour because they provide a public good. The National Association of Estate Agents (NAEA)[1] is just such a membership body in the UK that promotes and protects the integrity of the profession by requiring its members to comply with a specified code of practice. Similarly, it is accepted that engineering components such as bearings should comply with universal specifications to ensure safety, reliability and interchangeability. A market based on standardised, identical products leads to so-called perfect competition and the lowest market prices (Cramer & Heuser, 1960).

The challenge for the estate agents and the bearing manufacturers in their standardised worlds is to find a way to differentiate their products and services from the competition. They can invest in productivity to lower their costs and prices. They can invest in marketing to increase brand awareness. The bearing manufacturer could invent a new high-performance bearing and enjoy high prices under the legal patent monopoly for the next twenty years (see Chapter 6). It could share its patented inventions with its competitors in a 'patent pool'. Cooperative patent pooling is preferred to conflict in the technology industries where multiple patented inventions held by different companies are required for a single product (Kingsbury & Gamman, 2013). Notable examples of patent pooling for technology transfer and aggregation purposes include DVD, MPEG, RFID and smartphone technologies (Galetovic et al., 2018; Lampe & Moser, 2016). Sutherland (1949) was unequivocal in objecting to patent pools, and they occasionally attract the interest of competition authorities, but they are usually regarded as beneficial and legal because their cooperative purpose is to raise economic efficiency and to improve public welfare by bringing products to market at lower prices (World Intellectual Property Organisation [WIPO], 2014). Consequently, they are generally exempt from the competition laws.

All the above strategies are challenging and they require substantial invest-ment. It is much easier for competitors to merge into large conglomerates as advocated by Mond (1927). The competition authorities frequently scrutinise such mergers and sometimes either prevent them or impose conditions to pre-vent a monopolistic abuse of dominant position (CMA, n.d. b). It is easier still, far cheaper and therefore economically rational for the competitors to organise a few meetings with the objective of cooperating fully in the management of the market in order to maximise their collective profits (Connor & Lande, 2012). It is at this point that close cooperation becomes a secret monopoly and attracts the pejorative 'hard-core cartel' description (Harding, 2006).

What is a hard-core cartel?

The line between constructive cooperation and destructive collusion is not obvious. The Mond (1927) debate illustrates that the distinction rests on the purpose of the collaboration. The challenge for regulators is to distin-guish between positive collaborations in areas such as research, production and marketing, and anti-competitive agreements which undermine the free market and harm the consumer (OECD, n.d.). Farmers' cooperatives that collectively agree prices, and in some cases output quantities, are regarded as a pro-social way of rebalancing the power between the farming commu-nity and corporate buyers (Cseres, 2020). The purpose of exempting the agricultural sector from some aspects of competition law and encouraging cooperative cartels is to ensure the security of food supplies and thereby protect the welfare of citizens. Such arrangements are not tolerated in the estate agency or the ball bearing markets. This dependency on purpose or objective means that a precise definition of an illegal cartel remains elusive (Dunne, 2020).

The phrase 'hard-core cartel' is now commonly used to differentiate anti-social (welfare undermining) cartels from pro-social (welfare enhancing) cartels. The objective of hard-core cartels is to maximise members' profits at the expense of the consumer through agreements that harm competition. On the other hand, cartels that aim to improve market efficiency and enhance public welfare are exempt from competition law. Provided their objectives meet these pro-social conditions, cartel agreements such as patent pools and vertical distribution agreements are enabled by so-called block exemptions under European law (CMA, 2021). These exemptions are subject to periodic review to ensure their relevance and effectiveness (EC, 2020).

It is important to differentiate between vertical and horizontal agreements. Vertical distribution agreements within a supply chain are legal until they restrain competition through abuse of effective dominance. This can happen, for example, when a manufacturer contractually fixes its distributors' resale prices at the same level in a geographical market, restricts market segments or requires the distributors to sell tied or bundled products (Burns, 1993; EC, 2010). Competition authorities are less concerned about vertical arrangements because their impacts tend to be narrow in restricting 'intra-brand' competition, that is competition between distributors selling the same brand of product. There are, however, egregious vertical agreements that amount to abuse of dominant position. The EC fined Google €4.34 billion in 2018 because of its restrictive requirement for manufacturers of mobile phones and tablets to pre-install the Google Search app and Chrome browser (EC, 2018). This appears to be a peculiar Google strategy as Microsoft was fined €561 million in 2013 for a similar offence, tying computer devices into its Internet Explorer browser (EC, 2013).

The primary economic and welfare concern of the regulators is the horizontal agreement which distorts 'inter-brand' competition between corporate entities. Although the OECD definition is the most commonly used in this context, Harding (2004) points out that it confuses entities (cartels) and practice (agreements):

> Hard core cartels refers to anticompetitive agreements, concerted practices or arrangements by actual or potential competitors to agree on prices, make rigged bids (collusive tenders), establish output restrictions or quotas, or share or divide markets by, for example, allocating customers, suppliers, territories, or lines of commerce.
>
> (OECD, 1998)

Characterising hard-core cartels as 'the supreme evil of antitrust', Dunne (2020, p. 400) provides an in-depth discussion of the definitional problem and develops her own description to emphasise important features of cartels:

1   cartels comprise forms of horizontal collusion;
2   which restrict fundamental parameters of competition;
3   involving purely private profit-maximising behaviour; and
4   which almost invariably include some form of deliberate secrecy and/or deception on the part of participants.

The key behavioural features within this definition are collusion, secrecy and deception for gain. They are also notable characteristics of bribery and conspiracy to defraud offences. Dunne (2020, p. 392) further conceptualises the purpose of hard-core cartel activity as a form of fraud: '... involving a transfer of wealth from consumers to producers to which the latter are not entitled, and which is broadly equivalent to appropriating that money directly from customers'. This helps us to understand that hard-core cartel activities are a form of corruption as it involves an abuse of entrusted power for private gain (Transparency International, n.d.; United Nations, 2013). Cartels are in effect an alternative to corporate bribery with the same objective of financial gain and employing the same collusive, deceptive and secret behaviour. We can summarise these descriptions by defining hard-core cartels as follows.

> Hard core cartels are corrupt groups of independent corporate entities that undermine public welfare. They conspire to defraud customers by creating secret horizontal agreements that restrain trade in order to maximise their profits by price fixing, bid rigging, restricting outputs, or sharing or dividing markets.

Viewed in this way, Niamh Dunne's (2020) somewhat hyperbolic characterisation of cartels as a 'supreme evil' is understandable: they are massive white-collar frauds committed against the public. This is the kind of behaviour that criminologists have objected to when describing corporations as criminogenic (Coleman, 1992; Gelobovskiy, 2019).

International legal framework

As with bribery enforcement, America has led the way in policing cartels. America was the first to introduce antitrust laws with the Sherman Act in 1890 whilst the rest of the world regarded hard-core cartels as legitimate features of business practice (Harding, 2006; Roth, 2019). The Act outlaws the monopolisation of trade and criminalises horizontal cartel agreements that unreasonably restrain trade. The Clayton Antitrust Act of 1914 extended the list of proscribed activities to include anti-competitive mergers and anti-competitive vertical agreements in supply chains. Hard-core cartel activities remain criminal under the Sherman Act and they continue to be enforced under the exclusive jurisdiction of the Department of Justice (DOJ).

The European Union broadly followed American practices with the introduction of the TFEU in 1957 but avoided criminalising the offence so that it has followed a regulatory path. Article 101 prohibits the collusive practices of hard-core cartels. Article 102 prohibits the abuse of dominant position. The articles are enshrined in the national laws of EU member states: the Competition Act 1998 in the UK follows the TFEU wording almost verbatim. These laws were rarely enforced until the 1990s.

Accelerated globalisation in the late 20th century caused policy makers to adjust their attitudes, spurring a collective approach to tackling business cartels. As an independent intergovernmental organisation that shapes common policies, the OECD was called on to produce the Recommendation of the Council concerning Effective Action against Hard Core Cartels (OECD, 1998). The OECD framework focused on hard-core cartels and their anti-competitive horizontal agreements to set out a shortlist of recommendations based on the deterrence principle. It called for national laws that provide for effective enforcement procedures and adequate deterrence sanctions, and alignment of national laws and cross-border enforcement cooperation. The framework was enhanced in 2019 to reflect developments in cartel policy (OECD, 2021). The additional recommendations include:

- leniency programmes to increase detection;
- provision of protection for whistle-blowers;
- enhanced powers for competition authorities for conducting unannounced dawn raids, accessing electronic information and obtaining information from third parties;
- increase cooperation with more effective information exchange;
- incentivise early resolution by way of plea negotiation and early settlements;
- increase deterrence with criminal sanctions;
- enable victims of hard-core cartels to seek compensation for damages.

The majority of these recommendations have been implemented in many jurisdictions. To support implementation and to coordinate anti-cartel activities, the International Competition Network (ICN) was formed in 2001.[2] Illustrating how enforcement has become global, the ICN network now comprises 141 competition agencies. The European Competition Network (ECN) provides a similar coordinating function within the European Union.[3] Two contrasting enforcement models have emerged, both of which comply with the OECD framework. The American model is criminal orientated whilst the European model is regulatory orientated.

American criminal enforcement model

The American approach to the enforcement of hard-core cartels is unique as it is based on two linked limbs. The first limb is the criminalisation of cartel offences under the historic Sherman Act. The second limb is the restorative justice right of citizens to bring actions for damages against corporations. This structure suits the highly litigious nature of American life, where jurisprudence expects those harmed by cartels to pursue actions for damages against the offending corporations in the civil courts. The consequence is that the majority value of financial orders against offenders in the USA comes from civil cases brought by the antitrust regulator, the Federal Trade Commission (FTC) and the DOJ, rather than fines from criminal proceedings (Connor, 2016). The European model is the reverse, based mainly on the fines issued by non-criminal regulators.

The DOJ has carefully set out the justification for its criminal justice approach based on these two limbs (Werden et al., 2011). Under the criminalisation limb, its fundamental premise, like Dunne (2020), is that the hard-core cartel offence is a property crime like burglary and should be prosecuted as such because the threat of prison is a more powerful general deterrent than fines against corporations or individuals. The DOJ developed a carrot-and-stick approach with the introduction of its leniency programme in 1993 (DOJ, 1993, 1994). The programme allows the DOJ to offer immunity from prosecution to the first corporation and/or executive reporting and confessing to cartel activity. With the addition of the leniency tool, Werden et al. (2011) argue that the threat of prison is '.... the single greatest incentive to self-report through a leniency application and thereby escape sanctions .... [or] a powerful incentive to cooperate in exchange for a reduction in sentence' (Werden et al., 2011, p. 7). This argument clearly highlights the differences in methods to achieve the same cooperative end: the American system involves coercion by the spectre of executive imprisonment, the European approach is coercion by the threat of massive corporate fines for which the executives are responsible. In the American model, the cooperative executives are seeking to save themselves. In the European model, the cooperative executives are seeking to protect the interests of the company.

A key justification for maintaining the power to prosecute corporations is to support the second restorative justice limb, bringing actions for damages against the corporate offenders (Werden et al., 2011). Here they argue that the powers of inquiry and persuasion of the DOJ not only prove guilt for criminal sentencing purposes, these also simultaneously establish the liability of offenders in anticipation of any civil action. The criminal prosecutors are therefore providing a public service in enabling victims to sue offenders. A crucial component of this restorative justice objective is that the leniency programme does not offer immunity from civil action (Warrington, 2021). This strategy locks neatly into the US policy of imposing punitive treble damages for deterrence purposes. By co-opting victims to participate in crime control strategies, they are encouraged to serve as 'private attorneys general'.[4] The US Supreme Court noted in an antitrust case:

> The treble-damages provision wielded by the private litigant is a chief tool in the antitrust enforcement scheme, posing a crucial deterrent to potential violators.[5]

Ever innovative, the DOJ has recently added another tool to its prosecutorial inventory in cartel cases in 2013 (Bial et al., 2013). Deferred prosecution agreements (DPAs) have been used successfully in dealing with bribery cases in the US, UK and other jurisdictions (see Hock, 2020 and Chapter 2). To summarise the operation of the DPA, the prosecutor initially defers a prosecution and then withdraws it after a set number of years provided the accused pays a large fine and agrees to mend their errant ways by complying with certain conditions. In practice, therefore, DPAs are more like a regulatory justice model than traditional criminal justice. In this respect, the US is moving towards the European regulatory justice approach, which will be returned to later in this chapter.

The generic drug cartel scandal in America illustrates effective application of DPAs. The DOJ (2021) charged seven pharmaceutical companies and four senior executives for conspiring in cartels affecting over $1 billion of generic drugs sales. Three of the executives pleaded guilty. Five of the companies entered into DPAs with the DOJ to resolve the charges, under which they collectively paid $426 million in criminal penalties, which is nearly 50% of the affected sales. One of the firms, Taro Pharmaceuticals, was involved in two cartels and entered into a DPA, paying $206 million, the highest penalty to date for a domestic cartel offender. The five companies and executives agreed to cooperate in the cases against the remaining parties. Class action lawsuits have been launched which are likely to attract thousands of members as complainants (McAfee, 2021).

This example illustrates the use of criminal DPAs in support of the two-limbed strategy for enforcement against serious offending. The threat of prosecution encourages early settlement with penalties that can exceed the normal 20% fine. It also motivates conspirators to cooperate in the prosecution of cartel members who refuse to settle. Finally, if successful, it opens the door for victims to seek compensation.

European regulatory model

In contrast to the criminal approach in the USA, the regulatory model dominates OECD compliance in much of the rest of the world, including Europe (TFEU Article 101). Nevertheless, the regulators enjoy substantial powers. One advantage of this approach is the lower, civil standard of proof. However, the most prominent advantage is that the authority is the investigator, prosecutor and arbiter of the non-criminal cases. This is a form of administrative justice whereby allegations are investigated and sanction decisions are arrived at behind closed doors. This coherent approach raises the efficiency of the enforcement process, but arguably at the expense of traditional procedural justice. To assist in their evidence gathering, the EC and member authorities have the power to compel witness testimony, to force disclosure of materials, to enter businesses premises without a warrant, to seize evidence and to make interim orders for the protection of the public (CMA, 2020; EC, n.d. a).

Because most authorities cover all aspects of non-criminal cases from investigation to judgement, their sanction primary powers are limited to ordering a stop to cartel activity and imposing substantial fines. Once an authority has decided the outcome of cases, it issues its findings and proposed penalties to respondents, the 'Statement of Objection' in the European system, and allows the respondents access to the case files. The respondent corporations then have the opportunity to reply to the findings in writing or orally, which the authority considers before issuing its final decision. To guard against miscarriages of justice, respondents can appeal the decisions. Appeals are heard in Commission cases by the Court of Justice of the European Union. The Competition Appeal Tribunal hears appeals in the UK.

This process is based on restorative justice principles (Braithwaite, 2002), informed by the utilitarian calculation that the welfare of the public is far better served by the twin objectives of stopping the systematic harm and deterring others rather than becoming embroiled in complex and lengthy criminal prosecutions for retributive purposes. To this end, the authorities seek cooperation with offending parties from the outset. The leniency programme aligns with the US practices with the objective of increasing both detections and investigative efficiency. It incentivises cooperation by leveraging the threat of huge fines to offer full or partial immunity to the first member of a cartel that confesses. It is a key tool in providing authorities with the evidence to justify targeted inspections or dawn raids on other cartel members (CMA, 2020; EC, n.d. b). The first instance confession under the leniency terms can be after an investigation has been launched. During the subsequent investigations, the model then offers the carrot of reduced fines to incentivise cooperation and settlement with the remaining cartelists. Mirroring American practice, the leniency programme does not provide immunity from civil litigation (Warrington, 2021).

Leniency was obtained by the domestic cartelists in the estate agency case (CMA, 2019). One of the four estate agencies, Romans, brought the case to the CMA in 2018, confessed and cooperated with the investigation, providing voluntary access to its business records. This immediately led to dawn raids on the other three agencies. Romans avoided a fine. A second estate agency, Prospect, applied for leniency after a dawn raid. It was granted partial leniency for its cooperation leading to a 60% reduction in its fine to £269,000. The Hardy agency eventually admitted the offending and settled the matter at £143,000 with a 10% discount. The Worth agency was fined £194,000 and received no discount for cooperation and settlement. The case concluded in less than two years. Without the persuasive leverage of substantial fines, the leniency tool and the CMA's search powers the case would not have been launched in the first place or would have taken many years.

The European model has inched closer to the American strategy with respect to criminal prosecution and civil litigation. Although the EC remains purely an administrative regulator, national authorities have adopted powers of prosecution, but they are rarely used. For example, the UK's CMA has the power to prosecute individuals under the Enterprise Act 2002, however, it has conducted only seven criminal investigations between 2008 and 2021, just two of which led to prosecutions and the convictions of four directors (CMA, n.d. a). The CMA can also apply to the court for the disqualification of directors for up to 15 years, but rarely does so: just two directors were disqualified in 2019.

In 2014, the EU introduced the Damages Directive (2014/104/EU) which is aimed at harmonising the rights of victims of hard-core cartels to claim for damages across the EU. It has been incorporated into the Competition Act 1998 in the UK. The most striking aspect of this development is there is now an assumption that cartels cause harm; this transfers the burden of proof onto the defendant cartelist, which has to prove to the civil courts that it did not cause damage to claimants. No-win-no-fee law firms have emerged to represent multiple victims in civil cases, one is aptly named Cartel Damage Claims (CDC).[6] As in the US model, the risks for these law firms is greatly lowered and the chances of some redress for the victims is raised when actions are launched after the offender's liability has been proven by a competition authority. Following the €3.8 billion fine imposed by the EC on six European truck manufacturers in 2016 and 2017 (EC, 2014), CDC launched a civil claim against the companies on behalf of business that purchased or leased relevant trucks between 1997 and 2011, the 14-year duration of the conspiracy.[7] On the assumption that the action is successful, the value of the compensation is likely to be eye-watering. CDC's fee is 35% of the compensation.

Calculation of fines

The US criminal and European regulatory systems have adopted a similar approach to the determination of fines. They are both unusual in that they are based on economic calculations of rational deterrence. Becker (1968) first postulated the idea that rational economic calculations could be used to optimise sanctions for maximum deterrence. Recognising the utility of applying economic deterrence to economic crimes, Landes (1983) proposed that the optimal financial deterrence in antitrust cases should be the violation's net harm to others divided by the probability of detection and proof. Therefore, if the value of the overcharges from a hard-core cartel is £1 million and the chance of detection and proof is 33%, the value of the fine should be £3 million. Although the deterrence calculations have been much debated (see Davies & Ormosi, 2014), Landes' overall approach has been adopted and it explains why the fines are so large.

With the primary aim of deterrence, the sentencing guidelines in the USA set the fine at 20% of affected commerce, that is, the total value of the relevant sales during the period of the cartel operation (US Sentencing Commission, 2019). This is based on the assumption that the average overcharge is 10%, which then should be doubled for deterrence purposes. The EC's approach is more discretionary, allowing fines up to 30% of the affected sales to address the overcharge element plus an additional 15%–25% of one year's sales as the deterrence element (EU, 2006). The fine is capped so that it cannot exceed 10% of an offending firm's prior total turnover. The guidance for the UK's CMA (CMA, 2018) is the same except there is no specific percentage guidance for the deterrence element.

These large deterrence calculations highlight the tension between the regulatory component of restorative justice and the direct form of restorative justice, that is, compensating the victims. The high level of fines extracts resources from offenders and reduces the incentive to settle with victims. Following their €3.9 billion fine, the European truck companies are resisting settlement with the law firm CDC. The restorative principles are also undermined by the costs of the civil action. With the lawyers passing on just 65% of any recoveries, the victims remain 35% out of pocket. The OECD has acknowledged this issue, suggesting a regulatory procedure which combines the settlement with the authorities and the settlement for the victims in order to avoid unnecessary litigation delays and excessive costs (OECD, 2011). The problem is yet to be meaningfully addressed.

International enforcement

The membership of domestic cartels resides in a single jurisdiction. The estate agency case is a domestic cartel. International cartels, as in the bearing case, include corporate members from more than one country. They are the more damaging collusive groups due to their scale and reach, and because they are the most difficult to prosecute and close down (Connor, 2016). Consequently, they attract special attention from the competition authorities. Recognising that regulating the impacts on home markets required an international reach, extraterritorial enforcement emerged in the 1990s in America and Europe (Levenstein & Suslow, 2008). Competition authorities now regularly impose substantial penalties on corporations residing in foreign jurisdictions. These cases highlight the value of the common OECD framework in ensuring coordination rather than conflict between authorities.

The bearings cartel was originally detected in Japan by the JFTC (2013). It involved four Japanese manufacturers which collectively agreed price increases of 8%–10%. One of the manufacturers, JTEKT, obtained leniency for its cooperation with the JFTC and avoided a fine. The other three (Nachi, NSK and NTN) were fined ¥13.4 billion (€102 million) based on the impact on domestic sales in Japan. The case subsequently rippled around the world as regulators in Australia, Canada, Korea, Singapore and the USA shared information to impose extraterritorial fines on the Japanese manufacturers for the harms caused in their respective jurisdictions. JTEKT and NSK entered plea agreements with the US DOJ, pleaded guilty and were fined US$103 million and US$68 million, respectively (DOJ, 2013a,b).

The EC also took up the matter and expanded their enforcement to include two European cartel members, Schaeffler based in Germany and SKF based in Sweden (EC, 2014). The Commission found that the value of the affected sales in the EU was between €1 billion and €1.5 billion over a seven-year period to 2011. It imposed the largest collective fine of all the regulators at €953 million, mainly due to the involvement of Schaeffler and SKF as domestic producers with the largest local market share. The Commission fined Schaeffler and SKF £270 million and £315 million, respectively. JTEKT avoided an €80 million fine under the Commission's leniency programme.

The extent and impact of cartel crime

The bearings case clearly illustrates the extent of the harm that can arise from a powerful, international cartel scheme. As in all areas of crime, no data exists which accurately estimates the total cost of cartel crime. Aggregate regulatory fines and awarded civil damages are one rough way to gauge the level of cartel harm. Since 2000, when the EC became fully engaged in enforcement, it has imposed fines totalling €28 billion on 658 corporations involved in 127 hardcore cartel schemes (EC, 2021). This is about nine times the level of fines in North America (Connor, 2016). However, when civil damages are taken into account, the North American total exceeds Europe at $34 billion.

More thorough estimates of harm are available based on the open-access Private International Cartel (PIC) database assembled by Professor John Connor (Connor, 2020). Drawing on public documents from across the globe, the PIC is the most comprehensive dataset of international cartel enforcement, starting in 1990. It excludes domestic cases, such as the estate agency example. The database has been adopted by the OECD.[8] Using this data, Connor (2016) estimates that the total value of worldwide affected sales between 1990 and 2016 was between US$51 trillion and US$76 trillion involving 1,336 cartels and over 7,200 corporations. He further estimates that aggregate cartel overcharges over the 26 years at US$4.6 trillion. This compares reasonably well with the US Sentencing Commission's (2019) informed assumption of 10% of sales.

Economists have applied complex economic analyses to the PIC data to estimate the average level of overcharging at 10%–20%, and up to 50% in the worst cases (Tavares de Araujo, 2010). The fulsome analysis of Boyer and Kotchoni (2015) concludes the average overcharge is 16%. Applying this figure to the affected sales, the total value of overcharging up to 2016 was between US$7 trillion and $10 trillion, about double the Connor (2016) figure. To put this into clear perspective, these analyses imply that a small number of *detected* corrupt schemes (1,336) and *detected* corrupt corporations (7,200) have caused between $5 trillion and $10 trillion of fraudulent damage worldwide. A key dimension contributing to the harm is the duration of the schemes. Oindrila De (2010) estimates the average duration is eight years. This is seven times the 14-month duration of a typical occupational fraud scheme (Association of Certified Fraud Examiners [ACFE], 2020).

These estimates exclude undetected international cartels. However, economists have developed models that predict the cost of undetected international cartels at between two and four times the detected level (Davies & Ormosi, 2014). This implies that the total overcharging impact of international cartels between 1990 and 2016 was between US$10 trillion and US$40 trillion or between US$0.6 trillion and US$2.5 trillion per year. Proportioned to the size of the UK economy (GDP), the annual impact in the UK is between £16 billion and £62 billion. Although this analysis is limited to international cartels, it clearly explains why governments across the world have empowered their competition authorities to protect the public interest. It also explains why governments have responded positively to the OECD's call for cross-border cooperation against these archetypal white-collar crimes.

There is no equivalent data for domestic cartels due in part to regulatory effort being more focused on the high harm international cartels. It can also be partly explained by the priority domestic regulators place on reviewing business mergers that risk the creation of monopolies. The UK's CMA provides a useful example. In 2019, the CMA (n.d. a) concluded five cartel investigations, two with no adverse findings, one secured an agreement from car rental companies that they would change their online booking practices, and just two resulted in fines: £36 million to three companies supplying drainage products, and £3.4 million to two companies supplying bagged household fuels. On the other hand, the CMA completed 54 merger inquiries in the same year.

Consequential harms

Illegal price mark-ups do not only cause harm to buyers by overcharging, they also restrict access to products or services to those who cannot afford them (Tavares de Araujo, 2010). It is a particular concern when the practice restricts access to essential goods such as medicines. This is also a policy dilemma in relation to intellectual property (IP) rights. In order to incentivise innovation, owners of patented inventions are provided with legal monopoly rights for 20 years so that they can recoup their investments and make a profit (Howell & Bainbridge, 2014). The dilemma for policymakers is that IP rights can restrict access to essential pharmaceuticals, such as vaccines, especially in developing nations (Smith, 2007).

It might seem that a legal monopoly based on IP rights amounts to the same thing as an illegal cartel monopoly. However, it is important to emphasise again their respective purposes. The purpose of IP rights is to encourage innovation for the betterment of public welfare. In contrast, the purpose of cartels is solely to maximise the profit interests of corporations at the expense of public welfare. Indeed, the easy profits that can be earned from cartel conspiracies lead to a lack of innovation, lower efficiency and higher costs for business customers (London Economics, 2011).

However, the most obvious direct impact of unrestrained cartel activity is in the healthcare sector, where it deprives people of access to treatments, and this is not solely a healthcare problem for developing nations. The private sector dominates the healthcare system in America. Consequently, the authorities pay particular attention to healthcare providers and pharmaceutical firms because cartels directly harm the health of less wealthy, vulnerable Americans (DOJ, 2021).

Obstacles to compliance and enforcement

The foregoing discussion of the enforcement environment and its heavy deterrence penalties would suggest that competition authorities are having an effect. Indeed, with no evidence of repeat offending, it seems that competition authorities are successful in specific deterrence. However, most of the available data and research is based on enforcement against international cartels by authorities in developed nations with a functioning rule of law. We know little about domestic cartels and less about cartels in developing nations.

The estate agency case is an example of a very local cartel operating in the high street. We do not know the extent to which small cartels are operating in professional services in small towns, involving lawyers, accountants, consultants, dentists, architects and so on. Small firms emerge around large factories and other business centres to supply essential goods and services. We do not know the extent to which they fix local prices or secretly share out contracts through bid-rigging. It is feasible that small firms in such circumstances are motivated by survival rather than profiteering and would not regard it as illegal. A director interviewed by Shepherd (2016) did not know that fixing prices was illegal until he mentioned his practices to a former director of the Office for Fair Trading at a dinner party (the OFT became the CMA in 2014).

A CMA and ICM (2018) survey of 1,200 business organisations in the UK revealed that only 57% of the businesses knew that price fixing was illegal, 52% knew that bid-rigging was illegal and just 18% were aware of the leniency programme. The responses from small and large companies were very similar indicating that a large proportion of the business community at all levels does not understand that hard-core cartel behaviour is illegal. Indeed, for many it is an acceptable social norm (Stephan, 2010). The implication is that compliance is low and the number of detected domestic cartels is the tip of the iceberg.

The estate agency case illustrates how large crimes are committed on the high street, under our noses. Perpetrators get away with it because cartels are secret, administrative crimes. Unlike burglary, there are no broken windows to signal wrongdoing. Consequently, the authorities' main detection strategy is logical, based on the coupling of large fines with the leniency policy to prompt cartelists to turn on their co-conspirators and self-report. However, this strategy is severely undermined in the UK because over three quarters of businesses are unaware of the leniency programme, and nearly half are unaware that cartel practices are proscribed (CMA & ICM, 2018). For many, therefore, the practice remains socially acceptable or tolerated (Stephan, 2010). In order to make the deterrence policy work effectively, the challenge for the domestic authority is to develop more powerful normative messages supported by more than a couple of successful cases in a year. In doing so, it is important that the messages clearly distinguish between constructive, cooperative practice and destructive collusion.

Poly-criminality that protects the operation of cartels is another significant challenge. Examining the links between hard-core cartels and other forms of corruption in the Canadian construction industry, Reeves-Latour and Morselli (2017) observed that bribery assists in sustaining cartels in two ways. Firstly, to maintain trust and cooperation within bid-rigging schemes, the firm designated for securing a contract pays other members a kick-back fee. Secondly, bribing key employees of customers brings them into the trust network to ensure the cooperation of those who should be watching out for cartel abuse. A classic example is the domestic construction cartel that bribed the administrators in Laval, a city in Canada, including the Mayor, Gilles Vaillancourt, who was sentenced to six years imprisonment in 2016 (CBC, 2016). In this case, the cartelists reinforced their defences to detection by inviting key government officials to join the conspiracy. The Laval scheme involved four forms of economic crime: hard-core cartel price fixing and bid-rigging, bribery for which Vaillancourt and his associates received 2% of contract values (Reeves-Latour & Morselli, 2017), fraud by abuse of position as the city officials dishonestly signed contracts at inflated prices and money laundering. By 2019, the city had recovered almost CA$50 million from the offenders.

Regulators tasked with detecting hard-core cartels and enforcing the law are also susceptible to the lure of corruption. The director of the Hellenic Competition Commission (HCC), Panayiotis Adamopoulos, and two others were arrested in 2006 on bribery and blackmail charges (BBC News, 2006). They tried to exploit the leniency programme in Greece by demanding a €2.5 million payment from a dairy firm under investigation, Mevgal, to avoid a €25 million fine (Stephan, 2010). In this case, the cartelist refused the protection and reported the officials to the authorities. They were sentenced to 5.5 years in prison, and the cartelists, including Mevgal, were fined €50 million for price fixing (Ekathimerini, 2009). The multiple crimes in this scheme involved price fixing, bribery and attempted blackmail.

Both the Canadian construction and Greek dairy cartels are model examples of the insidious poly-criminality of economic crime. They clearly illustrate why academics, policy makers and law enforcers need to appreciate the broad spectrum of economic crime and the links between the different species of economic crime, particularly with respect to substantial white-collar crimes perpetrated by powerful business people.

Conclusion

This chapter has explained why Sutherland (1949) was justifiably anxious about white-collar crime in general and cartel crime in particular. The illegal gains obtained by a small number of corporate offenders are huge. The analysis suggests that international cartels alone are defrauding the public of up to $2.5 trillion per year due to overcharges of 16%. The proportionate impact on the UK economy is up to £62 billion per year. Realising that globalisation has amplified the disproportionate harm of international illicit cartels, the authorities across the world have refreshed their historic attitudes and have, since the 1990s, become more actively engaged. Governments now broadly agree that, if left unchecked, international hard-core cartels would concentrate selfish power and pose a structural threat to the free market economy, undermine efficiency and innovation and illegally deprive people of even essentials needed for their welfare.

Informed by the criminal approach of the US DOJ and the regulatory approach of the EC, the partially harmonised enforcement practices under the OECD framework centre on a bold deterrence policy, which couples large fines and a leniency programme, in order to modify the rational calculations of corporate executives in favour of the law. The absence of recidivism suggests that the authorities' focus on international hard-core cartels using this approach is successful as specific deterrence. However, its impact as a general deterrence is less clear. The effectiveness of the policy is most uncertain in relation to domestic cartels, in part due to very low enforcement rates. A major challenge in the domestic context is the lack of awareness of the deterrence policy and, crucially, what constitutes corrupt cartel activity as opposed to constructive cooperation. Regulation and enforcement in domestic markets needs considerable attention.

Notes

1 NAEA – www.naea.co.uk/.
2 International Competition Network – www.internationalcompetitionnetwork.org/.
3 European Competition Network – https://ec.europa.eu/competition/ecn/index_en.html.
4 Hawaii v. Standard Oil Co. of Cal., 405 U.S. 251, 262 (1972).
5 Mitsubishi Motors Corp. v. Soler Chrysler-Plymouth, Inc., 473 U.S. 614, 635 (1985).
6 Cartel Damage Claims – https://carteldamageclaims.com/.
7 Cartel Damage Claims – Trucks – https://carteldamageclaims.com/our-cases/on-going-cases/.
8 OECD International Cartel Database – https://qdd.oecd.org/subject.aspx?Subject=OECD_HIC.

References

ACCC. (2019). *Cartels: Deterrence and detection – A guide for government procurement professionals*. Retrieved from the APO website https://apo.org.au/node/275496
ACFE. (2020). *Report to the nations*. www.acfe.com/report-to-the-nations/2020/

BBC News. (2006). *Greek competition boss arrested.* http://news.bbc.co.uk/1/hi/business/5356064.stm

Becker, G. S. (1968). Crime and punishment: An economic approach. *The Journal of Political Economy, 76*(2), 169–217. www.nber.org/system/files/chapters/c3625/c3625.pdf

Bial, J., Nanni, A., & Ravas, S. (2013, March 4). *United States: Antitrust Division enters into first Deferred Prosecution Agreement.* Mondaq. www.mondaq.com/unitedstates/trade-regulation-practices/224902/antitrust-division-enters-into-first-deferred-prosecution-agreement

Boyer, M., & Kotchoni, R. (2015). *How much do cartel overcharge?* www.tse-fr.eu/sites/default/files/TSE/documents/doc/wp/2015/cartel_overcharges.pdf

Braithwaite, J. (2002). *Restorative justice & responsive regulation.* Oxford University.

Burns, J. W. (1993). Vertical restraints, efficiency, and the real world. *Fordham Law Review, 62*, 597. https://heinonline.org/HOL/Page?handle=hein.journals/flr62&div=28&g_sent=1&casa_token=&collection=journals

CBC. (2016). *'King of Laval' Gilles Vaillancourt sentenced to 6 years in prison.* www.cbc.ca/news/canada/montreal/laval-gilles-vaillancourt-1.3898029

CMA. (2018). *CMA's guidance as to the appropriate amount of a penalty.* https://assets.publishing.service.gov.uk/government/uploads/system/uploads/attachment_data/file/700576/final_guidance_penalties.pdf

CMA. (2019). *Case 50543 – Residential estate agency services in Berkshire.* www.gov.uk/cma-cases/provision-of-residential-estate-agency-services

CMA. (2020). *Guidance on the CMA's investigation procedures in Competition Act 1998 cases: CMA8.* CMA. www.gov.uk/government/publications/guidance-on-the-cmas-investigation-procedures-in-competition-act-1998-cases/guidance-on-the-cmas-investigation-procedures-in-competition-act-1998-cases#taking-urgent-action-to-prevent-significant-damage-or-to-protect-the-public-interest

CMA. (2021). *Retained block exemption.* CMA. www.gov.uk/government/publications/retained-block-exemptions/retained-block-exemptions

CMA. (n.d. a). *Competition and Markets Authority cases.* CMA. www.gov.uk/cma-cases

CMA. (n.d. b). *Mergers: Detailed information.* CMA. www.gov.uk/topic/competition/mergers

CMA & ICM. (2018). *Competition law research 2018.* https://assets.publishing.service.gov.uk/government/uploads/system/uploads/attachment_data/file/750149/icm_unlimited_cma_competition_law_research_2018.pdf

Coleman, J. (1992). The theory of white-collar crime: From Sutherland to the 1990s. In K. Schlegel & D. Weisburd (Eds.), *White-collar crime reconsidered* (pp. 53–77). Northeastern University Press.

Connor, J. M. (2016). *The rise of anti-cartel enforcement in Africa, Asia, and Latin America. Asia, and Latin America.* https://dx.doi.org/10.2139/ssrn.2711972

Connor, J. M. (2020). *Private international cartels full data 2019 edition.* Purdue University. https://doi.org/10.4231/G5GZ-0505

Connor, J. M., & Lande, R. H. (2012). Cartels as rational business strategy: Crime pays. *Cardozo Law Review, 34*, 427–490.

Cramer, D. L., & Heuser, W. L. (1960). Variations in the definitions of the degrees of competition. *The American Journal of Economics and Sociology, 19*(4), 383–397. www.jstor.org/stable/3484618

Cseres, K. (2020). "Acceptable" cartels at the crossroads of EU competition law and the Common Agricultural Policy: A legal inquiry into the political, economic, and social dimensions of (Strengthening Farmers') bargaining power. *The Antitrust Bulletin, 65*(3), 401–422. https://journals.sagepub.com/doi/pdf/10.1177/0003603X20929122

Davies, S., & Ormosi, P. (2014). *The economic impact of cartels and anti-cartel enforcement.* http://competitionpolicy.ac.uk/documents/8158338/8235397/CCP+Working+Paper+13-7+v2+%282014%29.pdf/75e1ba67-d52f-4bf5-ac39-11c687a8ed83

De, O. (2010). Analysis of cartel duration: Evidence from EC prosecuted cartels. *International Journal of the Economics of Business, 17*(1), 33–65. https://doi.org/10.1080/13571510903516946

DOJ. (1993). *Corporate leniency policy.* www.justice.gov/atr/file/810281/download

DOJ. (1994). *Individual leniency policy.* www.justice.gov/atr/individual-leniency-policy

DOJ. (2013a). *USA v NSK Ltd Plea Agreement.* www.justice.gov/atr/case-document/file/506606/download

DOJ. (2013b). *USA v JTEKT Corporation Plea Agreement.* www.justice.gov/atr/case-document/file/500241/download

DOJ. (2021). *Generic drugs investigation targets anticompetitive schemes – Division update Spring 2021.* www.justice.gov/atr/division-operations/division-update-spring-2021/generic-drugs-investigation-targets-anticompetitive-schemes

Dunne, N. (2020). Characterizing hard core cartels under Article 101 TFEU. *The Antitrust Bulletin, 65*(3), 376–400. https://journals.sagepub.com/doi/pdf/10.1177/0003603X20929121

EC. (2010). *Guidelines on vertical restraints (2010/C 130/0).* https://eur-lex.europa.eu/legal-content/EN/TXT/?uri=CELEX%3A52010XC0519%2804%29

EC. (2013). *Antitrust: Commission fines Microsoft for non-compliance with browser choice commitments.* https://ec.europa.eu/commission/presscorner/detail/en/IP_13_196

EC. (2014). *Case comp/39922 – Bearings.* https://ec.europa.eu/competition/antitrust/cases/dec_docs/39922/39922_2067_2.pdf

EC. (2018). *Antitrust: Commission fines Google €4.34 billion for illegal practices regarding Android mobile devices to strengthen dominance of Google's search engine.* https://ec.europa.eu/commission/presscorner/detail/en/IP_18_4581

EC. (2020). *Commission staff working document evaluation of the vertical block exemption regulation.* https://ec.europa.eu/competition/consultations/2018_vber/staff_working_document.pdf

EC. (2021). *Statistics on cartel cases.* Retrieved 13/06/2021 from https://ec.europa.eu/competition-policy/cartels/statistics_en

EC. (n.d. a). *Antitrust and cartels procedures.* https://ec.europa.eu/competition-policy/antitrust/procedures_en

EC. (n.d. b). *Leniency.* https://ec.europa.eu/competition-policy/cartels/leniency_en

Ekathimerini. (2009, April 14). *Three guilty of Mevgal blackmail.* www.ekathimerini.com/news/62885/three-guilty-of-mevgal-blackmail/

EU. (2006). *Guidelines on the method of setting fines imposed pursuant to Article 23(2)(a) of Regulation No 1/2003.* https://eur-lex.europa.eu/legal-content/EN/ALL/?uri=CELEX%3A52006XC0901%2801%29

Galetovic, A., Haber, S., & Zaretzki, L. (2018). An estimate of the average cumulative royalty yield in the world mobile phone industry: Theory, measurement and results. *Telecommunications Policy, 42*(3), 263–276. www.sciencedirect.com/science/article/pii/S0308596117302240

Glebovskiy, A. (2019). Inherent criminogenesis in business organisations. *Journal of Financial Crime, 26*(2), 432–446. https://doi.org/10.1108/JFC-01-2018-0010

Harding, C. (2004). Forging the European cartel offence: The supranational regulation of Business Conspiracy. *European Journal of Crime, Criminal Law and Criminal Justice, 12*(4), 275–300. https://doi.org/10.1163/1571817042523121

Harding, C. (2006). Business collusion as a criminological phenomenon: Exploring the global criminalisation of business cartels. *Critical Criminology, 14*(2), 181–205. https://link.springer.com/article/10.1007/s10612-006-9000-6

Hock, B. (2020). Policing corporate bribery: Negotiated settlements and bundling. *Policing and Society.* https://doi.org/10.1080/10439463.2020.1808650

Howell, C., & Bainbridge, D. (2014). *Intellectual Property Asset Management: How to identify, protect, manage and exploit intellectual property within the business environment.* Routledge. https://ebookcentral.proquest.com/lib/portsmouth-ebooks/detail.action?docID=1588654

JFTC. (2013). *The JFTC issued cease and desist orders and surcharge payment orders against bearing manufacturers.* www.jftc.go.jp/en/pressreleases/yearly-2013/march/130329_2.html

Kingsbury, A., & Gamman, J. (2013). Patent-collaboration: Licensing, patent pools, patents commons, open source and communities of innovation. *New Zealand Intellectual Property Journal,* 3–9. https://core.ac.uk/download/pdf/79181369.pdf

Lampe, R., & Moser, P. (2016). Patent pools, competition, and innovation—Evidence from 20 US industries under the new deal. *The Journal of Law, Economics, and Organization, 32*(1), 1–36. https://doi.org/10.1093/jleo/ewv014

Landes, W. M. (1983). Optimal sanctions for antitrust violations. *The University of Chicago Law Review, 50*(2), 652–678. www.jstor.org/stable/pdf/1599506.pdf

Levenstein, M. C., & Suslow, V. Y. (2008). International cartels. In *Issues in competition law and Policy* (pp. 1107–1126). American Bar Association. www-personal.umich.edu/~maggiel/files/aba.pdf

London Economics. (2011). *The nature and impact of hardcore cartels.* https://londoneconomics.co.uk/blog/publication/the-nature-and-impact-of-hardcore-cartels/

McAfee, D. (2021, March 9). *Teva generic price-fixing securities suit gets class status.* Bloomberg Law. https://news.bloomberglaw.com/class-action/teva-generic-price-fixing-securities-lawsuit-gets-class-status

Mond, A. (1927). International cartels. *Journal of the Royal Institute of International Affairs, 6*(5), 265–283. https://doi.org/10.2307/3014741

OECD. (1998). *Recommendation of the council concerning effective action against hard core cartels.* https://legalinstruments.oecd.org/en/instruments/OECD-LEGAL-0294

OECD. (2011). *Quantification of harm to competition by national courts and competition agencies.* www.oecd.org/daf/competition/QuantificationofHarmtoCompetition2011.pdf

OECD. (2021). *Recommendation of the council concerning effective action against hard core cartels.* https://legalinstruments.oecd.org/en/instruments/OECD-LEGAL-0452

OECD. (n.d.). *Cartels and anti-competitive agreements*. www.oecd.org/competition/cartels/

Reeves-Latour, M., & Morselli, C. (2017). Bid-rigging networks and state-corporate crime in the construction industry. *Social Networks, 51*, 158–170. https://doi.org/10.1016/j.socnet.2016.10.003

Roth, P. (2019). The continual evolution of competition law. *Journal of Antitrust Enforcement, 7*(1), 6–26. https://doi.org/10.1093/jaenfo/jny018

Shepherd, D. (2016). *Complicit silence: Organisations and their response to occupational fraud.* University of Portsmouth.

Smith, A. (2007). Intellectual property rights and the right to health: Considering the case of access to medicines. In C. Lenk, N. Hoppe, & R. Andorno (Eds.), *Ethics and law of intellectual property: Current problems in politics, science and technology* (pp. 47–72). Ashgate Publishing.

Stephan, A. (2010). Cartel laws undermined: Corruption, social norms, and collectivist business cultures. *Journal of Law and Society, 37*(2), 345–367. https://doi.org/10.1111/j.1467-6478.2010.00507.x

Sutherland, E. (1949). *White collar crime*. Dryden.

Tavares de Araujo, M. (2010). Improving deterrence of hard-core cartels. *Competition Policy International, 6*(2), 69–82. www.levysalomao.com.br/files/publicacao/anexo/20110720095356_cpiautumn2010ebook.pdf

Transparency International. (n.d.). *What is corruption?* www.transparency.org/en/what-is-corruption

United Nations. (2013). *A guide for anti-corruption risk assessment.* www.unglobalcompact.org/library/411

US Sentencing Commission. (2019). *Primer on antitrust.* https://sentencing.umn.edu/sites/sentencing.umn.edu/files/2019_us_antitrust_primer.pdf

Warrington, G. (2021). *UK anti-cartel laws and their enforcement.* www.pinsentmasons.com/out-law/guides/uk-anti-cartel-laws-and-their-enforcement

Werden, G. J., Hammond, S. D., & Barnett, B. A. (2011). Deterrence and detection of cartels: Using all the tools and sanctions. *The Antitrust Bulletin, 56*(2), 207–234. https://doi.org/10.1177%2F0003603X1105600202

WIPO. (2014). *Patent pools and antitrust – A comparative analysis.* www.wipo.int/export/sites/www/ip-competition/en/studies/patent_pools_report.pdf

Chapter 5

Economic cybercrime

Introduction

> Unfortunately the University has been impacted by a cyber incident. This has affected some of our IT systems, which remain offline whilst we work with expert support to investigate the issue and securely restore them. As part of this, we have taken the decision to close down the campus and many of our services in order to best protect our systems and information while the investigation is underway.

In the midst of writing this book in April 2021, the authors, along with several thousand staff and students received the communication above from the University they work for. The University of Portsmouth was under a cyber-attack, so this chapter was drafted during a real incident. There are several types of cybercrime that have become a menace to individuals and organisations. This chapter will begin by exploring what economic cybercrime is, before providing some real examples. The chapter will then move on to explore the extent of this type of crime and briefly explore its impact. The chapter will end with a brief consideration of the different types of perpetrators who become involved.

What is economic cybercrime?

'Cybercrime' is a very broad term that is used to describe any crime that involves digital technology, from criminals sending ransomware to make money, to school children trolling and abusing fellow pupils online, to state actors hacking into the defence systems of other governments (Holt & Bossler, 2014). Ibrahim (2016) and Lazarus (2019) set out a very useful tripartite typology of cybercrime: socioeconomic, such as hacking bank accounts and phishing frauds; psychosocial, such as online abuse; and geopolitical cybercrime, such as espionage. This chapter is concerned with the socioeconomic type of cybercrime.

DOI: 10.4324/9781003081753-5

There is also another important distinction to be made, that between cyber-enabled and cyber-dependent crime (Furnell, 2002; McGuire & Dowling, 2013). The former are crimes that do not require information communications technology (ICT) to commit them, but can be expanded by the use of such technology. For example, a lottery fraud could be perpetrated by traditional mail, but also by email. Cyber-dependent crimes, however, can only be perpetrated by ICT, such as hacking into a computer to cause damage or infecting a network with ransomware. Cyber-enabled fraud was largely dealt with in Chapter 2 on fraud. This chapter expands the discussion to include financially motivated cyber-dependent crime. Broadly this covers the following five types of behaviour:

- hacking;
- ransomware;
- distributed denial-of-service (DDoS) attacks;
- computer viruses/malware;
- doxing.

These types of cybercrimes can affect both individuals and organisations, so the scope of this chapter will cover both types of victims. It is also important to note that these crimes can also overlap with other economic crimes. Hacking can be used to secure information for 'cyber-enabled' frauds as well as to secure information for cyber-enabled espionage. It is therefore important not to consider these cybercrimes in isolation. It is also important to be aware of the overlap between cyber-dependent and cyber-enabled crime. An attack on a network that is a disruptive, data gathering cyber-dependent crime event may be a precursor to, for example, cyber-enabled fraud.

The five principal types of cybercrime above often attract their own specific criminal laws. In the UK (note legislation covers the whole of the UK), the principal offences fall under the Computer Misuse Act 1990 (CMA) as follows:

Hacking offences:

> Section 1: Unauthorised access to computer material.
> Section 2: Unauthorised access with intent to commit or facilitate commission of further offences.

Computer virus offences:

> Section 3: Unauthorised acts with intent to impair, or with recklessness as to impairing, operation of computer, etc.
> Section 3ZA: Unauthorised acts causing, or creating risk of, serious damage.

Section 3A: Making, supplying or obtaining articles for use in offence
under Section 1, 3 or 3ZA (Crown Prosecution Service, n.d.).

These offences can be committed alone, but are also often used to enable
other offences, which may be more serious. For example, hacking another
person's email account to just read their correspondence would be an offence
under Section 1. However, if the aim of the hacking is to secure details of
banking credentials to financially defraud the person or the bank, it would be
cyber-enabled fraud. Offenders could then be charged with fraud, or hacking
under Section 2 of the Computer Misuse Act, or both.

In the USA, the original legislation was the Computer Fraud and Abuse
Act of 1984, which has been amended several times since (Office of Legal
Education Executive Office for United States Attorneys, n.d.). The principal
offences from the legislation, as amended, are listed below:

- obtaining national security information;
- accessing a computer and obtaining information;
- trespassing in a government computer;
- accessing a computer to defraud and obtain value;
- intentionally damaging by knowing transmission;
- recklessly damaging by intentional access;
- negligently causing damage and loss by intentional access;
- trafficking in passwords;
- extortion involving computers.

Several other offences, depending upon the behaviours, can also be potentially utilised in the US, such as offences related to fraud (wire fraud), identity
theft and communication interference (Office of Legal Education Executive
Office for United States Attorneys, n.d.).

Examples of economic cybercrime

This section will provide some real examples of economic cybercrime against
both individuals and organisations to illustrate the seriousness and sophistication of this type of crime. It will consider malware, DDoS attacks, hacking,
ransomware and doxing. These methods are often used in combination to
maximise the impact of attacks. The deployment of malware is frequently
the first stage of sophisticated attacks using other methods. It was noted
earlier that the focus would be on socioeconomic cybercrime. In doing so it
is important to note this does not mean that the scope of this chapter is only
criminals who seek financial gain, it also includes cybercrime by actors whose
prime motivation is to inflict economic damage on the victim, for example,
hostile states, terrorist groups and extreme activists.

Malware

Most people have probably experienced a computer virus on one of their devices at some point and these can often be dealt with relatively easily with anti-virus software. 'Malware' (malicious software) is a broad term used to describe viruses, worms, software and applications produced for negative purposes (McGuire & Dowling, 2013). It is a primary tool in the armoury of cybercriminals. The purpose of some malware is just to cause malicious damage to computers and networks. However, most malware attacks have more pernicious purposes in remotely controlling systems, collecting information or inserting spyware to monitor activities. Malware is frequently the preliminary, facilitating tool in sophisticated DDoS, hacking, ransomware, and doxing attacks.

In a typical example, Bitdefender (a cyber security company) reported a spearfishing campaign in 2020 that targeted the oil and gas industry. The attacks impersonated established contractor emails which were directed to load spyware onto the victim organisations. It was speculated that the campaign had an economic purpose in gathering information on company responses to falling oil prices during the pandemic (Culafi, 2020). Until Europol and national enforcement agencies dismantled the infrastructure behind the Emotet malware, it was regarded as the world's most serious malware threats (Europol, 2021). The malware, which used emails as an attack vector, was particularly dangerous because it provided access to computer systems for any malicious purpose such as data theft or ransomware attacks. It proliferated rapidly because the gang controlling Emotet sold it to other cybercriminals (Europol, 2021).

Distributed denial-of-service attacks

DDoS attacks flood computers or networks with very high volumes of traffic to degrade or disable their performance (McGuire & Dowling, 2013). They are typically executed using botnets (robot network). Each bot is a legitimate device infected by a malware that becomes part of an infected network controlled by cybercriminals. The attacker instructs the botnet devices to send emails or network requests to specific IP addresses causing the target to become overwhelmed.

DDoS attacks are a means for a competitor or activist group to disrupt the activities of an organisation or individual. In 2004, MyDoom, a worm virus spread rapidly across the world via spam emails to such an extent it was estimated to account for a quarter of email traffic. The malware triggered massive DDoS attacks and opened backdoors to enable remote control of systems. The economic cost of the damage was estimated at US$26.1 billion in just one year (Insurance Times, 2004). Similarly, in 2012, six US banks were subjected to attacks that created 10–20 times the normal level of traffic, causing huge disruption to the banks and to their customers (CNN, 2012). In another example, the popular website for mothers, Mumsnet, was the victim of multiple cyberattacks, including a DDoS attack that disrupted the ability of many legitimate users to access the site (Cluley, 2015).

Hacking

'Hacking' is an umbrella term that means different things to different people. Some use it to describe a broad range of cybercrimes from digital data theft to DDoS attacks (McGuire & Dowling, 2013). Originally the term referred to finding better ways to solve problems and is still used in this sense. For example, the Ordnance Survey in the UK runs hacking conventions to stimulate innovative use of its digital maps.[1] Alan Turing and his team at Bletchley Park in the UK developed the world's first digital computer to crack the Enigma code used by the German military in the Second World War. The term emerged in the 1950s when Massachusetts Institute of Technology (MIT) students found ways to avoid using punch cards and directly programme early computers (Brenner, 2010). The term later became associated with accessing computers for malign purposes. We refer to hacking in the way set out in the CMA: the act of illegally accessing computers.

Hacking is one of the most common economic cybercrimes (ONS, 2021). Sometimes criminals hack into an organisation's network to gain control of the systems and cause damage, secure information for espionage (see Chapter 7), directly defraud the target, or to gather the personal information of customers and staff for subsequent use in fraud (Button et al., 2020). The value of personally identifiable information is such that it has become a commodity on the dark web: fraudsters can simply buy the information (UNODC, 2021).

One of the most common types of hacking attacks are those that aim to steal the personal information of an organisation's clients, customers and staff. Ideally, from the hacker's point of view, the information contains core identity details (e.g. national insurance numbers), banking details and account access credentials. These types of hacks are clearly cyber-dependent crimes in the first place, but the collected data is subsequently used for cyber-enabled crimes. Such attacks can not only be damaging to the organisation that is breached, in terms of reputation and customer loyalty, but they can also lead to significant fines by regulators. The GDPR (General Data Protection Regulation) implemented within the EU in 2018 includes potential fines for data breaches of 4% of global turnover or €20 million (£17.5 million), whichever is the greater (ICO, n.d.). Table 5.1 provides examples of some of the largest and most infamous breaches.

Hacking can also be used more directly to steal money from organisational victims' bank accounts, a form of cyber-enabled theft. In one case reported by Kaspersky in 2015 around 100 banks lost around US$1 billion to hackers.

Table 5.1 Selected major hacks

Equifax 2017: 147 million accounts (names, Social Security numbers, dates of birth, credit card numbers and even driver's license numbers). Equifax settled with regulators for US$700 million.

Dubsmash 2018: 161.5 million accounts (account holder names, email addresses and hashed passwords).

Zynga 2019: 218 million accounts (log-in credentials, the hacker accessed usernames, email addresses, log-in IDs, some Facebook IDs, some phone numbers).

Marriott 2018: 383 million accounts (names, addresses, contact information and passport numbers).

Adult Friend Finder 2016: 412.2 million accounts (very sensitive information as a website facilitating sex and swingers).

Yahoo 2013: 3 billion (user accounts names, email addresses, telephone numbers and dates of birth). Yahoo settled a class action lawsuit for US$117.5 million.

Sources: BBC News (2016a), CNBC (2019).

Malware described as 'Carbanak' was placed on the banks' systems enabling the hackers to monitor bank activities and after waiting several months, they then struck by transferring money to their own accounts (CNN, 2015).

It is not just big corporations that are targeted with hacking, many ordinary individuals are also victims. Individuals' computers or other devices are hacked using malware that exploits the vulnerabilities of technology. However, hackers are increasingly using sophisticated social engineering techniques (Button et al., 2020; UNODC, 2021). These methods involve building trust to deceive the victims into becoming unwitting participants in their own victimisation. The victims are enticed into handing over their identity credentials or banking details.

In the UK, there has been a spate of social engineering hacks involving offenders impersonating BT (a telecommunications company). The victims are cold-called, told they have a problem with their broadband that needs to be investigated and tricked into enabling the scammers to remotely control their computers (Button et al., 2020). After an 'investigation', the victims are told they are entitled to a refund which can be paid directly into their accounts. Victims then open their bank accounts in front of the scammers, thus enabling the criminals to access and empty the victims' accounts (Button et al., 2021).

Hacking can also be used to secure information to divert payments. For example, Button et al. (2020) found examples of several victims whose email had been hacked. The offenders then monitored and read emails and when a payment arose, created fake emails to divert the funds. In one case a small plumbing firm's invoices were resent to customers with the bank account details changed to the offender's account.

Hacking is frequently used as a means to disrupt an organisation. A common problem is hacking an organisation's website and defacing it to damage the reputation of the organisation. Button et al. (2020) found an example of a school whose website was briefly hacked diverting traffic to a porn site. In 2015, the computer manufacturer Lenovo's website was hacked and redirected to pictures of bored teenagers with High School Musical's 'Breaking Free' set to the background. Those clicking on the slideshow were redirected to the Twitter feed of the hacking group 'Lizard Squad' (Guardian, 2015).

Ransomware

At the time of writing, there would seem to be a burst in activity in this type of crime. It involves infecting a victim's computer with malware that prevents users from accessing their system or personal files, usually by encryption (UNODC, 2021). The victim is then presented with a time limited offer to pay a ransom to restore access to the systems. The attackers often demand payment by cryptocurrency (UNODC, 2021).

In 2021, Colonial Pipeline controversially paid a US$4.4 million ransom in Bitcoin to restore systems after such an attack (BBC News, 2021a). The initial reports of the attack and disruption led to a jump in fuel prices because the firm's pipelines distribute a significant amount of diesel, petrol and jet fuel in the USA. The attack was linked to a Russian group, Darkside. Unusually, however, the company, via the FBI, was able to recover US$2.3 million in Bitcoin it had paid (CNN, 2021).

The ransomware attackers do not just target large organisations with big budgets. In research conducted by Button et al. (2020), a small farmer had been the victim of such an attack. The farmer had advertised for a job and when the victim opened the CVs of applicants one contained ransomware. The attack culminated in the victim having to abandon that computer and return to paper-based systems for some activities. In another case, a theatre was targeted causing disruption for several days.

Doxing

The last type of economic cybercrime to be considered is doxing. This is the deliberate broadcasting of private data to the Internet. Douglas (2016) distinguishes three main types, largely orientated around individual victims:

- deanonymising doxing: the exposure of a previously anonymous individual;
- targeting doxing: disclosing previously private information about a person; and
- delegitimising doxing: releasing information that damages the credibility of an individual.

The above could also be applied to organisations, so the first could include exposure of an organisation privately funding a venture they did not wish to be in the public domain, the second could involve the sensitive plans of an organisation and the latter could be targeted at discrediting an organisation too, such as exposing regulatory or legal breaches. The latter category therefore deserves a variation of:

- whistleblowing doxing: exposing wrongdoing.

The motives for such attacks can be grudges against particular companies/persons, exposing wrongdoing but also financial, because a victim has refused to pay a ransom (Kivu, 2020). Doxing can be linked to hacking by external parties, intimate partners and friends but also insiders who have access to information. As such it is not always the result of a cyber-incident although the results of the exposure are likely to end up on the Internet.

Doxing can inflict significant damage on individuals and organisations, though sometimes it is well deserved. The Panama Papers leak in 2016 is an example of whistleblowing doxing. An anonymous whistleblower leaked over 11.5 million records held by Mossack Fonseca, a Panamanian law firm, to journalists working with the International Consortium of Investigative Journalists (Guardian, 2016; ICIJ, n.d.). Mossack Fonseca set up and ran hundreds of thousands of offshore shell companies and bank accounts for wealthy clients to legally avoid or illegally evade domestic taxes. Some of the clients were high profile politicians, including the Prime Minister of Iceland who was forced to resign. Others were crime bosses who used Mossack Fonseca to facilitate money laundering. The exposure led to the prosecution of American citizens for tax evasion, fraud and money laundering, the closure of the law firm and arrest warrants for its founders (Fitzgibbon, 2020, 2021).

Extent and impact

Most countries do not conduct regular victimisation surveys to measure the extent of cybercrime. England and Wales is one of the few jurisdictions where accurate measurement is being regularly conducted. The Crime Survey for England and Wales (CSEW) provides high-quality statistics for individual victimisation (ONS, 2021). The Cyber Security Breaches Survey provides data on organisational victimisation. Some of this data will now be considered (Department for Culture, Media and Sport & Ipsos MORI, 2021a,b).

Figure 5.1 illustrates the computer misuse statistics from the CSEW for 2016–2020. The graph shows a decline in computer misuse from just under 2 million in 2016 to just under one million in 2019 and then a steep rise to 1.6 million in 2020, which coincides with the Covid pandemic and a change in the methodology used for the CSEW. During the pandemic, there has been much anecdotal evidence of greater numbers of fraud and computer misuse

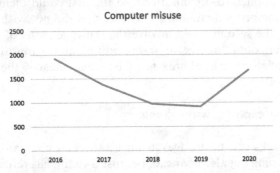

Figure 5.1 CSEW computer misuse 2016–2020 (thousands) (Reuters, 2018).

Table 5.2 Cyber security attacks experienced in previous 12 months in the UK 2017–2021

	2017	2018	2019	2020	2021
All businesses (%)	46	43	32	46	39
Large-sized businesses (%)	68	72	61	75	64
Medium-sized businesses (%)	66	64	60	68	65
Small-sized businesses (%)	52	47	40	62	39
Micro-sized businesses (%)	38	40	28	43	37
Charities (%)		19	22	26	26
Primary schools (%)				41	36
Secondary schools (%)				76	58
Further education/higher education (%)				80	75

Sources: Klahr et al. (2017), Finnerty et al. (2018, 2019), Department for Culture, Media and Sport & Ipsos MORI (2021a,b) and Department for Digital, Media, Culture and Sport & Ipsos MORI (2020a,b).

attacks as people moved from working in offices to their homes (Interpol, 2020). After fraud, computer misuse is the second most common crime against individuals in England and Wales.

The annual Cyber Security Breaches Survey estimates the level of offending experienced by organisations (Department for Culture, Media and Sport & Ipsos MORI, 2021a). Table 5.2 shows the percentage of organisations that have experienced at least one cyber-breach event between 2017 and 2021. The events include both successful and attempted breaches such as phishing emails, impersonation attempts, malware of all types, DDoS attacks, ransomware and hacking. As such it is not the same as the concept of computer misuse used in the CSEW, which is clearly focused around unauthorised access and malware attacks. It shows that between 2017 and 2021, in most years, over 40% of businesses experienced a breach, for large businesses it was usually around two thirds. Rates were also high in the education sector in secondary

Table 5.3 Recorded computer misuse offences England and Wales 2014–2020

	2014	2015	2016	2017	2018	2019	2020
Computer viruses/ malware	5,535	4,108	5,208	7,954	5,215	5,536	7,192
Denial-of-service attack	160	249	579	332	254	136	116
Denial-of-service attack (extortion)	55	134	400	291	224	30	71
Hacking – server	452	532	610	724	841	298	332
Hacking – personal	2,375	2,532	3,358	3,652	3,973	2,996	4,915
Hacking – social media and email	5,637	5,355	4,484	7,792	8,936	11,101	14,004
Hacking – PBX/dial through	507	575	524	372	230	102	132
Hacking (extortion)	601	862	1,071	1,037	3,710	2,936	2,889
Total computer misuse	15,322	14,347	16,234	22,154	23,383	23,135	29,651

Source: ONS (2021).

schools with well over half experiencing attacks and for further and higher education around three quarters, the highest rate of all the sectors in the table.

For recorded computer misuse, one of the first things to note is that reporting is very low (even lower than fraud) in comparison to actual victimisation (Wall, 2007). Many of the same reasons relating to fraud apply, but in addition, many incidents of computer misuse, are not reported to the authorities because they do not result in actual losses. Table 5.3 sets out the statistics for police recorded computer misuse in the UK from 2014 to 2020 organised by category (ONS, 2021). The recorded crime rates doubled over this period with the big increases in hacking of social media and email accounts, and malware. However, in the context of the victimisation surveys for both individuals and organisations, these figures are tiny. Indeed, the police recorded crime (29,651) is just 1.8% of the CSEW data (1,674,000) for 2020. Considering the recorded figure includes organisational victims, and the CSEW only captures individual victims, the actual proportion of offences reported to the authorities is far lower.

The cost of cybercrime has not been subject to recent high-quality scrutiny, although there are estimates to be found. The Cabinet Office and Detica (2011) report estimated the cost at £27 billion per year in the UK. Cybercrime has increased since 2011 and with it the total cost. Other estimates can be found, often produced for marketing purposes rather than based on robust research. For example, one report cited in the media in 2020 estimated the global costs of cybercrime to be US$6 trillion in 2021 but predicted to rise to US$10.5 trillion by 2025 (Cybercrime Magazine, 2020). Another report from 2020 by McAfee (2020) estimated the global costs of cybercrime to be in the region of US$1 trillion.

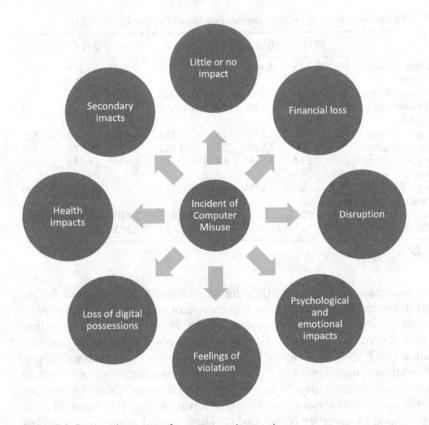

Figure 5.2 Potential impacts of computer misuse crime.

Chapter 2 noted some of the impacts of frauds on individuals and businesses. Research on cybercrime has shown similar impacts. Figure 5.2 illustrates the results of research by Button et al. (2021), which shows the range of impacts includes financial loss, disruption, psychological and emotional impacts, feelings of violation, loss of digital possessions, health impacts and secondary impacts such as damage to reputation.

The Cyber Security Breaches Survey found the average cost to organisations of cyber breaches is £8,460, rising to £13,400 for medium and large firms (Department for Culture, Media and Sport & Ipsos MORI, 2021a). However, the mean can hide the serious damage incidents inflict on organisations. For example, the disruption and financial damage caused by a ransomware attack was illustrated by the aluminium producer Norsk Hydro. The attack hit 22,000 computers in 170 sites, in 40 countries causing extensive disruption; resulting in the 35,000 strong workforce having to return to pen and paper. The incident caused disruption for several months and cost the company £45 million to deal with (BBC News, 2019).

Perpetrators

Much of the literature on cybercriminals has focused on types of hackers, their motivations and their skill levels. Barber (2001) described three types of hacker. 'Script kiddies' are teenage males with limited skills who are generally motivated by fun and the challenge. 'Hackers' are skilled individuals able to create sophisticated code and motivated by curiosity and the joy of discovery. 'Crackers' are skilled hackers with malicious intentions. Seebruck (2015) developed a more nuanced typology:

Coders – non-malicious, good skills, motivated by prestige

Novices – non-malicious, low skills, motivated by curiosity

Punks – malicious, average skills, motivated by revenge or thrill to cause damage

Crowdsourcers – malicious collectives, low skills, motivated by recreation, revenge or ideology to cause damage

Hacktivists – malicious, average skills, motivated by ideology to cause damage

Insiders – malicious, disgruntled (ex-)employees motivated by revenge to cause damage or criminal profit

Criminals – malicious, high skill, motivated solely by criminal profit

Cyber warriors – malicious, very high skill, motivated by ideology to cause damage or criminal profit

Six of these eight groups are involved in economic crime. The punks are essentially delinquents who cause economic harm through their deceptive disruption of systems. Crowdsourcers are collectives that gather information by various means, including open source data, to maliciously broadcast personally identifiable information about individuals (i.e. doxing). Hacktivists are typically motivated by politics or religion and include anarchists (Karagiannopoulos, 2018; Taylor, 2005). Insiders are current or former employees of organisations seeking revenge or seeking to profit from their opportunities to access the organisations' systems.

The criminal group uses their technical skills as an expeditious means of making an illicit profit, either by organising their own crimes or by selling their skills to others. There are illicit forums on both the Internet and dark web where such skills are discussed and traded (Holt, 2013). Cyber warriors possess the apex skill sets and are therefore potentially highly dangerous. This is where organised crime groups, terrorists and rogue states are most likely to find their best technical experts (Giantas & Stergiou, 2018; Leukfeldt et al., 2017). The nexus between cyber warriors and criminals represents the most dangerous cybercriminals: the highly skilled individuals with a strong profit motive and a psychopathic disregard for the harm caused to victims. Ideologically motivated cyber warriors provide the pool of expertise for terrorist groups, and the best candidates for rogue governments that engage in state-sponsored economic crime (Grabosky, 2015).

To illustrate the range of active economic cybercriminals, the following introduces some examples based on five types: lone operatives, hacktivist groups, organised crime groups, terrorist groups and state actors (i.e. governments). Discussion above some examples of perpetrators will be provided before offering more insight on the dark web.

Lone operatives

In 2021, a teenager was sentenced to three years jail after being convicted for hacking into various celebrity Twitter accounts, including those of Bill Gates and Joe Biden, which he then used to solicit Bitcoin from their followers, netting over US$100,000 (Guardian, 2021a). In another example, a young man from Cyprus was extradited to the USA and convicted after hacking various websites in the USA, securing personal data and then threatening to expose it unless the victim organisation paid a ransom (United States Department of Justice, 2021a). Earlier the cyberattack on Mumsnet, the website for mothers, was noted, which caused serious disruption to the company. The perpetrator of this attack was also a skilled teenager (BBC News, 2016b).

Hacktivist groups

There are many hacktivist groups with a wide range of different motives, often ideological. They target individuals, companies, international organisations and governments. LulSec is an example of one group, which sought to expose the weak security in organisations they had issues with. The group was an online community that never met and they targeted organisations as wide as Fox, PBS, the FBI and most famously Sony. They stole the data of 23.6 million PlayStation customers leading to the network having to shut down for several days. Their motive was to expose poor security and embarrass corporations, but their activities led to the risks of fraud from the data they released. Several members were caught and punished by US authorities (Guardian, 2013).

Organised crime groups

Cybercrime is top of Europol's (2021) serious and organised crime threat assessment. Earlier the ransomware attack on Colonial Pipeline was mentioned. This was undertaken by a group called DarkSide. Media reports suggest this group adopted very business-like practices: it started by building partnerships with expert cryptographers, then developed an effective platform to target victims and then reaped millions of dollars from attacks (Guardian, 2021b). Wall (2021) also explains that the groups perpetrating such attacks have developed new business models, which include recruiting affiliate partners to conduct such attacks, thereby increasing their capacity and earnings while also reducing the risk of arrest. He further observes specialisation with appropriately skilled persons contributing to each part of the business process: spamming, phishers, data brokers and so on. Hackers sell knowledge of vulnerabilities in systems to ransomware attackers, darkmarketers facilitate the selling of services through tools such as the Tor (The Onion Router) network and monetisers help launder the loot from the attack. There are also 'ransomware consultants' emerging who advise offenders at all stages of the attack for a fee. Just like traditional organised crime, organised cybercrime is becoming an organised industry with criminal entrepreneurs offering crime-as-a-service to other criminals (Europol, 2021).

An example of prosecution success centred around a Ukrainian national with a high-level role in the hacking group FIN7, which had over 70 persons working for it in various specialist functions. The group used a variety of means to hack the accounts and systems of victims causing estimated losses of over US$1 billion (US Department of Justice, 2021b). The Ukrainian crime boss was convicted and sentenced in 2021 to 10 years prison in the USA.

Terrorist groups

There is much debate over what constitutes terrorism with some definitions stretching to state acts, and some to extreme political groups that do not necessarily use violence. Giantas and Stergiou (2018) described how the Islamic State (ISIS) recruited skilled hackers and used them to target the systems of organisations to cause damage. After the Charlie Hebdo attacks in Paris in 2015, over 19,000 websites were targeted in France, which were largely defaced with Islamic State propaganda. However, a report investigating their capability concluded:

> Despite attracting a great deal of attention, particularly from mass media, experts largely agree that the Islamic State and the range of cyber actors and hackers that claim affiliation to the organization do not exhibit especially advanced cyberterrorism capabilities.
>
> (Alexander & Clifford, 2019)

State actors

There is also plenty of evidence of state actors' involvement in cybercrime (Centre for Strategic and International Studies, 2021). However, such is the opaque nature of involvement, typically using affiliates, it is difficult to provide authoritative accounts. States have a number of purposes for pursuing cybercrime, including infrastructure damage and industrial espionage (see Chapter 7). In 2021, it was widely reported that a cyberattack on an Iranian nuclear facility was carried out by the Israeli state (BBC News, 2021b). In

2021, three North Korean military personnel were indicted in a US$1.3 billion by the US Department of Justice for their involvement in a wide range of cyberattacks ranging from extortion to hacking to steal funds (US Department of Justice, 2021c).

Dark web

Much of the unindexed web is called the 'deep web', where legitimate and harmless databases, customer accounts and resources of private organisations exist (Wang et al., forthcoming). Our online accounts are secured within the deep web (Wang et al., forthcoming). However, the dark web or darknet is the unindexed part of the Internet that lies beneath the surface of the web and is accessible to anyone with a specialist browser such as Tor. The unindexed dark web cannot be accessed by normal web browsers and search engines. Despite its infamy, the dark web represents a tiny percentage of the entire web – just 0.0004% of total data (Wang et al., forthcoming).

Tor technology was originally developed by the US military for privacy purposes, and most dark web users are legitimate people using it for legitimate privacy purposes, for example, journalists (Kumar & Rosenbach, 2019). However, an increasing portion of the dark web is used by deviants and criminals to exploit the privacy features and remain hidden from the authorities. The dark web is used to facilitate a variety of criminal activities such as the sale of illicit goods and child pornography. One area that has emerged are services to facilitate cybercrime, variously called 'Crime-as-a-Service' (CaaS), 'Malware-as-a-Service' (MaaS) or 'Ransomware-as-a-Service' (RaaS). It is like business-to-business sales in legitimate commerce. The illicit products and service available include the rental of botnets to undertake DDoS attacks, kits to conduct ransomware, tools to help conduct hacking and lists of personal details and accounts for identity fraud (Bennett, 2020; Fink, 2018; Kumar & Rosenbach, 2019; Meland et al., 2020).

The dark web has expanded the capacity of the crime business, in particular the economic cybercrime business. It is a crime-as-a-service marketing platform offering tools and services which can be purchased by those without the necessary skills to conduct their chosen economic cybercrime provided they are motivated and have access to a computer and cryptocurrency. We can, therefore, add another dimension of hacker or cybercriminal to Seebruck's (2015) eight categories: the client cybercriminal with very limited skill but motivated to commit economic cybercrime.

Conclusion

This chapter has considered the problem of economic cybercrime. It began by defining this type of crime using five main types of cyber-dependent crime: hacking, malware, DDoS attacks, ransomware and doxing. Examples of such attacks were provided, before considering some of the estimates of the size and impact of the problem. The range of offenders was described based on motivation and technical skill. Finally, the chapter explained that technical skill is no longer a necessary prerequisite to economic cybercrime because the necessary tools and services can be purchased on the darknet by anyone. This has led to the emergence of the client cybercriminal.

Note

1 OS Map & Hack, virtual hackathon: www.ordnancesurvey.co.uk/business-government/developers/hackathon.

References

Alexander, A., & Clifford, B. (2019). Doxing and defacements: Examining the Islamic state's hacking capabilities. *CTC Sentinel, 12*(4), 22–28.

Barber, R. (2001). Hackers profiled—Who are they and what are their motivations?. *Computer Fraud & Security, 2001*(2), 14–17.

BBC News. (2016a). *Up to 400 million accounts in Adult Friend Finder breach*. www.bbc.co.uk/news/technology-37974266

BBC News. (2016b). *Mumsnet cyber-hacker ordered to do 200 hours' unpaid work*. www.bbc.co.uk/news/uk-england-surrey-36954673

BBC News. (2019). *How a ransomware attack cost one firm £45m*. www.bbc.co.uk/news/business-48661152

BBC News. (2021a). *First on CNN: US recovers millions in cryptocurrency paid to Colonial Pipeline ransomware hackers*. https://edition.cnn.com/2021/06/07/politics/colonial-pipeline-ransomware-recovered/index.html

BBC News. (2021b). *Iran nuclear attack: Mystery surrounds nuclear sabotage at Natanz*. www.bbc.co.uk/news/world-middle-east-56722181

Bennett, D. (2020). *The time I sabotaged my editor with ransomware from the dark web*. Bloomberg. www.bloomberg.com/features/2020-dark-web-ransomware/

Brenner, S. (2010). *Cybercrime: Criminal threats from cyberspace*. Greenwood Publishing Group.

Button, M., Blackbourn, D., Sugiura, L., Shepherd, D., Kapend, R., & Wang, V. (2021). Victims of cybercrime: Understanding the impact through accounts. In R. Leukfeldt & M. Kranenbarg (Eds.), *Cybercrime in context*. Springer.

Button, M., Sugiura, L., Blackbourn, D., Kapend, R., Shepherd, D., & Wang, V. (2020). *Victims of computer misuse*. University of Portsmouth. https://researchportal.port.ac.uk/portal/files/20818559/Victims_of_Computer_Misuse_Main_Findings.pdf

Cabinet Office and Detica. (2011). *The cost of cyber crime*. Retrieved from https://assets.publishing.service.gov.uk/government/uploads/system/uploads/attachment_data/file/60942/THE-COST-OF-CYBER-CRIME-SUMMARY-FINAL.pdf

Centre for Strategic and International Studies. (2021). *Significant cyber incidents*. www.csis.org/programs/strategic-technologies-program/significant-cyber-incidents

Cluley, G. (2015). *MumsNet hit by hack, DDoS attack and SWAT*. www.welivesecurity.com/2015/08/19/mumsnet-hack-ddos-swat/

CNBC. (2019). *The 10 biggest data hacks of the decade.* www.cnbc.com/2019/12/23/the-10-biggest-data-hacks-of-the-decade.html

CNN. (2012). *Major banks hit with biggest cyberattacks in history.* https://money.cnn.com/2012/09/27/technology/bank-cyberattacks/index.html

CNN. (2015). *Hackers stole from 100 banks and rigged ATMs to spew cash.* https://money.cnn.com/2015/02/15/technology/security/kaspersky-bank-hacking/index.html

CNN. (2021). *First on CNN: US recovers millions in cryptocurrency paid to Colonial Pipeline ransomware hackers.* https://edition.cnn.com/2021/06/07/politics/colonial-pipeline-ransomware-recovered/index.html

Computer Misuse Act. (1998). www.legislation.gov.uk/ukpga/1990/18/section/7/enacted

Crown Prosecution Service. (n.d.). *Computer Misuse Act.* www.cps.gov.uk/legal-guidance/computer-misuse-act

Culafi, A. (2020). *New spear phishing campaign targets oil and gas industry.* https://searchsecurity.techtarget.com/news/252482039/New-spear-phishing-campaign-targets-oil-and-gas-industry

Cybercrime Magazine. (2020). *Cybercrime to cost the world $10.5 trillion annually by 2025.* https://cybersecurityventures.com/hackerpocalypse-cybercrime-report-2016/

Department for Culture, Media and Sport & Ipsos MORI. (2021a). *Cyber security breaches survey 2021.* https://assets.publishing.service.gov.uk/government/uploads/system/uploads/attachment_data/file/972399/Cyber_Security_Breaches_Survey_2021_Statistical_Release.pdf

Department for Culture, Media and Sport & Ipsos MORI. (2021b). *Cyber security breaches survey 2021 – Education Annex.* www.gov.uk/government/statistics/cyber-security-breaches-survey-2021/cyber-security-breaches-survey-2021-education-annex

Department for Digital, Media, Culture and Sport & Ipsos MORI. (2020a). *Cyber security breaches survey 2020.* https://assets.publishing.service.gov.uk/government/uploads/system/uploads/attachment_data/file/875573/Main_report_-_Cyber_Security_Breaches_Survey_2020.pdf

Department for Digital, Media, Culture and Sport & Ipsos MORI. (2020b). *Cyber security breaches survey 2020 – Education Institutions Annex.* https://assets.publishing.service.gov.uk/government/uploads/system/uploads/attachment_data/file/875574/Education_annex_-_Cyber_Security_Breaches_Survey_2020.pdf

Douglas, D. M. (2016). Doxing: A conceptual analysis. *Ethics and Information Technology, 18*(3), 199–210.

Europol. (2021). *Serious and organised crime threat assessment.* Europol. www.europol.europa.eu/activities-services/main-reports/european-union-serious-and-organised-crime-threat-assessment

Fink, B. (2018). *Hackers for hire: The continued rise of malware-as-a-service.* www.humansecurity.com/blog/hackers-for-hire-the-continued-rise-of-malware-as-a-service

Fitzgibbon, W. (2020). *Germany seeks arrest of Panama Papers lawyers.* www.icij.org/investigations/panama-papers/germany-seeks-arrest-of-panama-papers-lawyers/

Fitzgibbon, W. (2021). *From front pages to prison time: Behind the scenes of a Panama Papers criminal case.* www.icij.org/investigations/panama-papers/from-front-pages-to-prison-time-behind-the-scenes-of-a-panama-papers-criminal-case/

Furnell, S. (2002). *Cybercrime: Vandalizing the information society*. Addison-Wesley.

Giantas, D., & Stergiou, D. (2018). *From terrorism to cyber-terrorism: The case of ISIS*. https://dx.doi.org/10.2139/ssrn.3135927

Grabosky, P. (2015) Organized cybercrime and national security. In R. Smith, R. Cheung, & L. Lau (Eds.), *Cybercrime risks and responses*. Palgrave Macmillan. https://doi.org/10.1057/9781137474162_5

Guardian. (2013). *LulzSec: What they did, who they were and how they were caught*. www.theguardian.com/technology/2013/may/16/lulzsec-hacking-fbi-jail

Guardian. (2015). *Lenovo website hacked and defaced by Lizard Squad in Superfish protest*. www.theguardian.com/technology/2015/feb/26/lenovo-website-hacked-and-defaced-by-lizard-squad-in-superfish-protest

Guardian. (2016). *What are the Panama Papers? A guide to history's biggest data leak*. www.theguardian.com/news/2016/apr/03/what-you-need-to-know-about-the-panama-papers

Guardian. (2021a). *Teen who hacked Joe Biden and Bill Gates' Twitter accounts sentenced to three years in prison*. www.theguardian.com/technology/2021/mar/16/florida-teen-sentenced-twitter-bitcoin-hack

Guardian. (2021b). *Welcome to DarkSide – And the inexorable rise of ransomware*. www.theguardian.com/commentisfree/2021/may/15/welcome-to-darkside-and-the-inexorable-rise-of-ransomware

Holt, T. J. (2013). Examining the forces shaping cybercrime markets online. *Social Science Computer Review, 31*(2), 165–177.

Holt, T. J., & Bossler, A. M. (2014). An assessment of the current state of cybercrime scholarship. *Deviant Behavior, 35*(1), 20–40.

Ibrahim, S. (2016). Social and contextual taxonomy of cybercrime: Socioeconomic theory of Nigerian cybercriminals. *International Journal of Law, Crime and Justice, 47*, 44–57.

ICIJ. (n.d.). *The Panama Papers: Exposing the rogue offshore finance industry*. www.icij.org/investigations/panama-papers/

ICO. (n.d.). *Penalties*. ICO. https://ico.org.uk/for-organisations/guide-to-data-protection/guide-to-law-enforcement-processing/penalties/#ib2

Insurance Times. (2004). *Mydoom virus costs stretch into billions of dollars*. www.insurancetimes.co.uk/mydoom-virus-costs-stretch-into-billions-of-dollars/1339721.article

Interpol. (2020). *Cybercrime: Covid 19 impact*. www.interpol.int/en/content/download/15526/file/COVID-19%20Cybercrime%20Analysis%20Report-%20August%202020.pdf

Karagiannopoulos, V. (2018). *Living with hacktivism: From conflict to symbiosis*. Springer.

Kivu. (2020). *What doxxing victims reveal about "targeted attacks"*. https://kivuconsulting.com/wp-content/uploads/2020/05/Kivu-Threat-Intel_What-Doxxing-Victims-Reveal-About-Targeted-Attacks_May2020.pdf

Kumar, A., & Rosenbach, E. (2019). *The truth about the Dark Web*. www.imf.org/external/pubs/ft/fandd/2019/09/pdf/the-truth-about-the-dark-web-kumar.pdf

Lazarus, S. (2019). Just married: The synergy between feminist criminology and the Tripartite Cybercrime Framework. *International Social Science Journal, 69*(231), 15–33.

Leukfeldt, E. R., Kleemans, E. R., & Stol, W. P. (2017). A typology of cybercriminal networks: From low-tech all-rounders to high-tech specialists. *Crime, Law and Social Change, 67*(1), 21–37.

McAfee. (2020). *New McAfee report estimates global cybercrime losses to exceed $1 trillion.* www.mcafee.com/enterprise/en-us/about/newsroom/press-releases/press-release.html?news_id=6859bd8c-9304-4147-bdab-32b35457e629

McGuire, M., & Dowling, S. (2013). *Cyber crime: A review of the evidence.* https://assets.publishing.service.gov.uk/government/uploads/system/uploads/attachment_data/file/246749/horr75-summary.pdf

Meland, P. H., Bayoumy, Y. F. F., & Sindre, G. (2020). The Ransomware-as-a-Service economy within the darknet. *Computers & Security, 92*, 101762.

Office of Legal Education Executive Office for United States Attorneys. (n.d.). *Prosecuting computer crimes.* Retrieved from www.justice.gov/sites/default/files/criminal-ccips/legacy/2015/01/14/ccmanual.pdf

ONS. (2021). *Crime in England and Wales: Appendix tables.* www.ons.gov.uk/peoplepopulationandcommunity/crimeandjustice/datasets/crimeinenglandandwalesappendixtables

Reuters. (2018). *Panama Papers law firm Mossack Fonseca to shut down after tax scandal.* www.reuters.com/article/us-panama-corruption-idUSKCN1GQ34R

Seebruck, R. (2015). A typology of hackers: Classifying cyber malfeasance using a weighted arc circumplex model. *Digital Investigation, 14*, 36–45.

Taylor, P. A. (2005). From hackers to hacktivists: Speed bumps on the global superhighway? *New Media & Society, 7*(5), 625–646.

UNODC. (2021). *Darknet cybercrime threats to Southeast Asia.* UNODC. www.unodc.org/southeastasiaandpacific/en/2021/02/darknet-cybercrime-southeast-asia/story.html

US Department of Justice. (2021a). *Cypriot hacker sentenced to federal prison for extorting website operators with stolen personal information.* www.justice.gov/usao-ndga/pr/cypriot-hacker-sentenced-federal-prison-extorting-website-operators-stolen-personal

US Department of Justice. (2021b). *High-level organizer of notorious hacking group sentenced to prison for scheme that compromised tens of millions of debit and credit cards.* www.justice.gov/opa/pr/high-level-organizer-notorious-hacking-group-sentenced-prison-scheme-compromised-tens

US Department of Justice. (2021c). *Three North Korean Military hackers indicted in wide-ranging scheme to commit cyberattacks and financial crimes across the globe.* www.justice.gov/opa/pr/three-north-korean-military-hackers-indicted-wide-ranging-scheme-commit-cyberattacks-and

Wall, D. (2007). *Cybercrime: The transformation of crime in the information age* (Vol. 4). Polity.

Wall, D. (2021). Inside a ransomware attack: How dark webs of cybercriminals collaborate to pull them off. *The Conversation.* https://theconversation.com/inside-a-ransomware-attack-how-dark-webs-of-cybercriminals-collaborate-to-pull-them-off-163015

Wang, V., Gee, J., & Button, M. (Forthcoming). Crime on the darknet – The case of brand abuse. In M. Gill (Ed.), *Handbook of security* (3rd ed.). Palgrave.

Chapter 6

Intellectual property crime and illicit trade

Introduction

Sutherland (1949, 1983) considered intellectual property (IP) crime to be a form of white-collar crime, devoting a whole chapter to violations involving patents, trademarks and copyright. Sutherland's research identified four forms of corporate malpractice. Firstly, he observed that corporations habitually infringed the IP rights of competitors. Ironically, this meant that corporations were frequently both perpetrators and victims of wrongdoing. Secondly, he criticised the way that corporations manipulated the IP laws to unfairly extend their exclusivity over rights. Thirdly, he was clearly dismayed at the way corporations used their power and abused the laws to threaten emerging competitors. Sutherland was particularly scathing with regard to the fourth type of abuse wherein powerful competitors share IP rights to support monopolistic cartels. He argued that these IP sharing clubs were in effect illegal restraint of trade policies that amounted to criminal racketeering.

Sutherland's research reflected how IP crime in the 20th century was a relatively rare, fringe phenomenon involving corporate malpractice and expensive corporate disputes. The landscape rapidly changed with globalisation, the industrialisation of China from 1990 and the rapid rise in Internet access from 2000 onwards. In 2000, just 6% of the world's population used the Internet, rising to 51% or about 4 billion people in 2019 (The World Bank, n.d.). The Internet, particularly Web 2.0, generates enormous social and economic benefits in providing open access to instant communications and information sharing. Within the business community, it enables even small companies and sole traders to embrace the digital business model and reach global markets with efficient marketing and logistics (Andriole, 2010).

However, open accessibility means that the Web fails to distinguish between good and bad actors. Wrongdoers are equally able to exploit the power of the Internet in order to facilitate unprecedented levels of IP crime, from cyber-enabled industrial espionage to digital piracy and the global trade in counterfeit goods (Wall & Large, 2010). Mass marketing websites such as AliExpress enable small workshops in the Far East to connect with individual consumers

DOI: 10.4324/9781003081753-6

anywhere in the world. As a result, the international illicit trade in physical counterfeits alone is worth $509 billion per year (OECD & EUIPO, 2019). The scale and reach of the problem illustrates that IP crime is no longer just a white-collar crime that results from corporate rivalry. IP crime has become a substantial social and economic problem. A counterfeit economy has emerged which competes with the legitimate economy. It reduces tax revenues, cuts legitimate business profit, destroys jobs and kills people.

This chapter provides an overview of the 21st-century IP crime problem: the illicit trade in IP infringing goods. As the essential component of IP crime is the breach of IP rights, it begins by introducing those rights. The subsequent discussion of academic and legal definitions of IP crime illustrates the lack of consensus in defining the offence. The nature, scale and impacts of the crime are then explored before the chapter concludes by introducing a typology of offenders.

Overview of intellectual property rights

The World Intellectual Property Organization (WIPO) describes IP as creations of the mind, such as inventions and designs, literary and artistic works, and symbols, names and images used in commerce (WIPO, n.d.). Hunter and Patterson (2012, p. 1) describe IP in terms of legal rights, 'a series of legal principles and domains that create exclusive rights in intangible "property of the mind"'. Drawing on these descriptive and legal principles, IP has three key components.

The creation – IP is a product of a person's intellect. It does not have to be a finished product; it can be a drawing of an invention rather than a manufactured item, it can be a music score rather than a recording.

The property rights – IP is like any other form of property asset. A person's rights over her IP include that it should not be stolen, or used in any way by someone else without permission. IP rights are also economic rights in that they allow IP owners a monopoly over the IP so that the owners can exclusively benefit from their work or investment in a creation for a defined period (WIPO, n.d.). Owners of IP can choose to give it away, allow others to use it for free, to licence it for a fee or to sell it to a new owner.

Legal recognition as property – IP becomes property when it is legally recognised as property. Some forms of IP are recognised in law at the moment they are produced in a tangible form, whilst others require registering. For some types of IP, the legal rights expire after a defined period, at which point the creation is no longer IP and it belongs to no one.

These characteristics of IP can be summarised as follows:

> Intellectual property is the unique creation of a person's mind which is recognised in law as valuable property exclusively owned by a person for a specified period. Intellectual property rights are the rights of owners to

exclusively use and control the idea or creative work during the specified period.

To avoid confusion and litigation whilst encouraging creativity and smooth trade, IP laws have been substantially, though not completely, harmonised across the world through World Trade Organization (WTO) and WIPO treaties. The WTO's 1994 Trade-Related Aspects of Intellectual Property Rights (TRIPS) agreement sets out the minimum level of IP law that has to be adopted by WTO's 164 member states. The key aspects of the treaties set out in Table 6.1 illustrate important differences in the laws associated with each of the main types of IP. The differences mean that the powers available to IP rights owners and law enforcement agencies depend on the type of IP and on national laws. For example, TRIPS only requires member states to criminalise commercial-scale infringement of copyright and trademarks. As a consequence, some countries, such as Germany and Spain, criminalise patent infringements, whilst others including the UK, USA and China do not (EUIPO, 2017; Koniger, 2016).

Patents provide owners of unique inventions with exclusive rights for 20 years. They have to be registered with national or international authorities and published so that others can avoid inadvertently replicating the invention whilst also learning from it. Industrial designs are unique physical creations, but they are not inventive. The design rights only apply to the form and appearance of an article, not to its technical or functioning features: the technical mechanism of a Bugatti kettle is not a design right, but its unique appearance is. The term of design rights varies between countries and depends on registration: the term of protection is 3 years in the UK and EU if it is not registered but extends to 25 years if it is periodically renewed. Infringement of design rights is a criminal offence in some jurisdictions including in the UK.

Table 6.1 Main types of intellectual property

IP type	Recognition	Term	Offence type
Patent – invention	Must be registered	20 years	Civil + criminal in some jurisdictions
Industrial design	Can be registered	10 years minimum if registered	Civil + criminal in some jurisdictions
Copyright	On creation	Life of creator + 50 years	Civil + criminal on commercial scale
Trademark	Can be registered	Indefinite if registration is renewed	Civil + criminal on commercial scale
Geographical indications	Must be registered	Indefinite	Civil + criminal in some jurisdictions
Trade secrets	On creation	Indefinite	Civil + criminal in some jurisdictions

Copyright covers literary and artistic works including books, journals, newspapers, music, musical scores, sound recordings, films, videos, web content, multimedia, advertisements, paintings, drawings, illustrations, sculpture. It also includes technical products such as computer programmes, databases, maps and technical drawings.

Trademarks are distinct identifiers that distinguish the goods or services of a person or enterprise. They can be a unique name, phrase, letters, numbers, colours, symbol, drawing, shape, squiggle, sound or a combination of these. Trademarks have significant value because they represent the reputation or brand image of individuals or organisations (Wilson & Sullivan, 2016). Trademarks do not have to be registered, but registration does provide additional protection. Geographical indications (GIs) are a form of collective trademark signal the origin and quality of products, for example, Champagne and Scotch Whisky. GIs do have to be registered and approved by authorities.

Trade secrets refer to the confidential information held by enterprises. It is a class of IP included in TRIPS, but it is very different from the other types of IP as it cannot be in the public domain and therefore cannot be registered. The types of information covered are very broad, including customer lists, sales methods, marketing plans, manufacturing methods and secret recipes. The laws vary widely, for example, the theft of trade secrets is a specific criminal offence under the US the Economic Espionage Act, but not in the UK where it is a civil offence.

What is illicit trade?

Illicit trade is often associated with the illegal arms trade, smuggling narcotics, human trafficking, trade in endangered species, illegal logging, smuggling tobacco, sanctions busting, counterfeit goods and so on. However, there is no single legal definition which adequately describes all forms of illicit or illegal trade. Oddly, the WTO does not have a working definition, whilst the World Health Organisation (WHO) provides a succinct definition in its Framework Convention on Tobacco Control (FCTC):

> Illicit trade means any practice or conduct prohibited by law and which relates to production, shipment, receipt, possession, distribution, sale or purchase including any practice or conduct intended to facilitate such activity.
>
> (FCTC, Article 1(a))

The WHO definition refers broadly to illegal acts involved in a supply chain but is vague as to the applicable law: illegal acts in one country are perfectly legal elsewhere. For example, the trade in whale meat is legal in Iceland and Japan, but illegal in the UK and USA; sanctions busting may be illegal in France and Australia, but not in Russia or China. The WHO definition also does not address the kind of applicable law, whether it is criminal, regulatory or civil, which varies between jurisdictions as Table 6.1 shows. Finally, the WHO definition does not adequately distinguish between illegal methods of trade and illegal goods. Legal firearms or legal tobacco only become illegal trade when they are smuggled into a country, bypassing import controls and excise duties. On the other hand, counterfeit goods are illegal at the point of manufacture.

TradeLab (2017) set out a modified version of the WHO definition to emphasise that illicit trade involves both legal and illegal products:

> Illicit trade means any commercial practice or transaction related to the production, acquisition, sale, purchase, shipment, movement, transfer, receipt, possession or distribution of:
>
> (i)   any illicit product defined as such by international law; or
> (ii) any licit product for non-licit purposes as defined by international law.
>
> Illicit trade also covers any conduct intended to facilitate such activities.

This definition distinguishes between illicit goods and illicit trading methods, but ignores local laws and does not acknowledge the criminal, regulatory and civil regimes. To address these shortcomings, this book uses the following typological definition of illicit trade:

> Illicit trade is a trade scheme which involves an illegal product and/or an illegal method of commercial trade. Method refers to any activity that enables the trade including production, labelling, packaging, acquisition, sale, purchase, shipment, movement, transfer, receipt, possession, distribution or facilitation. Illicit and illegal refer to all offences, whether criminal, regulatory or civil according to national or international laws.

What is intellectual property crime?

Presently, there is no consensus as to the definition of the term 'IP crime'. Albanese (2009) loosely defines IP crime as a form of deceptive white-collar crime. Yar (2005) describes IP crime narrowly and vaguely as violation of copyrights, patents and trademark rights. The UK's Intellectual Property Office (IPO) has adopted a similarly broad definition, which simply describes IP crime as illegal acts:

> The carrying out of acts restricted by intellectual property legislation without the permission of the rights holder.

These definitions are problematic for two reasons. Firstly, they do not address the kind of applicable law, whether criminal, regulatory or civil. Secondly, they do not describe the activities involved in the offences. Europol's (n.d.) deals with the activity problem by focusing on commercial-scale illicit trade:

> Intellectual property crime is committed when someone manufactures, sells or distributes counterfeit or pirated goods, such as such as (*sic*) patents, trademarks, industrial designs or literary and artistic works, for commercial gain.

Unfortunately, this definition is badly phrased, confuses the sale of goods with the sale of patents and other IP rights, only recognises the illicit trade or supply side of IP crime and does not acknowledge that IP offences do not always involve illicit trade. For example, precursor crime such as the theft of confidential product drawings is industrial espionage and a form of IP crime under TRIPS, but it is not an illicit trade (see Chapter 7). The illicit trade starts when product manufacturing using the stolen drawings commences. Furthermore, the definition does not acknowledge non-commercial violations or the public's consumption of illegal goods. The intersection between illicit trade and IP crime is illustrated in Figure 6.1.

IP crime is often defined as a binary classification, counterfeiting and piracy. However, there is no consensus as to which offences sit under each classification. For example, the EUIPO & Europol (2019) report classifies IP crime in the following way:

> Counterfeiting and piracy are used to describe a range of illicit activities, normally relating to registered trade marks and patents (for counterfeit goods) and copyright and design (for piracy). Together, these constitute IP offences.

This definition clearly classifies design violations as piracy. Europol (n.d.) classifies design violations as counterfeiting. Piracy is usually associated with copyright materials (Cordell et al., 1996; Gopal et al., 2004; IPO, 2016) associates copyright materials with piracy, but others call such infringements counterfeiting (Antonopoulos et al., 2011). Furthermore, patent infringements are rarely a component of counterfeit goods, especially if they are process or method patents rather than product patents.

The inconsistencies and inaccuracies in the definition of IP crime are an important issue as it indicates the IP protection and enforcement community does not have a common language for the problem. It is therefore important that we set out the definition and classification used in this book:

> IP crime is the unlawful violation of a person's or an organisation's intellectual property rights. Crime refers to all offences whether criminal, regulatory or civil. Unlawful violation refers to any illegal acquisition,

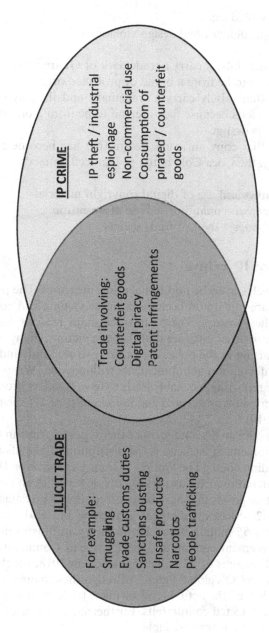

Figure 6.1 Intersection between illicit trade and IP crime.

use, consumption or illicit trade that infringes IP rights including IP theft, copyright, trademark, design and patent infringements.

IP crime is classified as:
Counterfeits – trademark and design violations

- Products that falsely carry a trademark or GI are counterfeits because they pretend to be from a brand or protected origin.
- Products that falsely carry a trademark and illegally copy a design are counterfeits because they pretend to be from a brand and are fake copies of its design.
- Products that copy an iconic design that has become a mark of the brand (e.g. the Coca Cola bottle or Duracell battery).

Piracy – unauthorised use of digital copyright material
Patent infringement – unauthorised use of invention
Industrial espionage – theft of trade secrets

The extent of IP crime

IP crime is not well served by traditional crime measures. The police recorded crime statistics are not useful because business victims and consumers tend not to report these crimes. There are three main reasons for this lack of reporting: they are often unaware that they are victims, many believe there is no point in reporting as the police are unlikely to respond, and many do not want to share information about incidents with anyone (Wilson et al., 2016). The low level of reporting inevitably leads to few offenders brought to justice. Just 445 offenders were prosecuted and found guilty of IP offences in the UK in 2017 (IPO, 2019).

IP crime does have an advantage over other types of crime in that a primary focus of law enforcement agencies is the disruption of the illicit trade by the seizure of offending goods. The World Customs Organization (WCO) collects seizure data from national authorities to provide statistics on the number, type and origin of illicit goods that have been seized. Based on data from 61 countries, the WCO (2019) reported 60,134 seizures of physical counterfeit goods in 2018 involving 55 million items. However, again illustrating inconsistencies in the enforcement community, the European Commission (EC, 2019) reported 69,354 seizures of 27 million products in 2018, nearly 10,000 more seizures than the WCO's global figure. Although these figures are substantial, they are a fraction of the actual level of illicit trade in counterfeits because they only reflect detected counterfeits. Furthermore, the inconsistency in the measures indicates they are unreliable.

IP crime is also different to other types of crime in that it is overwhelmingly centred in one country, China. The EC (2019) estimates that China (including

Table 6.2 Top four provenance economies for physical counterfeit goods

Provenance economy	Share in world exports of counterfeit goods %	Value of counterfeit exports $ billion
China + Hong Kong	63.4	322.2
India	3.4	17.4
United Arab Emirates	3.0	15.5
Singapore	2.6	13.1
All other countries	27.6	140.8
Total	100	509.0

Source: OECD & EUIPO (2019).

Hong Kong) is the largest provenance country accounting for 60% of the volume and 79% of the value of seized counterfeit goods. The Organisation for Economic Co-operation and Development (OECD) has developed an economic approach to valuing the international trade in counterfeit goods. The General Trade-Related Index of Counterfeiting (GTRIC) combines a risk assessment, customs seizure data and total trade values for each country to estimate the value of counterfeit goods originating in each country. Though it is regarded as a crude estimate, it is the best available (Spink & Leventes Fejes, 2012). Using this method, the OECD & EUIPO (2019) estimate the total annual value of the international trade in physical counterfeit goods at $509 billion or 3.3% of world trade. China contributes 63% or $322 billion to the trade. The top four provenance economies account for 73% or $368 billion (Table 6.2). It is estimated that the UK imported £13.6 billion ($18 billion) in 2016, mainly from China (OECD & IPO, 2019). Considering the organisation, distribution networks and number of people required to enable this volume of illicit trade within the UK, it is clear that a meagre of 445 sentenced offenders is just scratching at the surface.

The OECD & EUIPO (2019) estimate only covers the international trade in counterfeit goods; it does not measure the domestic trade in counterfeits, piracy or consequential impacts. The International Chamber of Commerce report (ICC & Frontier Economics, 2016) provides the best available data for piracy and domestically produced and consumed counterfeit goods. These categories are included in Table 6.3. The estimated total global value of counterfeits is $861 billion per year, piracy is worth $213 billion per year and the combined total is just over $1 trillion per year.

The top 20 product categories for international trade in physical fakes are tabulated in OECD & EUIPO (2019, p. 47). It omits domestically produced and consumed physical fakes and online piracy. The top seven product groups represent 62% of the trade in physical counterfeits (Table 6.4).

The list makes it eminently clear that IP crime is not just about attractive bags and perfumes, it includes electrical equipment, machinery, vehicle parts,

Table 6.3 Global financial impact of counterfeit and pirated goods

		$ billions/year	$ billions/year	Source
International trade counterfeits			509	1
Domestic trade counterfeits			352	2
Copyright piracy	Music	160	213	2
	Movies	29		2
	Software	24		2
Total value			**1,074**	

Sources: (1) OECD & EUIPO (2019). (2) ICC & Frontier Economics (2016).

Table 6.4 World trade in physical counterfeits and online piracy

Product group	Share of trade %	Value of trade $ billion
Electrical machinery and electronics	27.1	138.0
Jewellery and watches	10.6	54.0
Clothing, footwear, accessories	10.3	52.3
Optical, photographic, medical apparatus	5.2	26.7
Machinery and mechanical appliances	3.9	19.7
Toys and games	3.0	11.8
Furniture	2.2	11.5
All other products	38.3	195.0
Total	100	509

Source: OECD & EUIPO (2019).

medical goods and pharmaceuticals. The scale and breadth of the illicit trade in counterfeit and pirated goods illustrates that the trade has become an illegal economic sector which competes with the legitimate economy.

Though the impact on the revenues of legitimate businesses is clearly huge, it is not equivalent to the trade in counterfeit and pirated goods. A key issue is the consumers' substitution rate, that is, the proportion of illicit purchases which displace legal purchases (OECD, 2017). The illicit traders target two market segments (OECD & EUIPO, 2019; Spink et al., 2013). Primary markets are those in which the criminals aim to deceive consumers into thinking the products are genuine and sourced from a reputable brand. Products are close copies of genuine items, are packaged in the same way as the genuine brand, carry the fake trademarks, and prices are closer to those of the legitimate products. The buyers of these counterfeits are in effect victims of fraud. Thus, every sale on a primary market represents a direct loss for genuine manufacturers. The OECD & EUIPO (2019) report estimates that 42% of counterfeits are substitute, primary market sales.

The 58% of counterfeits sold on the secondary market are not designed to deceive the consumers. Unlike the defrauded primary market consumers, the secondary market buyers are willing participants in the illegal transactions: they are the cooperative offenders on the consumption side who choose to sustain the trade. Therefore, only a small fraction of secondary market sales represent substitute sales. It is reasonable to assume that the overall substitution rate covering both the primary and secondary markets is at least 42%.

A further illustration of the scale of the illicit trade in counterfeit and pirated goods can be gleaned from the disruption and enforcement activities that are taking place every day on the Internet. To date, there have been over 10 billion interventions by just two providers due to IP infringements. Google processes requests for removing content and delisting URLs from search results due to IP infringements across all its services, including Google Search, YouTube, Google Ads and Google Shopping Google (n.d. a). As of 18 March 2021, Google had processed just over 5 billion requests to delist URLs for copyright infringement under the US Digital Millennium Copyright Act (DMCA) at the rate of 1.53 million requests per day (Google, n.d. b). In its efforts to disrupt the sale of counterfeit goods on its platform, Amazon blocked over 6 billion suspected bad listings and over 2.5 million accounts in 2019 (Amazon, 2020). Facebook (n.d.) is less active than Google and Amazon, removing a relatively meagre of 8.9 million pieces of content in 2019.

Impact of IP crime

Impact on individuals

The most obvious and prevalent impact on individuals is that those who purchase illicit goods on the primary market are victims of fraud, sometimes spending hundreds or thousands of dollars on low quality, fake and potentially dangerous fake goods. The total value of the fraudulent primary market in physical counterfeit goods is $362 billion per year (42% of $861 billion). However, the most insidious aspect of the trade in counterfeits is the deliberate recklessness of the criminal enterprises which export injury, ill health and death. ICC & Frontier Economics (2011) estimated the economic costs of deaths alone at $18 billion per year.

The most obvious impact on individuals relates to counterfeit medicines. There are many cases of substandard, illicit medicines causing deaths and serious injuries (Newton et al., 2010). The WHO (2006) reckons that counterfeit medicines represent 10% of all global medicines trade and are clear about the impacts:

> People don't die from carrying a fake handbag or wearing a fake t-shirt. They can die from taking a counterfeit medicine.

The WHO (2017) reports that 72,000 children die each year from pneumonia due to substandard and fake antibiotics, and fake antimalarials lead to 116,000 deaths from malaria in sub-Saharan Africa. The volume and value of fake medicines is increasing. It is worth $4.4 billion (OECD & EUIPO, 2019). Counterfeiters are producing an increasingly diverse range of counterfeit medicines, including cancer medication (EUIPO & Europol, 2019). Erectile dysfunction medicines are among the most commonly counterfeited medicines, but the supply of fake medicines for the treatment of serious illnesses is increasing. Perhaps most unnerving is the finding that most fake pharmaceutical products (69%) are sold through the primary markets (OECD & EUIPO, 2019). The significant health implication is that two-thirds of people who purchase illicit medicines are probably unaware that they are fake, substandard and dangerous.

The international trade in fake cosmetic products is worth $5.4 billion (OECD & EUIPO, 2019). They attract customers because they are a fraction of the price of genuine products. However, with the low price comes substantial health risks. Like the fake pharmaceuticals, they are manufactured in unhygienic conditions by criminal enterprises that pay no heed to the damage they cause. Contaminants found in fake cosmetics include lead, arsenic, mercury, cyanide, bacteria, urine and faeces (Mackey, 2018).

Illicit food and drink is sometimes referred to as *food fraud*. The total value of fake foods is estimated at $6.2 billion (OECD & EUIPO, 2019). Mostly, the illicit food does not threaten health but misleads consumers by incorrect labelling. In Europe in 2013, several EU countries found horsemeat in products fraudulently labelled as beef (O'Mahoney, 2013). In other instances, the foodstuffs lead to widespread illness and death. A counterfeit beverage caused the deaths of 23 people in Turkey in 2005 (Paun, 2011). In China in 2008, melamine contamination of baby milk powder resulted in illness to 298,000 individuals, 50,000 hospitalisations and six deaths (Bouzembrak et al., 2018). The 2005 illegal use of Sudan Red I, an industrial, carcinogenic red dye, in chicken products in China, and the 2009 illegal use of clenbuterol hydrochloride in animal feed caused many foodborne illnesses (Zhang & Xue, 2016).

It is not just fake pharmaceuticals and foodstuffs which cause death and serious injury. A danger evident in Table 6.4 is the presence of high volumes of electrical, mechanical and medical equipment that pose serious safety risks. Counterfeit, substandard vehicle parts are on the increase, including safety critical items such as airbags, tyres, wheel rims, brake pads, batteries and helmets (EUIPO & Europol, 2019). The number of seized components in the EU has increased dramatically to 422,218 (EUIPO & Europol, 2019) and the value of this market worldwide is $10 billion (OECD & EUIPO, 2019). Yar (2005) suggested 3% of fatal car crashes are due to faulty, counterfeit parts. He estimated that it causes 36,000 deaths and 1.5 million injuries per year. Counterfeit aircraft parts have been implicated in 174 crashes and accidents between 1973 and 1996 (Yar, 2005), and about 24 crashes since 2010 (McKenzie, 2017). The cause of the fatal Concorde crash in 2000 which killed

109 people was attributed to a counterfeit part that fell off an airplane prior to the departure of the Concorde (UNICRI, 2011).

In addition to financial and health impacts, IP crime is also linked to cybercrime. Many piracy-related websites are associated with malware that put the user at risk of privacy invasion, lost data, damaged computers, fraud and ransomware (BSA, 2018). Downloading low-cost or free pirated digital products such as software, music, videos and games may appear attractive to consumers, but they are too often inviting bad actors into their computers and digital lives with consequential impacts ranging from disruptive viruses to fraud and highly intrusive webcam spying (Button et al., 2020). To illustrate the scale of the risk, BSA (2018) estimates that pirated software accounts for 37% of software installed on PCs across the world with a total commercial value of $46.3 billion.

Impact on business

As Table 6.4 illustrates the impact of IP crime on legitimate businesses is huge and plagues virtually every industry (Wilson et al., 2016). The most direct threat to legitimate companies is the loss of sales due to counterfeit, pirated or patent infringing products. In addition to these direct losses, there are the more subjective economic harms to reputation and brand. Branded counterfeits carrying the attributes of a legitimate brand threaten the reputation of the brand and the reputation of the company which owns the brand (Wilson & Grammich, 2020). Furthermore, the problem does not just impact the manufacturers, it also harms legitimate distributors, wholesalers and retailers. IP crime is thus a structural threat to legitimate commerce in that it threatens the profitability and sustainability of businesses, investment in innovation and growth, and employment throughout the supply chain.

In order to protect themselves, many firms implement brand protection strategies (Wilson et al., 2016). These may be simple reaction strategies when a counterfeit or pirated product is detected, but these responses can be very expensive, especially when they involve lawyers and the courts. Others spend a great deal of money on prevention strategies and compliance costs which involve product design, packaging and labelling, continuous surveillance, membership of trade bodies and the costs of employing brand protection professionals.

Impact on governments, society and the environment

The damage to businesses in turn flows through to impact on governments and society. For governments, the most direct cost of IP crime and illicit trade is reduced tax revenues. The OECD & IPO (2019) report estimates that the UK government lost £4 billion in tax revenue due to counterfeit products in 2016: £3.1 billion from the retail and wholesale sector, and £0.9 billion from rights holders. This is equivalent to 0.5% of the total UK tax revenue which could otherwise be invested in public services.

As well as reducing tax revenues, IP crime and illicit trade increases the costs of governments in establishing and enforcing the law, resourcing the police and customs agencies, developing policies and contingency plans. None of these enforcement activities would be necessary if people did not routinely commit these crimes. In addition, lower sales reduce the demand for labour and increase unemployment, further increasing government costs through welfare benefits. At least 86,300 jobs in the UK were lost due to counterfeiting and piracy in 2016, equivalent to 1.4% of all employees (OECD & IPO, 2019).

It could be argued that the trade in illicit goods transfers jobs to where they are needed the most. However, the trade contributes to poverty in some countries in poverty. The low prices of illicit goods is sustained by low-cost labour in countries such as China, India, Pakistan and Indonesia, where the working conditions and safety standards can be poor, owners exploit child labour and wages are at poverty levels (OECD & EUIPO, 2019). Furthermore, multinational corporations with significant resources to invest in these regions are unlikely to do so if there is a risk that their IP will be abused by local businesses. It is ironic that in seeking to find an entrepreneurial way out of poverty, business practices are tolerated that deter inward investment which would make a difference. A financial figure cannot be put to these kinds of harm.

Turning to the ecology, a growing trade in illicit pesticides and agrochemicals has emerged with a significant link to environmental crimes. Like the fake pharmaceuticals, many of these products are substandard with heavily diluted active ingredients that reduce farming yields. Others contain excessive amounts of toxic ingredients which destroy crops and fields, and can seriously affect the health of farmers and consumers (EUIPO & Europol, 2019). The high level of criminality has a substantial impact on the industry sector: illicit trade takes nearly 14% of the market worth €1.3 billion (EUIPO, 2017). Europol's Operation Silver Axe seized a record 1,346 tonnes of illicit pesticide in 2020, sufficient to spray 207,000 km^2, equivalent to more than all the farmland in Germany. It seems that many farmers are content to use high-risk materials to save money.

Offenders

There has been very little research into IP crime offenders, their activities and types. It is clear from the foregoing that most offenders are individual consumers on the demand side, and the supply side comprises organised businesses that engage in illegal activities. The Serious Crime Act 2007 in the UK defines the term organised crime group (OCG) as a group which has at its purpose, or one of its purposes, the carrying on of criminal activities, and consists of three or more people who agree to act to further that purpose.

Table 6.5 Typology of IP crime and illicit trade offenders

Individual		Group				
Consumers Employees Delinquents	Sole traders	Delinquent groups	Legitimate companies	Criminal enterprises	Organised crime groups	Terrorist groups
Occasional or Habitual	Habitual	Habitual	Occasional	Habitual	Habitual	Habitual

For the purpose of offender analysis, this definition is too broad as it encompasses three distinct organised groups. It encapsulates crime gangs and transnational OCGs that typically perpetrate multiple crimes including violence (FBI, n.d.). It describes legitimate businesses that purposefully engage in criminal activities, for example, the historic business models at Airbus and Alstom relied on criminal bribery (Hock, 2020). It also captures many of the businesses involved in the manufacture and distribution of counterfeit goods. Building on the approach of Spink et al. (2013), which helpfully distinguishes between OCGs and criminal enterprises, an alternative typology of IP crime offenders is developed in Table 6.5. It shows that IP crime is no longer solely a white-collar crime.

The typology also allows offenders to be examined according to the types of individuals and the types of organisations. It categorises offenders according to their level of organisation (individual or group) and offending frequency (occasional or habitual). The criminal threats increase with the level of organisation and the frequency of offending. Lone, occasional offenders are the lowest threat level. The organised crime and terrorist groups pose the greatest threat due to the poly-criminality.

Individuals – consumers

Consumers who engage in IP and illicit trade offences are ordinary citizens who, for example, exceed customs allowances, import/export illicit goods, knowingly purchase counterfeit products, download pirate music or stream illegal broadcasts. These consumers choose to support the secondary market in physical fakes, which is 58% of the total market (OECD & EUIPO, 2019). Some consumers are opportunistic, infrequent offenders, perhaps purchasing a counterfeit product whilst on vacation. Others are habitual offenders. Motivations include saving money, obtaining things they could not otherwise afford and ideological protest.

There is a substantial body of research indicating the willingness of large numbers of consumers to purchase counterfeit, pirated and illicit goods. Although such action is generally not a criminal offence, it is illegal and can be addressed by civil or regulatory action. There have been many surveys of the public asking if they have bought counterfeit or pirated goods and services. For example, a European IPO (EUIPO, 2017) study found:

- 7% of those surveyed had purchased counterfeit products intentionally.
- This rises to 15% of 15- to 24-year-old group who had purchased counterfeit products intentionally.
- 10% had intentionally accessed, downloaded or streamed content from illegal websites.
- This rises to 27% of the 15- to 24-year group who had intentionally accessed, downloaded or streamed content from illegal websites.

The same research also tested the attitudes towards different types of counterfeiting and piracy across the EU and in individual states. The results showed significant acceptance of these types of behaviour. For example:

- 27% agreed that it is acceptable to purchase counterfeit products when the price for the original and authentic product is too high (41% in the 15–24 age group).
- 24% agreed it is acceptable to buy counterfeit products when the original product is not yet available where they live (39% in the 15–24 age group).
- 35% thought it was acceptable to obtain content illegally from the Internet when it is for personal use.
- 31% thought it is acceptable to obtain content illegally from the Internet when there is no immediately available legal alternative (43% in the 15–24 age group).
- 45% of the 15–24 age group consider that consuming counterfeit products is an act of protest against the market-driven economy and premium brands (EUIPO, 2017).

Numerous other studies have also found similar attitudes towards counterfeiting and piracy. In an overview of 15 studies, the Center for Intellectual Property Understanding (2019, p. 16) found:

> If there is one common theme that can be gleaned from the various studies of intellectual property awareness conducted around the world, it is that most people generally understand that IP is important, but not why IP is important. The consumer studies considered in this report show that consumers have a general understanding of the importance of IP but find it more convenient to purchase counterfeits or access content in response to cost or availability concerns. Despite a feeling that counterfeit purchases are unethical and pose a threat to legitimate businesses, intentional purchases of counterfeits continue.

These studies might underestimate the problem, because even though they are usually based upon anonymous questionnaires, people are still often reluctant to admit to such behaviours. Nevertheless, it is clear that at least a substantial minority of people are prepared to engage in counterfeiting and piracy. It might seem strange that so many people are deliberately deviant. However, other studies have exposed significant sections of the community who find illegal behaviour acceptable. For example, in their study of 'everyday crimes', Karstedt and Farrall (2007) found that 61% of people in the UK have at some time committed at least one minor crime, such as stealing something from work, falsely claiming refunds or padding an insurance claim. These findings concerning widespread acceptance of illegal behaviours have important implications in explaining criminal behaviour, which will be returned to in Chapter 9. In particular, the findings link to Hirschi's question: 'Why do most of us not commit crime?' (Hirschi, 1969, p. 34).

The first important aspect of understanding IP crime and illicit trade offenders is that the majority of offenders are the knowing consumers, those that support the secondary counterfeit market, which is over half of the total market. They are ordinary people from all sections of society who are willing to engage in what Karstedt and Farrall (2006) call 'everyday crime'. This is a primary reason that counterfeiting and piracy are so prevalent and the traders are so successful. The organised counterfeiters and the copyright thieves exploit the human weakness for shiny things such as high brand watches and clothing, and sometimes they exploit the need for low-cost necessities such as medicines.

Individuals – employees

Some employees, sometimes called insiders, steal products or IP from their employers for money or other gains. The motivation for these crimes can be straightforward, to obtain money. They can also be quite complex. The primary employee threats in the context of IP are who steal and sell their employers' products, which is a form of illicit trade, and those who steal or leak their employers' proprietary information (trade secrets). An employee who steals products to sell is usually concerned with obtaining money, although the driving motivations may be more complex. They are usually one-off opportunistic offenders rather than habitual. In a large US study, Hollinger and Claike (1983) found that one-third of employees commit a fraud or theft offence against their employer at least once per year. Most of the perpetrators are occasional offenders; however, they also found that 7% of employees are habitual, offending at least 50 times per year.

Another form of employee IP crime is where an insider sells or publicises proprietary information of an organisation. This is a type of industrial espionage, sometimes called corporate or economic espionage. It has been estimated that 85% of trade secret thefts are committed by someone familiar to the owner (Wilson & Grammich, 2020). In some cases, the espionage is initiated by other organisations which approach and engage the employee. In other cases, the employee initiates arrangement by approaching the recipient organisation. These two situations are relatively clear cut. However, it can be less clear when an employee is recruited by a competitor or starts up their own business in the same market.

Insiders or employees of an organisation working in key areas may have access to sensitive proprietary information that would be very beneficial to a third party. Some motivated by greed, alienation with their organisation or political motives may decide to use that information to their advantage by sharing it with a third party resulting in serious harm to the rights owner.

Based on a study of 48 IP theft cases, Moore et al. (2011) propose a model of two types of insider:

> *Entitled Independent Model* – the insider has had a role in the development of the IP and is motivated by growing *dissatisfaction* fuelled by lack of pay rise, promotion or recognition.

> *Ambitious Leader Model* – here the motive is not dissatisfaction but *gain* and the insider is motivated to use his or her position to secure proprietary information for a competitor to then reap higher rewards and greater status. The competitor may be an existing company that the person joins or it may be a start-up business formed by the offender.

Moore et al. (2011, p. 31) also found that 56% of the offenders held technical positions, 75% were current employees when they committed the IP theft and 65% had already accepted positions with another company at the time of the theft. Organisations are most vulnerable to this type of IP crime when there is a toxic mix of dissatisfaction or greed, a desire to move elsewhere and opportunity.

Individuals – delinquents

The delinquent group comprises individuals with considerable IT skills who break IP laws for fun, for the challenge, fame or notoriety, or because they have an ideological belief that digital products should be freely available. They typically breach copyright protections to freely use and share digital products. They are usually habitual offenders, but their motivation is often not money. Some libertarians believe IP law is a restrictive instrument of overbearing governments, an affront to personal freedom and hinders creativity (Kinsella, 2009).

Individuals – sole traders

Sole traders are individuals who run small businesses supplying goods at local markets, small shops or online. They typically sell their illicit wares to opportunistic consumers. Sole traders often belong to informal underground networks for sourcing counterfeit goods. They tend to be habitual, professional offenders as the illegal income is all or a substantial portion of their earnings. Treadwell (2011) conducted a small study involving interviews with 10 criminals who sold counterfeit goods online, mainly fashion goods. He found that some had emerged from traditional criminal careers such as burglary and fencing and often combined their trading in counterfeits with selling stolen goods, tax evasion, welfare fraud, and small-scale drug dealing. He also observed that they were working-class entrepreneurs who exploited low-risk, high reward opportunities. Some consumers view such trade as a rebellion against corporate excess and regard the sole traders as 'Robin Hoods' who make expensive, luxury items affordable (Sugden, 2007).

Delinquent groups

Delinquent groups are loose networks of individuals who cooperate to breach copyright protections and freely share digital products. So-called warez groups, for example, specialise in the distribution of pirated movies, music, games and software on the Internet (Urbas, 2006). They are typically habitual offenders motivated by fame and notoriety rather than money. Such groups often do not regard their acts as criminal which is accompanied by an ideological motivation orientated against the corporate world. The 'DrinkOrDie' warez group brought down by law enforcement agencies across the globe in 2001 included corporate executives, university network administrators, employees of hi-tech companies and government employees (Urbas, 2006).

Legitimate companies

Legitimate ordinary companies breach IP rights to introduce or support revenue streams with reduced development costs. Money is their motivation. Patent and copyright infringements are frequently a source of disputes between companies; they are usually settled by civil rather than criminal action. However, it can be difficult to distinguish between legitimate and illegitimate companies. Sullivan and Wilson (2017) researched counterfeit products entering the US military supply chain. Using prosecution data, they found three quarters of the cases detected by the authorities involved legitimate businesses running counterfeit products alongside their legitimate work and half involved shell companies to hide activities. Illustrating the significant overlap with other types of economic crime, 9 of the 31 offenders were charged with IP offences, whilst the remaining 22 were charged with fraud, money laundering and smuggling.

Criminal enterprises

Criminal enterprises are the organised group version of the sole trader. They are the small factories in the Far East, and the organised distributors, wholesalers and retailers and the piracy traders. They are habitual, professional offenders whose primary income is counterfeit or illicit goods. They are distinguished from organised crime gangs in that they do not engage in violence, extortion and corruption (Spink et al., 2013).

Organised crime groups

OCGs are similar to criminal enterprises in that they are professional offenders and crime is their primary source of income. They are motivated by money and, to some extent, power. OCGs are distinguished from criminal enterprises in that they engage in violence, extortion and corruption to achieve their aims (Spink et al., 2013). They also have an opportunistic *polycrime* approach in engaging in a wider range of money generating criminal enterprises, including counterfeiting, drugs, alcohol, arms and antiquities smuggling, money laundering, people trafficking, illegal gambling, burglary and art theft. In particular, the EUIPO & Europol (2019) threat assessment report noted that OCGs are involved in counterfeit food and drink, luxury products, clothes and accessories, pharmaceuticals, vehicle parts and piracy.

Terrorist groups

Terrorist groups are the most violent type of criminal group. They are motivated by power, ideology, politics and money. They are opportunistic in generating criminal income by any convenient means including counterfeiting and smuggling illicit goods. For example, the 1993 World Trade Centre attack was partially funded from counterfeiting activities (Spink et al., 2013). Lowe (2006) suggests that the IRA was one of the first terrorist groups to spot the opportunities from counterfeiting. Around 1990, two IRA members Brian Ruddy and Paeder Hamill provided $60,000 to set up a drug laboratory in Miami to produce fake Ivomec, a livestock antiparasite drug manufactured by Merck. The fake drug, which contained only water, was distributed unwittingly by a legitimate company, Life Services Inc. Lowe (2006) also describes how Arab families based in Paraguay raised millions of dollars for Hezbollah through counterfeit and illicit CDs, DVDs, software, electronic equipment and tobacco.

Facilitators

The final group of actors that need to be considered are the facilitators who assist criminal enterprises, OCGs and terrorists in enabling illicit trade shipments and transactions, avoiding the enforcement authorities and laundering the proceeds of crime. Some unwittingly facilitate the crimes, but others are deliberate facilitators. The line between the two is somewhat blurred, for example, by legitimate organisations which turn a blind eye to criminality or which deliberately choose to operate an ineffective enforcement policy.

Government agencies can unwittingly facilitate IP crime and illicit trade. For example, Companies House in the UK maintains the national register of companies. It allows companies to be incorporated without formal checks. This enables criminals to create new business identities and the appearance of respectability. Legitimate businesses in the financial sector, for example banks, are important facilitators in enabling the transfer of criminal funds and money laundering (UNICRI, 2011). Anti-money laundering laws such as the EU's Anti-Money Laundering Directive require financial firms to implement prevention systems, including reporting suspicious activity to the authorities (Suspicious Activity Report – SAR). Consequently, criminals are migrating to other methods. Cryptocurrencies are unregulated, and consequently, they have emerged as significant enablers for criminals because their secrecy makes it more difficult to detect and trace criminal activity. Foley et al. (2019) estimate that one-quarter of bitcoin users are involved in illegal activity. These users conduct 46% of bitcoin transactions amounting to $76 billion of criminal activity per year.

There are numerous types of deliberate facilitators ranging from lawyers and accountants to lorry drivers and transport companies, and of course the large hi-tech companies in China that operate the mass marketing websites such as AliExpress and DHgate. Deliberate facilitation often involves corruption and is usually an integral feature of crime groups (UNICRI, 2011). Petty corruption in particular is used to bribe public officials for permits and approvals and to dissuade them from enforcing the law (Button et al., 2018).

Governments

Although not included in the typology (Table 6.5), government involvement in IP crime and illicit trade needs to be briefly mentioned as major facilitators. There is increasing evidence that governments are involved in or sponsor IP crimes to support their own industries whilst undermining the industries and economies of primarily democratic nations. Western governments accuse Russia and China in particular of economic espionage, for example, in relation to Covid-19 research (BBC News, 2020; Giglio, 2019).

Conclusion

Early criminologists such as Sutherland (1949) regarded IP crime as a white-collar crime perpetrated by the respected bosses of corporations seeking competitive advantage. This chapter has shown that it is now a far more pervasive problem in all levels of society. Population growth, globalisation, the industrialisation of China and the Internet have created innumerable low-risk opportunities to commit IP crime. The scale and breadth of the illicit trade in counterfeit and pirated goods illustrates that the problem is no longer a matter of businesses seeking an illegal advantage over competitors, it has become a $500 billion economic crime economy in direct competition with the legitimate economy. Criminal enterprises, particularly factories in China, are at the forefront of the counterfeit economy supplying nearly two-thirds of counterfeit products with apparent impunity. Individual consumers on the demand side sustain the counterfeit economy: a large minority are victims of fraud, but the majority are willing, complicit buyers especially in the younger age groups, nearly half of whom regard it as a legitimate act of protest. The consequences are immeasurable but huge: it costs jobs, reduces investment, undermines public service and harms the environment, but worst of all, it exploits and sustains poverty, and exports avoidable injury, ill health and death.

References

Albanese, J. (2009). Combating *piracy*: Intellectual *property theft and fraud*. Transaction Publishers.

Amazon. (2020). *Amazon establishes Counterfeit Crimes Unit to bring counterfeiters to justice*. https://press.aboutamazon.com/news-releases/news-release-details/amazon-establishes-counterfeit-crimes-unit-bring-counterfeiters

Andriole, S. J. (2010). Business impact of Web 2.0 technologies. *Communications of the ACM, 53*(12), 67–79.

Antonopoulos, G. A., Hobbs, D., & Hornsby, R. (2011). A soundtrack to (illegal) entrepreneurship: pirated CD/DVD selling in a Greek provincial city. *The British Journal of Criminology, 51*(5), 804–822.

BBC News. (2020, July 16). *Coronavirus: Russian spies target Covid-19 vaccine research*. www.bbc.co.uk/news/technology-53429506

Bouzembrak, Y., Steen, B., Neslo, R., Linge, J., Mojtahed, V., & Marvin, H. J. P. (2018). Development of food fraud media monitoring system based on text mining. *Food Control, 93*, 283–296. https://doi.org/10.1016/j.foodcont.2018.06.003

BSA. (2018). *Global software survey*. https://gss.bsa.org/

Button, M., Shepherd, D., & Blackbourn, D. (2018). Co-offending, bribery and the recruitment of participants to corrupt schemes and the implications for prevention. *Security Journal, 31*(4), 882–900. https://doi.org/10.1057/s41284-018-0139-0

Button, M., Sugiura, L., Blackbourn, D., Kapend, R., Shepherd, D., & Wang, V. (2020). *Victims of computer misuse*. University of Portsmouth. www.port.ac.uk/news-events-and-blogs/news/new-home-office-funded-report-urges-greater-action-for-cybercrime-victims

Center for Intellectual Property Understanding. (2019). *IP awareness and attitudes: A summary of research and data*. www.understandingip.org/wp-content/uploads/2019/11/IP-Awareness-and-Attitudes.pdf

Clarke, R. (1983). Situational crime prevention: Its theoretical basis and practical scope. In M. Tonry & N. Morris (Eds.), *Crime and justice: An annual review of research* (Vol. 4). Chicago University Press.

Cordell, V., Wongtada, N., & Kieschnick, R. J. (1996). Counterfeit purchase intentions: Role of lawfulness attitude and product traits as determinants. *Journal of Business Research, 35*(1), 41–53. https://doi.org/10.1016/0148-2963(95)00009-7

EC. (2019). *Report on the EU customs enforcement of intellectual property rights: Results at the EU border, 2018.* https://ec.europa.eu/taxation_customs/business/customs-controls/counterfeit-piracy-other-ipr-violations/ipr-infringements-facts-figures/facts-figures-archive_en

EUIPO. (2017). *European citizens and intellectual property: Perception, awareness and behaviour.* https://euipo.europa.eu/tunnel-web/secure/webdav/guest/document_library/observatory/documents/IPContributionStudy/2017/european_public_opinion_study_web.pdf

EUIPO & Europol. (2019). *Intellectual property threat assessment 2019.* www.euipo.europa.eu/ohimportal/en/news/-/action/view/5180317

Europol. (n.d.). *Intellectual property crime.* www.europol.europa.eu/crime-areas-and-trends/crime-areas/intellectual-property-crime

Facebook. (n.d.). *Intellectual property.* https://transparency.facebook.com/intellectual-property

FBI. (n.d.). *Transnational organized crime.* www.fbi.gov/investigate/organized-crime#:~:text=The%20FBI%20defines%20a%20criminal,engaged%20in%20significant%20criminal%20activity.

Foley, S., Karlsen, J. R., & Putniņš, T. J. (2019). Sex, drugs, and bitcoin: How much illegal activity is financed through cryptocurrencies?. *The Review of Financial Studies, 32*(5), 1798–1853. https://doi.org/10.1093/rfs/hhz015

Giglio, M. (2019, August 26). China's spies are on the offensive. *The Atlantic.* www.theatlantic.com/politics/archive/2019/08/inside-us-china-espionage-war/595747/

Google. (n.d. a). *Content delistings due to copyright.* https://transparencyreport.google.com/copyright/overview?hl=en_GB

Google. (n.d. b). *Removing content from Google.* https://support.google.com/legal/troubleshooter/1114905

Gopal, R., Sanders, G., Bhattacharjee, S., Agrawal, M., & Wagner, S. (2004). A behavioral model of digital music piracy. *Journal of Organizational Computing and Electronic Commerce, 14*(2), 89–105. https://doi.org/10.1207/s15327744joce1402_01

Hirschi, T. (1969). *The causes of delinquency.* University of California Press.

Hock, B. (2020). Policing corporate bribery: Negotiated settlements and bundling. *Policing and Society.* https://doi.org/10.1080/10439463.2020.1808650

Hunter, D., & Patterson, D. (2012). *Oxford introductions to U.S. law: Intellectual property.* OUP. https://oxford.universitypressscholarship.com/view/10,1093/acprof:osobl/9780195340600.001.0001/acprof-9780195340600-chapter-001

ICC & Frontier Economics. (2011). *Estimating the global economic and social impacts of counterfeiting and piracy.* https://iccwbo.org/content/uploads/sites/3/2016/11/ICC-BASCAP-Global-Impacts-Full-Report-2011.pdf

ICC & Frontier Economics. (2016). *Estimating the global economic and social impacts of counterfeiting and piracy.* https://iccwbo.org/publication/economic-impacts-counterfeiting-piracy-report-prepared-bascap-inta/

IPO. (2016). *Protecting creativity, supporting innovation: IP enforcement 2020.* www.gov.uk/government/publications/protecting-creativity-supporting-innovation-ip-enforcement-2020

IPO. (2019). *IP crime and enforcement report 2018 to 2019.* https://assets.publishing. service.gov.uk/government/uploads/system/uploads/attachment_data/file/842351/ IP-Crime-Report-2019.pdf

Karstedt, S., & Farrall, S. (2006). The moral economy of everyday crime: Markets, consumers and citizens. *British Journal of Criminology, 46*(6), 1011–1036. https:// doi.org/10.1093/bjc/azl082

Karstedt, S., & Farrall, S. (2007). *Law abiding majority? The everyday crimes of the middle classes, Briefing 3, June 2007.* Centre for Crime and Justice Studies. www. crimeandjustice.org.uk/opus45/Law_abiding_Majority_FINAL_VERSION.pdf

Kinsella, S. (2009). *The case against IP: A concise guide.* Mises Institute. https://mises. org/library/case-against-ip-concise-guide

Koniger, K. (2016). The European patent with unitary effect—What about unitary criminal sanctions for infringement? *Journal of Intellectual Property Law & Practice, 11*(3), 153–153. https://doi.org/10.1093/jiplp/jpv251

Lowe, P. (2006). Counterfeiting: Links to organised crime and terrorist funding. *Journal of Financial Crime, 13*(2), 255–257. https://doi.org/10.1108/13590790610660944

Mackey, J. (2018). *The dangerous, toxic ingredients found in counterfeit cosmetics.* Red Points. https://blog.redpoints.com/en/dangerous-ingredients-are-being-found-in-counterfeit-cosmetics

McKenzie, V. (2017, September 20). *Who's policing counterfeit airplane parts? The crime report.* https://thecrimereport.org/2017/09/20/faa-warned-boeing-777-737-ntsb-airplane-parts-china/

Moore, A. P., Cappelli, D. M., Caron, T. C., Shaw, E., Spooner, D., & Trzeciak, R. F. (2011). *A preliminary model of insider theft of intellectual property (no. MU/SEI-2011-TN-013).* Carnegie Mellon University. https://resources.sei.cmu.edu/asset_ files/TechnicalNote/2011_004_001_15362.pdf

Newton, P. N., Green, M. D., & Fernández, F. M. (2010). Impact of poor-quality medicines in the 'developing' world. *Trends in Pharmacological Sciences, 31*(3), 99–101. https://doi.org/10.1016/j.tips.2009.11.005

OECD. (2017). *Trade in counterfeit products and the UK economy: Fake goods, real losses.* www.oecd-ilibrary.org/governance/trade-in-counterfeit-products-and-the-uk-economy_9789264279063-en

OECD & EUIPO. (2019). *Trends in trade in counterfeit and pirated goods.* https:// euipo.europa.eu/ohimportal/en/web/observatory/trends-in-trade-in-counterfeit-and-pirated-goods

OECD & IPO. (2019). *Trade in counterfeit products and the UK economy.* www.oecd. org/gov/risk/trade-in-counterfeit-products-and-the-uk-economy-2019.htm

O'Mahoney, P. (2013). Finding horse meat in beef products – A global problem. *An International Journal of Medicine, 106*(6), 595–597. https://doi.org/10.1093/qjmed/ hct087

Paun, C. J. (2011). Between collaboration and competition: Global public-private partnerships against intellectual property crimes. TranState *working papers* 149. www.econstor.eu/bitstream/10419/48277/1/664237320.pdf

Spink, J., & Levente Fejes, Z. (2012). A review of the economic impact of counterfeiting and piracy methodologies and assessment of currently utilized estimates. *International Journal of Comparative and Applied Criminal Justice, 36*(4), 249–271. https://doi.org/10.1080/01924036.2012.726320

Spink, J., Moyer, D. C., Park, H., & Heinonen, J. A. (2013). Defining the types of counterfeiters, counterfeiting, and offender organizations. *Crime Science, 2*(8), 1–10. https://doi.org/10.1186/2193-7680-2-8

Sugden, J. (2007). Inside the grafters' game: An ethnographic examination of football's underground economy. *Journal of Sport and Social Issues, 31*(3), 242–258. https://doi.org/10.1177/0193723507301050

Sullivan, B. A., & Wilson, J. M. (2017). An empirical examination of product counterfeiting crime impacting the US military. *Trends in Organized Crime, 20*, 316–337. https://doi.org/10.1007/s12117-017-9306-7

Sutherland, E. (1949). *White collar crime*. Dryden.

Sutherland, E. (1983). *White collar crime: The uncut version*. Yale University Press.

The World Bank. (n.d.). *Individuals using the Internet*. https://data.worldbank.org/indicator/IT.NET.USER.ZS

TradeLab. (2017). *Illicit Trade and the World Trade Organization: Raising awareness, identifying limitations and building strategies*. https://tradelab.legal.io/guide/5942ae1fe93c1b021a000f89/Illicit+Trade+and+the+World+Trade+Organizaion+Raising+awareness+identifying+limitations+and+building+strategies#_ftnref170

Treadwell, J. (2011). From the car boot to booting it up? eBay, online counterfeit crime and the transformation of the criminal marketplace. *Criminology & Criminal Justice, 12*(2), 175–191. https://doi.org/10.1177/1748895811428173

UNICRI. (2011). *Counterfeiting: A global spread, a global threat*. www.unicri.it/sites/default/files/2019-11/Report%20on%20the%20Counterfeiting%20and%20Organized%20Crime.pdf

Urbas, G. (2006). Cross-national investigation and prosecution of intellectual property crimes: The example of "Operation Buccaneer". *Crime, Law and Social Change, 46*(4–5), 207–221. https://doi.org/10.1007/s10611-007-9060-x

Wall, D. S., & Large, J. (2010). Jailhouse frocks: Locating the public interest in policing counterfeit luxury fashion goods. *The British Journal of Criminology, 50*(6), 1094–1116.

WCO. (2019). *Illicit trade report 2018*. www.wcoomd.org/-/media/wco/public/global/pdf/topics/enforcement-and-compliance/activities-and-programmes/illicit-trade-report/itr_2018_en.pdf?db=web

WHO. (2006). *Counterfeit medicines: The silent epidemic*. www.who.int/mediacentre/news/releases/2006/pr09/en/

WHO. (2017). *A study on the public health and socioeconomic impact of substandard and falsified medical products*. www.who.int/medicines/regulation/ssffc/publications/SE_Study_EN.pdf

Wilson, J. M., & Grammich, C. A. (2020). Brand protection across the enterprise: Toward a total-business solution. *Business Horizons*. https://doi.org/10.1016/j.bushor.2020.02.002

Wilson, J. M., Grammich, C., & Chan, F. (2016). Organizing for brand protection and responding to product counterfeit risk: An analysis of global firms. *Journal of Brand Management, 23*(3), 345–361. https://doi.org/10.1057/bm.2016.12

Wilson, J. M., & Sullivan, B. A. (2016). Brand owner approaches to assessing the risk of product counterfeiting. *Journal of Brand Management, 23*(3), 327–344. https://doi.org/10.1057/bm.2016.10

WIPO. (n.d.). *What is intellectual property?* www.wipo.int/about-ip/en/

Yar, M. (2005). A deadly faith in fakes: Trademark theft and the global trade in counterfeit automotive components. *Internet Journal of Criminology*, *1*, 1–33.

Zhang, W., & Xue, J. (2016). Economically motivated food fraud and adulteration in China: An analysis based on 1553 media reports. *Food Control*, *67*, 192–198. https://doi.org/10.1016/j.foodcont.2016.03.004

Chapter 7

Industrial and economic espionage

Introduction

In the previous chapter, intellectual property crime was considered. Linked to this type of crime, but deserving a separate chapter is economic and industrial espionage. Some intellectual property crimes might be preceded by espionage, but not all, and there are motives beyond gaining insights on intellectual property for espionage. Most economic crimes in this book are not high on the list of politicians, but economic and industrial espionage is one that has reached the 'top table'. In running for election, Donald Trump sought to raise the importance of the problem and pursue policy to try and address it. On 28 September 2011, he tweeted: 'China is stealing our jobs. We need to demand China stop manipulating its currency and end its rampant corporate espionage'.[1] In government, President Trump also continued to see this as an important issue. However, this has been unusual with most senior politicians ignoring the issue and it has been largely neglected by researchers. There have been a handful of research monographs and practical guides published on the subject over the last 40 years by Heims (1982), Bottom and Gallati (1984), Cornwall (1991), Nasheri (2005), Hannas et al. (2013), Roper (2013) to name the most significant, as well as a handful of studies which will be referred to in this chapter.

This chapter will commence by defining economic and industrial espionage. It will then illustrate this by providing some cases of it before illustrating some of the techniques used. The scale and impact of the problem will then be explored before ending with a consideration of some of the different types of actors who become involved in it.

Defining economic and industrial espionage

Many companies are investing huge sums of money in research and development (R&D) to develop new products that will reap profits in the future. According to Statista (2021), the three biggest R&D spenders in 2018 were Amazon (US$22.6 billion), Alphabet (US$16.2 billion) and Volkswagen

DOI: 10.4324/9781003081753-7

(US$15.8 billion) (Statista, 2021). This expenditure leads to trade secrets, innovations, patented inventions and new products and services. These corporations (and the many other companies that develop new ideas and products) are targets for unscrupulous individuals and organisations who are not willing or able to invest such sums.

Economic and industrial espionage is about information, the unlawful gathering of information from one party, for the benefit of another. All organisations gather information on competitors, but some cross legal and ethical lines (Crane, 2005). It is a crime that involves state intelligence services, private investigators, hackers to ordinary criminals and employees to name some. It is also a problem that cuts across many of the other economic crimes in this book: fraud, bribery, hacking, for example.

To illustrate it in its simplest form, consider the following example. Pharmaceutical company X invests in research to develop an antiviral drug to treat Covid. The investment pays off and they secure promising data from trials. Company Y had tried the same, but their trials were negative, so they decide to try and find out how company X's drugs work. They convene a secret group to try and gain access to the information trying cyber methods and then ultimately paying a corrupt insider in company X for information. They then use this to develop their own drug. This would be an example of industrial espionage based upon trade secrets, but it can also be for confidential information. Many organisations hold sensitive information which would be useful to competitors. This could be lists of clients to accounting information. For example, imagine a stock market trader is interested in a company that he suspects may have financial difficulties, which are not yet public. It would be very beneficial to the trader to secure access to financial information before it hits the public domain. Private information has value and some are prepared to secure that value by unlawful means.

Therefore, the essence of economic and industrial espionage is the unlawful gathering of information which will be of benefit to another, with the distinction between economic and industrial being: the former is state sponsored, the latter is a private initiative. Button and Knickmeier (forthcoming) define them:

> Economic and industrial espionage refers to targeting or acquiring trade secrets and confidential information from domestic companies or government entities to knowingly benefit a foreign state in the case of the former and a private entity in the case of the latter.

Some also use the term 'corporate, cyber and commercial' with espionage, instead of industrial. Economic and industrial espionage are also unusual in not always having a specific criminal offence, such as the UK. Some countries have, however, created specific statutes relating to economic espionage and sometimes industrial espionage too, such as Austria, Germany and

Switzerland (Button & Knickmeier, forthcoming; Konopatsch, 2020) which criminalise disclosing certain types of information to a foreign state official or person. The USA also passed specific legislation in 1996 titled the Economic Espionage Act which created offences for both:

- the theft of the trade secret to benefit a foreign government, instrumentality or agent and
- more common commercial theft of trade secrets, regardless of who benefits (US Department of Justice, 2015).

The lack of a specific offence in the UK does not mean it is legal; rather other criminal offences are used to deal with it, such as the following:

- stealing sensitive documents: theft offences;
- hacking of competitor's computer: computer misuse offences;
- bugging a room: wireless offences;
- paying a member of staff for information: bribery offences; and
- securing confidential client information: data protection offences.

There is therefore a debate – beyond the scope of this chapter – on whether special offences are necessary. As with so many other economic crimes, civil remedies are also very common. The victim can pursue the alleged perpetrator for damages or to secure some remedy to stop the organisation using the information gained. An example is a case from 2012 involving Dyson, where they launched a civil claim against Bosch, who it was claimed had placed an insider in Dyson to steal secrets (Guardian, 2012). Such cases are often settled out of court with no publicity, so it is difficult to know the outcome. This also makes it difficult to determine the number of cases that are dealt with by the civil courts too, an issue which will be returned to.

Economic and industrial espionage have been occurring for a long time. The industrialisation that began in the 18th century led to an increase of industrial espionage (Drescher, 2019). In one of the most significant acts of industrial espionage ever, in the 1800s the British East India Company hired the botanist, Richard Fortune, to smuggle tea cuttings, seeds etc. out of China which were used to help grow a tea industry in India, eclipsing the Chinese in a few decades (Rose, 2010). Economic and industrial espionage are still significant problems for many countries and companies today, although techniques have moved on since Fortune disguised himself as a Chinese merchant to conduct his work.

Cases of economic and industrial espionage

Knowledge about modern cases of industrial espionage does not always reach the public domain for a variety of reasons that include:

- Company may not even release it was a victim.
- Knowledge of incident could adversely affect their share price.
- Knowledge of the incident could be embarrassing or reveal other sensitive information.
- Criminal prosecution is unlikely so there is no desire to report.
- Prosecution/legal action might occur using offences/torts not easily linked to economic and industrial espionage (Button & Knickmeier, forthcoming; Lee et al., 2020).

For all these reasons, cases do not reach the public domain very often, but some do and the following cases provide a snapshot. The first case involves the theft of client data. In 2020, Ticketmaster was fined US$10 million by the US Department of Justice for intrusions into a competitor's computer system, where two employees (one who had previously worked for the competitor) had illegally entered the other company's computer system using stolen passwords to access client data to use for Ticketmaster's advantage (BBC News, 2020).

The impact on a share price of revealing such incidents is illustrated by the next case. The Austrian company AMSC Windtec experienced one of their engineers selling important source code to a Chinese competitor. This case reached the public domain, resulting in a loss of US$1 billion to the company, a significant reduction in the share price and 700 staff losing their jobs (US Department of Justice, 2018).

In the 1990s, the American manufacturer of adhesive products, Avery Dennison, was victim of a significant case of industrial espionage. Throughout the 1990s, two Taiwanese business executives running a rival company had paid an employee of Avery Dennison over $160,000 to pass on trade secrets on the formulas for adhesives and new innovations. The scheme was estimated to have cost Avery Dennison over $200 million in lost revenues by the FBI (Los Angeles Times, 1999).

The Avery Dennison case was the result of a corrupt insider, but the next case known as the 'Night Dragon' attacks was perpetrated by hacking. In this case, Chinese hackers working 9–5 in Beijing were able to access sensitive information, such as proposed bidding plans from five companies operating in the oil, gas and petrochemical sectors (Reuters, 2011). The Reuters report cites the original writer of the report into the incidents from McAfee as stating, 'That information is tremendously sensitive and would be worth a huge amount of money to competitors'.

The final case involves the dispute between British Airways (BA) and Virgin Atlantic in the early 1990s, where industrial espionage was exposed in a libel case that emerged from it (which was settled before trial). A wide range of 'dirty tricks' were illustrated and some relating to espionage showed BA had set up a specialist unit whose task was to secure confidential information from the computer systems of Virgin. A newspaper report on the case claimed

Virgin realised, '... BA employees had been directly engaged in poaching passengers, as well as tampering with company files designated "confidential"' (Independent, 2015).

The approaches to economic and industrial espionage

Some of the discussion so far has alluded to the behaviour of those who engaged in espionage. It is first important to note that in some contexts it might even be pursued through lawful means, through what is known as 'business intelligence' (Crane, 2005). But the further down the list below, the more clearly illegal it becomes and moves into the realms of economic and industrial espionage.

Open-source intelligence: trade shows, industry reports and publications, press articles, company websites and announcements, social media, online photos are used to gather intelligence legitimately.

Hiring employees of competitors: this is a common tactic and although they may have contractual limitations, the offers from a new employer might make them open to revealing secrets. One famous case involves Starwood Hotels suing Hilton hotels over the development of a new brand, which arose from Hilton hiring key employees from Starwood. Hilton eventually settled in an out of court settlement worth US$150 million with restrictions on their future activities in this area also agreed (Jameson, 2011).

Dumpster diving: this is less prevalent as data is increasingly shared in digital format, but some information is produced in paper forms which is sometimes not destroyed securely enabling sensitive information to sometimes been found.

Social engineering of employees: another method is trying to trick employees into sending or disclosing information or enabling malware to be downloaded for purpose of hacking, often through a human mistake in a technical system (Greitzer et al., 2014; Sadok et al., 2019).

Illegal surveillance: placing recording devices in rooms where meetings are held, in the devices of employees or using other technical methods to listen in on discussions are all tactics which have been used. One case that arose to illustrate this involved a dispute involving members of the Barclay family who own the *Telegraph* newspaper, among many other companies. In the legal case that emerged from the dispute, it was revealed the conservatory at the Ritz had been extensively bugged to secure information to advantage one side in the dispute (Guardian, 2021).

Cultivating insiders and former insiders: employees with access to information are often cultivated to gain access to it using promises of jobs, bribes to blackmail. Some disgruntled employees may just leak information because they are alienated from the company. Some employees are fired or made redundant and hold information from their employment or have access to systems which can be exploited (Winkler, 1996).

Placing insiders: another tactic is to place a person in a competitor organisation with a view to securing information. In one simulation in a company in the USA it was possible, after research, to get a temporary employee within the target organisation who through a variety of methods within a day was able to secure access to US$1,000,000,000 worth of information (Winkler, 1996).

Hacking: unauthorised access to computer systems by hackers to secure information is another common tactic. In a case from the USA involving two rival insurers it was revealed that one company had hired a hacker to get inside the competitors code that develops quotes, so they could then beat them (Sussman, 2021). Botnets and other methods have also been found to be used to gather such information (Bederna & Szadeczky, 2020).

Many of these acts are clearly criminal, but some are not. Determined spies may use multiple methods to try and achieve their aims.

The extent and impact of economic and industrial espionage

Cases of economic and industrial espionage that reach the public domain are only the 'tip of the iceberg' (Hou & Wang, 2020). The few cases that are publicly reported add to the challenges of gauging the size of the problem. The measurement of most crimes is fraught with challenges, but at least with a crime such as burglary, there are the recorded cases in police statistics and often more accurate measures from victim surveys. As already noted, economic and industrial espionage is not always a crime and thus even if there were extensive statistics it would still be only a partial picture. Additionally, there are the challenges of non-reporting and victims not knowing how they came to be or even if they are victims. In the UK where there are no specific offences gauging the extent of the problem, it would be very difficult to secure such information, as one would have to search through information on other criminal cases to determine if they were industrial espionage related. Searching civil cases would be even more challenging because many do not directly refer to the problem in the case title and often they are settled out of court. Gauging the size of the problem through criminal and court statistics is therefore of limited use.

Victim surveys are another indication of the size of a crime problem, but very few have touched upon industrial and economic espionage. These are very rare related to this crime type and the authors are only aware of a handful of studies, most of which focus upon cyber, which may or may not be espionage related. A survey of 583 German small- and medium-sized enterprises (SMEs) in the manufacturing sector found in the previous five years 22% suspected an incident to have occurred, 13% had experienced one incident and 9% multiple incidents (Bollhöfer & Jäger, 2018, p. 31).

Possibly the best indicators of the size of the problem have been some of the estimates of the costs of economic and industrial espionage. The sizeable investments many companies make to develop intellectual property create lucrative targets for those willing to engage in such acts. Indeed, the technological revolution of the last two decades has provided many more opportunities to pursue such acts, for both state and corporate actors, which for some can be done without even setting foot physically in the country or firm's premises.

The definitional issues always create a challenge in estimating the magnitude of the problem, but those few estimates that have been offered provide little doubt to the substantial size of this global problem. The US Intellectual Property Commission (2017) estimated trade secret theft costs 1%–3% of GDP, meaning that the cost to the $18 trillion US economy was between $180 billion and $540 billion. In the UK, a £27 billion estimate of the cost of cybercrime suggested that £7.6 billion could be attributed to industrial espionage, including £2 billion financial services, £1.2 billion aerospace and defence and £1.6 billion mining (Cabinet Office & Detica, 2011). However, as cybercrime is only one means to perpetrate espionage, this is an under-estimate. A report by the European Centre for International Political Economy (2018) estimated the costs of cyber-espionage in the EU to be €55 billion, putting 289,000 jobs at risk.

A good illustration of the value or cost of this problem is the activities of the Stasi in the former state of East Germany. The Stasi perpetrated economic espionage on an industrial scale. Unique analysis of their activities against the West between 1970 and 1989 found substantial economic advantages for East Germany, such that the 'East-to-West German TFP (Total Factor Productivity) ratio would have been 13.3 percent lower at the end of the Cold War had East Germany not engaged in industrial espionage' (Glitz & Meyersson, 2020, p. 1055).

Another example to illustrate the size and cost is from 2012 when the head of MI5 (the state security service in the UK) noted how one company had suffered an £800 million loss from a state-sponsored cyberattack resulting in lost intellectual property and suffered disadvantages in contract negotiations (Shah, 2012).

Perpetrators of economic and industrial espionage

Research on who engages in industrial espionage has been rare, but drawing upon anecdotal evidence, the section below provides the main sources:

Competitors: the staff or contractors of companies in some cases have been tasked to undertake such activities. The BA/Virgin case above is a good example of this where staff in a small group had this responsibility. Organisations, however, may lack the expertise to conduct such activities, so turn to contractors (Gregory, 2010).

Contractors: sometimes contractors might be used, most commonly unethical private investigators or cyber-experts willing to push ethics or even break the law. In 2007, in the UK, six men were convicted, including two former police officers, for running a private investigation firm – Active Investigation Services – which offered a range of illegal services, some of which included hacking for the purposes of industrial espionage (House of Commons Home Affairs Committee, 2012, Ev 82). The press hacking scandal in the UK and the subsequent Leveson Inquiry exposed how some private investigators were willing to conduct illegal surveillance for a fee (Leveson, 2012; Serious Organised Crime Agency, 2008). In another example from 2008, an Israeli firm of private investigators was found guilty in a criminal court of stealing commercial information for a competitor by sending spyware to competitors (Government Technology, 2008). The BA/Virgin case briefly described earlier involved the use of private investigators (Gregory, 2010).

Organised criminals: some criminals of varying level of sophistication and organisation become involved in this type of activity too. Criminals may target companies looking for information to sell to competitors or to secure information to enable secondary criminal activities to take place. Wall (2015, p. 113) notes such groups scan security systems for weakness to sell gaps to other organised criminals for further use.

States: some states have been linked to espionage and either through clearly linked staff or proxies have perpetrated espionage. For example, in 2020, an official report claimed Russian state-backed hackers 'Cozy Bear' were attempting to hack medical research organisations in the UK, USA and Canada developing a vaccine for Covid-19 to secure data useful for Russian bodies also attempting to do this (National Cyber Security Centre, 2020). The Chinese state has also been linked to extensive economic espionage with a RUSI report stating, 'in the US, economic cyber-espionage is thought to be Chinese government policy, and the Chinese the most active and persistent practitioners of cyber-espionage in the world' (Jeffray, 2014). Defence is another area where state-backed espionage has been implicated with Hannas et al. (2013, p. 78) arguing China is pursuing:

> a deliberate, state-sponsored project to circumvent the costs of research, overcome cultural disadvantages and 'leapfrog' to the forefront by leveraging the creativity of other nations.

Insiders: due to their insider knowledge, the activities of internal offenders can be particular risky, as they know the worth of trade secrets, usually have easier access to them and are difficult to detect, if they, for example, take photos of trade secrets with their mobile or transfer data to their USB-stick (Knickmeier, 2020, p. 48). At another level, they might be careless leading to a leak of information. A member of staff might click on a link to an email that enables the computers to be hacked, they might leave information in a public place or put secure documents in a bin un-shredded. Insiders can also more purposefully seek to pass information on. It is not just staff insiders who pose a risk, but also students from other countries. There have been repeated reports of students from countries such as China engaging in espionage to steal information from sensitive research projects at the cutting edge of technology (NBC News, 2020).

Former insiders: another source of information can be former insiders. These can be a more fruitful source to cultivate particularly if they have been sacked or made redundant and have a grudge. In a case of espionage against the telecom company Ericsson, a former employee, Afshin Bavand (along with others), was convicted for passing information to Russian intelligence officers. A programme designed to help him find work had meant he still had access to the company intranet, email and telephone systems and he was able to access technical information on existing and future projects (Holmström, 2010).

Conclusion

This chapter has considered the fascinating problem of economic and industrial espionage. It is a very costly problem that has a low profile in research. Some politicians such as former President Trump have taken an interest in it, but this is unusual. The chapter defined the problem, illustrated some examples, the common techniques and the scale and impact of it. The chapter ended with a brief exploration of those who become involved in perpetrating such acts.

Note

This chapter draws on parts of Button, M., & Knickmeier, S. (Forthcoming). Economic and industrial espionage: Characteristics, techniques and response. In Gill, M. (Ed.), *Handbook of security* (3rd ed.). Palgrave.

Note

1 https://twitter.com/realDonaldTrump/status/119116243537113088.

References

BBC News. (2020). *Ticketmaster fined $10m for business 'intrusions'*. BBC News. www.bbc.co.uk/news/entertainment-arts-55496891

Bederna, Z., & Szadeczky, T. (2020). Cyber espionage through Botnets. *Security Journal, 33*(1), 43–62.

Bollhöfer, E., & Jäger, A. (2018). *Wirtschaftsspionage und Konkurrenzausspähung – Vorfälle und Prävention bei KMU im Zeitalter der Digitalisierung*. Max-Planck-Instituts für ausländisches und internationales Strafrecht.

Bottom, N. R., & Gallati, R. R. (1984). *Industrial espionage: Intelligence techniques and countermeasures*. Butterworth.

Button, M. (2020). Editorial: Economic and industrial espionage. *Security Journal,* *33*(1), 1–5.

Button, M., & Knickmeier, S. (Forthcoming). Economic and industrial espionage: Characteristics, techniques and response. In M. Gill (Ed.), *Handbook of security* (3rd ed.). Palgrave.

Cabinet Office & Detica. (2011). *The cost of cyber crime.* https://assets.publishing.service.gov.uk/government/uploads/system/uploads/attachment_data/file/60942/THE-COST-OF-CYBER-CRIME-SUMMARY-FINAL.pdf

Cornwall, H. (1991). *The industrial espionage handbook.* Century.

Crane, A. (2005). In the company of spies: When competitive intelligence gathering becomes industrial espionage. *Business Horizons, 48*(3), 233–240.

Drescher, J. (2019). *Industrie- und Wirtschaftsspionage in Deutschland.* LIT Verlag.

European Centre for International Political Economy. (2018). *Stealing thunder: Cloud, IoT and 5G will change the strategic paradigm for protecting European commercial interests. Will cyber espionage be allowed to hold Europe back in the global race for industrial competitiveness?* https://ecipe.org/publications/stealing-thunder/

Glitz, A., & Meyersson, E. (2020). Industrial espionage and productivity. *American Economic Review, 110*(4), 1055–1103.

Government Technology. (2008). *Private eyes jailed in industrial espionage spyware case.* www.govtech.com/security/Private-Eyes-Jailed-in-Industrial-Espionage-Spyware_Case.html

Gregory, M. (2010). *Dirty tricks: British Airways' secret war against Virgin Atlantic.* Random House.

Greitzer, F. L., Strozer, J. R., Cohen, S., Moore, A. P., Mundie, D., & Cowley, J. (2014). Analysis of unintentional insider threats deriving from social engineering exploits. In *2014 IEEE security and privacy workshops* (pp. 236–250). IEEE.

Guardian. (2012). *Dyson accuses Bosch of paying research spy.* www.theguardian.com/business/2012/oct/24/dyson-accuses-bosch-paying-research-spy#:~:text=Dyson%20has%20accused%20its%20German,its%20high%2Dsecurity%20research%20division.&text=%22Dyson%20has%20confronted%20Bosch%20with,technology%2C%22%20the%20company%20said.

Guardian. (2021). *Barclay family calls truce to end Ritz espionage case in high court.* www.theguardian.com/media/2021/jun/04/barclay-family-calls-truce-to-end-ritz-espionage-case-in-high-court

Hannas, W. C., Mulvenon, J., & Puglisi, A. B. (2013). *Chinese industrial espionage: Technology acquisition and military modernisation.* Routledge.

Heims, P. A. (1982). *Countering industrial espionage.* 20th Century Security Education.

Holmström, L. (2010). *Industrial espionage and corporate security: The Ericsson case.* www.theseus.fi/bitstream/handle/10024/86735/Rapotteja_87_holmstrom.pdf?sequence=1

Hou, T., & Wang, V. (2020). Industrial espionage – A systematic literature review (SLR). *Computers & Security, 98*, 102019. https://doi.org/10.1016/j.cose.2020.102019

House of Commons Home Affairs Committee. (2012). *Private investigators.* Retrieved from https://publications.parliament.uk/pa/cm201213/cmselect/cmhaff/100/10002.htm

Jameson, D. A. (2011). The rhetoric of industrial espionage: The case of Starwood v. Hilton. *Business Communication Quarterly, 74*(3), 289–297.

Jeffray, C. (2014). *The threat of cyber-crime to the UK RUSI Threat Assessment*. https:// rusi.org/sites/default/files/201406_bp_the_threat_of_cyber-crime_to_the_uk.pdf

Knickmeier, S. (2020). Spies without borders? The phenomena of economic and industrial espionage and the deterrence strategies of Germany and other selected European countries. *Security Journal, 33*, 6 26.

Konopatsch, C. (2020). Fighting industrial and economic espionage through criminal law: Lessons to be learned from Austria and Switzerland. *Security Journal, 33*(1), 83–118.

Lee, S., Lee, J., & Jung, J. (2020). An exploration of the necessary competencies of professional police investigators for industrial espionage cases in South Korea. *Security Journal, 33*, 119–138.

Leveson, B. H. (2012). *An inquiry into the culture, practices and ethics of the press: Executive summary and recommendations [Leveson report]*. The Stationery Office.

Los Angeles Times. (1999). *2 Taiwanese convicted in economic spy case*. www.latimes. com/archives/la-xpm-1999-apr-29-fi-32206-story.html

Nasheri, H. (2005). *Economic espionage and industrial spying*. Cambridge University Press.

National Cyber Security Centre. (2020). *Annual review 2020*. www.ncsc.gov.uk/files/ Annual-Review-2020.pdf

NBC News. (2020). *American universities are a soft target for China's spies, say U.S. intelligence officials*. www.nbcnews.com/news/china/american-universities-are-soft-target-china-s-spies-say-u-n1104291

Reuters. (2011). *Chinese hackers infiltrated five energy firms: McAfee*. www. reuters.com/article/us-energy-cyber-china/chinese-hackers-infiltrated-five-energy-firms-mcafee-idUSTRE7190XP20110210

Roper, C. (2013). *Trade secret theft, industrial espionage, and the China threat*. CRC Press.

Rose, S. (2010). *For all the tea in China*. Penguin.

Sadok, M., Welch, C., & Bednar, P. (2019). A socio-technical perspective to counter cyber-enabled industrial espionage. *Security Journal, 33*(1), 27–42.

Serious Organised Crime Agency. (2008). *Private investigators: The rogue element of the private investigation industry and others unlawfully trading in personal data*. SOCA.

Shah, S. (2012). *Corporate espionage on 'an industrial scale' targeting the UK*. Retrieved from www.computing.co.uk/ctg/news/2187123/corporate-espionage-an-industrial-scale-targeting-uk

Statista. (2021). *Ranking of the 20 companies with the highest spending on research and development in 2018*. www.statista.com/statistics/265645/ranking-of-the-20-companies-with-the-highest-spending-on-research-and-development/

Sussman, B. (2021). *Company hires hacker for corporate espionage*. www.secureworldexpo. com/industry-news/company-hires-a-hacker-for-corporate-espionage

The Independent. (2015). *British Airways spying scandal: New logo, new routes, new bosses – But the stench remains*. www.independent.co.uk/news/uk/home-news/ british-airways-spying-scandal-new-logo-new-routes-new-bosses-but-the-stench-remains-10076755.html

The US Intellectual Property Commission. (2017). *The theft of American intellectual property: Reassessments of the challenge and United States policy*. www.nbr.org/ program/commission-on-the-theft-of-intellectual-property/

US Department of Justice. (2015). *Introduction to the Economic Espionage Act*. www. justice.gov/archives/jm/criminal-resource-manual-1122-introduction-economic-espionage-act

US Department of Justice. (2018). *Chinese company Sinovel Wind Group convicted of theft of trade secrets*. www.justice.gov/opa/pr/chinese-company-sinovel-wind-group-convicted-theft-trade-secrets

Wall, D. S. (2015). Dis-organised crime: Towards a distributed model of the organization of cybercrime. *The European Review of Organised Crime*, 2(2).

Winkler, I. S. (1996). Case study of industrial espionage through social engineering. In *Proceedings of the 19th information systems security conference* (pp. 1–7).

Chapter 8

Money laundering

Introduction

The problem of money laundering is vast and complex. Money laundering is always associated with criminal assets. These criminal assets come from variety of sources and are derived from a range of criminal activities, including the sales of illegal drugs, human trafficking, fraud, corruption and many other acquisitive crimes. The variety of sources of criminal assets and predicate crimes present key conceptual and practical challenges.

The 'Essentials of money laundering' section explores what money laundering is by examining the money laundering process and relevant definitions. The section will then analyse key predicate crimes of money laundering and its scale. The 'Enablers and vulnerabilities of money laundering' section provides an analysis of key enablers and vulnerabilities using a typology developed for this book. The 'Policing money laundering' section discusses how money laundering is tackled by both public institutions and private entities. We will see how the criminal justice system has been increasingly tasking financial institutions and other obliged entities to prevent and detect money laundering. The section will also explore the effectiveness of anti-money laundering (AML) compliance programmes.

Essentials of money laundering

This section guides the reader through key perspectives that will support their independent thinking about the nature of money laundering and an appropriate response. We will start by discussing the money laundering process, key definitions and modalities of this economic crime. We will then consider key issues associated with measuring money laundering.

Money laundering process

In its core, money laundering is the false representation of criminal earnings as legitimate earnings. The false representation can often, though not always,

DOI: 10.4324/9781003081753-8

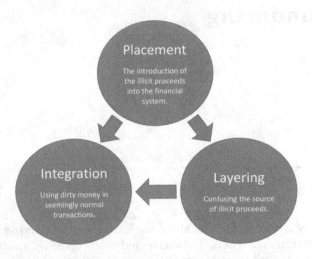

Figure 8.1 Traditional three-stage model of money laundering.

be illustrated as a procedural model of turning, disguising and moving criminal money into legitimate money. This process typically includes three stages: placement, layering and integration as illustrated in Figure 8.1 (see Cassella, 2018; Europol, 2015, p. 9).

Figure 8.1 illustrates the three stages of money laundering. The first is *placement*. In this stage, criminals introduce criminal assets into the financial system. This may involve multiple methods such as cash smuggling, involving cross-border physical movement of cash, and smurfing, involving multiple small deposits each under the reporting threshold (Europol, 2015; Soudijn & Reuter, 2016; Zali & Maulidi, 2018, p. 44). Smurfing may involve relatively simple schemes based on the activities of money mules, hired to deposit criminal assets (Raza et al., 2020; Soudijn, 2014) as well as sophisticated schemes. Organised crime groups (OCGs), for example, often 'outsource' money laundering activities to professional intermediaries, such as lawyers, accountants, real estate agents and company and trusts service providers (Europol, 2020; Lord et al., 2019).

The second is *layering*. In this stage, criminals add layers of financial transactions to separate criminal assets from their original source. These activities are often associated with the secretive world of offshore banking and facilitated by professional money launderers and corrupt intermediaries such as company service providers, lawyers and accountants (Lord et al., 2018). These professionals may take advantage of lax regulations that often allow them to use shell companies to layer corporate ownership (Gilmour, 2020; Lord et al., 2019). Layering may also involve the conversion of funds into different forms, for example, investing in real estate (De Sanctis, 2017),

Table 8.1 Insider trading and money laundering

The US authorities brought actions against SpaceX engineer J. R. Jones, who pleaded guilty for selling insider information on the dark web. According to the complaint, traders paying in bitcoins purchased his tips on the dark web and ultimately traded based on the information (SEC, 2021).

Although this case features many interesting questions, including the crime of insider trading, securities fraud and the use of dark web as an enabler of economic crime, our focus here are the implications of this to money laundering. Let us consider the following, hypothetical scenario, that could be associated with cases similar to the Jones case.

- 'A' is an investor who purchases advanced inside information on the dark web and accordingly sells many shares quickly in order to avoid a loss.
- 'A' has benefitted from their crime that of receiving and dealing in insider information-by the amount that they avoided losing, for example the equivalent of £1 million.
- 'A' transfers the proceeds of the early share sales, £1 million, to their account in the name of 'A'. The £1 million remains in the account for 4 years.
- 'A' has laundered the proceeds of their crime-that of receiving and dealing in advanced insider information – through their bank account.
- However, there has been no placement, no layering and no integration.

---

reselling high-value goods (Gilmour, 2016) and using cryptocurrencies (Albrecht et al., 2019).

The third is *integration*. In this stage, criminal assets re-enter the economy and are used in seemingly normal transactions. This can be associated with the purchase of high-value goods such as luxurious cars, jewellery and artwork. More complex, and in many ways serious, integration processes are associated with the infiltration of OCGs in the legitimate economy (Levi, 2015). Hulme et al. (2021) and Europol (2021) provide strong evidence of how the majority of OCGs invest into the legal economy, abusing legal business structures and using corruption on a regular basis.

The three-stage model cannot explain all types and forms of money laundering. A number of crimes, including almost all frauds, result in criminal proceeds that are already within the financial system. Moreover, the line between layering and integration stages might be blurred in complex laundering schemes, as actual integration of criminal proceeds can, in fact, present another stage of layering. Table 8.1 provides a case study illustrating limitations of the three-stage model.

Legal definition of money laundering

The common understanding of money laundering – the false representation of criminal earnings as legitimate earnings – is not followed by international and domestic legislation, which includes the mere possession or any form of handling criminal assets (Gelemerova, 2021). Consider the United Nations Convention against Transnational Organized Crime (2000), which provides the definition of money laundering for the purposes of criminal law in Article 6(1). The key features of the definition include:

1   The conversion or transfer of property for the purpose of:
     a   concealing or disguising the illicit origin of the property; or
     b   helping any person who is involved in the commission of the predicate offence to evade the legal consequences of his or her action;
2   The concealment or disguise of the true nature, source, location, disposition, movement or ownership of or rights with respect to property;
3   The acquisition, possession or use of property, knowing, at the time of receipt, that such property is the proceeds of crime;
4   Complicity or conspiracy to commit any of the offences.

It is important to note that the knowledge that property is the proceeds of crime is the condition of criminal liability.

The catch-all character of this legislative definition offers an opportunity to policing authorities to present many forms and types of criminality as money laundering. On this reading, the response to money laundering forms the response to the predicate crimes, and the underlying money laundering regulatory measures have cross-cutting character. Confiscations, civil recovery orders and other similar tools that are conventionally used to disrupt predicate crimes, including drug trafficking, fraud and corruption, are primarily money laundering tools. These orders, however, are not equivalent to criminal prosecutions, and international organisations such as the OECD have criticised the UK for using civil recovery orders too often instead of criminal laws (OECD, 2012; Ryder, 2013a).

Yet, this broad definition also blurs important differences associated with predicate crimes. Gelemerova (2011, 2021) argues that understanding the entry point of the crime proceeds into the legitimate economy is crucial from an investigative point of view – crimes are not the same in methodology. For example, the proceeds of tax evasion have very different character from cash-intense human trafficking. In addition, harm caused by these crimes is also different. The elasticity of such a broad definition of money laundering indicates that the AML regime consists of constantly shifting conceptual, operational and normative platforms (*ibid.*). Table 8.2 provides examples of key predicate crimes.

The scale of money laundering

The issues associated with the inclusive character of the money laundering definition are also reflected in the struggle to credibly measure the scale of the problem. While some areas, such as organised crime and money laundering, are relatively well understood (Europol 2021; Hulme et al., 2021), measuring

Table 8.2 Predicate crimes of money laundering

Examples of key predicate crimes		Notable works
Illicit drugs and arms trafficking	Illicit drugs and arms trafficking are traditional predicate crimes of money laundering. These predicate crimes are often associated with activities of OCGs that traditionally use cash-intensive businesses. While there are knowledge gaps, this area provides comparatively strongest evidence on how, and in what scales, proceeds of crime are laundered.	Hughes et al. (2020), Soudijn (2016), UNODC (2020)
Human trafficking and modern slavery	The abuse and exploitation of people remains an important problem associated with organised crime, globalisation and the exploitation of alternative remittance systems.	Sarkar (2015)
Environmental crime	Environmental crimes such as illegal fishing, illegal logging and illegal wildlife trade present a global challenge with criminal justice systems struggling to respond effectively.	United Nations Environment Programme (2016), FATF (2020)
Fraud	Although fraud is a major predicate crime of money laundering, more research needs to be done to better understand many linkages between fraud, including tax fraud and money laundering.	Phillips (2017)
Tax evasion	Tax evasion is a complex economic crime that often overlaps with fraud, corruption and money laundering. Tax evasion is often enabled by professionals that use complex corporate structures through offshore jurisdictions.	Hock (2021)
Cybercrime	The advancement of technology enables new forms and types of crime. Issues such as malwares, hacking and the misuse of virtual currencies belong to this category.	Custers et al. (2019)
Corruption	Corruption, including its various forms such as corporate bribery and nepotism, presents a broad category of improper conduct. Many forms of corruption such as international bribery are economically motivated and involve businesses channelling money to foreign government officials. The corporations and corrupt politicians then need to set up the system to launder corporate bribes.	Lord and Levi (2017)

the scale of money laundering presents a huge problem (Halliday et al., 2019; Levi, 2020; Walker & Unger, 2009). Key issues include:

1   The quality of empirical data is very weak in this area; overall we mainly see very rough and imprecise estimates (see Table 8.3). Halliday et al. (2019) argue that international organisation, transgovernmental networks and nation states have been providing reports based on inconsistent approaches and dubious methodologies;
2   Walker and Unger (2009, p. 821) argue that 'measuring global money laundering, the proceeds of transnational crime that are pumped through the financial system worldwide, is still in its infancy'. Existing methods of measurement mainly included: case studies, proxy variables and models for measuring the shadow economy;
3   Although we know about the existence of various typologies and methods, what we struggle with is how different predicate crimes compare and how various money laundering vulnerabilities and enablers play a role in different sectoral and other contexts (Levi & Soudijn, 2020).
4   Some of the more recent approaches include 'Gravity Models' inspired by an international trade theory (see Ferwerda et al., 2020; Walker & Unger, 2009). These models estimate the flows of criminal proceeds that need to be laundered.

Moreover, though it is clear that different types of money laundering flows lead to different enforcement challenges (Ferwerda et al., 2020), the global nature of crime and money laundering presents a challenge too (see Moiseienko & Keatinge, 2019). From the perspective of the UK regulator, for example, money laundering can take three different 'territorial' forms:

Table 8.3 Reviewing the scale of money laundering

Reviewing the scale of money laundering	
The United Nations Office on Drugs and Crime (UNODC, 2017)	Every year up to 5% ($2 trillion), of the global GDP have been introduced into the legal financial system by means of money laundering activities
NCA (2019)	The scale of money laundering impacting the UK annually could be over £100 billion
Pol (2019)	The amount of criminal funds identified and stopped is 0.1% or less.
Ferwerda et al. (2020)	Most money laundering happens in the USA and the UK. These countries are responsible for 40% of all money laundering in 36 OECD countries that were studied. Money laundering generally amounts to about 1.9% for OECD countries, while the World average is 3%.

1   laundering of the proceeds of UK crime;
2   laundering of the proceeds of overseas crime that are invested in the UK and
3   laundering of the proceeds of overseas crime via the use of UK business infrastructure.

Just based on the 'territoriality' criterion, we may assume important practice as well as normative implications in measuring and responding to money laundering. For example, policing money laundering associated with the UK illicit drugs market have both economic rationales and important health and security implications. Disturbing dirty money being channelled through the UK banking sector from, for example, Russia to Colombia, necessitates not only different practical responses than the UK illicit drugs market, but also different moral, economic and societal justifications.

Enablers and vulnerabilities of money laundering

Relevant work on money laundering provides multiple formal titles such as enabler, facilitator, vulnerability, method, type etc., that attempt to explain who, how and why conduct money laundering, what makes money laundering easier to undertake and who and what is vulnerable to money laundering. It is important to note that this terminology is often inconsistent, and some works have started avoiding them to prevent confusion (see FATF, 2018, p. 10).

In this work, we operate with two key terms 'vulnerability' and 'enabler'.

*   **Vulnerability** – *people, things or processes within an organisation, a specific sector or country that create opportunities and/or attract threat actors to target. Vulnerabilities are required for money laundering to occur.*

This definition aligns with the definition provided by HM Treasury and Home Office (2020, p. 7) in the National Threat Assessment for Money Laundering and Terrorist Financing essentially focused on the opportunity that can be exploited by threat actors. More broadly, this also applies in an organisational, or even national, context. In other words, vulnerabilities are individual, organisational, systemic and national factors that attract threat actors.

*   **Enablers** – *people or things that make vulnerabilities for frauds/money laundering easier to exploit. Unlike vulnerabilities, enablers are not required for money laundering to occur.*

Enablers such as the dark web and the use of shell companies can aid criminals to exploit vulnerabilities. They are, however, not necessary for money laundering to occur. Figure 8.2 illustrates this further.

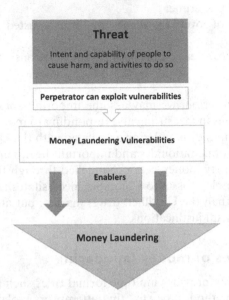

Figure 8.2 Enablers and vulnerabilities of money laundering.

Vulnerabilities

This section illustrates key examples of money laundering vulnerabilities. The main aim is to illustrate how our conceptual framework helps structure the thinking about more specific opportunities that attract money laundering. Firstly, we highlight sectoral vulnerabilities. Secondly, we will discuss general vulnerabilities including organised crime, ineffective legislation, and organisational vulnerabilities.

Sectoral vulnerabilities

Money laundering undermines market competition and legitimate business. Nevertheless, not all economic sectors present the same opportunity to money launderers. To make an AML policy effective, national states and supranational organisations such as the EU conduct regular assessments of how, and to what extent, economic sectors are vulnerable to money laundering. For example, the UK's 2020 National Risk Assessment confirms that traditionally high-risk sectors are vulnerable, including financial services, money service businesses as well as new sectors such as financial technology firms (HM Treasury and Home Office, 2020).

The Traditional Financial Sector, including banks and other financial institutions, has been the main focus in the money laundering area. Given the volume of business transactions and the globalisation of business, the financial sector will remain the key sector vulnerable to money laundering.

Moreover, we see significant innovation led by the so-called *Financial Technology (Fintech) sector*, which has emerged as an alternative to traditional banking and non-banking institutions. New technological solutions, however, come with their own risk, including, the misuse of virtual assets (Albrecht et al., 2019).

Professional services such as lawyers, auditors, and consultants have been under an increasing regulatory scrutiny. The sectoral regulators such as the Solicitor Regulation Authority have started closely monitoring the effectiveness of money laundering prevention of its members. However, the effects of these efforts remain unclear (Levi, 2021). Historically, we have seen strong evidence that lawyers and other professionals are willing to take risks and turn a blind eye on suspicious clients and transactions (Helgesson & Mörth, 2019).

The real estate sector has been an attractive alternative for oligarchs, corrupt politicians and other criminals that often misuse the real property market to launder their ill-gotten gains (Zavoli & King, 2020). The UK, and especially London, faces high risk of money laundering through real estate. Some studies indicate that, for example, 31% of land titles in the City of Westminster are owned by anonymous companies and 91% of overseas company-owned London property was bought through secure jurisdictions (Transparency International, 2016). While the UK law and other laws and regulations are expanding beyond their traditional focus, to regulate real estate agents and other professionals, luxury property still presents an opportunity to clean large sums of money, especially through anonymous companies.

There are many other sectors potentially vulnerable to money laundering such as gambling, including the remote and non-remote casinos and betting, online gaming, hospitality, creative arts and high-value portable commodities such as gold, jewellery and diamonds.

General vulnerabilities

Money laundering is attracted by more general vulnerabilities, which individually and together provide varying opportunities for criminals to launder the proceeds of their crimes. Organised crime and the operations of OCGs present one such vulnerability. Although it might appear that criminal enterprises are predominantly the matter of less developed countries, it is not the case. In the UK, for example, there are over 4,500 OCGs (National Audit Office, 2019). Supported by skilful professional intermediaries (see Lord et al., 2019), these groups become particularly powerful when they are able to infiltrate legitimate economies, and thus corrupt entire economic sectors. States that cannot deal effectively with organised crime are more vulnerable to money laundering (Europol, 2021; Hulme et al., 2021).

Globalisation creates multiple opportunities too, as it allows criminals to attack national economies from secure jurisdictions and hide their criminal proceeds in huge amounts of international business transactions. Although many countries have adopted AML policies to prevent and detect money laundering, their efforts need to go beyond their own national borders. Mitigating these risks often require extraterritorial policing activities and international cooperation. These responses are, however, associated with numerous political, economic, and practical challenges (see Gelemerova, 2011).

Many challenges are associated with insufficient regulation and enforcement, when criminals are more attracted by jurisdictions tolerating corporate anonymity. This is indeed a very broader category widely covered by relevant literature referred to throughout this chapter. Some of the most important vulnerabilities include:

- Legislative gaps and inadequate enforcement of AML legislation;
- National culture tolerating anonymity and secrecy;
- The lack of cooperation and coordination between national authorities as well as between individual states;
- Ineffective regulatory supervision;
- Inadequate system of state inspection and audit; especially in the context of international trade;
- Ineffective reporting system and public-private collaboration.

An important part of the global fight against money laundering is organisations' resilience to money laundering. Businesses with weak internal compliance programmes are more vulnerable to economic crimes, including money laundering. The question of organisational vulnerabilities is closely connected with the effectiveness of AML compliance programmes, which are discussed later in this chapter.

Enablers

This section discusses payment methods, technology, international trade, and offshore secrecy as key examples of money laundering enablers, meaning people or things that make money laundering vulnerabilities easier to exploit.

Cash remains the most significant commodity used by criminals to infiltrate the legal economy (see Europol, 2015). Despite new technological opportunities to launder money, most of the laundering schemes are based on the use of cash. This is either because criminal activities such as drug trade generate cash profits (see Soudijn & Reuter, 2016), or because criminals decide to change their assets into cash in order to disguise the crime from its proceeds. For example, cybercriminals will transfer the proceeds of their cybercrime to money mules, who will then withdraw proceeds in cash and place money to different accounts held by criminals. This creates additional difficulties for enforcement authorities which generally struggle to trace physical cash money movements (see Europol, 2015).

Furthermore, new technological advancements make some forms of money laundering easier. On the one hand, we see illicit infrastructure such as underground forums and the dark web providing a platform for trading tools and knowledge of how to launder criminal proceeds (Europol, 2020). On the other hand, legitimate forms of assets such as virtual currencies and innovative payment services such as e-money products have become popular enablers of money laundering. For example, mobile digital payments systems, digital wallets, and prepaid cards pose additional compliance risks that Fintech firms need to address (FCA, 2018a).

International trade is an increasingly important enabler of money laundering. While the financial system and various forms of money and money-related services have always been leading enablers of money laundering, the regulatory scrutiny has been increasing. This is why OCGs have been increasingly using alternatives such as trade-based money laundering (TBML) (Hataley, 2020). TBML is based on the movements of value through trade transactions in an attempt to legitimise its illicit origins (see Table 8.4). The complexity of

Table 8.4 Trade-based money laundering

The core of TBML is the misrepresentation of the price of goods, its quantity, quality and nature. Some basic fraudulent techniques include over-invoicing and under-invoicing of goods, over/under-shipment of goods and falsely described goods.
Consider two hypothetical TBML scenarios, in which you are able to compare prices associated with export of tablets and import of cut emeralds.

Import/Export	Product	Country	Selling price	World average price
Scenario 1 UK export (at low average prices)	Tablets	X	£20	£200
Scenario 2 UK import (at high average prices)	Emeralds	Y	£1,000/carat	£50/carat

Scenario 1 provides data that indicate under-invoicing. An OCG based in the UK needs to launder the proceeds of drug sales and human trafficking and move these proceeds to Country X. One way to achieve this objective is to purchase a large amount of tablets for an average world price of £200 and make arrangements to export those tablets to their co-conspirators in Country X. In doing so, however, the UK OCG will fraudulently under-invoice the tablets at £20 each. The co-conspirator then sells the goods at their true market value in Country X.
In Scenario 2, foreign exporter from Country Y sells emeralds for £1,000/carat to the UK-based colluding importer. However, foreign exported fraudulently over-invoice emeralds that otherwise cost £50/carat. This trade-related fraud will allow the transfer of illegal funds to the UK.
TBML might distort prices on certain goods in certain markets. Clearly, a country's average price of certain goods that is significantly higher or lower than the world average prices might indicate the presence of high volumes of TBML (see Ferwerda et al., 2020; Walker and Unger, 2009).

Table 8.5 Enablers associated with offshore secrecy and corporate transparency

Offshore secrecy enablers	Description
Shell company	Anonymous companies with no independent operations; used for stock holding and asset shifting but also to layer corporate structure and conceal the identity of the real beneficial owners.
Front company	Fully functioning company serving as a venue to infiltrate legitimate markets; the purpose is to re-introduce money to the legitimate economy.
Offshore financial centres (OFCs)	OFCs usually have many financial institutions, disproportionately large amounts of external assets and liabilities as compared to domestic finance, low taxation and lax financial regulation.
Free trade zones	Economic areas with special regulatory and tax conditions. Post Brexit, the UK created multiple freeports; spaces to store assets with lower custom duties with a view to encourage local and foreign investment (see Gilmour, 2021).

international trade and the ease to fraudulently false documentation and declaration of traded goods makes TBML one of the most challenging forms of money laundering to detect and investigate (GAO, 2020).

Offshore secrecy and other factors that hinder corporate transparency present another typical group of money laundering enablers. It is well documented how professional money launderers hide beneficial ownership and conceal illicit wealth through offshore jurisdictions (Gilmour, 2020). In their experimental study focusing on incorporation services in 177 countries and 1,722 US firms, Findley et al. (2015) show how easy it is to incorporate confidential business, with 19% of firms globally not requiring ID documents and 36% not requiring notarised ID documents. These professionals take advantage of lax regulations in some jurisdictions that allow for an effective use of shell entities and trust arrangements to hide beneficial owners and anonymise illicit assets. Table 8.5 provides an overview of these arrangements.

Policing money laundering

The global AML regulatory arena is vast and complex. This section explains the most important aspects of this complexity, and especially the institutional setup based on the interaction between public policing and the AML compliance activities of private obliged entities. The public-private interdependence and the responsibilisation of the private sector are core elements of this system of policing.

The evolution of AML law

The importance of the private sector in policing money laundering has been apparent since the emergence of powerful criminal syndicates in the USA in 1920s and 1930s. Consider the infamous Al Capone who was able to buy loyalties of public authorities and allow his criminal enterprise to exploit many crime opportunities, including the illegal sales of alcohol during the US alcohol prohibition. While this criminal enterprise often enforced its will by the use of violence, Al Capone was charged with income tax related violations. The key role in this case played the cooperation of private sector firms (Gelemerova, 2021; Mendlow, 2018).

The first major AML statute, the US Bank Secrecy Act of 1970 (BSA), obliges the private sector to participate in policing money laundering. In its core, the BSA makes it more difficult for criminals to misuse financial institutions for the purposes of money laundering by requiring financial institutions to report suspicious activities and provide relevant documentation to regulators. This model has inspired other AML laws adopted in the USA and overseas. The BSA was accompanied by the Racketeering Influenced and Corrupt Organizations Act of 1970 (RICO), which enables enforcement authorities to tackle large criminal schemes undertaken through OCGs and similar criminal enterprises. Figure 8.3 illustrates the evolution of AML laws.

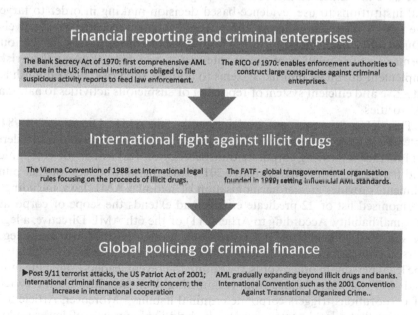

Figure 8.3 The evolution of AML laws.

In its early stage, the international AML regime focused primarily on the fight against illegal drugs under the Vienna Convention of 1988 and subsequently moved into regulating criminal finance flows more broadly. The foundation of the Financial Action Task Force (FATF) in 1989 led to further strengthening and expansion of regulatory standards and operational measures for combating money laundering.[1] The Convention Against Transnational Organized Crime subsequently created the domestic criminal offence of money laundering and established the framework for extradition of criminals, mutual legal assistance and law enforcement cooperation.

Following the 9/11 terrorist attacks and the adoption of the Patriot Act of 2001, we see that the problem of international criminal finance has become a national security issue (Ryder, 2015). States started cooperating more closely on the matters related to transnational crime and adopting and applying new extraterritorial forms of economic crime laws (see Hock, 2020). Furthermore, a series of corporate scandals in the late 1990s led to the adoption of the Sarbanes-Oxley Act (2002), which catalysed a wave of corporate reforms associated with the expansion of corporate ethics and compliance programmes.

These developments have also translated into the AML regulatory arena in Europe, including the EU AML directives and other regulations. Most importantly, the 4th AML Directive 2015/849 established the so-called risk-based approach to money laundering. The EU Member States and the UK have implemented measures that require obliged entities such as financial institutions to use 'evidence-based decision-making in order to target the risk of money laundering and terrorist financing […] more effectively' (Directive, 2015/849, para. 22). This provision opens doors for various forms of self-regulation of the private sector, which must assess their risk, implement adequate internal systems to address such risk, and establish an effective and efficient system of reporting of suspicious activities to national authorities.

This EU regime is still evolving with 5th AML Directive 2018/843 extending the AML obligations to virtual currency providers and art traders, and further improving corporate transparency on real owners of companies and trusts. The 6th AML Directive 2018/1673 then introduces tougher punishment, provides greater harmonisation of national AML laws, including a harmonised list of 22 predicate crimes, and extends the scope of corporate criminal liability. According to Article 5(1) of the 6th AML Directive, a legal person shall be held liable if a person in a leading position within the legal person commits money laundering and associated crimes for the benefit of the legal person. In other words, the failure to prevent leaders ('directing mind and soul') of corporations from committing illicit activities for the benefit of corporations triggers corporate criminal liability.[2] Moreover, Article 5(2) provides that a legal person can also be held liable for acts of lower-ranked employees, provided that the lack of supervision or control by persons in leading positions has made possible the commission of money laundering and associated crimes for the benefit of that legal person.

In the UK, the Proceeds of Crime Act (2002) (POCA) requires obliged entities to submit Suspicious Activity Reports to the National Crime Agency (NCA). The MLR 2017 then obliged supervisory authorities such as the FCA to ensure the compliance with the AML legislation and regulations within their sectors. In doing so, supervisory bodies use a number of tools such as warning notices and guidelines. Yet, the system of prevention and detraction of criminal finance is largely in the hands of the private sector, which needs to develop its own AML standards and practices.

The legal provisions focusing on the prevention and detection of money laundering by private actors are accompanied by criminal AML tools, focusing on the criminal liability for money laundering and its predicate crimes. Moreover, this second type of AML laws aims to facilitate the forfeiture of finance linked to crime. In this context, the POCA defines money laundering for the purposes of criminal law and allows competent authorities to seek the detention and freezing of assets, and ultimately their recovery or confiscation.[3]

The rise of AML enforcement

AML laws and regulations have been increasingly enforced in recent years. Importantly, however, the key focus of enforcement has not been criminals that generate proceeds of crimes, but rather prosecuting entities lacking adequate and effective AML systems and controls. Many European and US banks such ING, HSBC, Goldman Sachs, Standard Chartered, Deutsche Bank, Wells Fargo, Danske Bank, and BNP Paribas paid billions to resolve their failures to comply with AML laws and regulations. Facilitating money laundering, turning a blind eye on suspicious activities and the lack of willingness to prevent money laundering have become more costly worldwide. In the UK, for example, the so-called statutory AML supervisors – HMRC, FCA, and Gambling Commission – have concluded a number of high-profile cases in recent years (see Table 8.6).

In addition to the high-profile cases conducted by the UK statutory regulators, we see an increase in AML enforcement by some of the 25 legal and accountancy professional body supervisors such as the Solicitors Regulation Authority (SRA), which is undertaking AML compliance campaigns and reviews of firms, including conducting interviews with fee earners and reviewing client matters (Solicitors Regulation Authority, 2018). The SRA can also issue relatively small fines for minor breaches and refer larger cases to the Solicitors Disciplinary Tribunal. It is important to note that professional AML supervisors are supervised by the Office of Professional Body AML Supervision (OPBAS). The OPBAS aims to ensure robust and consistent standards of AML supervision in the legal and accountancy sectors

Table 8.6 High-profile cases concluded by the UK statutory supervisors

Entity	UK authorities	Sanction	Background
Goldman Sachs International (22/10/2020)	FCA and Prudential Regulation Authority (PRA)	£96.6 million	Part of $2.9 billion global resolution (including US and Singapore) with the bank. The bank ignored signs of fraud and bribery in a bond scheme arranged for a Malaysian state-owned entity.
Commerzbank AG (17/06/2020)	FCA	£37.8 million	Failing to put adequate AML systems and controls in place. For example, failing to verify beneficial ownership details in relation to high-risk clients, significant number of clients not subject to timely KYC checks, and weaknesses in automatized tools for transaction monitoring.
Standard Chartered Bank (05/02/2019)	FCA	£102.2 million	Failure to establish and maintain risk-sensitive policies and procedures (especially in the context of its branches in the United Arab Emirates, and in the context of correspondent banking). Serious shortcomings in AML controls relating to CDD and ongoing monitoring.
Deutsche Bank AG (31/01/2017)	FCA	£163 million	Significant deficiencies throughout the bank's AML control framework, and especially its Corporate Banking and Securities division. For example, it performed inadequate CDD, used flawed risk methodologies, lacked automated AML systems etc.
MT Global Limited (07/01/2021)	HMRC	£23.8 million	A money transfer company failed in carrying out adequate risk assessment and CDD, and also failed to maintain adequate policies, controls and procedures.
Caesars Entertainment UK (02/04/2020)	Gambling Commission	£13 million	Not carrying out adequate source of funds checks on customers and enhanced CDD associated with VIP practices. In addition, part of the case relates to social responsibility failings.

and facilitate cooperation between both statutory supervisors, professional supervisors and law enforcement agencies (FCA, 2018b).

Moreover, a very important part of the AML enforcement system is the use of the so-called ancillary orders, including confiscation orders, restraint orders, freezing orders, civil recovery orders and unexplained wealth orders. Although there are many challenges associated with the use of these orders, the fact is that the value of frozen and confiscated assets has been growing in Europe, which indicates they might be effective. For example, in 2019/2020, £208 million was collected under POCA, which represents an 8% increase since 2014/2015 (Home Office, 2020).

The effectiveness of AML law and regulations

It is well documented that policing money laundering is challenging. While we have seen a rapid increase of AML laws, regulations and standards, the effectiveness of the AML regime in terms of decreasing levels of money laundering is difficult to assess (Levi, 2020; Levi et al., 2018). Despite the increase in regulatory and enforcement activities, the prevalence and costs of money laundering are not decreasing (ibid.; Gelemerova, 2021).

Here, the definitional problems and issues associated with the measurement of money laundering appear again. National states and international organisations such as the EU operate not only with a very inclusive definition of money laundering but also with broad effectiveness criteria.[4] While there is no major controversy in the problem-solving and objective-achieving character of the AML regime, the money laundering problem is too complex. Any measuring of effectiveness needs to identify more specific and measurable sub-problems (National Audit Office, 2019).

However, it is hard to find any clear methodology on evaluating effectiveness of the AML regime, and this task has not been clearly prioritised by nation states and other relevant institutions such as the EU Commission (Halliday et al., 2019; Levi et al., 2018). The fact that national and supranational AML policies are not based on specific objectives is a significant shortcoming.

To improve the effectiveness of AML laws and regulations, the complexity associated with the cross-cutting character of AML regulatory instruments should be better understood, exploited and monitored by relevant authorities. Measures associated with policing international bribery, online fraud, and tax evasion overlap with those that can be used for money laundering. Furthermore, the money recovery function of AML regulation as well as the policing of underlying predicate crimes present a different part of the money laundering problem as compared to the disruption of professional money launderers who specialise in active money laundering. The foundations of many solutions will lay in identifying these cross-cutting issues and determining the core of AML policy.

Secondly, the question is how, and to what extent, the use of confiscations, civil recovery orders, and other similar tools alongside criminal prosecutions of individuals and organisations is proportionate. It is clear that recovering proceeds of crime is a better alternative than non-enforcement of AML laws. However, one needs to consider the tendency of enforcement authorities to use recovery orders as a substitute to the prosecution of criminals. Moreover, the question is how recoveries associated with two different crimes, for example, illicit drugs and global economic sanctions, compare when we consider their deterrence effect.

Thirdly, the question is what constitutes an effective system of private engagement in AML policing. On the one hand, the fact that businesses are legally held responsible for adequate money laundering prevention and detection is an important feature of the existing regime. How does this administrative/regulatory feature of the regime, however, interact with a more qualitative/analytical approach to AML policing? Clearly, the private reporting of suspicious activity is in place to feed effective law enforcement activities. Yet, academic research provides strong evidence that obliged entities tend to focus on regulatory risk over financial crime risk, which leads to too many suspicious activity reports that do not meet the needs of criminal justice system agencies. For example, private actors tend to focus on box-ticking and submit a report if there is any suspicion in order to be protected from regulators (Ryder, 2013b, pp. 62–63; Zavoli & King, 2021, pp. 762–764).

Lastly, AML cooperation, whether it is international cooperation of states, national agencies, public-private partnerships, or private-private initiatives, is a key issue in this area. However, any initiatives supporting such AML partnerships should consider that states, their agencies, and firms are political actors, in the sense that they have their own interests. This is why rational actors often struggle to pursue a collective interest, which ultimately leads to all players being worse-off (see Hock, 2020). This means that some partnerships, and especially public-private partnerships, will have higher potential to be successful than other partnerships. In other words, public-private partnership is not a value-neutral mechanism and policy-makers should invest their resources in promoting those that have potential to sustain and improve wide societal interest rather than private interests.

The effectiveness of AML compliance

The policing of money laundering is largely based on the interaction between public policing and the AML compliance activities of private obliged entities. The public-private interdependence and responsibilisation of private sectors is closely associated with the notion of AML compliance. Typically, international AML standards and international AML legislation require states to implement regulations that require businesses to undertake efforts internally to prevent and detect money laundering. A well-managed organisation will typically maintain an adequate AML compliance programme.

Relevant laws and regulations indicate that an effective AML compliance programme should be risk-based. This is associated with the risk-based approach to money laundering, which is the core of AML regulatory regime. Paragraphs 22 and 23 of the 4th AML directives, for example, provides, in relation to both the Member States and obliged entities, that:

> The risk of money laundering and terrorist financing is not the same in every case. Accordingly, a holistic, risk-based approach should be used. [...] It involves the use of evidence-based decision-making in order to target the risks of money laundering and terrorist financing [...] more effectively. Underpinning the risk-based approach is the need [...] to identify, understand and mitigate the risks of money laundering and terrorist financing that they face.

While the risk-based approach is reflected at the national level by the National Risk Assessment (see HM Treasury and Home Office, 2020), it also presents the core of an effective compliance programme.

Obliged entities must take appropriate steps to undertake assessment of their money laundering risks, taking into account various risk factors associated, for example, with their customers, products and services, transactions, delivery channels and geographical areas. AML supervisors have started releasing various guidance documents to clarify how they plan to assess the effectiveness of these programs, the FCA (2015), for example provides, that:

> Central to meeting your AML obligations is a risk assessment of your firm's business, as it will help you develop effective and proportionate prevention procedures. As the risks change over time, your risk assessment will need to be kept up-to-date. Once these procedures are in place, you will need to make sure that your employees understand and comply with them. You will also need to keep monitoring the procedures to ensure that they continue to be appropriate for your business as it develops, and that they work well.

The risk-based approach to money laundering compliance explains why there remains significant space for corporations to self-regulate.

Clearly, every business will face specific risks, and businesses are best placed to understand those risks. Moreover, defining risk appetite is largely the business decision and should be part of discussions with senior management. The core of these considerations is incorporated into the so-called risk formula.

Figure 8.4 Risk formula.

Figure 8.4 illustrates the risk formula, a model including conventional money laundering risk methodology (see Wolfsber Group, 2015, pp. 7–16). The so-called inherent risk includes risk that exists without any controls in place. Organisations must undertake their own risk assessment and identify appropriate risk mitigation tools, including compliance policies and procedures, due diligence measures, technology, training etc. so as to reduce their risk to an acceptable level. The residual risk, or also 'real risk', is the amount of risk after the application of a mitigation programme. It is up to the organisation and its senior management whether its residual risk meets its risk appetite. Should the residual risk exceed the risk appetite, the organisations might need to reconsider its inherent risk or increase the level of its mitigation programme.

The above discussion illustrates that a thorough understanding of money laundering risk is necessary to determine proportionate and effective systems and controls. While the supervisory bodies often feature sector-specific guidance documents and thematic reviews, there remains significant ambiguity allowing for the heterogeneity of approaches. It is true that the private sector will often criticise public authorities for not being sufficiently specific in what exactly is required in terms of AML compliance. Yet, academic literature has long documented that the significant space for corporations to self-regulate is in general beneficial for businesses (see Gilad, 2014).

Conclusion

This chapter has considered the problem of money laundering and the AML regime. It began by analysing the money laundering process and its limitations. Examples of how money laundering takes place in various stages of the process were provided, before considering the inclusiveness of the legal definition of money laundering. While the common understanding is that money laundering includes the false representation of criminal earnings as legitimate earnings, the legal definition includes the mere possession or any form of handling criminal assets. The catch-all character of this legislative definition offers an opportunity to policing authorities to present many forms and types of criminality as money laundering. Yet, this broad definition also blurs important differences associated with predicate crimes and harm caused by these various crimes. This is ultimately reflected in the struggle to credibly measure the scale of the problem and the effectiveness of the response.

While there is no major issue in the problem-solving and objective-achieving character of the AML regime, the money laundering problem is too complex to be value neutral. Clear and transparent policy choices associated with concrete problems are needed to allow for a more credible assessment of the effectiveness of AML responses. The chapter offers new conceptual-isation of many money-laundering issues as 'vulnerabilities' and 'enablers'. Finally, the chapter offers an analysis and evaluation of the AML regime, the regime based on an intensive interaction between public policing and private policing, and alludes to issues associated with the effectiveness of AML laws, regulations and compliance systems.

Legislation and regulation

Bank Secrecy Act of 1970, No. 91-508, 84 Stat. 1114-2 aka 84 Stat. 1118.

Convention Against Illicit Traffic in Narcotic Drugs and Psychotropic Substances, 20 December 1988, www.unodc.org/pdf/convention_1988_en.pdf

Directive 2015/849 of the European Parliament and of the Council of 20 May 2015 on the prevention of the use of the financial system for the purposes of money laundering or terrorist financing, 2015 O.J. (L 141).

Directive 2018/843 of the European Parliament and of the Council of 30 May 2018 amending Directive (EU) 2015/849 on the prevention of the use of the financial system for the purposes of money laundering or terrorist financing, and amending Directives 2009/138/EC and 2013/36/EU, 2018 O.J. (L 156).

Directive 2018/1673 of the European Parliament and of the Council of 23 October 2018 on combating money laundering by criminal law, 2018 O.J. (L 284).

Racketeer Influenced and Corrupt Organization Act (RICO) of 1970, no. 91-452, 84 Stat. 922-3 aka 84 Stat. 941.

Sarbanes-Oxley Act of 2002, No. 107-204, 116 Stat. 745.

United Nations Convention Against Transnational Organized Crime, 15 November 2000, www.unodc.org/documents/treaties/UNTOC/Publications/TOC%20Convention/TOCebook-e.pdf

Uniting and Strengthening America by Providing Appropriate Tools Required to Intercept and Obstruct Terrorism (US Patriot Act) Act of 2001, No. 107-56, 115 Stat. 272.

Notes

1 See the discussion in Chapter 10, section 'Transgovernmental networks – the case of Financial Action Task Force'.

2   Please note that the UK has opted out from complying directly with the 6th AML Directive.
3   See Chapter 10, section 'National laws against economic crime'.
4   See section 'Legal definition of money laundering' above.

References

Albrecht, C., Duffin, K. M., Hawkins, S., & Morales Rocha, V. M. (2019). The use of cryptocurrencies in the money laundering process. *Journal of Money Laundering Control, 22*(2), 210–216.

Cassella, S. D. (2018). Toward a new model of money laundering: Is the "placement, layering, integration" model obsolete? *Journal of Money Laundering Control, 21*(4), 494–497.

Custers, B. H. M., Pool, R. L. D., & Cornelisse, R. (2019). Banking malware and the laundering of its profits. *European Journal of Criminology, 16*(6), 728–745.

De Sanctis, F. M. (2017). *International money laundering through real estate and agribusiness: A criminal justice perspective from the panama papers.* Springer.

Europol. (2015). *Why is cash still king? A strategic report on the use of cash by criminal groups as a facilitator for money laundering.* www.europol.europa.eu/publications-documents/why-cash-still-king-strategic-report-use-of-cash-criminal-groups-facilitator-for-money-laundering

Europol. (2020). *Internet Organised Crime Threat Assessment (IOCTA 2020 report).* www.europol.europa.eu/activities-services/main-reports/internet-organised-crime-threat-assessment-iocta-2020

Europol. (2021). *European Union Serious and Organised Crime Risk Assessment (SOCTA 2021).* www.europol.europa.eu/activities-services/main-reports/european-union-serious-and-organised-crime-threat-assessment

FATF. (2018). *Professional money laundering (FATF report).* www.fatf-gafi.org/media/fatf/documents/Professional-Money-Laundering.pdf

FATF. (2020). *Money Laundering and the Illegal Wildlife Trade (FATF report).* www.fatf-gafi.org/publications/methodsandtrends/documents/money-laundering-wildlife-trade.html

FCA. (2015). *Money laundering and terrorist financing.* www.fca.org.uk/firms/financial-crime/money-laundering-terrorist-financing

FCA. (2018a). *Money laundering and terrorist financing risks in the e-money sector.* www.fca.org.uk/publications/thematic-reviews/tr18-3-money-laundering-and-terrorist-financing-risks-e-money-sector

FCA. (2018b). *Office of Professional Body Anti-Money Laundering Supervision (OPBAS).* www.fca.org.uk/opbas

Ferwerda, J., van Saase, A., Unger, B., & Getzner, M. (2020). Estimating money laundering flows with a gravity model-based simulation. *Scientific Reports, 10*(1), 18552.

Findley, M. G., Nielson, D. L., & Sharman, J. C. (2015). Causes of noncompliance with international law: A field experiment on anonymous incorporation. *American Journal of Political Science, 59*(1), 146–161.

GAO. (2020). *Trade-based money laundering (report).* www.gao.gov/assets/gao-20-333.pdf

Gelemerova, L. (2011). *The anti-money laundering system in the context of globalisation: A panopticon built on quicksand?* Wolf Legal Publishers.

Gelemerova, L. (2021). *The ultimate goal of effective money laundering is to make it harder for crime money to be enjoyed by criminals and provide leads to underlying crime such as human trafficking, thus disrupting it.* Risk & Compliance Platform Europe. www.riskcompliance.biz/news/dr-liliya-gelemerova-the-ultimate-goal-of-effective-money-laundering-is-to-make-it-harder-for-crime-money-to-be-enjoyed-by-criminals-and-provide-leads-to-underlying-crime-such-as-human-traf/

Gilad, S. (2014). Beyond endogeneity: How firms and regulators co-construct the meaning of regulation. *Law & Policy, 36*(2), 134–164.

Gilmour, N. (2016). Understanding the practices behind money laundering – A rational choice interpretation. *International Journal of Law, Crime & Justice, 44*, 1–13.

Gilmour, P. M. (2020). Lifting the veil on beneficial ownership: Challenges of implementing the UK's registers of beneficial owners. *Journal of Money Laundering Control, 23*(4), 717–734.

Gilmour, P. M. (2021). Freeports: Innovative trading hubs or centres for money laundering and tax evasion? *Journal of Money Laundering Control.* https://doi.org/10.1108/JMLC-01-2021-0002

Halliday, T., Levi, M., & Reuter, P. (2019). Anti-money laundering: An inquiry into disciplinary transnational legal order. *UC Irvine Journal of International, Transnational, and Comparative Law, 4*, 1–25.

Hataley, T. (2020). Trade-based money laundering: Organized crime, learning and international trade. *Journal of Money Laundering Control, 23*(3), 651–661.

Helgesson, K. S., & Mörth, U. (2019). Instruments of securitization and resisting subjects: For-profit professionals in the finance–security nexus. *Security Dialogue, 50*(3), 257–274.

HM Treasury and Home Office. (2020). *National risk assessment of money laundering and terrorist financing 2020.* https://assets.publishing.service.gov.uk/government/uploads/system/uploads/attachment_data/file/945411/NRA_2020_v1.2_FOR_PUBLICATION.pdf

Hock, B. (2020). *Extraterritoriality and international bribery.* Routledge.

Hock, B. (2021). *The Interconnections between Tax Crimes and Corruption in the United Kingdom'* <https://1476934c-816f-43d8-852e-50afda7e77a9.filesusr.com/ugd/860044_bc1241719cfb44869be6fc8aa623b902.pdf

Home Office. (2020). *Asset recovery statistical bulletin.* https://assets.publishing.service.gov.uk/government/uploads/system/uploads/attachment_data/file/923194/asset-recovery-financial-years-2015-to-2020-hosb2320.pdf

Hughes, C. E., Chalmers, J., & Bright, D. A. (2020). Exploring interrelationships between high-level drug trafficking and other serious and organised crime: An Australian study. *Global Crime, 21*(1), 28–50.

Hulme, S., Disley, E., & Blondes, E. L. (Eds.) (2021). *Mapping the risk of serious and organised crime infiltrating legitimate businesses (final report).* European Commission. https://op.europa.eu/en/publication-detail/-/publication/ab3534a2-87a0-11eb-ac4c-01aa75ed71a1/language-en

Levi, M. (2015). Money for crime and money from crime: Financing crime and laundering crime proceeds. *European Journal on Criminal Policy & Research, 21*(2), 275–297.

Levi, M. (2020). Evaluating the control of money laundering and its underlying offences: The search for meaningful data. *Asian Journal of Criminology, 15*(4), 301–320.

Levi, M. (2021). Making sense of professional enablers' involvement in laundering organized crime proceeds and of their regulation. *Trends in Organized Crime, 24*(1), 96–110.

Levi, M., Reuter, P., & Halliday, T. (2018). Can the AML system be evaluated without better data? *Crime Law & Social Change, 69*, 307–328.

Levi, M., & Soudijn, M. R. J. (2020). Understanding the laundering of organized crime money. *Crime & Justice, 49*, 579–631.

Lord, N., Campbell, L. J., & Van Wingerde, K. (2019). Other people's dirty money: Professional intermediaries, market dynamics and the finances of white-collar, corporate and organized crimes. *British Journal of Criminology, 59*(5), 1217–1236.

Lord, N., & Levi, M. (2017). Organizing the finances for and the finances from transnational corporate bribery. *European Journal of Criminology, 14*(3), 365–389.

Lord, N., van Wingerde, K., & Campbell, L. (2018). Organising the monies of corporate financial crimes via organisational structures: Ostensible legitimacy, effective anonymity, and third-party facilitation. *Administrative Sciences, 8*(2), 1–17.

Mendlow, G. S. (2018). Divine justice and the library of Babel: Or, was Al Capone really punished for tax evasion? *Ohio State Journal of Criminal Law, 16*(1), 181–206.

Moiseienko, A., & Keatinge, T. (2019). *The scale of money laundering in the UK (briefing paper)*. RUSI. https://rusi.org/sites/default/files/20190211_moiseienko_and_keatinge_extent_of_money_laundering_web.pdf

National Audit Office. (2019). *Tackling serious and organised crime.* www.nao.org.uk/wp-content/uploads/2019/03/Tackling-serious-and-organised-crime.pdf

NCA. (2019). *National Economic Crime Centre leads push to identify money laundering activity.* www.nationalcrimeagency.gov.uk/news/national-economic-crime-centre-leads-push-to-identify-money-laundering-activity

OECD. (2012). *Phase 3 report on implementing the OECD anti-bribery convention in the United Kingdom.* www.oecd.org/daf/anti-bribery/UnitedKingdomphase3reportEN.pdf

Phillips, C. (2017). From 'rogue traders' to organized crime groups: Doorstep fraud of older adults. *British Journal of Criminology, 57*(3), 608–625.

Pol, R. F. (2019). The global war on money laundering is a failed experiment. *The Conversation.* https://theconversation.com/the-global-war-on-money-laundering-is-a-failed-experiment-125143

Raza, M. S., Zhan, Q., & Rubab, S. (2020). Role of money mules in money laundering and financial crimes a discussion through case studies. *Journal of Financial Crime, 27*(3), 911–931.

Ryder, N. (2013a). To confiscate or not to confiscate? A comparative analysis of the confiscation of the proceeds of crime legislation in the United States and the United Kingdom. *Journal of Business Law, 8*, 767–798.

Ryder, N. (2013b). *Money laundering – An endless cycle? A comparative analysis of the anti-money laundering policies in the United States of America, the United Kingdom, Australia and Canada.* Routledge.

Ryder, N. (2015). *The financial war on terrorism: A review of counter-terrorist financing strategies since 2001.* Routledge.

Sarkar, S. (2015). Trade in human beings: Evidence of money laundering from sex trafficking in India and the UK. *Journal of Transnational* Management, 20(2), 107-125.

SEC. (2021). *SEC charges California-based fraudster with selling "insider tips" on the Dark Web.* www.sec.gov/news/press-release/2021-51

Solicitors Regulation Authority. (2018). *Preventing money laundering and financing of terrorism.* www.sra.org.uk/sra/how-we-work/reports/preventing-money-laundering-financing-terrorism/

Soudijn, M. R. J. (2014). Using strangers for money: A discussion on money-launderers in organized crime. *Trends in Organized Crime, 17*(3), 199–217. http://doi:10.1007/s12117-014-9217-9

Soudijn, M. R. J. (2016). Rethinking money laundering and drug trafficking: Some implications for investigators, policy makers and researchers. *Journal of Money Laundering Control, 19*(3), 298–310.

Soudijn, M. R. J., & Reuter, P. (2016). Cash and carry: The high cost of currency smuggling in the drug trade. *Crime, Law and Social Change, 66*(3), 271–290.

Transparency International. (2016). *London property: A top destination for money launderers.* https://issuu.com/transparencyuk/docs/final_s041329_v8_hrnc__1_

United Nations Environment Programme. (2016). *Strategic report, environment, peace and security, a convergence of threats.* https://wedocs.unep.org/20.500.11822/17008

UNODC. (2017). *Money laundering.* www.unodc.org/unodc/en/money-laundering/overview.html

UNODC. (2020). *Global study on firearms trafficking.* www.unodc.org/unodc/en/firearms-protocol/firearms-study.html

Walker, J., & Unger, B. (2009). Measuring global money laundering: "The walker gravity model". *Review of Law and Economics, 5*(2), 821–853.

Wolfsberg Group. (2015). *The Wolfsberg frequently asked questions on risk assessments for money laundering, sanctions and bribery & corruption.* www.wolfsberg-principles.com/sites/default/files/wb/pdfs/faqs/17.%20Wolfsberg-Risk-Assessment-FAQs-2015.pdf

Zali, M. & Maulidi, A. (2018). Fighting against money laundering. *BRICS Law Journal, 5*(3), 40–63.

Zavoli, I., & King, C. (2020). New development: Estate agents' perspectives of anti-money laundering compliance-four key issues in the UK property market. *Public Money & Management, 40*(5), 415–419.

Zavoli, I., & King, C. (2021). The challenges of implementing anti-money laundering regulation: An empirical analysis. *Modern Law Review, 84*(4), 740–771.

Chapter 9

Explaining economic crime

Introduction

One of the author's sons plays cricket and in the course of watching him, one would not expect to hear largely middle class parents openly talking about engaging in criminality. However, over the years, these are some of the stories that have been recounted. 'Our house was burgled and we knew part of our loss was not covered, so we had to exaggerate the claim by adding a whole series of fictitious items' (insurance fraud); 'X Builders are very good and they will always give you a discount for cash!' (tax fraud); 'I know a very good merchant in Hong Kong who can make any cricket, football, rugby shirt you like and they are as good as the real thing!' (intellectual property [IP] crime). One of the authors was recently on a commuter train to London and two men dressed in suits sat in front were discussing their different strategies for fiddling their travel expenses and avoiding detection (fraud).

Now imagine if those same parents at the cricket had been discussing how they experienced problems climbing through their neighbours window to steal their jewellery (burglary) or the two men on the train had been discussing their plans for robbing the local betting shop. Society's perception of economic crime is very different from traditional volume crimes, viewed by many as not a real crime. Just as Sutherland (1945) was stirred by this kind of social apathy to ask, 'Is "white collar crime" crime?', this chapter asks, 'Is "economic crime" crime?'

The chapter uses the analogy of a ladder to describe the steps a person descends in order to reach the crucial point where he or she commits the economic crime act. Not all these steps are essential but they illustrate a range of factors that make decisions to commit economic crimes easier and more palatable than traditional volume crimes. The chapter starts by considering social perceptions of the status of economic crimes. It then moves on to explore why, in comparison to traditional acquisitive crimes, people find it easier to rationalise that economic crime is not morally wrong. An essential component of all economic crimes, opportunity, is then considered along with the capability required to exploit opportunities. Three theories are then

DOI: 10.4324/9781003081753-9

introduced, which seek to explain key social influences that lead people to accept economic crime as a socially acceptable, reasonable and appropriate course of action. The chapter subsequently uses strain theory to briefly discuss the motivational pressures driving people to contemplate economic crime. The final step on the ladder to the commission of an economic crime is the rational choice perspective where the individual considers whether the crime is worth taking the risks.

Is 'economic crime' crime?

Knowledge they are crimes

If you were to walk into a classroom of school children and ask them if stealing from a shop or breaking into another person's house to steal their laptop was wrong and a crime, there would likely be near universal agreement they are both crimes. However, ask them about a series of economic crimes and there might be more confusion.

Such is the nature of some economic crimes; some people do not even realise they are crimes. Some contractors do not realise that colluding in contract bidding is market manipulation and a crime. Indeed, Shepherd (2016) interviewed a director of a company who did not realise such market collusion was illegal. There are a variety of IP crimes that some might consider as roguish or mischievous, but not really wrong, such as selling counterfeit Manchester United shirts. Some people might not realise that exaggerating income or omitting certain information on a mortgage application is fraud. Many, like the fellow train passengers, do not even realise that exaggerating expense claims is a crime because it is so common (Bristol Post, 2021).

Money mules might not realise that allowing their bank accounts to be used to receive cash is a criminal offence. Indeed, the uptake in such activity led Cifas, UK Finance and the police to launch a campaign highlighting the criminality of such activities, 'Don't be fooled – don't become a money mule' (see https://moneymules.co.uk/). Imagine that a friend tells you that his employer is about to announce a major discovery that causes the company's share price to rocket. It would be rational for you to buy shares now and cash them in after the announcement, but this would be an insider dealing offence. Such is the nature and everyday circumstances of these kinds of economic crime that many people do not know they are crimes. People learn from an early age that stealing, robbing and breaking into another's house are wrong. However, young children are not taught about market collusion, IP crime, application fraud, money laundering, insider dealing and data privacy.

Willingness to engage in economic crime

Many people are willing to perpetrate economic crime because they do not realise it is crime. Furthermore, even when some people are aware the acts are proscribed, they do not regard them as 'real' crimes. The social pathway to accepting economic crime as reasonable and appropriate behaviour is discussed later in this chapter. The large Ipsos MORI (2017) survey in the UK found that fraud and commercial crime are their lowest priorities, lower than online abuse, anti-social behaviour and other non-crimes. The regular Institute of Business Ethics (2018) surveys provide further evidence from across the European Union (EU) on attitudes to petty misconduct. For example, 9% think that minor exaggeration of travel expenses is acceptable. Karstedt and Farrall (2007) found that the majority (61%) of people in the UK have at some time committed at least one minor 'everyday crime', such as stealing something from work, falsely claiming refunds or padding an insurance claim. They further found that a significant minority of the public is willing to engage in such everyday crimes: for example, 22% of the public in England and Wales, and 40% in Germany, would consider padding insurance claims (Karstedt & Farrall, 2006). Similarly, research in America discovered one in four think it is acceptable to exaggerate an insurance claim (Accenture Newsroom, 2003).

Public attitudes are also more accepting of bribery. Transparency International (2021) research in the EU found that 7% of public service users had paid a bribe in the previous 12 months, with Romania one of the highest at 20% and Bulgaria at 19%. At the lower end Denmark, Finland and Sweden had rates of 1%, Germany 3% and France 5%, with mid-range countries such as Belgium at 10% and Austria at 9%. Globally, Transparency International (2017) found one in four have paid a bribe to access public services. The context of bribery is such that some people might have been forced to pay bribes to access public services, but not all, and some would have willingly paid. In a study of convicted bribery offenders, Button et al. (2018a) interviewed one senior executive who recalled how the sales training he received during the 1980s and 1990s included training on how to bribe. Another convicted senior manager rationalised that paying bribes to win contracts is a normal part of commerce in some countries:

> My own view was always … if you don't like it, don't go there. But if you do like it, and you want to go there, and you need the business, then keep your mouth shut and play by the rules … And we might find their laws archaic and whatever, but they are the laws. And if it's perceived as the way to do business, well then you must be prepared to do it.
>
> (Button et al., 2018a, p. 895)

IP crime is one of the economic crimes that people are most open to. In part, this reflects that it is not a criminal offence in most countries to intentionally purchase counterfeit products or download pirated products for personal consumption. The European Union Intellectual Property Office (EUIPO, 2017) study in 2017 found:

- 7% of those surveyed had purchased counterfeit products intentionally.
- This rises to 15% of 15–24 of the year old group who had purchased counterfeit products intentionally.
- 10% had intentionally accessed, downloaded or streamed content from illegal websites.
- This rises to 27% of the 15–24 year group who had intentionally accessed, downloaded or streamed content from illegal websites (EUIPO, 2017).

The same research also tested the attitudes towards different types of counterfeiting and piracy across the EU and in individual states. The results showed significant acceptance of these types of behaviour, and they reveal a range of rationalisations that excuse the behaviour:

- 27% agreed that it is acceptable to purchase counterfeit products when the price for the original and authentic product is too high (41% in the 15–24 age group).
- 24% agreed it is acceptable to buy counterfeit products when the original product is not or not yet available where you live (39% in the 15–24 age group).
- 35% thought it was acceptable to obtain content illegally from the Internet when it is for personal use.
- 31% thought it is acceptable to obtain content illegally from the Internet when there is no immediately available legal alternative (43% in the 15–24 age group).
- 30% consider that consuming counterfeit products is an act of protest against the market-driven economy and premium brands (45% in the 15–24 age group).

There is also evidence from a body of experimental research – often with students – that shows many people will engage in dishonest, fraudulent-type behaviours and bribery. For example, Dan Ariely has conducted extensive experiments to test the dishonesty of people under different conditions (Ariely, 2012). One experiment explored whether signing a statement of honesty at the start or at the end of a form impacts on levels of dishonesty (Shu et al., 2012); it found that cheating was lowest (37%) when participants signed at the start, compared to 79% who cheated when signing at the end. In a role-playing experiment, Köbis et al. (2017) found that participants were prepared to pay bribes to win a game. There are clearly limitations with these kinds of gaming-based experiments, but they do provide further support for the propensity of people to cheat when given the opportunity.

Some studies have involved deep investigations into how a society can develop a culture of corruption, which normalises a wide variety of petty corrupt acts, such as Smith's (2010) anthropological study of Nigeria. Organisational studies have also illustrated how occupational economic crimes can become normalised within organisational cultures (see Ditton, 1977; Mars, 1982). In an extensive study involving 9,175 employees of 45 organisations, Hollinger and Clark (1983) found that one-third of employees offend at least once per year. This result again indicates that fraud is committed by ordinary people as they go about their daily lives. Their data suggests that most employee fraudsters are occasional offenders, but a small minority of around 7% are habitual offenders who perpetrate 68% of the frauds. Indeed, developing strong ethical cultures has been identified as a key component to reducing fraud (Suh & Sim, 2020).

Rationalisation and neutralisation

There are some individuals whose morality and respect for normative social values is so weak that they have no inhibitions in contemplating deviance or even very serious crime. These psychopathic individuals lack human empathy and any sense of guilt for their egregious behaviour (Hare, 1999). Despots and vicious murderers are obvious examples. Some economic criminals are similarly psychologically defective in lacking any sense of morality or guilt in stealing victims' life-savings. However, most people do have strong attachments to society and the prevailing social norms. Their sense of social morality acts as a restraint against contemplating deviant or criminal behaviour. Consequently, for most offenders, overcoming these inhibitions is a key step on the pathway to criminality.

Ordinary, otherwise law-abiding citizens sideline any sense of wrongness in their planned behaviour by constructing justifications for the behaviour. This cognitive process of constructing rationalisations for deviance was first identified by Ernest Jones, a psychotherapist (Jones, 1908). It is a recognised symptom of some personality disorders that can lead to anti-social attitudes and behaviours (Vinkers et al., 2011). Sutherland (1940) acknowledged the role of rationalisation in community-based crime and white-collar crime. It is also a key component of Cressey's (1953) fraud theory.

In their study of delinquents, Sykes and Matza (1957) later argued that the *rationalisations* are important in *neutralising* a person's inhibitions in choosing a deviant course of action. The terms rationalisation and neutralisation now tend to be used interchangeably. They described five techniques of neutralisation (i.e. rationalisations): denial of responsibility, denial of injury, denial of victim, condemnation of condemners and appeal to higher loyalties. White-collar crime researchers have identified additional techniques, most notably that corporate crime is normal (Benson, 1985) and the intention of the fraudster is to borrow money and not steal it (Cressey, 1953). These seven techniques are briefly described in Table 9.1 using scenarios to illustrate their application in economic crime and traditional crime. Either in isolation or in combination, the techniques enable the offender to rationalise their deviant or criminal behaviour as morally acceptable. Defining the behaviour

Table 9.1 Techniques of neutralisation applied to organisational settings

Rationalisation technique	Example rationalisations for economic crimes	Example rationalisations for traditional crimes
Denial of responsibility: offenders accept the act is wrong but believe they have no choice or are pressured to do it by others	Senior management pressure me to pay the bribes because they need the contract	It was not my fault, my friends dragged me into peddling the drugs
Denial of injury: the act is not wrong because no one is harmed by it	The company makes huge profits, so exaggerating the expenses will not harm it	Stealing the laptop was not an issue; the company has just bought hundreds and will not miss a few
Denial of the victim: the victim is not really a victim and deserves it	Insurance companies always deny paying out claims, so they deserve to be defrauded	Banks overcharge customers, so they deserve to be robbed
Condemnation of the condemners: the act is justified because those condemning the behaviour are the problems	The politicians are corrupt, so they cannot criticise paying bribes to win business	The energy companies rip everyone off, so they cannot blame me for stealing electricity
Appeal to higher loyalties: the act is justified by a higher moral standard	We should get involved in the price-fixing cartel, otherwise the company might collapse and lots of workers will lose their jobs	I lost my job so I had to burgle the pawnbroker for my family
Normal: everybody does it	It is acceptable to do these things because everybody pads insurance claims, exaggerates expenses, buys counterfeits, downloads pirated products and pays bribes in some countries	Everybody is a thief, so it is acceptable to shoplift videos and software
Borrowing: the money was borrowed, not stolen	The frauds are a way for me to borrow money from my employer, and I will pay it back	I broke into the school to borrow the money, not steal it

as morally acceptable thus neutralises the restraining effects of internal and external social controls. It frees the offender to engage in deviance or crime whilst maintaining his or her moral self-image. Compared to traditional crime, the absence of physical force makes economic crimes well-suited to rationalisations or techniques of neutralisation.

The organisational context of all the scenarios in Table 9.1 means that the offences are impersonal and therefore easier to rationalise. Nevertheless, the rationalisations for the economic crimes are more acceptable than the traditional crimes. There is some plausibility in the excuses for the economic crimes, but the traditional crimes are clearly not right. The piracy example is particularly illuminating. It is far easier to rationalise downloading pirated videos or software than it is to rationalise shoplifting videos and software, yet they lead to the same outcome, the theft of a rightful owner's property.

To a lesser extent, these differences in perceived acceptability also apply to crimes against individuals. Consider the difference between a fraud and a mugging committed against a female pensioner.

Fraud

A fraudster targets a victim with a phone call, wins her confidence and tricks her into handing over her banking details, which enables him to empty the victim's bank account. The fraudster is able to rationalise his actions are not wrong and neutralise his self-control inhibitions as follows: denial of injury (no physical attack, she will get the money back from the bank), denial of victim (she willingly gave information over) and appeal to higher loyalties (the money is needed for food for the fraudster's family).

Mugging

A mugger sees a woman walk away from an ATM outside a bank, snatches her bag causing her to fall over and runs off with the money she has just withdrawn. This is much harder to rationalise and neutralise as there is immediate, physical harm to a proximal victim, and the criminal has to physically engage with her and hear her screams as he runs off. He may have even physically hurt her. It is harder to justify that she deserves the attack and the damage inflicted justified the placing of food on the table.

Economic crimes are therefore much more susceptible to rationalisations that make the offences feel justifiable, which in turn neutralises external controls and internal restraints. A substantial body of work has examined rationalisation in the context of economic crime (Albrecht et al., 1982; Braithwaite, 1992; Coleman, 2006; Cressey, 1953; Ditton, 1977; Goldstraw-White, 2011; Mars, 1982; Shepherd & Button, 2018; Wolfe & Hermanson, 2004) and has identified the following types:

- The victim deserved it.
- Management treats us badly and deserves it.
- I am underpaid and undervalued.
- It is normal, everybody else does it.

- This is normal behaviour in those countries.
- It had to be done to save the company.
- Excessive taxation by a wasteful government.
- It is a small amount of money that will not be missed.
- Just borrowing the money: the money will be repaid.
- The proceeds of the crime were used for a better purpose.
- Nobody was physically hurt.
- They are overcharging for these products.
- They will be reimbursed by the banks.
- The victims are in another country where they are all rich.

Opportunities to commit economic crimes

A fundamental step on the ladder to explaining any type of crime is opportunity: a crime cannot be committed if there is not the opportunity to do so. There has been a great deal of research to illustrate how crime is related to opportunity (for example, Clarke, 1980; Mayhew et al., 1976). In one study conducted by the UK's Home Office, the researchers found that changing the fuel supply from toxic town gas to non-toxic natural gas reduced the suicide rate because it removed the opportunity for the preferred method of suicide:

> It seems reasonable, therefore, to conclude that the overall decline of the national rate of suicide for England and Wales in the 1960s and 1970s was due to the elimination of domestic gas poisoning as a method, and, further, that this observation constitutes powerful evidence of the role of opportunity in suicide.
>
> (Clarke & Mayhew, 1989, p.36)

A great deal of academic research and the efforts of practitioners are devoted to identifying opportunities. They are the risks that security and compliance specialists seek to eliminate or mitigate. Cressey (1953) famously based his fraud theory on opportunity, rationalisation and financial pressure. It should be emphasised that the theory focuses on employee fraudsters who perpetrate their crimes alone, and not in collaboration or conspiracy with anyone else. The theory stipulates that the three conditions need to be present for a lone employee to commit fraud against their employer: an employee under personal financial pressure with the opportunity to commit the fraud, and rationalisations to justify the fraud (Figure 9.1). Occupational fraudsters have the opportunities because they are employees and because they have access to the organisations' systems and assets. Albrecht et al. (1982) later described Cressey's theory as the fraud triangle. Wolfe and Hermanson (2004) later included 'capability' as an additional dimension to highlight that a person needs the capability or skills to exploit the opportunity.

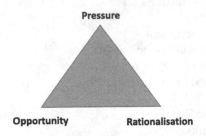

Figure 9.1 Fraud triangle.

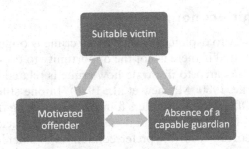

Figure 9.2 Routine activity theory.

Opportunity became a core feature in explaining crime for many academics and practitioners. In particular, Cohen and Felson (1979) noticed how crime rates in America increased due to increased prosperity because prosperity provides many more opportunities for crimes: there are more potential victims with more money, cars and other possessions. Focusing on traditional, acquisitive crimes, they developed routine activity theory, which explains how crimes occur during the everyday routine activities of victims and offenders. Crime occurs when three factors coincide at a particular time and place: a motivated offender, a suitable victim and the absence of a capable guardian (Figure 9.2). The target victim and the absence of the capable guardian can be considered as components of the opportunity: a victim's home presents the opportunity to a burglar, and weak security enables the opportunity to be exploited. Several researchers have linked routine activity to economic crimes such as IP crime, fraud and cybercrime (Hollis et al., 2015; Hollis & Wilson, 2014; Leukfeldt & Yar 2016; Pratt et al., 2010).

People are confronted every day with relatively easy opportunities to commit economic crimes for themselves or for their employers. Ordinary people have hundreds of opportunities a year to potentially engage in economic crime. Consider an ordinary worker, who is a homeowner and engages in a typical range of routine activities. In their working life, they might make expense claims, over-time claims, and have access to sick pay, all of which provide opportunities for fraud. At home, they falsify their car insurance application to reduce the premiums and pad the house insurance claim following a water leak. They have a sideline in buying counterfeit goods from China and selling them online. They falsify their tax returns by failing to declare this additional income.

Many people have even more valuable opportunities. An accountant might have sole responsibility for the transfer of his employer's money. A buyer presides over the decisions to award contracts, thus providing opportunities for bribery. Some staff members have access to sensitive product development data on the organisation's IT systems that could be sold to a competitor. False advertising just requires a few strokes on a keyboard. A person owning an electrical contractor might play football with competitors leading them to discuss rigging a competitive bid for a contract. Business executives routinely talk to their competitors, so it is easy to slip into the conversation the idea of agreeing with minimum prices. Compared to traditional acquisitive crime, the growing complexities of modern life provide far more people with far more routine opportunities to commit economic crime, and with the potential for far greater financial reward.

The emergence of the digital economy has also provided career criminals and organised crime groups with innumerable opportunities to engage in economic crime within the routine activities of our digital lives (May & Bhardwa, 2017). The immediacy and reach of the connected world has facilitated unprecedented levels of economic crime as a business. It is very easy to advertise non-existent items on eBay or dishonestly exaggerate product descriptions. Shop and drop logistics makes it very easy to set up a simple website and sell counterfeit products sourced from China (see Chapter 6). It is easy to create bogus invoices to defraud organisations and consumers. Most company logos are instantly available online to facilitate the creation of false trademarks and false documents. Phone numbers, emails and credit card details can be purchased on the dark web (Wang et al., forthcoming). Romance frauds are perpetrated remotely using false identities (Cross & Holt, 2021). Indeed, all these crimes can be perpetrated with no physical presence, in a distant place beyond the gaze or reach of law enforcement.

The volume of opportunities for cyber-enabled economic crime, the ease with which they can be perpetrated, and the low risks of encountering law enforcement stand in sharp contrast to traditional 'professional' crimes such as drug dealing, arms trafficking and burglary. These physical world crimes require particular skills, organisation and a physical presence; they are also higher risk from the perspective of the criminal as they attract the attention of policing agencies.

Capability

Wolfe and Hermanson (2004) highlighted the importance of capability in perpetrating frauds. This observation also applies to other economic crimes. Cyber-enabled and dependent economic crimes require the offender to have specialist skills, or access to someone with specialist skills. Bribery and cartel offences require negotiating capabilities. Producing counterfeits requires specialist design, manufacturing and logistics skills. However, many economic crimes do not require specialist skills. Lying on application forms, padding insurance claims, falsifying invoices and buying and selling counterfeits are all easy crimes to commit. Furthermore, as Chapters 2 and 5 illustrated, it is becoming increasingly easy to purchase some skills. The simplicity of the cheating and deceptions required for many economic crimes distinguishes them from traditional crimes that yield similar returns. Burglary, for example, requires a particular set of skills in planning, execution and escape that few people possess (Nee & Meenaghan, 2006).

Personality determinants of economic crime

Unlike conventional criminals, there has been very little research into the personality traits of economic criminals. Collins and Schmidt (1993) conducted a survey of 365 imprisoned white-collar offenders and comparable white-collar non-offenders in America and found that the offender sample had greater tendencies towards low conscientiousness involving irresponsibility, lack of dependability and disregard for rules. In contrast, a study of 76 German white-collar offenders by Blickle et al. (2006) found they were more likely to have high conscientiousness, but low behavioural self-control, high hedonism and high narcissism. A smaller study of 17 convicted occupational offenders by Nee et al. (2019) indicated that occupational offenders involved in bribery are personable liars with higher than usual self-control.

No overall conclusions can be drawn from these results because they are contradictory, based on small samples of serious offenders who have come to the attention of the authorities, and based solely on occupational offenders. The findings therefore do not at all reflect the broad population of economic crime offenders. There is not as yet a persuasive body of research about the personality determinants of economic crime. The sociological determinants discussed in the next section are, however, better understood.

Social pathway to economic crime

Cressey's (1953) research into the aetiology of fraud narrowly focused on a specific type of offender, a lone employee, and a specific type of offence, fraud against an employer, and a specific motivation, a secret financial pressure. The theory does not consider the social trajectory of offenders that leads to the contemplation and commission of crime other than that they are experiencing financial distress. This section discusses three related concepts: differential association, pathogen theory and differential rationalisation. All three theories explain important social influences that lead people to accept economic crime as a socially acceptable, reasonable and appropriate course of action.

Differential association

Sutherland's theory of differential association is a very important social learning theory that has been used to explain both white collar and other types of criminality (Sutherland et al., 1992, p. 88). The essence of the theory is that criminality is learnt, and that if a person is exposed to more cues favouring a particular course of action than not, they are more likely to engage in it. Proximal social groups such as family, communities, gangs and workplaces provide the behavioural cues for engaging in or rejecting criminality. Individuals are more likely to become criminals when they associate more with those who favour crime over those who disapprove of crime.

In an organisational context, employees conform to the ethical climate and prevailing normative values of their employers. Consequently, if the ethical climate is corrupt to the extent that it normalises and promotes illegal activities such as bribery and cartel price-fixing, then employees are more likely to rationalise that economic crime is normal (Benson, 1985). The theory extends to market sectors and national cultures. Research has illustrated how subcultures nurture and normalise economic crime in organisational, community and family contexts. Sutherland (1949) demonstrated how young adults embarking on their professional careers were inducted into white-collar criminality by their managers and colleagues. Ditton (1977) and Mars (1982) later showed how occupational fraud is learnt from colleagues in the workplace. Smith (2010) has shown how youths are sucked into the '419' mass-marketing scam community in Nigeria, whilst Button et al. (2017) exposed the importance of local communities in engaging in cash-for-crash insurance fraud. These studies illustrate that economic crime is a very social activity, one that is learnt from others and is very frequently perpetrated in conspiracy with others.

Differential rationalisation

Differential association explains that people are more likely to acquire criminal ways within communities, subcultures and organisations that actively promote criminality rather than actively condemn it. In a study of organisational cultures, Shepherd and Button (2018) found that positive messaging in favour of criminality is not necessary for economic crime to emerge and thrive. A culture of economic criminality can emerge in a reputable organisation because of the absence of messages that condemn economic crime, even when the organisation is a victim of the crimes. It therefore relates to the messages in policies, procedures and training that espouse an organisation's values. However, more importantly, it is concerned with the meaningful messages that are represented in the way that an organisation resources and organises its security systems, and most importantly in how an organisation responds to economic crime incidents by enforcing its rules and the law.

Shepherd and Button (2018) found that public and private sector organisations construct rationalisations for not dealing with economic crime. Managers find justifications and excuses for avoiding the difficulties of tackling economic crime and investigating incidents properly. These avoidant rationalisations are very similar to the rationalisations that the criminal uses to engage in the crimes; for example, protecting the organisation's reputation from adverse publicity (higher loyalty); not dealing with an offender because she is an effective employee (higher loyalty); economic crime is normal; it is just a budgeted business cost (denial of injury). Although the avoidant rationalisations do not actively promote criminality, they encourage the acceptance of criminality and excuse weak guardianship, which makes organisations more vulnerable.

Differential rationalisation theory states that economic crime is more likely to occur in an organisation when messages in favour of ignoring the crime are in excess of the messages calling for the rules and the law to be enforced. These positive messages do include the proclamations of executives espousing positive ethical values, but the loudest messages are delivered when the law is visibly enforced. Conversely, the most destructive messages are heard when the law is ignored.

Corruptor pathogen theory

Corruptor pathogen theory is a particular form of differential association in the organisational context because it uses an interactive social network approach to examine relationships between people and organisational controls. It was developed by Button et al. (2018a) to explain bribery. The theory states that there must be relationships between at least three components to successfully complete a bribe: a human corruptor pathogen, a human submissive pathogen, and a resident system pathogen. The corruptor pathogen is the person seeking to engage in a corrupt conspiracy (e.g. bribery) with another. The submissive pathogen is the person who submits to the corrupt invitation of the corruptor pathogen. The resident pathogen is the latent weakness within the operational controls of an organisation, and which is exploited by the two human pathogens.

Corruptor pathogens use a wide range of strategies to carefully groom and recruit submissive pathogens. The simplest and most common inducement is money, the so-called kickback, but it can be anything of value, such as a holiday, car or school fees. Sometimes coercive strategies call on higher loyalty rationalisations that emphasise the needs of a business and job security (Sykes & Matza, 1957), sometimes they involve direct threats (Button et al., 2018a).

However, the success of the corrupt relationship does rely on the opportunity provided by weaknesses in organisational controls, and the capability of a conspirator to exploit the weaknesses. Organisations with robust and resilient controls are less susceptible to corrupt infections because they minimise the opportunities. On the other hand, where a weak ethical climate is indifferent to corruption, or where inadequate controls allow the infection to spread, employees, suppliers and customers come to learn that corruption is normal in the organisation. The environment thus provides them with the rationalisations to perpetrate the crimes whilst they learn how to commit them by way of differential association.

Although the theory originally focused on bribery, it can be applied to any kind of economic crime conspiracy where corrupt relationships are groomed and nurtured, including fraud conspiracies and hard-core cartels (see Chapters 3 and 4). There has been no research into the process of forming hard-core cartels; nevertheless, their reliance on secrecy and a small, select group of trusted individuals makes them amenable to pathogen theory. Although the theory provides a general explanation for the emergence of economic criminality within a subculture, such as an organisation, an industry, or a local community, it does not explain the sole, individual offender. Furthermore, it does not explain the underlying motivations and pressures that push people onto the path of economic criminality.

Motivation and pressure

Turning now to motivational pressures, motivation is an essential psychological component of nearly all crimes, except perhaps those involving negligence. It is a core component of both the fraud triangle and routine activity theory. Motivation is a slippery concept because it comes in a myriad of forms from boredom to poverty and ideology. In the context of economic crime, Karstedt (2016) conveniently summarises motivations as need, greed or lure. Greed and lure are arguably just forms of need: greed is the need to acquire an excessive amount of assets, and lure is the need to acquire a shiny trinket, designer brand or work of art. Financial distress is frequently cited as an understandably powerful motivational need (Albrecht et al., 1982; Cressey, 1953; Wolf & Hermansen, 2004).

However, other motivations often lie beneath these financial pressures, such as excessive debt, undue family or peer pressure, fear of failing, gambling or addictions (Albrecht et al., 1983; Coleman, 1992; Duffield & Grabosky, 2001). Motivations are often altruistic or ideological, for example, the need to support one's employer and colleagues' jobs, or the need to protest against the perceived evils of capitalism. The pressures can also be very malign, involving coercion or outright blackmail (Button et al., 2018a; Donegan & Ganon, 2008). A common feature of all these motivations is the psychological strain to obtain something or achieve something.

Strain theory

The basis of strain theory is Merton's (1938) anomie theory. It is concerned with the broad societal pressures for individuals to achieve a set of socially prescribed goals. These goals are increasingly focused upon materialistic issues such as the accumulation of consumer goods, a house, a car and regular holidays. It is sometimes described as 'keeping up with the Joneses'. However, not everyone has the ability or access to the legitimate opportunities to achieve the socially prescribed lifestyle, sometimes characterised as the 'American dream' (Tierney, 2013). The combination of societal expectations and frustrated ambitions can create sufficient psychological strains that some people resort to illegitimate means to achieve those objectives (Newburn, 2017). Agnew (1992) later expanded the theory to include the strains arising from more localised and personal pressures from family, friends, colleagues and managers to succeed, not to let others down, and at the very least not to fail.

Strain is a psychological phenomenon and therefore blind to the socio-economic status of people. At the lower end of the social spectrum, the strain may be poverty that means insufficient food for a family. Unprecedented rates of innovation have brought the strain of acquiring the latest gadget, cable TV and designer brands. At the higher end of the social spectrum, global competition has increased the pressure to deliver more profit to justify keeping a well-paid job. In some cases, these strains combine into powerful forces; for example, an owner of a struggling business faces the strain of losing her income, not providing for her family, making employees redundant with the impact on their families, not paying small suppliers, letting customers down and facing the stigma of failure.

Strain theory is well suited to many economic crimes as they provide relatively easy ways for individuals to resolve the psychological strains. Bribery, fraud and hard-core cartels deliver the results at work. Welfare fraud relieves the pressure on a parent to support the family. Buying shiny counterfeit brands enables consumers to keep up with their friends. Operating boiler room scams provides the funds for high living. One of the offenders interviewed by Button et al. (2019, p. 147) explained the aspirational strains that motivated his engagement in occupational corruption:

> And so I just wanted to not be the normal, live in three bed semi land, no disrespect to anyone who lives in three bed semi land, but I had a picture in my head when I was 15, 16 of what I wanted and I was going to

do everything I possibly could to get it. Growing up I established myself
in the early 80s, it was a time where greed was good, debt was good,
getting into debt was the best thing to do because it made you get up
in the morning and work hard. I took all the Americanisms and did it,
Thatcher's child and everything else. And I decided that I was going to
make £1m by the time I was 30, and so I got into finance. But being that
I was … I wasn't accepted in the circles that my brain should've allowed
me to be accepted in, if that makes sense.

This quote from a successful businessman illustrates how strain created
motivations to succeed. Once he became successful, strain spurred him on
to seek more wealth and higher status by corrupt means. Strain theory also
explains why some individuals' hunger for power leads them to illegitimate
methods. Organised crime groups and despots are driven by wealth and
power. Terrorist groups are driven by power and ideology and will adopt the
most wicked methods to realise their ambitions.

Critical perspectives

There is a strong vein criminology scholarship preoccupied with criticism
of capitalism and the inherent criminogenic consequences of such economic structures (see Bittle et al., 2018; Gordon, 1973). They argue that the
competition inherent in the structure of the free market economy creates
strains within businesses that inevitably lead to white-collar criminality,
thus furthering the wealth and power interests of the elite at the expense
of the workers (Barnett, 1981; Gordon, 1973). Coleman (1992) describes
corporations as criminogenic because managers are pressured into delivering
profits and returns to shareholders by any means including crime. He argued
that corporations have to ethically numb employees to deliver these goals.
Differential association and shared rationalisations are the sociological
processes for creating this numbness within weak ethical climates. Tombs
and Whyte (2015) argued that the only way to combat the pressures that
create immoral corporate environments is to abolish corporations in their
current form. Although these perspectives are somewhat extreme, they do
support Sutherland's (1940) more measured assertion that, for example, the
secret bribery and hard-core cartel offences of corporations are financially
huge and do cause widespread harm.

The profit motive of capitalism also creates strains outside the business
environment, within those who ideologically object to capitalism, especially the
power enjoyed by the mega-corporations. These strains can lead to economic
crime against corporations assisted by denial of victim rationalisations: the
corporations deserve it because they overcharge, are too powerful and create
social inequality. These ideological motives and rationalisations are apparent
in the 30% of citizens who regard purchasing counterfeits as an act of protest

against the market-driven economy and premium brands (EUIPO, 2017). Some piracy groups are strongly motivated by an ideology that rejects IP rights, claiming that the laws serve the selfish interests of the big corporations. So-called warez groups believe that online access to movies, music, games and software should be free to all and not just to those who can afford it (Urbas, 2006).

Deterrence and rational choice

Standing on the last run of our ladder, the potential offender considers the chances of getting caught and punished. The central question is whether these risks are sufficient to deter the offender. *Deterrence theory* is a cornerstone of justice systems. The idea is that crime control is achieved through *specific* and *general* deterrence (Paternoster & Bachman, 2012). Specific deterrence is where an offender is subjected to punishments which deter them from acting in the same way again. General deterrence is where persons see others getting caught and punished for crimes and therefore view such activities as too risky and wrong. Thus, for deterrence to work most effectively, the following would be required:

- Laws that designate behaviours as wrong and are widely understood.
- Law enforcement that always catches lawbreakers.
- Punishments that are severe enough to deter such behaviours.

Deterrence is based on *rational choice theory*: the assumption that most people are rational and calculate the risks of being caught against the benefits of the crime (Newburn, 2017). Becker (1968) argued that people will commit an offence if the 'expected utility' of the crime is positive, i.e. the advantages outweigh the disadvantages. The desired benefit may be money, a car, a computer or illegal software; it may also be excitement, fun, prestige, defiance or sexual gratification. The costs can include the monetary cost or effort required to perpetrate the crime, the risks of being caught, the level of punishment and more subtle consequences such as the disapproval of others. Deterrence and rational choice clearly link to opportunity theory in that an opportunity vaporises if a potential offender rejects it as too risky. However, it is important to emphasise that this would be the subjective view of one person; another person may well accept the risk. Therefore, opportunities cannot usually be viewed in a binary fashion (opportunity or not), because they depend on the subjective perceptions of offenders (Cornish & Clark, 2003).

As previously explained, the required investment in effort, skills and costs to commit many economic crimes is low. In these situations, the rational choice calculation for a contemplated economic crime is the chance of being caught by the authorities. Unfortunately, economic crime is not a police priority, so it attracts much less resource than traditional crimes (Cross & Blackshaw, 2015;

Leukfeldt et al., 2013; Skidmore et al., 2020). In England and Wales, there is plenty of evidence that only a tiny proportion of frauds result in a successful criminal prosecution, as the Skidmore et al. (2018, p. 4) noted:

> While 3.2 million frauds were estimated to have taken place in 2017-18, just 638,882 frauds were recorded by the police and industry bodies. For every crime reported just one in 13 was allocated for investigation and in that same period only 8,313 cases resulted in a charge/summons, caution, or community resolution, representing just three per cent of the number reported to the police.

For both cyber-dependent crime and bribery, there are usually less than 100 cases prosecuted per year out of tens of thousands of incidents that occur (see Chapter 1). Similar low levels of convictions can be found across most economic crimes. There is also evidence that some economic criminals who do face criminal sanctions are treated more leniently compared to other volume property offenders (Levi, 2010). Consequently, the deterrence effect is minimal and the overall positive utility associated with economic crime encourages offending.

However, this is not to say that economic criminals are not caught at all. Reflecting Sutherland's (1940) criticism that elite white-collar criminals do not face criminal prosecution, most apprehended economic crime offenders face some kind of regulatory or administrative justice irrespective of their social status. Crimes of deception have become democratised in that they are accessible to all sections of society, and enforcement is dominated by non-criminal means, modest fines and administrative sanctions. Button et al. (2018b) found that out of 1 million sanctioned fraudsters in the UK, less than 9,000 were brought to justice by the police and the Serious Fraud Office. The vast majority were dealt with by regulatory or private, administrative means, see Table 9.2.

There is a debate to be had – which is beyond the scope of this chapter – on how much of a deterrent these alternatives are. However, whatever the debate, a habitual career offender who does rationally calculate the utility of crime is very likely to conclude that the utility of economic crime is higher than traditional crime due to the high rewards and lower sanction risks. Similarly, ordinary citizens who contemplate one-off or occasional acts are likely to conclude that the punishment risks are not an obstacle to the anticipated benefits.

Control theory and descending the ladder to economic crime

Readers familiar with criminological theory will have spotted elements of control theory in this chapter. This turns the question of why do people commit

Table 9.2 Total number of sanctioned fraud offenders (average of 2014–2015)

Enforcement type	Justice route	Offenders	%	%
Criminal	TV licensing	162,869	15.6	17.1
	Police + CPS + SFO	8,860	0.8	
	DWP	6,105	0.6	
	HMRC	716	0.1	
	Government profession regulators	15	0.0	
	Contempt of court (civil courts)	12	0.0	
Regulatory – general public	NHS	606,063	57.9	70.0
	TfL	100,113	9.6	
	HMRC	14,760	1.4	
	DWP	10,155	1.0	
	Insolvency Service	1,122	0.1	
Regulatory – professions	Government regulators	110	0.01	0.03
	Delegated regulators	226	0.02	
	Self-regulators	66	0.01	
Database record	Cifas	135,485	12.9	12.9
Total [1]		1,046,675	100	100

1 Rounding errors from average calculation

Source: Adapted from Button et al. (2018b, p. 63).

crime on its head to ask Hirschi's famous question, 'Why do most of us not commit crime?' (Hirschi, 1969, p. 34). Control theory is a broad group of ideas that are based on the classicist notion that we are all born into this world with an equal propensity to criminality. Control theory seeks to understand the interaction between internal self-restraint controls and external controls (Gottfredson & Hirschi, 1990). The external controls are broadly divided into two areas, informal and formal controls.

Informal controls are the non-regulatory social controls which guide individuals into conformance with normative values; they include the controlling influences of family, friends, colleagues, managers, mass media and so on. Control theory leans heavily on social learning theory in postulating that the informal controls of positive nurturing by parents, schools, communities and other institutions promote strong attachments to normal society and the internalisation of the controls, which in turn leads to self-restraint and compliance with social norms (Jones, 2017). Effective nurturing is based on positive encouragement and rewards for moral behaviour as well as constructive discipline for errant behaviour. Conversely, ineffective nurturing weakens the bonds to normal society, leading to delinquency and crime (Hirschi, 1969).

Formal controls are those exercised by regulators and law enforcement agencies. These controls assist in the development of self-restraint by formally identifying behaviour that transgresses normative social values. They then reinforce the internal controls by public acts of enforcement. This aspect of control theory is essentially deterrence theory as the formal controls are exercised when internal control has failed and a person has committed a crime. Nevertheless, a key point of control theory is that external, formal controls are required to intervene whenever informal social controls and ultimately internal, self-restraint controls fail.

Unfortunately, as this chapter has explained, social controls in relation to economic crime are weak because:

- Young people are not nurtured to understand that economic crime is wrong.
- Economic crime is broadly regarded as not a real crime.
- Moral justifications are readily constructed to neutralise any residual inhibitions (rationalisation).
- It is viewed as socially acceptable (differential association and differential rationalisation).
- The perceived risks of being caught and criminally punished are very low (rational choice and deterrence).

The weaknesses of social controls mean that societies across the world were unprepared for the proliferation of opportunities for cyber-enabled economic crime as a result of globalisation and the Internet. The scale of the problem is such that law enforcement agencies tend to focus on the most serious economic crimes. Consequently, the impact of these formal controls in preventing people from slipping into economic crime is marginal, and their influence in developing social values that wholeheartedly reject economic crime is negligible.

Some researchers have discussed the descent into forms of economic crime as a 'slippery slope', where circumstances and pressures draw an individual to crime (Levi, 2016). The authors of this book propose a ladder metaphor (Figure 9.3). The ladder is an idealised representation of how an otherwise law-abiding citizen descends in steps towards the commission of an economic crime.

At the top rung of the ladder, social learning and environmental influences have led a potential offender to believe the act is not a crime or a 'real crime'; rather it is a socially acceptable course of action.

At the second step, those that internally acknowledge the deviance or criminality of economic crime rationalise that it is morally justified in order to neutralise any residual internal controls.

Having decided that contemplated acts are appropriate, the potential offender encounters on the third rung a multitude of opportunities during the everyday, routine activities of his or her life.

The fourth step represents the offender identifying opportunities which match his or her capabilities.

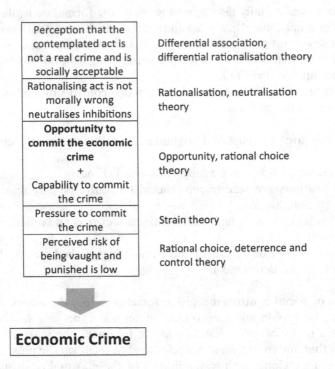

Perception that the contemplated act is not a real crime and is socially acceptable	Differential association, differential rationalisation theory
Rationalising act is not morally wrong neutralises inhibitions	Rationalisation, neutralisation theory
Opportunity to commit the economic crime + Capability to commit the crime	Opportunity, rational choice theory
Pressure to commit the crime	Strain theory
Perceived risk of being vaught and punished is low	Rational choice, deterrence and control theory

Economic Crime

Figure 9.3 Descending the ladder to economic crime.

At the fifth step, the potential offender concludes that the chance of being caught and punished is low.

Leading to the final jump off the ladder to commit the act.

The chronology of the steps is purely hypothetical: individuals will follow different sequences, and some of the influences, such as the social learning aspects of differential association are typically gradual, taking effect over months or many years. Some individuals will omit steps. For example, a small shop owner confronted with an opportunity to purchase counterfeit Manchester United shirts to sell might jump straight to the bottom without thinking about the other steps. An organised criminal, who does not care about the illegality, immorality or harm of an act, may only consider opportunity, capability and the risk of detection.

However, the most important aspect of all economic crimes is opportunity: there can be no crime without opportunity. In the absence of adequate social controls, the social approach to controlling economic crime overwhelmingly relies on potential individual and organisational victims preventing the crimes by removing opportunities, mitigating opportunities and disconnecting opportunities from potential offenders (Button & Gee, 2013; Graycar &

Felson, 2010; Tunley et al., 2018). Unfortunately, too many individuals and organisations do not have adequate protections. Studies show that individuals fail to comprehend the risks and adopt appropriate measures against fraud and cybercrime (Button & Cross, 2017; Chen et al., 2017; Deliema et al., 2020; Holt & Bossler, 2008). Similarly, organisations frequently fail to grasp the problem and secure their operations (ACFE, 2020; Buil-Gil et al., 2021; Button & Gee, 2013; Department for Culture, Media and Sport & Ipsos MORI, 2021; Timofeyev, 2015).

Cross-border economic criminals

Much of this chapter has been written from the perspective of offending in the home country. It is, however, important to recognise that all types of economic crime cross borders. Many economic criminals are based in countries where social controls and law enforcement are especially weak due to culture, other priorities, state corruption or state acquiescence (Button, 2012; Cross, 2020). Law enforcement may be completely disinterested in these places if the criminals are targeting overseas victims. In some cases, offenders engaged in industrial espionage are loyally following the instructions of their governments (Rettman, 2020).

Thus, cyber-criminals in Russia and 419 fraudsters operating out of West Africa have the distinct advantage that their victims are across the world in an alien jurisdiction. Their social learning environment may well be based on endemic corruption within the broad social structures and the political leadership of their countries. They may even have a grudge against former colonial powers or cold war rivals to add to the many rationalisations already available. The globalisation of trade and instant communications has created innumerable opportunities across the world for fraudsters, bribers, money launderers, counterfeiters, cyber warriors, economic spies and cartel members based in lawless places to operate with impunity.

Conclusion

This chapter has explored some of the research and criminological theories that seek to explain economic crime. It used the crime ladder metaphor to illustrate key determinants in the descent to economic criminality. Weak social controls create the perception that economic crime is not a real crime and is socially acceptable. Compared to traditional acquisitive crimes, it is far easier to construct rationalisations that morally justify economic crime and neutralise any residual inhibitions. Globalisation and the complexities of everyday life create innumerable opportunities, which are exploited to satisfy a wide range of motivational pressures, and which the authorities overwhelmingly fail to deter due to ineffective enforcement.

References

Accenture Newsroom. (2003). *One-fourth of Americans say it's acceptable to defraud insurance companies, Accenture Survey Finds.* http://newsroom.accenture.com/article_display.cfm?article_id=3970.

ACFE. (2020). *Report to the nations.*www.acfe.com/report-to-the-nations/2020/.

Agnew, R. (1992). Foundation for a general theory of crime and delinquency. *Criminology, 30*(1), 47–87.

Albrecht, W., Howe, K. & Romney, B. (1983). *Deterring fraud: The internal auditor's perspective.* The Institute of Internal Auditor's Research Foundation.

Albrecht, W. S., Romney, M. B., Cherrington, D. J., Payne, I. R., & Roe, A. V. (1982). *How to detect and prevent business fraud.*Prentice-Hall.

Ariely, D. (2012). *The (honest) truth about dishonesty.* Harper Collins.

Barnett, H. C. (1981). Corporate capitalism, corporate crime. *Crime and Delinquency, 27*(1), 4–23.

Becker, G. S. (1968). Crime and punishment: An economic approach. The Journal of Political Economy, 76(2), 169–217. www.nber.org/system/files/chapters/c3625/c3625.pdf

Benson, M. (1985). Denying the guilty mind: Accounting for involvement in a white-collar crime. *Criminology, 23*(4), 583–607.

Bittle, S., Snider, L., Tombs, S., & Whyte, D. (Eds.). (2018). *Revisiting crimes of the powerful: Marxism, crime and deviance.* Routledge.

Blickle, G., Schlegel, A., Fassbender, P., & Klein, U. (2006). Some personality correlates of business white-collar crime. *Applied Psychology: An International Review, 55,* 220–233.

Braithwaite, J. (1992). Poverty, power and white-collar crime: Sutherland and the paradoxes of criminological theory. In K. Schlegel & D. Weisburd (Eds.), *White-collar crime reconsidered.* Northeastern University Press.

Bristol Post. (2021). *The 40 crimes most people commit without even realising.* www.bristolpost.co.uk/news/bristol-news/crimes-committed-without-realising-everyday-228790.

Buil-Gil, D., Lord, N., & Barrett, E. (2021). The dynamics of business, cybersecurity and cyber-victimization: Foregrounding the internal guardian in prevention. *Victims and Offenders, 16*(3), 286–315.

Button, M. (2012), Crossborder fraud and the case for an "Interfraud". Policing: An *International Journal, 35*(2), 285–303. https://doi.org/10.1108/13639511211230057.

Button, M., Brooks, G., Lewis, C., & Aleem, A. (2017). Just about everybody doing the business? Explaining 'cash-for-crash' insurance fraud in the United Kingdom. *Australian and New Zealand Journal of Criminology, 50*(2), 176–194.

Button, M., & Cross, C. (2017). *Cyber frauds, scams and their victims.* Routledge.

Button, M. & Gee, J. (2013). *Countering fraud for competitive advantage.* Wiley.

Button, M., Shepherd, D., & Blackbourn, D. (2018a). Co-offending and bribery: The recruitment of participants to corrupt schemes and the implications for prevention. *Security Journal, 31*(4), 882–900.

Button, M., Shepherd, D., & Blackbourn, D. (2018b). 'The iceberg beneath the sea', fraudsters and their punishment through non-criminal justice in the 'fraud justice network' in England and Wales. *International Journal of Law, Crime and Justice, 53*(1), 56–66.

Button, M., Shepherd, D., & Blackbourn, D. (2019). Explaining the causes of bribery from an offender perspective. In L. Pasculli & N. Ryder (Eds.), *Corruption in the global era*. Routledge.

Chen, H., Beaudoin, C. E., & Hong, T. (2017). Securing online privacy: An empirical test on internet scam victimization, online privacy concerns, and privacy protection behaviors. *Computers in Human Behavior, 70*, 291–302.http://doi:10.1016/j.chb.2017.01.003.

Clarke, R. (1980). Situational crime prevention: Theory and practice. *British Journal of Criminology, 20*(2), 136–147.

Clarke, R., V., & Mayhew, P. (1989). Crime as opportunity. a note on domestic gas suicide in Britain and the Netherlands. *British Journal of Criminology, 29*(1), 35–46.

Cohen, L., E., & Felson, M. (1979). Social changes and crime rates: A routine activities approach. *American Sociological Review, 44*, 588–608.

Coleman, J. (1992). The theory of white-collar crime: From Sutherland to the 1990s. In K. Schlegel & D. Weisburd (Eds.), *White-collar crime reconsidered* (pp. 53–77). Northeastern University Press.

Coleman, J. (2006). *The criminal elite: The sociology of white-collar crime* (6th ed.). St. Martin's Press.

Collins, J.M., & Schmidt, F.L. (1993). Personality, integrity and white collar crime: A construct validity study. *Personnel Psychology, 46*, 295–311.

Cornish, D., & Clarke, R. (2003). Opportunities, precipitators and criminal decisions: A reply to Wortley's critique of situational crime prevention. *Crime Prevention Studies, 16*, 41–96. https://popcenter.asu.edu/sites/default/files/Responses/crime_prevention/PDFs/Cornish&Clarke.pdf.

Cressey, D. (1953). *Other people's money*. Wadsworth Publishing.

Cross, C. (2020). 'Oh we can't actually do anything about that': The problematic nature of jurisdiction for online fraud victims. *Criminology and Criminal Justice, 20*(3), 358–375. https://doi:10.1177/1748895819835910.

Cross, C., & Blackshaw, D. (2015). Improving the police response to online fraud. *Policing: A Journal of Policy and Practice, 9*(2), 119–128.

Cross, C., & Holt, T. J. (2021). The use of military profiles in romance fraud schemes. *Victims and Offenders, 16*(3), 385–406.

Deliema, M., Shadel, D., & Pak, K. (2020). Profiling victims of investment fraud: Mindsets and risky behaviors. *Journal of Consumer Research, 46*(5), 904–914.

Department for Culture, Media and Sport and Ipsos MORI. (2021). *Cyber security breaches survey 2021*. https://assets.publishing.service.gov.uk/government/uploads/system/uploads/attachment_data/file/972399/Cyber_Security_Breaches_Survey_2021_Statistical_Release.pdf.

Ditton, J. R. (1977). *Part-time crime: An ethnography of fiddling and pilferage*. Springer.

Donegan, J. J., & Ganon, M. W. (2008). Strain, differential association, and coercion: Insights from the criminology literature on causes of accountant's misconduct. *Accounting and the Public Interest, 8*(1), 1–20.

Duffield, G., & Grabosky, P. (2001). *Red flags of fraud: Trends and issues in crime and criminal justice*. Australian Institute of Criminology. www.aic.gov.au/publications/tandi/tandi200

EUIPO. (2017). *European citizens and intellectual property: Perception, awareness and behaviour.* https://euipo.europa.eu/tunnel-web/secure/webdav/guest/document_libr ary/observatory/documents/IPContributionStudy/2017/european_public_opinion_ study_web.pdf.

Goldstraw-White, J. (2011). *White-collar crime: Accounts of offending behaviour.* Springer.

Gordon, D. M. (1973). Capitalism, class, and crime in America. *Crime and Delinquency, 19*(2), 163–186.

Gottfredson, M., & Hirschi, T. (1990). *A General Theory of Crime.* Stanford University Press.

Graycar, A., & Felson, M. (2010). Situational prevention of organised timber theft and related corruption. In K. Bullock, R. Clarke & N. Tilley (Eds.), *Situational crime prevention of organised* crimes. Willan.

Hare, R. D. (1999). *Without conscience: The disturbing world of the psychopaths among us.* Guilford Press.

Hirschi, T. (1969). *The causes of delinquency.* University of California Press.

Hollinger, R., & Clark, J. (1983). Deterrence in the workplace: perceived certainty, perceived severity and employee theft. Social Forces, 62(2), 398–418. https://doi. org/10.1093/sf/62.2.398

Hollis, M. E., Fejes, Z. L., Fenoff, R., & Wilson, J. (2015). Routine activities and product counterfeiting: A research note. *International Journal of Comparative and Applied Criminal Justice, 39*(3), 257–272.https://doi.org/10.1080/01924036.2014.973055.

Hollis, M. E., & Wilson, J. (2014). Who are the guardians in product counterfeiting? A theoretical application of routine activities theory. *Crime Prevention and Community Safety, 16*(3), 169–188.https://doi.org/10.1057/cpcs.2014.6.

Holt, T. J., & Bossler, A. M. (2008). Examining the applicability of lifestyle-routine activities theory for cybercrime victimization. *Deviant Behavior, 30*(1), 1–25.

Institute of Business Ethics. (2018). *Ethics at work. 2018 survey of employees. Europe.* www.ibe.org.uk/uploads/assets/ba9cd14a-a195-4c79-b12c68f7b06fd203/IBESurvey ReportEthicsatWork2018surveyofemployeesEuropeINT.pdf.

Ipsos MORI. (2017). *Public perceptions of policing in England and Wales 2017: Report for Her Majesty's Inspectorate of Constabulary and Fire & Rescue Se*rvices. www. ipsos.com/ipsos-mori/en-uk/public-perceptions-policing-england-and-wales-2017.

Jones, E. (1908). Rationalisation in everyday life. *Journal of Abnormal Psychology, 3*(3), 161–169.

Jones, S. (2017). *Criminology.* Oxford University Press.

Karstedt, S. (2016). Middle-class crime: Moral economies between crime in the streets and crime in the suites. In S. Van Slyke, M. Benson & F. Cullen (Eds.), *The Oxford handbook of white-collar crime.* Oxford University Press.

Karstedt, S., & Farrall, S. (2006). The moral economy of everyday crime: Markets, consumers and citizens. *British Journal of Criminology, 46*(6), 1011–1036.

Karstedt, S., & Farrall, S. (2007). *Law abiding majority? The everyday crimes of the middle classes, Briefing 3, June 2007.* Centre for Crime and Justice Studies. www. crimeandjustice.org.uk/opus45/Law_abiding_Majority_FINAL_VERSION.pd.

Köbis, N. C., van Prooijen, J. W., Righetti, F., & Van Lange, P. A. (2017). The road to bribery and corruption: Slippery slope or steep cliff? *Psychological Science, 28*(3), 297–306.

Leukfeldt, E. R., & Yar, M. (2016). Applying routine activity theory to cybercrime: A theoretical and empirical analysis. *Deviant Behavior, 37*(3), 263–280.

Leukfeldt, R., Veenstra, S., & Stol, W. (2013). High volume cyber crime and the organization of the police: The results of two empirical studies in the Netherlands. *International Journal of Cyber Criminology, 7*(1), 1–17.

Levi, M. (2010). Hitting the suite spot: Sentencing frauds. *Journal of Financial Crime, 17*(1), 116–132.

Levi, M. (2016). *The phantom capitalists: The organization and control of long-firm fraud*. Routledge.

Mars, G. (1982). *Cheats at work: An anthropology of workplace crime*. Allen and Unwin.

May, T., & Bhardwa, B. (2017). *Organised crime groups involved in fraud*. Springer.

Mayhew, P., Clarke, R. V. G., Sturman, A. & Hough, J. M. (1976). *Crime as opportunity*. HMSO.

Merton, R. (1938). Social structure and anomie. *American Sociological Review, 3*, 672–682.

Nee, C., Button, M., Shepherd, D., Blackbourn, D. & Leal, S. (2019). The psychology of the corrupt: Some preliminary findings. *Journal of Financial Crime, 26*(2), 488–495. https://doi.org/10.1108/JFC-03-2018-0032.

Nee, C., & Meenaghan, A. (2006). Expert decision making in burglars. *British Journal of Criminology, 46*(5), 935–949.

Newburn, T. (2017). *Criminology*. Routledge.

Paternoster, R., & Bachman, R. (2012). Perceptual deterrence theory. In F. Cullen & P. Wilcox (Eds.), *The Oxford handbook of criminological theory*. Oxford University Press.

Pratt, T. C., Holtfreter, K., & Reisig, M. D. (2010). Routine online activity and internet fraud targeting: Extending the generality of routine activity theory. *Journal of Research in Crime and Delinquency, 47*(3), 267–296.

Rettman, A. (2020). *China suspected of bio-espionage in 'heart of EU'*. EUobserver. https://euobserver.com/science/148244.

Shepherd, D. (2016). *Complicit silence: Organisations and their response to occupational fraud*. University of Portsmouth.

Shu, L. L., Mazar, N., Gino, F., Ariely, D., & Bazerman, M. H. (2012). Signing at the beginning makes ethics salient and decreases dishonest self-reports in comparison to signing at the end. *Proceedings of the National Academy of Sciences, 109*(38), 15197–15200.

Skidmore, M., Goldstraw-White, J., & Gill, M. (2020). Understanding the police response to fraud: The challenges in configuring a response to a low-priority crime on the rise. *Public Money and Management, 40*(5), 369–379.

Skidmore, M., Ramm, J., Goldstraw-White, J., Barrett, C., Braleaza, S., Muir, R., & Gill, M. (2018). *Improving the police response to fraud*. The Police Foundation. www.police-foundation.org.uk/project/improving-the-police-response-to-fraud-2/.

Smith, D. J. (2010). *A culture of corruption*. Princeton University Press.

Suh, J. B., & Shim, H. S. (2020). The effect of ethical corporate culture on anti-fraud strategies in South Korean financial companies: Mediation of whistleblowing and a sectoral comparison approach in depository institutions. *International Journal of Law, Crime and Justice, 60*, 100361. https://doi.org/10.1016/j.ijlcj.2019.100361.

Sutherland, E. (1940). White-collar criminality. *American Sociological Review*, 5(1), 1–12.

Sutherland, E. (1945). Is "white-collar crime" crime? *American Sociological Review*, 10(2), 132–139.

Sutherland, E. (1949). White collar crime. Dryden.

Sutherland, E., Cressey. D. & Luckenbill, D. (1992). *Principles of criminology* (11th ed.). General Hall.

Sykes, G. & Matza, D. (1957). Techniques of neutralization: A theory of delinquency. *American Sociological Review*, 22(6), 664–670.

Tierney, J, (2013). *Criminology: Theory and context* (3rd ed.). Pearson Longman.

Timofeyev, Y. (2015). Analysis of predictors of organizational losses due to occupational corruption. *International Business Review*, 24(4), 630–641.

Tombs, S., & Whyte, D. (2015). *The corporate criminal: Why corporations must be abolished*. Routledge.

Transparency International. (2017). *People and corruption: Citizens' voices from around the world*. https://images.transparencycdn.org/images/GCB_Citizens_voices_FINAL.pdf.

Transparency International. (2021). *Global Corruption Barometer European Union 2021*.https://images.transparencycdn.org/images/TI_GCB_EU_2021_web_2021-06-14-151758.pdf.

Tunley, M., Button, M., Shepherd, D., & Blackbourn, D. (2018). Preventing occupational corruption: Utilising situational crime prevention techniques and theory to enhance organisational resilience. *Security Journal*, 31(1), 21–52.

Urbas, G. (2006). Cross-national investigation and prosecution of intellectual property crimes: The example of "Operation Buccaneer". *Crime, Law and Social Change*, 46(4–5), 207–221.

Vinkers, D. J., De Beurs, E., Barendregt, M., Rinne, T., & Hoek, H. W. (2011). The relationship between mental disorders and different types of crime. *Criminal Behaviour and Mental Health*, 21(5), 307–320.

Wang, V., Gee, J., & Button, M. (Forthcoming). Crime on the Darknet – the case of brand abuse. In M. Gill (Ed.), *Handbook of security* (3rd ed.). Palgrave.

Wolfe, D. T., & Hermanson, D. R. (2004). *The fraud diamond: Considering the four elements of fraud*. https://digitalcommons.kennesaw.edu/cgi/viewcontent.cgi?article=2546&context=facpubs.

Chapter 10

Economic crime: law and regulation

Introduction

Economic crime, including its various forms such as bribery, fraud and money laundering, presents a regulatory challenge. While criminologists see the primary response to crime and criminal behaviour in criminal justice systems, many norms that influence this response are present beyond the remit of criminal law. In other words, limiting the discussion about economic crime regulation to criminal law would be short sighted. Clearly, there is not a single statute containing a comprehensive set of legal norms against economic crime. Economic crime regulation stems from a broad range of sources.

This chapter explains the complexity of law and regulation relevant to economic crime. It seeks to provide a guide for the reader to orient themselves in many layers of legal rules governing economic crime, starting from national measures, going through to international and finishing in new forms of regulation beyond the nation state. The chapter also discusses the notion of compliance and its links to economic crime regulation. This analysis does not attempt to define the notion of economic crime regulation. Instead, the chapter discusses economic crime regulation in a reasonably broad manner, and the reader is invited to independently contemplate the themes and arguments to gain a more comprehensive view on 'Economic Crime Regulation'.

The remainder of this chapter is structured as follows. The first section focuses on the concept and purpose of law and regulation, including legal sources and origins of law. The second section introduces key sources of economic crime regulation, including international law, European Union (EU) law as well as state legislation and regulation. The third section discusses economic crime regulation that goes beyond the state centric system, including various transgovernmental networks, self-regulatory activities and compliance standards.

DOI: 10.4324/9781003081753-10

Theory of economic crime law and regulation

Good understanding of criminal justice system response to the problem of economic crime requires an elementary understanding of the concepts of law and regulation. This part guides the reader through some key perspectives and theories that will support their independent thinking about economic crime regulation.

What is law?

A classic legal research primarily focuses on questions such as how the state establishes, applies and enforces legal rules. This discussion is often prescriptive in terms of what the law is and what it is not. For the purposes of our discussion, we define the terms 'the law' and 'law' in the following manner (Cambridge Dictionary, n.d.):

- **the law**: *the system of rules of a particular country, group or area of activity*
- *law: a rule, usually made by a government, that is used to order the way in which a society behaves*

While laws of many jurisdictions differ in their content, they often have similar conceptual grounds. Especially Western legal theory traditionally attempts to identify universal principles associated with, for example, the role of state in law-making, the rule of law, justice, legality and legitimacy (see Hart, 2012). Scholars, however, stress the importance of the socio-economic context in which the law operates as well as the transnational reach of national laws (Husa, 2018).

These considerations challenge the validity of universal approaches to law and regulation as well as the centrality of the state in the creation of the law.

Example of law principle: the rule of law

> The core of the rule of law principle is that all actors within the state, be it the government, judges, regulators, businesses, politicians, ordinary people, etc., should be bound by laws and enjoy the rights those laws provide. At the same time these laws should be publicly made, have general effect in the future, and they should be enforced by independent and impartial courts.
>
> (see Bingham, 2011)

Despite different schools of thought, however, legal practitioners traditionally associate the concept of law with the system of state rules, meaning rules issued by the legislator and, in common law countries, co-created by judges.

In other words, a conventional view is that the central actor in articulating a collective goal of communities is the state.

A typical example of the law created and enforced by the state is UK criminal law. This subsystem of UK law consists of laws that relate to crime and criminal procedure. Bribery of foreign public officials, for example, is a criminal offence under Section 6 of the UK Bribery Act 2010 (the Bribery Act). This criminal law statute provides that a conduct that consists of promising, offering or giving a financial or other advantage to a foreign public official, either directly or through a third party, in order to obtain or retain business or other advantage in the conduct of business, is a crime. As other criminal law statutes, the Bribery Act prescribes conduct considered as harmful and specifies sanctions of those that violate criminal laws. Under this view of the law, the law is a set of rules that are legitimately applied by the state. And the state has the final authority to use a coercive power to enforce legal rules.

Facilitative and expressive role of the law

Modern legal theory is dominated by the belief that the law and legal rules cause social phenomena (Griffiths, 1979). Consider, for example, the UK's Competition Act 1998 that under section 2 prohibits cartels, that is, agreements between undertakings, decisions by associations of undertakings or concerned practices which directly or indirectly fix purchase or selling prices or any other trading conditions. The law was introduced to facilitate the elimination of cartels that affect trade in the UK.

This facilitative role of the law stands behind multiple economic crime-related statutes. By introducing new statutes and other legal rules, the state hopes to shape the behaviour of relevant actors and solve practical problems. The nation states have played an instrumental role in creating laws and regulations in the area of fraud, bribery and corruption, antitrust, money laundering, intellectual property (IP) crime, and industrial and economic espionage. Whether these state laws lead to a desired societal change is an arguable question that goes beyond the remit of traditional legalistic approaches. The traditional legalistic approaches rather focus on the second important role which the law takes – the expressive role.

In its expressive role, the law institutionalises values. Without anti-bribery laws, for example, certain forms of corruption and bribery could be considered as positive phenomena. Some economists discuss bribery as an efficient solution to certain problems. For example, corruption could in some instances be considered as an efficient phenomenon that serves to overcome the dysfunctional inefficiencies of bad administrations (Huntington, 1968). It was only after the adoption of the United Nations Convention against Corruption (UNCAC) when bribery and corruption were universally rejected as immoral, and in most cases also illegal, phenomena (see Zagaris, 2015, pp. 137–138).

To summarise, the law's function is not only associated with behavioural change, the law also institutionalises values. In fact, laws and regulations often lead to various unintended consequences, which makes the facilitative role of law less relevant as opposed to its expressive role (Griffiths, 1979).

Theories of regulation

Unlike the study of the law and legal principles, the concept of regulation has become a key topic beyond legal research. Be it criminologists, economists, political scientists, sociologists, historians and other social scientists, regulation has become the subject of interdisciplinary research (Baldwin et al., 2010, 2012).

The discussion about regulation includes a technical dispute about terminology. For example, legalistic definitions of regulation that stress the importance of a public authority are under-inclusive in that they do not consider wider forms of social control. Selznick (1985, p. 363) explains that regulation is 'the sustained and focused control exercised by a public authority over activities valued by the community'. Other approaches are over-inclusive as they consider all forms of social and economic mechanisms, such as private rules associated with business information management, that influence behaviour as regulatory (Baldwin et al., 2010, 2012, p. 3).

In the following discussion, we aim to offer a useful introduction to the study of economic crime regulation and avoid a technical use of terminology. As the working definition, the notion of 'regulation' should be understood as:

> [...] the sustained and focused attempt to alter the behaviour of others according to defined standards or purposes with the intention of producing a broadly identified outcome or outcomes, which may involve mechanisms of standard-setting, information gathering and behaviour-modification.
>
> (Black, 2002, p. 20)

The above definition includes two key elements: *a control element* and a *problem-solving element*. A *control element* is based on the capacity of a system to perform three functions:

1   Capacity for standard-setting to produce rules that allow recipients see the difference between what is a preferred state of affairs and what is not.
2   Capacity for information gathering to produce knowledge about the standard and its changes (monitoring).
3   Capacity for behaviour modification (enforcement components) (see Morgan & Yeung, 2007, p. 3; Hood et al., 2001, p. 23)

Moreover, the definition also includes a *problem-solving element* of regulation, which is similar to the discussion above about the facilitative role of the law. The problem-solving element should be a sustained and focused attempt to alter the behaviour rather than an ad hoc event (Black, 2002).

The following section explains two key academic discussions about regulation. The first discussion focuses on the question whether and when private actors should regulate relevant actors instead of the state. The second discussion focuses on the emergence of regulations and how they interact.

Good regulation – public vs private

A key regulatory issue is whether and when the state should defer to private systems of regulation by businesses or other non-state entities. Such systems are commonplace, in particular when the state fails to provide effective order. In some developing countries, for example, it is relatively common that state institutions fail to sufficiently support economic activities in certain territories, which then leads to the emergence of non-state institutions such as terrorist groups (Hock & Gomtsian, 2018).

Self-regulation by outlaw groups is not new. Pirates in late seventeenth- and early 18th-century, for example, were successful in their pursuit of economic profit due to their sophisticated and well-defined rules (Leeson, 2009). They created pirate codes and systems of democratic check and balances that held the captains accountable. Similarly, present day organised crime groups such as the mafia operate according to informal codes laid down and enforced by the crime bosses (Pomeroy, 2007).

Examples of private regulation pervade many areas of social and economic activity, including professional associations such as the Law Society, business associations such as the Chamber of Commerce, and local sports clubs, all of which function alongside established state laws. Professional sports are typically governed by sophisticated self-regulatory regimes. For example, the Fédération Internationale de Football Association (FIFA) has established its own regulatory order. This regime is highly independent of state interference and players, clubs, and other actors are bound by FIFA's rules. Football disputes are resolved by special arbitration tribunals rather than state courts, and their determinations are backed by special non-state sanctions (Gomtsian et al., 2018).

While most private regulatory regimes are desirable, they are often left free of accountability to governments or civil society. States generally only interfere in the operation of these regimes when they fail to protect the broader interests of society. For example, repeated failures of self-regulation in the financial services sector in the UK led to the imposition of increased state regulation (Richardson et al., 2010). Similarly, the Sherman Act in the USA and the Competition Act 1998 in the UK were introduced to combat the secret, antitrust agreements between corporations that make markets less competitive (see Chapter 4).

Governments, however, in many cases face trade-offs when deciding whether, and how, to be involved in a particular regulatory area. While antitrust law and its enforcement can ensure better functioning of market competition, it could also undermine innovation and the value-maximising results of cooperation between businesses (Richman, 2009). A massive academic effort across various disciplines has been devoted to examining the circumstances when the state should defer to private self-regulation, generally concluding that governments should intervene only when they are sure about the inefficiency and ineffectiveness of private self-regulation (see Ellickson, 2016; Katz, 1996).

Moreover, another big question is whether and when should the state intervene in the internal functioning of organisations. Coming back to FIFA's private regime, we can see that while it has been very effective, and by far the best alternative for all involved actors, FIFA has evolved into an enterprise with an elitist structure that extensively exploits its powers (Hock & Gomtsian, 2018). In the so-called FIFA-gate scandal, a major anti-corruption investigation exposed massive bribes, money laundering and other economic crimes (see Department of Justice, 2015). The scandal illustrates the need for national governments to intervene and enforce the law whenever self-regulation fails, especially when the private orders themselves are corrupt. In other circumstances, governments frequently prefer a lighter touch intervention, requiring or suggesting internal governance and compliance improvements to otherwise effective and efficient self-regulatory regimes.

The private and public modes of regulation usually interact and influence each other. The nature and extent of government interaction with otherwise legitimate forms of private regulatory systems often lead to a complex form of co-regulation. The state often cooperates with the private sector with the aim of finding an optional regulatory solution. This relates to the second major question: how economic crime regulations emerge and interact.

How do regulations emerge and interact?

Another major question about regulation is how various rules and legal processes emerge and interact. This is important for the economic criminologists because the behaviour of organisations and individuals is influenced by a mix of legal and societal rules. Standards that attempt to alter behaviour, for example, ordering businesses to prevent fraud, take the form of legal rules adopted by multiple states, but they also take a form of more informal rules and business practices. The behaviour of relevant actors, for example whether to engage in crime, or not, is then shaped by a mix of overlapping laws, regulations and societal practices.

Numerous theories of regulation provide frameworks that can be applied to economic crime problems to understand a mix of overlapping laws, regulations and practices and suggest what to do to better mitigate economic crime (see Morgan & Yeung, 2007, p. 53). We present the following three schools of thought that can help economic criminologists understand the complexity of problems related to economic crime regulation.

Regulatory space

Hancher and Moran (1989) suggested the analytical device of 'regulatory space' to understand economic regulation. The space itself and the allocation of power within this space is influenced by various legal, political and economic factors. In this space, we see a mixture of interests, and especially those of powerful state organisations and firms.[1] From this perspective, the biggest firms are often so powerful that they resemble public governing institutions. For example, the regulation of telecom services and the Internet has been dominated by the interests of powerful private institutions that are able to influence state regulation as well as to create and enforce their own regulation. Looking at some economic crime problems from the perspective of 'regulatory space' can allow economic criminologists to identify the distribution of interests in the structures of economic crime regulation, which can help assess the appropriateness of existing policing tools and regulatory measures. A prominent example is the identification and assessment of interests and influences in the development of out-of-court resolutions in corporate crime cases.

Responsive regulation

Crime control and the policing of economic crime may be well captured by the interests of the private sector, which can harm the public interest. On the other hand, excessive state regulation can hamper economic growth and innovation. The idea of responsive regulation indicates how different industry structures require different degrees and forms of regulation to avoid harmful forms of regulatory capture and ensure an effective functioning of the market (Ayres & Braithwaite, 1992).

Ayres and Braithwaite (1992) have developed a number of conceptual and normative tools such as 'tripartism', which looks at interactions between regulatory agencies, firms and public interest groups (PIGs) Tripartism is based on an assumption that regulatory choices are primarily determined by the state and business. Unless these choices are influenced by the third parties – PIGs – regulation will become corrupt and captured by business interests. This idea is further translated into a number of 'regulatory pyramids' that serve as conceptual grounds for appropriate regulatory response.[2] This approach to regulation has become dominant in examining the regulation of corporate crime, including what triggers a regulatory response and what the regulatory response will, and should, be (see Schell-Busey et al., 2016).[3]

Global legal pluralism

The economic criminologist should also consider regulations that cross borders. One theory that helps to identify and understand how various transnational regulatory sources operate in the global economy is the idea of global legal pluralism. Teubner and Fischer-Lescano (2004) argue that this idea not only suggests that laws, regulations and policies are often in collision and conflict, but mainly that behind those norms, laws and regulations stand deeper collision of society-wide rationalities. For example, when the US criminalised the bribery of foreign government officials and started sanctioning conduct of corporations in developing countries, these regulatory processes were in conflict with local practices. Many countries that experienced the US enforcement tolerated corporate bribery by, for example, considering many bribes as acceptable gifts (see Chapter 3).

The global legal pluralism agenda is looking at the fragmentation of various laws and regulations in the global space and how existing conflicts can be resolved. This view complements 'regulatory space' and 'responsive regulation' perspectives in a way that it considers global aspects of regulations and their conflicts.

Sources of economic crime regulation

Economic regulation stems from multiple sources that compete, complement each other and co-exist in many different ways. These sources emanate from state activities that adopt various forms of economic crime laws and regulations, state organisations such as the United Nations (UN) and the EU, as well as from private actors such as business associations and non-governmental organisations (NGOs) (Conforti & Labella, 2012, pp. 1–3). In this section, we provide key sources of economic crime regulation and exemplify their content and linkages.

Sources of economic crime laws

The legal-centric view of law offers a well-established hierarchy of legal sources. Most importantly, these sources include international law, including EU law, primary legislation such as acts of parliament, and secondary legislation passed by, for example, regulatory agencies. The following discussion exemplifies these sources of economic crime laws.

International law and economic crime

Arguably, international law stands on the top of the legal norms' hierarchy. As the threat of global economic crime is increasing, the need to cooperate is associated with the ever-growing number of international treaties concluded by nation states. Some international treaties are signed and implemented by multiple states and have regional or even universal reach. The United Nations General Assembly, for example, adopted the United Nations Convention Against Transnational Organized Crime (UNTOC) with 147 signatory countries as well as the UNCAC with 140 signatories. In addition, we can see a number of regional efforts to fight economic crime. These efforts often involve oversight by regional organisations such as the Council of Europe and international organisations with a specific mission, for example the OECD primarily focuses on efficiency of international markets and the level playing field.

While international treaties present a crucial source of economic crime regulation, their effectiveness largely depends on the willingness of states to comply with them. The more inclusive an international treaty is in terms of its membership, the vaguer and softer its content will likely be.

European Union law and economic crime

The EU law represents one specific international legal regime. While it is true that the EU produces a lot of regulation, it is often done in cooperation with the EU Member States. This means that in some cases EU institutions lead a regulatory effort and enforce regulation, such as in the area of EU competition law, and in other areas the Member States take the lead, such as in criminal law enforcement. Whether the EU or Member States take the lead is largely determined by the competence of the EU institutions, which are generally very limited in the area of criminal law. When it comes to economic crime regulation, we can see three main types of competences that Member States transferred in various degrees to the EU institutions: to legislate in the area of substantive and procedural criminal law, the protection of the EU's financial interests and the protection of internal market, including market competition and free movements.

EU CRIMINAL LAW: EURO-CRIMES

Economic crime is to a large extent tackled through national criminal law enforcement. This is a sensitive policy field that the Member States largely keep for themselves. The EU, however, significantly complements national efforts to tackle economic crime. In this area, the EU brings significant value, especially in economic crime cases that transcend borders.

The EU and its Member States can rely on the legal framework established by the so-called Lisbon Treaty to develop, together with its Member States, criminal law legislation. This includes substantive criminal law such as harmonised definitions of various economic crimes as well as procedural measures focusing on, for example, exchange of information and the formation of joint-investigation teams. The Member States have significant powers to influence this process and potentially block the adoption of regulations if they consider that such regulation would hamper fundamental aspects of their national criminal justice systems.

In the broadest sense, the EU can adopt under Article 83 of the Treaty on the Functioning of the European Union (TFEU) directives with minimum rules on EU criminal law for different crimes. This means that the system does not allow for a full harmonisation of national criminal laws and the EU is only allowed to provide the so-called minimal rules on, for example, the definitions of criminal offences and sanctions.[4] Article 83(1) includes a list of the so-called Euro-Crimes which include money laundering, corruption, organised crime and terrorism. These crimes have been deemed by the EU and its Member State so serious that they require an EU approach. In addition, Article 83(2) allows the EU to legislate when it comes to offences related to ensuring the effective implementation of EU policies, which includes, for example, Directive 2014/57 (2014) focusing on serious cases of insider dealing, market manipulation and unlawful disclosure of insider information.

PROTECTION OF EU FINANCIAL INTERESTS

The EU has a vital interest to protect its financial interests and its budget. This is why it includes specific obligations and regulatory measures to deliver the best value for the EU money. Under Article 325(4) TFEU, the EU budget should be protected not only on the basis of administrative measures but also by means of criminal law, especially counter-fraud laws. This is specified in Directive 2017/1371 (2017) on the fight against fraud to the Union's financial interests by means of criminal law.

The EU counter-fraud regime goes way beyond criminal law, especially because criminal law enforcement is still largely in the hands of the Member States. On the revenue side, the EU relies on value added tax (VAT)-based resources, certain custom duties and the gross national income resources. This is why fraud that takes place in these areas is naturally of EU-wide interest. This is why the EU adopts various action plans, setting-out non-criminal measures to tackle fraud, and supports nation states in cooperation and investigations of frauds.

Consider, for example, the case of VAT related evasions that is illustrated in Figure 10.1. Historically, a very pervasive form of the VAT fraud is the so-called Missing Trader Intra-Community Fraud (MTIC) that costs approximately €60 billion annually in tax losses across the EU (Europol, n.d.). This type of fraud exploits the possibility to trade across the Member States without accounting for the VAT right-away. In exploiting this opportunity, criminal's set-up a chain of companies, including a shell corporation that will later disappear without paying VAT to authorities (the so-called missing trader). The missing trader purchases goods from a company registered in

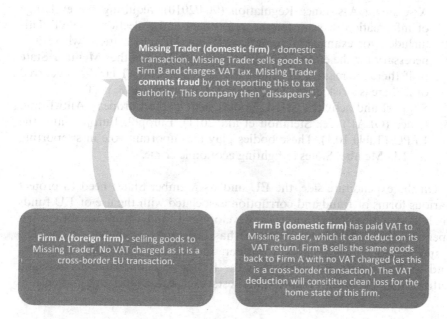

Figure 10.1 Carousel fraud.

another EU country. As this is a cross border EU transaction, no VAT is charged on this transaction. The Missing Trader then re-sells goods to a conspiring domestic company and charges this company a VAT. This tax, however, will not be declared and the Missing Trader will disappear without paying the VAT amount. The conspiring firm then re-sells goods back to the foreign firm without the need to pay VAT, and claim the reimbursement of VAT payments that never actually occurred.

Considering the above example, we can see that committing carousel fraud is a criminal offence under laws of all EU Member States. The role of the EU in tackling fraud, however, goes way beyond criminal law. To successfully tackle this type of fraud, numerous other regulatory mechanisms are needed. These include, for example:

1   Quick Reaction Mechanism: based on the Directive 2015/849 (2015) on the prevention of the use of the financial system for the purposes of money laundering or terrorist financing. Under Article 199b a Member State can, in cases of imperative urgency, change a standard process of charging the VAT. They can apply the domestic reverse charge mechanism to prevent criminals from disappearing before paying the VAT due to authorities. Under this emergency regime, domestic suppliers cannot temporarily charge the VAT on their invoices.

2 Assessment Assistance Regulation (904/2010): requiring the exchange of information relevant for the assessment and collection of VAT. This includes, for example, automatic exchange of information 'where it is necessary for the effectiveness of the controls in another Member State or if there are reasons to believe that a breach of VAT law has occurred or if there is a risk of tax loss' (Ceci & Lamensch, 2018, p. 30).

3 Support and activities of EU bodies such as the European Anti-Fraud Office (OLAF) (see Stefanou et al., 2011), Europol, Eurojust and the EPPO (Table 10.1). These bodies play an important role in supporting the EU Member States in fighting economic crime.

On the expenditure side, the EU and its Member States need to protect various forms of fraud and corruption associated with the use of EU funds such as structural funds and rural development funds. To protect improper spending of the EU money, the EU has developed a number of counter-fraud measures and policies. Consider, for example, the Early Detection and Exclusion System that protects the EU against unreliable persons and entities who threaten its financial interests, exclude such persons and entities

Table 10.1 European public prosecutor's office

Nature and aims	EPPO is a Europe-wide body that focuses on large-scale transnational crime against the EU budget and associated crimes. Its status, role and competences are set out in Council Regulation (EU) 2017/1939 of 12 October 2017 implementing enhanced cooperation on the establishment of the European Public Prosecutor's Office
1. Powers	The EPPO has direct powers to investigate, prosecute and bring to judgment the perpetrators of offences against the Union's financial interests under the Directive 2017/1371 of the European Parliament and of the Council. Subject to a unanimous decision of the European Council, it is possible to extend this competence to include serious crimes having a cross-border dimension (Regulation 2017/1939, para 11 and Article 4)
Operation	The EPPO is an independent and decentralised prosecution office. Its work is based on the combination of the EU and national enforcement. It is organised at two levels: a central level and a decentralised level. The central level includes the European Chief Prosecutor who organises the work, the College of Prosecutors which is responsible for strategic matters and Permanent Chambers that supervise investigations and prosecutions. The decentralised level includes European Delegated Prosecutors located in the Member States. These prosecutors undertake actual investigation and prosecution in their country (Regulation 2017/1939, Section 1)

from receiving EU funds, and allows for an imposition of financial and other penalties (European Commission, n.d.). The fight against fraud is also the competence of several EU institutions and bodies such as the OLAF, which investigates fraud against the EU budget, as well as the European Court of Auditors, which audits the EU budget in terms of revenue and spending.

Economic crime as the threat for EU internal market

The third key area in which the EU plays an important role in regulating economic crime is regulation associated with the protection of the internal market. This includes the protection of four main EU freedoms and fair and equal competition between businesses. Economic crimes such as cartels and fraud in large public procurement projects are sources of unacceptable market distortions. These areas are therefore of large interest to EU institutions.

Unlike in the area of criminal law and measures associated with the protection of the EU financial interests, some forms of economic crime threatening the internal market can be directly regulated by EU institutions. Consider the area of competition law that focuses on the fight against cartels (see Chapter 4). Cartel activity consisting of agreements between undertakings, decisions by associations of undertakings or concerned practices which directly or indirectly fix purchase or selling prices or any other trading conditions is prohibited in all EU Member States as well as the UK. Many countries including the UK have also criminalised cartels.

In addition to the national laws and anti-cartel enforcement, cartels that can affect trade between the EU Member States are prohibited under Article 101(1) of the TFEU. While the EU does not have competence to impose criminal sanctions, the European Commission can directly impose heavy fines on cartel members, which are subject to appeal and review by the Court of Justice of the EU (see Whelan, 2012). The national competition authorities, however, are also competent to enforce the EU law and their national competition rules (see Council Regulation 1/2003). This area is an important example of co-regulation and how this regulatory space is filled by various national and European rules. All actors, in fact, act as a network of co-regulators within this space.

National laws against economic crime

Despite an increasing number of international legal instruments emerging with the aim of mitigating economic crime, the primary responsibility for the enforcement of laws and regulations lies in the hands of nation states. By enforcement we mean investigations, prosecution, and the sanctioning of individuals and corporations for violations of economic crime laws and regulations. The following discussion focuses on key concepts and mechanisms associated with the enforcement of national laws and regulations.

Primary and secondary legislation

National regulations have a hierarchical structure. This means that some legal sources have more authority than other sources. This authority is given by, for example, the binding character of these sources and their validity. Primary legislation such as Acts of Parliament have more authority than secondary legislation passed by government's ministries and regulatory agencies. Secondary legislation passed by such bodies has to be in compliance with primary legislation and it can be reviewed by courts.

For example, the primary UK anti-money laundering (AML) legislation is the Proceeds of Crime Act 2002 (POCA) and the Criminal Finances Act 2017, which both oblige relevant entities to report suspicious activities to the National Crime Agency (NCA). The NCA and a range of other agencies such as the Serious Fraud Office (SFO) and the Crown Prosecution Service are involved in the criminal law enforcement response to economic crimes such as money laundering, corruption and bribery.

Furthermore, the obligations set by the primary legislations are usually further specified by secondary legislation. In the area of money laundering, for example, the POCA's obligations to report suspicious activities are specified by the Money Laundering Regulations 2017 (MLR 2017) implemented by HM Treasury. This secondary legislation includes requirements for risk assessment and controls, checking for politically exposed persons as well as the compliance with global sanctions. These regulations oblige a number of regulatory bodies to supervise relevant persons and entities within their regulatory remit. The MLR 2017 obliges three statutory supervisory authorities, the Financial Conduct Authority (FCA), Her Majesty's Revenue and Customs (HMRC) and the Gambling Commission, to ensure compliance with the AML legislation and regulations within their sectors. In addition, the MLR 2017 requires 25 professional bodies to act as supervisory authorities, ensuring compliance with AML laws within their specific regulatory areas. For example, the Solicitors Regulation Authority (SRA) supervises the compliance of solicitors. This second regulatory layer means that there are many regulators responsible for supervising obliged persons and enforcing AML laws.

Supervisory bodies are empowered to use a number of tools such as guidelines, warning notices and sanctions. For practicing professionals, the sanctions can be severe, including financial penalties and suspension, restriction of practice or professional banishment by withdrawal of membership (see SRA, 2019). All these supervisory bodies are coordinated by the Office for Professional Body Anti-Money Laundering Supervision, which also issues further regulatory instruments (see Wood, 2019).

The categorisation of the state legal sources to the primary legislative sources and secondary legislative sources is not exhaustive but provides a reasonably comprehensive picture of the sources of state law associated with economic crime. It is important to note that there are additional authoritative sources of national law such as case law. Moreover, this space is filled in by various non-binding instruments such as guidelines and policy notices with various degrees of authority. All these sources create a complex set of laws and regulations.

National law enforcement

Economic crime is not only immoral but causes societal and economic harms to individuals and the society at large. Criminal law response to economic crime has traditionally centred around punishment of criminals and the deterrence effect of criminal laws. This approach is based on an assumption that laws deter bad behaviour when the risks and penalties outweigh the benefits of the misconduct (Becker, 1968). Yet, the effectiveness of criminal law measures to fight complex economic crimes is often limited. Some issues relate to the independence and professionalism of enforcement authorities such as the SFO in the UK and the Department of Justice (DOJ) in the USA. These authorities need an appropriate budget to be successful.

A criminal conviction implies much higher pressure and standard of investigation and prosecution than civil proceedings. Unlike in civil cases, enforcement authorities have to provide evidence of conduct that goes beyond reasonable doubt and have to present such evidence during a time-consuming criminal trial. This is why enforcement authorities are increasingly relying on alternatives that require a lower level of judicial scrutiny and transparency. These alternatives to traditional criminal law enforcement are: (a) civil enforcement such as recovery orders; (b) non-trial resolutions such as deferred prosecution agreements (DPAs); (c) making a corporation liable for illicit acts of others, such as its overseas subsidiaries.

CIVIL ENFORCEMENT AND RECOVERY ORDERS

The key focus of civil recovery orders is not the crime itself but the recovery of property obtained through criminal conduct. This allows enforcement authorities to focus on the maximisation of revenue gains and move away from questions of appropriate punishment and deterrence effect. This strategy does not require a risky, expensive court hearing to achieve a criminal conviction; an enforcement authority only has to show on the balance of probabilities that the property was obtained through unlawful conduct. This is naturally much easier than, for example, proving bribery beyond reasonable doubt or, in cases of corporate criminal liability, proving that such bribery was undertaken by a person who is a directing mind and will of the corporations (the so-called identification doctrine).

The use of civil recovery orders instead of criminal law sanctions in foreign bribery cases was harshly criticised, for example, by the OECD in its monitoring reports:

> [...] civil recovery orders alone are *prima facie* insufficient when additional criminal penalties are available. If confiscation is the only sanction imposed, then the defendant is merely returned to the position he/she would have been in had the crime not been committed. Additional criminal penalties, if available, should thus be imposed as deterrence.
>
> (OECD, 2012, p. 33)

This criticism has been rectified by the introduction of new offences by the Bribery Act 2010 as well as by the use of DPAs.

DPAS AS A QUASI-CRIMINAL LAW ENFORCEMENT

Since the late 2010s, there has been a rapid spread of non-trial resolutions in economic crime cases. These non-trial resolutions are based on an agreement between enforcement authorities and alleged corporate offenders. Instead of litigating their case, corporations cooperate with enforcement authorities by self-disclosing their alleged conduct and cooperating with enforcement authorities by, for example, providing details of their violations following internal corporate investigations (Hock, 2021; Søreide & Makinwa, 2020).

In the UK, DPAs were introduced in 2014 under Schedule 17 of the Crime and Courts Act 2013 to enable the Crown Prosecution Service and the SFO to seek the court's approval for settlement agreements with organisations accused of specific economic crime offences: money laundering, fraud, bribery and failure to prevent facilitation of foreign tax evasion. Unlike in other countries such as the USA, the UK system requires DPAs to be reviewed and approved by the judge who must determine whether a DPA is likely to be in the interest of justice, and whether it is fair, reasonable, and proportionate (see Chapter 3, Figure 3.3). In 2020, the SFO published detailed guidance on DPAs (Serious Fraud Office, 2020a).

DPAs are designed to be an appropriate, effective and efficient alternative to prosecution of an organisation. Indeed, the introduction of DPAs has allowed the SFO, and a number of other enforcement authorities across the world, to complete several high-level cases of international corruption. For example, Airbus, an aerospace corporation, settled allegations of massive bribery perpetrated in countries such as China, Malaysia, Taiwan and Ghana. Instead of being prosecuted and facing a criminal trial, Airbus settled with the French, UK and US authorities and paid penalties amounting to £3 billion (Serious Fraud Office, 2020b).[5] In addition, Airbus also completed a massive internal investigation. In exchange, Airbus was not prosecuted and was not barred from competing for public contracts (Hock, 2020).

Despite DPAs helping increase the enforcement of economic crime laws, there remain questions whether DPAs are sufficient alternatives to criminal prosecutions. It is clear that high sanctions and other requirements associated with DPAs, such as that a DPA may require an organisation to improve its internal compliance programme, are a vital alternative to criminal enforcement. However, the impact of DPAs in lowering the rate of prosecutions, which arguably weakens deterrence, is seen by some scholars as major limitations (Hawley et al., 2020).

LIABILITY FOR ACTS OF OTHERS

Another alternative to traditional criminal law enforcement has been the focus on policing the organisations that are in some way associated with economic crime. These organisations do not directly commit the primary crime but are failing to prevent it. The key issue here is that the primary focus of enforcement authorities is not the investigation and prosecution of the original crime but rather the investigation and prosecution of other acts that facilitate it. Consider, for example, the adoption of the 'failure to prevent bribery' offence in the area of foreign anti-bribery law. Under Section 7 of the Bribery Act, what is prosecuted is not actual bribery but the failure to prevent bribery perpetrated by an associated person. Associated person under Section 8(1) is 'a person who performs services for or on behalf of' a company. This can be an employee, a subsidiary or even a foreign agent (Bribery Act, section 8(3)). This model of corporate liability has been also adopted in the area of tax evasion: sections 45 and 46 of the Criminal Finance Act 2017 introduced two offences of failure to prevent the facilitation of tax evasion, which is both a domestic offence and a foreign offence.

This alternative model of corporate criminal liability extends the powers of national enforcement authorities to hold organisations liable. Especially in the UK, the introduction of these new offences has helped to overcome some limitations of the corporate criminal liability model based on the identification doctrine. This doctrine suggests that corporations can be held liable only if enforcement authorities can prove that illegal acts, such as bribery, are committed by individuals who are 'directing the mind and will' of the corporation. This, however, covers only members of the board of directors, a managing director and other superior officers (OECD, 2012, pp. 14–18).

The failure to prevent offences are not the only type of offences in this category. Typically, in the area of tax fraud, we have seen for many years' the emergence of hybrid forms of regulation that focuses on third parties with some business connection to alleged fraudsters. Sellers, intermediaries and warehouse keepers are not only responsible for crime prevention but, as the consequence of potential fraud, they might be liable for the revenue lost through fraud. As de la Feria (2020) argues, the effectiveness of these measures is questionable because of a limited deterrence effect on crime and the liability being imposed on subjects who are only remotely connected with fraudsters. On the other hand, as is discussed in the following section, this type of regulation has incentivised organisations to implement internal compliance measures and self-regulate in this area.

Beyond state regulation – international standards, self-regulation and compliance

An increasingly important source of economic crime regulation are instruments created by informal state organisations and non-state actors such as international private organisations, non-profit organisations and business associations. In line with the above-discussed theories of regulation – regulatory space, responsive regulation, and global legal pluralism – this space is filled by a mixture of regulatory sources, and especially those reflecting interests of powerful states, state organisations, and firms (Ayres & Braithwaite, 1992; Hancher & Moran, 1989). The following sections discuss two key examples of these regulatory activities: transgovernmental networks and corporate compliance standards.

Transgovernmental networks – the case of Financial Action Task Force

Many sources of economic crime regulation are not created by nation state and international organisations, but rather by transgovernmental networks. Unlike formal negotiations, these informal networks are based on peer-to-peer ties and provide opportunities for frequent interactions. Informal and flexible exchange of experience and information improve the effectiveness of state response to common societal problems (OECD, 2013). This makes these networks well-suited to resolve practical problems associated with economic crime regulation and its enforcement.

The Financial Action Task Force (FATF) is an example of a transgovernmental network that has acquired a huge degree of authority. The FATF sets non-binding regulatory standards and operational measures for combating money laundering and the financing of terrorism. Besides standard setting, the FATF promotes effective implementation of these standards, monitors countries' progress in implementing the FATF Recommendations (see FATF, 2019), reviews criminal techniques and counter-measures and promotes global implementation of FATF Recommendations (FATF, n.d.).

For example, Recommendation 29 indicates that each country should establish a financial intelligence unit (FIU).[6] These national units should, for example, be able to receive and analyse suspicious activity reports and disseminate the results of that analysis (FATF, 2019, p. 24). This recommendation stands behind the formation of the so-called Egmont Group, an informal network of Financial Intelligence Units that facilitates information exchange, training and the sharing of information. The FATF is only one of many transgovernmental networks that create standards, for example, the Basel committee on Banking Supervision, the International Association of Insurance Supervisors, and the International Competition Network also create standards in their respective areas.

While these networks may have a positive impact on regulating certain aspects of economic crime, they are subject to criticism. The most authoritative of these networks create accountability and participation concerns, especially when their decisions have impact on parties that are excluded from a decision-making process. For example, the aim of FATF's Non-Cooperative Countries and Territories (NCCT) initiative was to incentivise non-FATF members to comply with the FATF recommendations. Following the criticism of the NCCT blacklist, the FATF currently maintains a list of 'High-Risk Jurisdictions subject to a Call for Action' and a list of 'Jurisdictions under Increased Monitoring'. These lists have provided economic and reputational incentives for the 39 Members of the FATF as well as non-members to comply with non-binding FATF standards (Blazejewski, 2008). This leverage to extend the standard on non-participating countries is one of the reasons why the FATF standards have influenced AML regulation worldwide.

Self-regulation and corporate compliance

Businesses and other organisations regulate economic crime in different ways. The discussion is limited to two key examples. Firstly, businesses find it sometimes beneficial to form a collective action initiative. Secondly, businesses must implement corporate compliance programmes in response to the public policing of economic crime.

Collective action initiatives

A collective action initiative is an alliance of organisations who adhere to common anti-economic crime principles, rules and standards. These initiatives can take many forms and actual requirements can range from a mere declaration to much more ambitious initiatives associated with third-party monitoring. Collective actions can take the following forms (see OECD, 2020):

1   Statement or declaration: These include public commitments to prevent economic crime. This may be related to a project or a single transaction. The compliance relies on the trust of involved actors, reputation and self-enforcement.
2   Integrity pact: These are mainly aimed to reduce the risk of economic crime in public procurement. While public procurement laws provide a minimum level of assurance that public authorities are purchasing goods,

services and works from the market in an effective, efficient and transparent way, they have many limitations. Integrity pacts provide additional assurance as they include an agreement between public buyers and bidding businesses to refrain from economic crimes. These agreements also usually include a process of reporting and resolving integrity issues and independent monitoring. For more information, see some of the established initiatives such as the B20 Collective Action Hub (Basel Institute on Governance, n.d.).

3   Standard-setting initiatives and certifications: Many business activities are governed by standards that concern the different aspects of crime prevention and sustainable operations of businesses. These standards are developed not only under auspices of states and international organisations such as the UN but also in combination with private bodies, and by transnational private-sector networks. One such standard-setting body is the International Organization for Standardization (ISO) that issued the ISO 37001 Anti-Bribery Management System standard (International Organization for Standardization, n.d.). The release of this standard is associated with a system of certification led by various accredited consultancies, which undertake independent audits. This standard and underlying certification processes are closely linked with the necessity of businesses to implement effective compliance programmes. This last example of how states invite private actors to self-regulate is discussed in the following section.

Corporate compliance

Typically, state regulation may require businesses to undertake efforts internally to prevent and detect violations of economic crime laws and regulations. The compliance function is often associated with the necessity to implement internal processes by which organisations seek to adapt behaviour to applicable laws, regulations and social norms (Griffith, 2016, p. 2082). As illustrated in Table 10.2, these internal processes are distributed across an organisation, which is often conceptualised as the 'Three Lines of Defence'.

A well-managed organisation needs to implement its compliance function through ethics and compliance programmes (Treviño & Weaver, 2003). These programmes include compliance policies which symbolise internally as well as externally the organisational commitment to prevent and detect economic crime. These programmes should also clearly establish measures and procedures of how the policy commitments are to be implemented (Miller, 2015). An important fact that stands behind the adoption of compliance programmes is that an initial incentive to implement them does not come from the board of directors or corporate law, but is imposed upon organisations by enforcement authorities (Griffith, 2016).

Table 10.2 Internal controls: three lines of defence

First line of defence	**Operational units – managers carrying out business** Not compliance professionals. Maintaining internal controls on a day-to-day basis. Cascading responsibility structure.
Second line of defence	**Monitoring and control units – chief compliance officer/ general counsel/chief risk officer** Compliance professionals responsible for monitoring and control activities. Responsible for prevention and detection of economic crime as well as for the risk appetite and risk-taking. They define roles, goals and responsibilities and provide guidance and training.
Third line of defence	**Internal audit** Providing comprehensive assurance – scanning the entire organization. Highest level of independence and objectivity.

Sources: See Miller (2015) and IIA (2013).

Enforcement authorities have a key role in incentivising organisations to implement ethics and compliance programmes. This trend originates in the USA, where corporate governance has been linked to out-of-court settlements, such as DPAs, since the 1990s. The level of compliance has a very important influence on the outcomes of settlement negotiations: corporations can, for example, get leniency if they can show their compliance programmes are effective, or if they show willingness to rectify any existing weaknesses in their compliance programmes. This formal recognition of a role of compliance programmes during the enforcement of economic crime cases has spread to multiple other countries such as the UK, France and Brazil (Hock, 2021; Pasculli, 2021; Søreide & Makinwa, 2020).

What constitutes an effective compliance programme, however, has been subject to significant ambiguity. It is true that various enforcement authorities have started releasing various guidance documents to clarify how they plan to assess the effectiveness of these programmes.[7] There, however, remains a huge space for corporations to develop their own approaches and self-regulate.

Conclusion

Economic crime regulation is an umbrella term for a complicated package of laws, regulations, industry standards and private norms. While criminal law can be understood as the key response to economic crime, in practice, it is not the case. In this chapter, we have illustrated some of the key concepts of economic crime regulation and its different sources.

Good understanding of criminal justice system response to the problem of economic crime requires an elementary understanding of the concepts of law. The legalistic definition of 'the law' indicates that the law is the system of rules of a particular country, group or area of activity. The purpose of such a system is not only to change behaviour but also to institutionalise societal values. There are many legal sources of economic crime regulation ranging from international law, EU law, and national laws and regulations.

Unlike the study of the law and legal principles, the concept of regulation has become a key topic beyond legal research. Here the discussion about economic crime becomes much more interesting for criminologists and other social scientists. When studying regulation, social scientists are examining the broad range of attempts to alter behaviour according to defined standards. These standards can be in the form of legal rules adopted by the state, but they can also take a form of more informal rules and practices that originate from private actors. In this context, economic crime regulation emerges and interacts within a specific sphere of life. These interactions are explained by multiple theories on regulation such as Regulatory Space (Hancher & Moran, 1989), Responsive Regulation (Ayres & Braithwaite, 1992) and Global Legal Pluralism (Teubner & Fischer-Lescano, 2004).

The understanding of various sources of economic crime regulation and their interactions is key for better understanding of an appropriate policy response. When discussing an appropriate response to bribery, money laundering, fraud, IP crime or cartels, we need to understand an entire system of regulatory responses. Being limited to resources existing in only one sphere would necessarily lead to inappropriate simplification.

It is important to note that the above discussion has largely focused on legal and other economic crime rules as they exist in books. While the understanding of such complexity is very important, it does not say much about the compliance with these rules and how they are enforced by competent actors. As these questions are very much context dependent, they are dealt with in the chapters discussing specific types of economic crime.

Statutes and treaties

Bribery Act 2010, c. 23.
Crime and Courts Act, 2013, c. 22.
Criminal Finances Act 2017, c. 22.
Competition Act 1998, c. 41.
Consolidated Version of the Treaty on the Functioning of the European Union. 15, May 9, 2008, 2008 O.J. (C 115) 47.
Foreign Corrupt Practices Act of 1977, 15 U.S.C. s 78dd-1 ff.
Fraud Act 2006, c. 35.
Money Laundering Regulations 2017, No. 692.
OECD Convention on Combating Bribery of Foreign Public Officials in International Business Transactions, 17 December 1997, www.oecd.org/daf/anti-bribery/ConvCombatBribery_ENG.pdf

Proceeds of Crime Act 2002, c. 29.

United Nations Convention Against Transnational Organized Crime, 15 November 2000, www.unodc.org/documents/treaties/UNTOC/Publications/TOC%20Convention/TOCebook-e.pdf

United Nations Convention against Corruption, 31 October 2003, www.unodc.org/documents/brussels/UN_Convention_Against_Corruption.pdf

EU law

Council Directive 2010/24/EU of 16 March 2010 concerning mutual assistance for the recovery of claims relating to taxes, duties and other measures, 2010 O.J. (L 84).

Council Directive 2013/42/EU of 22 July 2013 amending Directive 2006/112/EC on the common system of value added tax, as regards a Quick Reaction Mechanism against VAT fraud, 2013 O.J. (L 201).

Council Regulation 2017/1939 of 12 October 2017 implementing enhanced cooperation on the establishment of the European Public Prosecutor's Office, 2017 O.J. (L 283).

Council Regulation 1/2003 of 16 December 2002 on the implementation of the rules on competition laid down in Articles 81 and 82 of the EC Treaty, 2003 O.J. (L 1).

Directive 2014/57 of the European Parliament and of the Council of 16 April 2014 on criminal sanctions for market abuse (market abuse directive), 2014 O.J. (L 173).

Directive, 2015/849 of the European Parliament and of the Council of 20 May 2015 on the prevention of the use of the financial system for the purposes of money laundering or terrorist financing, 2015 O.J. (L 141).

Directive 2017/1371 of the European Parliament and of the Council of 5 July 2017 on the fight against fraud to the Union's financial interests by means of criminal law, 2017 O.J. (L 198).

Directive 2018/1673 of the European Parliament and of the Council of 23 October 2018 on combating money laundering by criminal law, 2018 O.J. (L 284).

Notes

1 It must be noted that this analytical device still stresses the importance of the nation state as the key player that determines regulation and its space dimension (see also Inversi, 2019).
2 In general, the role of the nation state under this line of thinking is less important than under the regulatory space framework.
3 See the website on responsive regulation highlighting many practical implications of this perspective for policing of economic crime. Braithwaite (n.d.) Responsive Regulation http://johnbraithwaite.com/responsive-regulation/.

4   Hence, for example, these rules will only require the implementation of certain sanction types, such as fines and imprisonment, to be available to national enforcement authorities (European Commission, 2011). This is also associated with the nature of an EU directive as an instrument that does not have any direct legal effect on EU citizens. Directives specify only desired goals and minimum standards that the EU Member States are required to implement into their national legislations.
5   For more information about global settlements and global character of enforcement see Chapter 3.
6   Please note that the FATF provides 40 recommendations.
7   Consider, for example, the Evaluation of Corporate Compliance programmes document released by the DOJ (Department of Justice, 2019).

References

Ayres, I., & Braithwaite, J. (1992). *Responsive regulation: Transcending the deregulation debate*. Oxford University Press.

Baldwin, R., Cave, M., & Lodge, M. (2010). *The Oxford handbook of regulation*. Oxford University Press.

Baldwin, R., Cave, M., & Lodge, M. (2012). *Understanding regulation: Theory, strategy, and practice*. Oxford University Press.

Basel Institute on Governance. (n.d.). *B20 collective action hub*. https://baselgoverna nce.org/b20-collective-action-hub.

Becker, G. S. (1968). Crime and punishment: An economic approach. In C. A. Fielding & N.G. Witt (Ed.). *The economic dimensions of crime*. Palgrave Macmillan.

Bingham, T. H. (2011). *The rule of law*. Penguin.

Black, J. (2002). Critical reflections on regulation. *Australian Journal of Legal Philosophy, 27*(1), 1–36.

Blazejewski, K. S. (2008). The FATF and its institutional partners: Improving the effectiveness and accountability of transgovernmental networks. *Temple International and Comparative Law Journal, 22*(1), 1–62.

Braithwaite (n.d.) Responsive Regulation http://johnbraithwaite.com/responsive-reg ulation/.

Cambridge Dictionary (n.d.) Law. https://dictionary.cambridge.org/dictionary/english/law

Ceci, E., & Lamensch, M. (2018). *Vat fraud: Economic impact, challenges and policy issues*. European Parliament. www.europarl.europa.eu/cmsdata/156408/VAT%20 Fraud%20Study%20publication.pdf.

Conforti, B., & Labella, A. (2012). *An introduction to international law*. Martinus Nijhoff.

Davies, R., Richardson, P., Katinaite, V., & Manning, M. (2010). *Evolution of the UK banking system. Bank of England*. www.bankofengland.co.uk/quarterly-bulletin/ 2010/q4/evolution-of-the-uk-banking-system.

de la Feria, R. (2020). Tax fraud and selective law enforcement. *Journal of Law and Society, 47*(2), 240–270.

Department of Justice. (2015). *Nine FIFA officials and five corporate executives indicted for racketeering conspiracy and corruption*. www.justice.gov/opa/pr/nine-fifa-officials-and-five-corporate-executives-indicted-racketeering-conspiracy-and.

Department of Justice. (2019). *Evaluation of corporate compliance programs*. www.justice.gov/criminal-fraud/page/file/937501/download.

Ellickson R.C. (2016). When civil society uses an iron fist: The roles of private associations in rulemaking and adjudication. *American Law and Economics Review, 18*(2), 235–271.

European Commission. (2011). *Towards an EU criminal policy: Ensuring the effective implementation of EU policies through criminal law*. https://eur-lex.europa.eu/legal-content/EN/TXT/?uri=celex%3A52011DC0573.

European Commission. (n.d.). *Early detection and exclusion system*. https://ec.eur opa.eu/info/strategy/eu-budget/how-it-works/annual-lifecycle/implementation/anti-fraud-measures/edes_en.

Europol. (n.d.). *MTIC (Missing Trader Intra Community) Fraud*. www.europol.europa.eu/crime-areas-and-trends/crime-areas/economic-crime/mtic-missing-trader-intra-community-fraud.

FATF. (2019). *The FATF recommendations*. www.fatf-gafi.org/media/fatf/documents/recommendations/pdfs/FATF%20Recommendations%202012.pdf.

FATF. (n.d.) *What we do*. www.fatfgafi.org/about/whatwedo/#:~:text=Starting%20with%20its%20own%20members,of%20the%20FATF%20Recommendations%20globally.

Gomtsian, S., Balvert, A., Hock, B., & Kirman, O. (2018). Between the green pitch and the red tape: The private legal order of FIFA. *Yale Journal of International Law, 43*, 85–113.

Griffith, S. J. (2016). Corporate governance in an era of compliance. *William and Mary Law Review, 57*, 2075–2140.

Griffiths, J. (1979). Is law important? *New York University Law Review, 54*(2), 339–375.

Hancher, L., & Moran, M. (1989). Organizing regulatory space. In L. Hancher, M. Moran (Eds.), *Capitalism, culture and regulation* (pp. 371–300). Oxford University Press.

Hart, H. L. A., & Green, L. (2012). *The concept of law* (3rd ed.). Oxford University Press.

Hawley, S., King, C., & Lord, N. (2020). Justice for whom? The need for a principled approach to deferred prosecution in England and Wales. In T. Søreide & A. Makinwa (Eds.), *Negotiated settlements in bribery cases: A principled approach* (pp. 309–346). Edward Elgar Publishing.

Hock, B. (2020). *Airbus – How the UK and France learned to investigate and sanction international corruption*. European Compliance Center. https://complianter.eu/air bus-international-corruption/.

Hock, B. (2021). Policing corporate bribery: Negotiated settlements and bundling, *Policing and Society, 31*(8), 950–966

Hock, B., & Gomtsian, S. (2018). Private order building: The state in the role of the civil society and the case of FIFA. *International Sports Law Journal*, 17, 186–204.

Hood, C., Rothstein, H., & Baldwin, R. (2001). *The government of risk: Understanding risk regulation regimes*. Oxford University Press.

Huntington, S.P. (1968). *Political order in changing societies*. Yale University Press.

Husa, J. (2018). *Advanced introduction to law and globalisation*. Edward Elgar Publishers.

IIA. (2013). *The three lines of defense in effective risk management and control* (IIA Position Paper). https://na.theiia.org/standards-guidance/Public%20Documents/PP%20The%20Three%20Lines%20of%20Defense%20in%20Effective%20Risk%20Management%20and%20Control.pdf.

International Organization for Standardization. (n.d.). *ISO 37001 – Anti-bribery management systems* www.iso.org/iso-37001-anti-bribery-management.html.

Inversi, C. (2019). *Exploring the concept of regulatory space: Employment and working time regulation in the gig-economy* [Doctoral dissertation, University of Manchester]. www.research.manchester.ac.uk/portal/files/122870775/FULL_TEXT.PDF.

Katz A. (1996). Taking private ordering seriously. *University of Pennsylvania Law Review, 144*(5), 1745–1763.

Leeson, P.T. (2009). *The invisible hook: The hidden economics of pirates.* Princeton University Press.

Miller, G. P. (2015). The compliance function: An overview. In J. N. Gordon & W. G. Ringe (Eds.), *The Oxford handbook of corporate law and governance* (pp. 981–1002). Oxford University Press.

Morgan, B., & Yeung, K. (2007). *An introduction to law and regulation: Text and materials.* Cambridge University Press.

OECD. (2012). *Phase 3 report on implementing the OECD anti-bribery convention in the United Kingdom.* www.oecd.org/daf/anti-bribery/UnitedKingdomphase3reportEN.pdf.

OECD. (2013). *International regulatory co-operation: Addressing global challenges.* OECD Publishing.

OECD. (2020). *Collective action and the fight against corruption* (Policy Briefing Note). OECD www.oecd.org/south-east-europe/programme/Collective-Action-and-Fight-Against-Corruption-Policy-Briefing-Note-May2020.pdf.

Pasculli, L. (2021). The responsibilization paradox: The legal route from deresponsibilization to systemic corruption in the Australian financial sector. *Policing: A Journal of Policy and Practice,* https://doi.org/10.1093/police/paab068

Pomeroy, R. (2007, November 8). *Mafia code reveals gangsters' 10 commandments.* Reuters. www.reuters.com/article/oukoe-uk-italy-mafia-idUKL0819930320071108.

Richman, B. D. (2009). The antitrust of reputation mechanisms: Institutional economics and concerted refusals to deal. *Virginia Law Review, 95*(2), 325–387.

Schell-Busey, N., Simpson, S.S., Rorie, M., & Alper, M. (2016). What works? A systematic review of corporate crime deterrence. *Criminology and Public Policy,* 15(2), 387–416.

Selznick, P. (1985). Focusing organisational research on regulation. In R. Noll (Ed.), *Regulatory policy and the social sciences* (pp. 363–367). University of California Press.

Serious Fraud Office. (2020a). *SFO operational handbook: Deferred prosecution agreements.* www.sfo.gov.uk/publications/guidance-policy-and-protocols/sfo-operational-handbook/deferred-prosecution-agreements/.

Serious Fraud Office. (2020b). D*eferred prosecution agreement. SFO v. Airbus.* www.sfo.gov.uk/download/airbus-se-deferred-prosecution-agreement-statement-of-facts/#.

Søreide, T., and Makinwa, A. (eds.) (2020). *Negotiated settlements in bribery cases: A principled approach.* Edward Elgar Publishing.

SRA. (2019). *Anti money laundering.* www.sra.org.uk/risk/outlook/priority-risks/anti-money-laundering/.

Stefanou, C., White, S., & Xanthaki, H. (2011). *OLAF at the crossroads: Action against EU fraud.* Hart Publishing.

Teubner, G., & A. Fischer-Lescano (2004). Regime-collisions: The vain search for legal unity in the fragmentation of global law. *Michigan Journal of International Law, 25*(4), 999–1046.

Treviño, L. K., & Weaver, G. R. (2003). *Managing ethics in business organizations: Social scientific perspective*. Stanford University Press.

Whelan, P. (2012). Legal certainty and cartel criminalisation within the EU member states. *Cambridge Law Journal, 71*(3), 677–702.

Wood, H. (2019). *Supervising the UK AML supervisors: The office for professional body anti-money laundering supervision* (First Annual Report). Centre for Financial Crime and Security Studies https://rusi.org/commentary/supervising-uk-aml-supe rvisors-office-professional-body-anti-money-laundering-supervision.

Zagaris, B. (2015). *International white collar crimes: Cases and materials*. Cambridge University Press.

Chapter 11

State and transnational policing of economic crime

Introduction

The policing of economic crime is a highly contentious issue. Sutherland (1949) argued that economic crimes should be brought under the jurisdiction of law enforcement agencies and criminal prosecutors rather than left to regulatory and civil justice. On the other hand, Braithwaite (2002) argued in favour of these non-criminal, restorative justice approaches. The reality in the UK accords with Braithwaite's view in that the vast majority of fraud and corruption offences are handled by regulatory bodies, and only very few are investigated by the police and prosecuted (Button et al., 2018; Levi, 2013). Levi (1986b) predicted 35 years ago that the lack of criminal enforcement would result in fraud becoming a major area of crime, and he was right. The Roskill Report of 1986 severely criticised the fractured institutional arrangements for policing fraud in the UK, calling for a unified body to investigate and prosecute fraud, and for non-jury trials (Levi, 1986a). A study conducted 25 years ago in 1996 by the UK police themselves concluded that the service lacked a strategy and was reluctant to commit resources to deal with inter-county crimes, never mind cross cross-border crimes (Doig et al., 2001). The Fraud Review in 2006 (Attorney General, 2006) laid bare the failures of the uncoordinated approach to fraud in the UK.

It appears that little has changed since the Fraud Review. Fisher (2010) continued to describe the arrangements for fighting economic crime as lamentable. A HMICFRS (2019) report eviscerated the police for its weak response to fraud in the UK. One consequence of these continued systematic institutional failures is that the vast majority of victims cannot access justice, leading some to take matters into their own hands (Shepherd, 2020). A second consequence predicted by Doig et al. (2001) is that the enforcement of the law would be increasingly taken out of the public sphere and privatised (see Chapter 12).

The two institutional areas subject to repeated criticism are the courts and the police. The courts and the prosecution services in the UK and elsewhere struggle to deal effectively with complex economic crime cases (Attorney General, 2006; Fisher, 2010; Fraud Advisory Panel, 2010; Levi, 1986a; Smith

DOI: 10.4324/9781003081753-11

& Shepherd, 2019; Wright, 2003). The courts are the primary cause of the bottleneck which deters the police and causes victims to find alternative forms of justice (Button et al., 2015). Even governments, including the UK government, have sought alternatives such as the confiscation powers under the Proceeds of Crime Act 2002, Deferred Prosecution Agreements (DPAs), Unexplained Wealth Orders (UWOs) and huge administrative fines for cartel offences (Chapter 8). The second primary area of criticism is the inadequacies of the police forces. The consistent complaints are low priority, inadequate resources and fractured structures (HMICFRS, 2019; Levi, 2010; Skidmore et al., 2018).

Furthermore, Levi's work has demonstrated that globalisation and the Internet have pumped high octane fuel into all forms of economic crime, not just fraud, to cause global harm (Levi, 1986b). The complexity of trans-national forms of corruption, bribery, intellectual property crime, money laundering and other economic crimes analysed in this book indicates that simply focusing on state policing is reductionist. In many instances, state policing occupies dual roles as both national policing and global policing, including extraterritorial policing and policing coordinated by international organisations. The nature of transnational policing actors and the effective-ness of transnational policing is an under-researched area.

This chapter sets out the role of the *police* in the wider context of *policing* both nationally and internationally and discusses the apparent economic crime paradox: despite the scale of the economic crime problem and the extent of the harm caused, it is a low priority on the police agenda. The chapter will begin by analysing state policing and the police. It will then move on to explore national policing of economic crime, before examining police priorities. The chapter will end by considering transitional forms of policing, including the role of international organisations and extraterritorial forms of national enforcement.

Policing and the police

Policing

It is important to distinguish between the terms 'police' and 'policing' (Dowling et al., 2019). Policing refers to the activities of organisations that are directed at maintaining social order. As Chapter 12 will explain, these social control activities are not restricted to the police. All organisations employ control processes of some form that are aimed at regulating the activities of their members and the interactions with broader society (Button, 2019). Without the controls, businesses, schools and hospitals would descend into chaos. Sensible organisations create rules to maintain order and apply dis-ciplinary sanctions to enforce compliance. For broader control purposes, statutory regulators such as the Financial Conduct Authority (FCA) in the

UK and the Australian Prudential Regulation Authority impose order on their respective finance industries. Similarly, most professions are governed by regulatory bodies with rulebooks and sanction powers, for example, the Solicitors Regulation Authority (SRA) in the UK and the Nederlandse orde van advocaten (NOvA) in Holland. Although the scope of their control is very different, individual organisations, industry regulators and profession regulators all do policing. Button (2019, p. 10) lists five core policing functions common to all organisations involved in policing:

- maintenance of order/keeping the peace;
- prevention of deviant acts;
- surveillance for deviant acts;
- investigation of deviant acts;
- application of sanctions and referral for sanction for breaches.

Loader (2000) developed a different approach, defining policing according to an organisational typology:

> *Policing by government* – usually recognised as the police. The category includes the national police forces and other law enforcement bodies, such as the FBI in the US, the Gendarmerie in France, the Carabinieri in Italy and the National Crime Agency in the UK.
> *Policing through government* – policing services controlled and provided by government but supplied by others, such as functions contracted out to the private security industry.
> *Policing above government* – international developments in policing such as Interpol and Europol. They are also known as intergovernmental organisations.
> *Policing beyond government* – the growing market for private policing services, for example when residents on estates purchase their own private patrols.
> *Policing below government* – organised surveillance encouraged by the state, such as neighbourhood watch, as well as vigilantism.

Thus, we can see that the term 'policing' encompasses a wide range of activities (Button, 2019) and a wide range of organisational types (Loader, 2000). The scope and powers of the organisations that are doing the policing depend very much on the social context. However, they all have the same universal aim in maintaining order through the exercise of social control (Bowling et al., 2019).

The police

The term 'police' refers to a particular type of institution involved in social control (Bowling et al., 2019). The police are the most visible and familiar agents of control: a body of men and women, usually uniformed, who patrol public spaces, intervene when disorder occurs, investigate crimes and apprehend offenders (Reiner, 1994). The modern police service is a special type of policing agency in that the scope of its control remit is very wide: from patrolling the streets, tackling terrorism to responding to serious road accidents. They are controlled and funded by governments to provide an omnibus, catch-all public service whilst having access to coercive powers including the legitimate use of force (Bittner, 1980). These powers are specified in national legislation but are also limited by the same legislation in modern societies to ensure that those powers are not abused by the police themselves, nor by the governments that fund and empower the police. Carefully balancing these powers is essential to maintaining the legitimacy of the public police and the social contract between the institutions and the public they serve (Cohen & Feldberg, 1991).

The police regularly draw on their powers to deal with criminal incidents; however, the majority of their time is consumed with non-criminal social work. The police are most often called upon to manage traffic flows, provide directions, provide a reassuring presence at public events, act as a clearing house for minor community complaints and intervene before disputes get out of hand (Hough & Roberts, 2017; Reiner, 2010).

National policing of economic crimes

All countries are unique in the way that they structure their laws and public policing arrangements for fighting economic crime. However, there is a common trend in the development of specialist functions that focus on economic crime. Some of the functions are completely separate from the police, some are specialised police forces and others are specialist units within the police. There has been considerable debate for decades over the policing of economic crime in the UK with repeated calls for more resources and greater integration (Button, 2008, 2021; Button et al., 2011; Doig et al., 2001). Table 11.1 shows that the very low level of police resources dedicated to economic crime compared to the scale of the fraud problem recorded by the UK government, and in comparison to other crimes. The March 2020 Crime Survey of England and Wales reported a total of 10.2 million crimes, 36% of which were fraud offences, yet only 0.5% of prosecuted cases involved fraud (Home Office, 2020a; MOJ, 2020; ONS, 2020). It is clearly no coincidence that just 0.6% of police officers in England and Wales are dedicated to economic crime (Home Office, 2020b). It is therefore very tempting to conclude that more resources are required to increase capacity and accelerate the number of justice outcomes. However, the structure of policing is equally important. This section describes three approaches: the highly integrated approach in Italy, the consolidated practices in the USA and the segregated structure in the UK.

Table 11.1 Crime and police headcount in England and Wales in 2020

	All crime	Fraud	%
Crime survey offences	10.2 million	3.7 million	36.3
Recorded offences	5,003,557	748,326	15.0
Disseminated to forces by Action Fraud/NFIB		29,634	
Prosecuted	1,339,898	7,670	0.5
Convicted	1,159,388	6,986	0.6
Police officers	129,110	820	0.6
Police staff	72,330	798	1.1
	201,440	1,618	0.8

Sources: Home Office (2020a,b), MOJ (2020), ONS (2020).

Integrated police structure – Italy

Italy's approach to policing economic crime is highly centralised under the Guardia di Finanza (GdF), which literally means guard of finance. The GdF is a militarised police force of 80,000 men and women controlled by the Ministro dell'Economia e delle Finanze (Ministry of Economy and Finance) and commanded by generals. It is one of three police forces in Italy alongside the Polizia di Stato (State Police) and the Carbinieri, a gendarme type of military force. The GdF has a very broad remit covering border protections, coastguard operations, alpine search and rescue, and territorial law enforcement. Its economic crime responsibilities include cartel offences, corruption, fraud, illicit trade, IP crime, money laundering, tax evasion and terrorist financing (Nussbaum & Doherty, 2021).

Consolidated police structure – USA

The American approach is structurally less integrated with a range of police and regulatory agencies tasked with fighting economic crime. The country's federal structure also adds to the complexity as each state has a high degree of independence in how they enforce the law. A myriad of local, city, state and federal police agencies are tasked with tackling economic crimes, which are typically referred to as white-collar crimes. The City of Portland Police, for example, has a White Collar Crimes Unit that deals with fraud, identity theft, IP crime and marketing scams. At the federal level, regulatory agencies and law enforcement agencies are involved in tackling economic crime.

The US Internal Revenue Service (IRS) is a regulatory agency within the US Department of Treasury and has general administrative powers for enforcing tax collection. It also has a criminal investigation (CI) division staffed by Treasury Agents. The CI's primary purpose is to support other agencies in tackling all types of economic crime, including tax evasion, fraud, corruption, illicit trade and money laundering (IRS:CI, 2020). The Financial

Crimes Enforcement Network (FinCEN) also sits within the US Treasury. It is a Financial Intelligence Unit (FIU) that provides intelligence and analytical support to domestic and foreign law enforcement agencies. The Office of Foreign Assets Control (OFAC) sits alongside FinCEN enforcing economic and trade sanctions.

The Federal Trade Commission (FTC) is the US regulator charged with enforcing consumer protection laws aimed at fraudulent business practices, counterfeit goods, cyber scams and antitrust cartels. As part of their product safety remits, the Consumer Product Safety Commission (CPSM) and the Food and Drug Administration (FDA) also deal with counterfeit goods. The Customs and Border Protection (CBP) agency investigates and seizes illicit goods at the borders. Its sister agency within the Department for Homeland Security, Immigration and Customs Enforcement (ICE), has a specialist group that focuses on pursuing and disrupting transnational criminal organisations using a wide range of financial crime and illicit trade laws.

The Securities and Exchange Commission (SEC) regulates the stock market in the US to protect investors. It enforces federal securities laws covering listed firms, investment advisors, brokers and stock exchanges by administrative and civil means. It transfers criminal fraud cases to the Department of Justice (DOJ). The Commodity Futures Trading Commission (CFTC) has jurisdiction over future trading in commodities such as agricultural products and metals. Its regulatory role is similar to the SEC, enforcing federal laws through administrative and civil powers. The US Postal Inspection Service (USPIS) is the regulatory arm of the US Postal Service. It is unique amongst the American economic crime regulators in having its own specialised police force, the US Postal Security Force, that deals with cybercrime, fraud, identity theft and money laundering involving the postal services.

Whilst all the regulators are empowered to enforce the law through administrative and civil justice regimes, the criminal case work of all the US regulators and police forces are channelled through the DOJ, the public prosecutor and its US Attorneys. However, the DOJ is very different from the Crown Prosecution Service (CPS) in the UK, which focuses solely on prosecuting cases in criminal courts. The DOJ is a catch-all enforcement agency with respect to economic crimes. Firstly, the DOJ also initiates and conducts its own investigations. Secondly, and more potently, the Federal Bureau of Investigations (FBI), the Drug Enforcement Agency (DEA) and the Bureau of Alcohol, Tobacco, Firearms and Explosives (ATF) are all frontline police agencies within the DOJ that have responsibilities for economic crime. Thirdly, the DOJ has two specialist divisions that provide gateways to partner agencies: the Antitrust Division is a pathway for the FTC and the Tax Division is the pathway primarily, but not exclusively, for the IRS.

Thirdly, the DOJ is not limited to criminal prosecution. It also acts like the regulatory agencies: its Civil Division enforces the law by seeking appropriate remedies through the civil courts. It litigates to force individuals or organisations to comply with the law, and it sues economic criminals to recoup money lost through fraud and the abuse of federal funds. This consolidated two-limbed approach, using criminal and civil procedures, provides the DOJ with a breadth of options to deliver justice using its own resources or in cooperation with the regulators. These powers also enable the DOJ to support class action victims who launch claims for damages in the civil courts (see Chapter 4 – cartels).

Segregated police structure – UK

The segregated policing structure in the UK bears no similarity with the integrated Italian model. It is closer to the consolidated US model. Like the USA, the UK does not have a single agency that deals with economic crime. The City of London Police (CoLP) has been tasked to be the lead force for economic crimes, and it incorporates specialist units: the Action Fraud national call centre and the National Fraud Intelligence Bureau (NFIB) that processes the reports, DCPCU, IFED and PIPCU (Table 11.2). The CoLP also oversees the integrated national process for handling fraud and cyber-crime reports from the public. The reports are received by the Action Fraud call centre. The reports are then analysed by the NFIB and disseminated to local forces for investigation.

The Regional Organised Crime Units (ROCUs) investigate instances of serious economic crime when they involve organised crime groups (OCG). The only national force covering economic crime is the National Crime Agency (NCA), which is modelled on the FBI and, again, its focus is serious and organised crime. Its National Economic Crime Centre (NECC) does, however, specialise in economic crimes. The NECC manages a national reporting process for suspected money laundering, which is similar to the CoLP's fraud system. The UKFIU receives and analyses all the Suspicious Activity Reports (SAR) from regulated financial businesses in support of NCA operations.

Table 11.3 is a list of non-police agencies in the UK whose remit includes economic crime. The list is not exhaustive, but it contains the most prominent agencies and regulators including the public prosecutors. There are two key differences between the US and UK models with respect to the public prosecutor. Firstly, there are three principal, independent prosecution services in the UK: the CPS covering England and Wales, the Procurator Fiscal in Scotland and the Public Prosecution Service (PPS) in Northern Ireland.

The second key difference lies in the powers of the public prosecutors. The DOJ has very wide-ranging powers and tools at its disposal covering investigation, direct support from the FBI, civil litigation as well as prosecution. With the objective of maintaining the legitimacy of the police and the social contract with the public, the prosecutors are not directly involved in investigative policing and matters involving civil law.[1] The prosecutors cannot therefore

Table 11.2 Economic crime structure of the UK police

Local police forces	
Police forces of England and Wales (n=43) Police Scotland Police Service of Northern Ireland (PSNI)	Economic crimes investigated by generalist investigators or specialist economic crime teams
Regional police units	
Regional Organised Crime Unit (ROCU) (n=10)	Drawn from local forces. Investigate serious organised crime
Sector police	
British Transport Police (BTP)	Ticket fraud, funded by the rail industry
Ministry of Defence Police (MDP)	Civilian police force within the MoD
Within the City of London Police	
Dedicated Card and Payment Crime Unit (DCPCU)	Funded by the finance industry
Insurance Fraud Enforcement Department (IFED)	Funded by the insurance industry
Police Intellectual Property Crime Unit (PIPCU)	Funded by the Intellectual Property Office (IPO)
National police forces	
National Crime Agency (NCA)	Investigates serious organised crime.
International Corruption Unit (ICU)	Within the NCA, investigates foreign corruption and bribery
Coordination units	
Within the City of London Police	
Action Fraud	National call centre for fraud and cybercrime
National Fraud Intelligence Bureau (NFIB)	Analyses Action Fraud reports and disseminates cases to local police forces
Within the NCA	
National Economic Crime Centre (NECC)	Coordinates the UK's response to economic crime
UK Financial Intelligence Unit (UKFIU)	Analyses and disseminates Suspicious Activity Reports (SAR) from regulated firms
Foreign Bribery Clearing House	Coordinates transnational bribery investigations
International Anti-Corruption Coordination Centre (IACCC)	Supports grand corruption investigations conducted by agencies in foreign jurisdictions
Joint Money Laundering Intelligence Taskforce (JMLIT)	Public-private sector information exchange partnership

initiate and pursue alternative investigative strategies, or seek civil remedies at a lower standard of proof. The single-lane role of the CPS, Procurator Fiscal and PPS inevitably causes a bottleneck to justice (Button et al., 2015). The Serious Fraud Office (SFO) was created in 1987 to overcome these problems for serious fraud and bribery cases. The SFO mirrors the DOJ in that it is both an investigator and prosecutor. However, it has had a chequered history

Table 11.3 Economic crime structure of UK non-police government agencies (principal)

Border and coastal law enforcement

Border Agency	Customs and immigration fraud, counterfeit goods and illicit trade
Maritime and Coastguard Agency (MCA)	Ship and seafarer certification fraud, fisheries fraud and illicit trade

Government regulators

Competition and Markets Authority (CMA)	Antitrust cartels
Department of Work and Pensions (DWP) – Counter Fraud, Compliance and Debt (CFCD)	Welfare benefit fraud
Driver and Vehicle Licensing Agency (DVLA)	Driving licence fraud
Driver and Vehicle Standards Agency (DVSA)	Commercial vehicle licence, document, tachograph fraud
Financial Conduct Authority (FCA)	Finance industry and stock market fraud, money laundering
Food Standards Agency (FSA)	Food fraud
Gambling Commission	Gambling industry fraud and money laundering
Her Majesty's Revenue and Customs (HMRC) – Fraud Investigation Service (FIS)	Tax fraud, money laundering
Intellectual Property Office (IPO) Intelligence Hub	Coordinates IP crime investigations
Local Authority Trading Standards (n=192)	Consumer fraud, counterfeit goods and illicit trade, rogue trading
Office of Financial Sanctions Implementation (OFSI)	Within HM Treasury, ensures sanctions are enforced in the UK

Principal prosecution agencies

Crown Prosecution Service (CPS)	Main public prosecutor in England and Wales
Procurator Fiscal	Public prosecutor in Scotland
Public Prosecution Service (PPS)	Public prosecutor in Northern Ireland
Serious Fraud Office (SFO)	Investigates and prosecutes serious fraud and bribery

as it prosecutes so few cases, 17 in 2018–2019 and just 3 in 2019–2020, and its conviction ratio is just 62% (de Grazia, 2008; Jolly, 2021; SFO, 2020, 2021).

Another notable difference between the UK and US models is that some of the UK regulators have criminal prosecution powers: CMA, FCA, FSA, Gambling Commission, FCA and MCA. However, this power is not particularly relevant as they rarely bring criminal prosecutions. Therefore, the public prosecutor in effect performs the same criminal prosecution function as the DOJ for the police and the regulators. The Department of Work and Pensions (DWP) and the Her Majesty's Revenue and Customs (HMRC) initiate the

Table 11.4 DWP and HMRC compliance and fraud cases in 2019–2020

	DWP	HMRC	Total
Compliance cases	332,000	338,000	670,000
Fraud investigations	46,000	864	46,864
Prosecutions	c.2,000	691	2,691

Sources: DWP (2020), HMRC (2021).

vast majority of regulator prosecutions as part of their programmes to prevent and deter welfare benefit fraud and tax crimes. The public sector in the UK employs 15,000 counter-fraud professionals (HMG, n.d.), nearly ten times as many as the police. Most of these professionals work for the DWP and HMRC: 8,000 in the Counter Fraud, Compliance and Debt group within the DWP, and 4,500 in the HMRC's Fraud Investigation Service (DWP, 2020; HMRC, 2021). The majority of their work is aimed at forcing compliance and providing evidence for administrative penalties rather than bringing people to court. Overall in 2019–2020, 7% of compliance cases turned into fraud investigations and just 0.4% resulted in about 2,700 prosecutions (Table 11.4). Nevertheless, the DWP and HMRC together accounted for one-third of all prosecutions in 2020 (see Table 11.1). This blend of enforcing regulatory compliance, a form of restorative justice, and hard criminal justice is an increasingly common feature of economic crime (Button et al., 2018) and is most clearly expressed with the introduction of Civil Recovery Orders (CROs), UWOs and DPAs.

Criticisms of the segregated structure

Button (2011) described the architecture of fraud policing in the UK as flawed, fragmented and under-resourced. Importantly, he also observed how the entities dealing with these crimes lack resilience. They are frequently reorganised, merged, demerged, resourced and then stripped of resources in response to the fluid priorities of local forces. He also observed how the triage processes and criteria used to identify and select cases for investigation are highly inconsistent and often illogical. Consequently, some high harm cases are totally ignored, whilst low harm are taken on. One reason that deserving cases are not taken on by a local police force is confusion over which force or regulatory entity should deal with it (Button et al., 2008). It is unclear whether cases should be allocated according to the type of economic crime, the seriousness of the crime or the geographic jurisdiction.

The jurisdictional issue can be a particularly vexed problem when the victim is in one county and the offender is in another, or when the victim is a business with multiple operating centres. This does not serve victims well as it can send them on a merry-go-round trying to find a force or agency to take on their cases (Button et al., 2013; Shepherd, 2020). The globalised digital era has exacerbated this problem as economic crime has no respect for jurisdictional boundaries (HMICFRS, 2019). Button et al. (2008) proposed the solution is a centralised, national police force dedicated to economic crime, or more radically a national body staffed by civilian investigators.

Some centralisation has been brought about with the nomination of the CoLP as the lead force, and the introduction of Action Fraud and the NFIB as the call centre and initial triage functions. However, the problems remain because all the local forces, the ROCUs, the NCA and the SFO have a high degree of independence over their resource allocations and which cases they take on. The result is, as the HMICFRS (2019) noted, that large-scale crimes, which should be investigated, still bounce around between forces and agencies with no one taking responsibility. Too often police staff see their role as finding reasons not to take on cases, even when there is good evidence, in order to reduce demand (HMICFRS, 2019). The problem that centralised reporting has not addressed is the fractured structure of the entities which are tasked to investigate the crimes (Skidmore et al., 2018). They concluded that all economic crimes investigated by the police should be handled by regional units that sit alongside the existing ROCUs. They also recommended that this regional model should be coordinated and tasked centrally by the CoLP.

Addressing the resource and structural issues requires the commitment of policy makers. However, police leaders rarely see economic crime as a priority because it does not 'bang, bleed, or shout', which means that the police does little to prevent fraudsters from committing further offences (HMICFRS, 2019, p. 5). Skidmore et al. (2018) suggest that the even bigger problem is that the policy makers who direct the police do not prioritise economic crime. Perhaps the biggest question is why they do not see economic crime as a priority, a question that will be returned to later in the chapter.

Cooperation and specialisation

Greater integration of the entities involved in fighting economic crime is one way to increase efficiency and effectiveness. However, it could lead to unintended outcomes if the aim is to create a coordinated group of catch-all generalists who can be assigned to all types of economic crime. Whilst some of the investigative skills are common to all crimes, the particular skills and tools required for investigating online piracy, corporate bribery and money laundering are very different. The alternative to integration is to increase the level of cooperation and coordination between existing entities. Action Fraud and the NFIB are a step towards coordination, though they presently fail to ensure coordination between the entities at the business end.

The UK governments 'Economic Crime Plan' is based on making better use of public and private sector resources through cooperation and coordination (HM Treasury and Home Office, 2019). The coordination units within the

NCA are key components of the strategy (Table 11.2). The JMLIT consists of 40 financial firms, Cifas,[2] the FCA, HMRC, the SFO, the CoLP and the Metropolitan Police. The private sector has been co-opted into fighting economic crime through legislation in the areas of anti-money laundering, bribery and tax evasion. The three sector specific teams within the CoLP are functioning examples of very close cooperation. The DCPCU and IFED are funded by the finance sector and the insurance industry, respectively. PIPCU is funded by a government agency, the IPO. All three units provide a specialist gateway into the police that avoids Action Fraud. PIPCU is different from the other two in that anyone can contact PIPCU to report an IP crime. The IPO also runs the Intelligence Hub which collects IP crime information from any source and disseminates it to the police, Trading Standards, brand owners and trade bodies.

Pragmatic criminal justice

Wishing to exploit increased cooperation and coordination, yet unwilling to tamper with the operation of the criminal justice system, the UK policy makers have introduced legislation that aims to circumvent the criminal process and provide law enforcement with more tools. The Proceeds of Crime Act 2002 introduced CROs to remove the ill-gotten gains of criminals under civil rules, without the need for criminal convictions. CROs are obtained in civil courts presided over by a judge, but no jury, and using the lower civil standard of proof, the balance of probabilities. CROs are nevertheless not viable when evidence is difficult to obtain, for example, when a money launderer is protected by an overseas regime (Schalchi, 2021). To address this international problem, UWOs were introduced in 2017 to go a step further and place the burden of proof on suspects to explain how they obtained their property. If the suspect fails to explain how they legitimately obtained the assets, CROs can be obtained without any proof of criminal activity.

The value and impact of UWOs is yet to be determined (Schalchi, 2021), and based on the UK's experience with DPAs, it may take some time. Borrowing from the DOJ, the UK government introduced DPAs in the Crime and Courts Act 2013 to enable settlement of bribery, fraud and tax evasion cases. Unlike in the US, where DPAs can be used to settle cases with individuals and companies, they can only be used in the UK when the accused is a company. To summarise their operation, the prosecutor initially defers a prosecution and then withdraws it after a set number of years provided the accused pays a large fine and agrees to mend their errant ways by complying with certain conditions. In practice, therefore, DPAs, CROs and UWOs are more like a regulatory justice model than traditional criminal justice. Illustrating the SFO's leaning towards this type of civil rather criminal justice approach, the SFO obtained just three convictions in 2019–2020 compared to 17 in 2018–2019 but secured a clear record in financial penalties of £880 million: £852 million from DPAs and

£13 million from CROs (SFO, 2020, 2021). The SFO is now a very substantial revenue generator and is clearly more than funding itself. The implication is that a pragmatic regulatory or restorative justice approach to economic crime is likely to be more successful in delivering justice than hammering against the doors of the criminal courts.

Police priorities

The police and the policy makers are repeatedly criticised for the low priority they accord economic crime (Button, 2011; HMCFRS, 2019; Skidmore et al., 2018). Firstly, it is important to note that their priorities are not hidden, they are proclaimed on websites and publications for the public to see. The leaders of the police are very clear. The National Police Chiefs' Council (NPCC, n.d.) is working with the democratically elected Police and Crime Commissioners on its 'Policing Vision 2025' reform and transformation programme to meet the needs of the public. Its headline priorities are child safeguarding, domestic abuse, serious and organised crime, human trafficking, terrorism and cyber-crime. It does not mention economic crime nor business victims.

The mission of the Metropolitan Police (Mayor of London, 2017) is to 'keep London safe for everyone' by focusing on 'what matters most to Londoners'. Its priorities are keeping children and young people safe, violence against women and girls, hatred, intolerance and extremism. The West Midlands Police (n.d.) crime plan, 'Your Police, Your Priorities' leads with safer roads and public transport, then focuses on deflecting younger people from crime, 'adverse childhood experiences' and their causes, modern slavery and knife crime. The Kent Police (2021) strategic plan is called 'Safer in Kent'. The priority crimes for Kent Police are domestic abuse, violence, sexual exploitation and human trafficking. It has expanded its traditional safety objectives to include pastoral care with the guiding principle that 'people suffering from mental ill health need the right care from the right person'.

These plans were written by elected officials: the Mayor of London and local Police and Crime Commissioners. They all contain very reasonable priorities that reflect the democratic will of local people. They also illustrate the ongoing debate over whether the police is a force or a social service (Mawby, 2011). It is therefore unsurprising to find that just a quarter (24%) of the calls that the police respond to are crime incidents, 12% involve deviant antisocial behaviour and two-thirds (64%) do not involve crime or deviance (National Audit Office, 2018). The plans clearly support the Hough and Roberts (2017) assertion that the public influences the direction and nature of criminal justice.

Research suggests that the forces are making the right priority choices in maintaining the social contract between the police and the public. A recent Belgian study found that the public is more concerned about the moral wrongfulness of crime types rather than the consequential extent of the harm

Table 11.5 UK public crime priorities

Crime	Crimes within top 3 (%)	Highest priority (%)
Violent crime	61	28
Terrorism/extremism	54	36
Sexual offences	49	16
Serious and organised crime	34	9
Burglary, theft	22	3
Domestic abuse	13	2
Antisocial behaviour and other non-crime incidents	11	2
Drug offences	10	1
Arson and criminal damage	7	1
Stalking and harassment	5	1
Online abuse	5	1
Fraud	4	1
Commercial/business crime	2	<0.5

Source: Ipsos MORI (2017).

that a crime causes (Adriaenssen et al., 2020). Consequently, the public ranks personal crimes that physically or psychologically harm individuals, such as violence, burglary and theft, as the most serious and economic crime that can impact many people as the least serious. An Ipsos MORI (2017) survey asked 12,662 UK citizens which three crimes should be prioritised by the police. The results set out in Table 11.5 are similar to the Adriaenssen study. The UK public ranks violence at the top and economic crime (fraud and commercial/business crime) as the lowest priority, below online abuse, antisocial behaviour and other non-crime incidents.

Despite their astonishing prevalence and the number of people victimised every year, economic crimes do not disrupt the peaceful coexistence of the citizens within Belgium and the UK. Their primary concerns are physical, personal crimes and antisocial behaviour that have direct impacts on their everyday lives. For most people, it seems that economic crime is not a real crime. These findings demonstrate that politicians and the law enforcement agencies follow the public's agenda (Hough & Roberts, 2017). They suggest that ploughing substantial additional resources into tackling economic crime would be democratically unsustainable. The findings are an explanation for the economic crime paradox: despite the scale of the economic crime problem and its attendant harms, it is low on the police agenda because it is low on the public's agenda.

This perspective is, of course, very Western Euro-centric and public opinion in other parts of the world may be very different. Institutional and political corruption in some countries does agitate citizens to the extent that it stimulates anti-corruption campaigns. Corrupt favouritism based on prebendalism and ethnicity fuels rivalries and conflict (Aluko, 2020; Goldman, 2008). Politicians in these countries frequently weaponise anti-corruption, proclaiming their anti-corruption credentials during election campaigns, but fail to deliver on their promises when they are in power or often continue with the practices (Amundsen & Jackson, 2021). Most peaceful, democratic nations are fortunate in not suffering this cycle of corruption, broken promises, violence and more corruption. Consequently, election campaigns in these places are rarely based on anti-corruption manifestos. They are never based on anti-money laundering, anti-cartel and anti-counterfeiting policies.

Transnational policing

Foreign bribery, online piracy, industrial espionage, money laundering and cartel offences do not respect national boundaries. For example, corruption and bribery prevalent in developing countries is not just a local problem. It is in part fuelled by corrupt foreign firms who bribe foreign government officials to obtain and retain lucrative business deals (Goldman, 2008; Stapenhurst et al., 2017).[3] Moreover, these illicit activities are further enabled by professional money launderers and corrupt intermediaries such as company service providers, lawyers and accountants. These professionals may take advantage of lax regulations that often allow them to use shell companies to layer corporate ownership (see Chapter 8). To mitigate transnational economic crime effectively, national policing authorities are required to extend their jurisdiction beyond their national borders as well as to adopt more structured, collective approaches to confront the threats through systems of policing above government (Loader, 2000).

Extraterritoriality and economic crime

While a collective action of multiple national enforcement authorities, or even a centralised transnational policing body formed by national states might have potential to be effective in mitigating some forms of transnational economic crime, oftentimes states fail to cooperate. In fact, the area of transnational economic crime has been dominated by powerful national states' efforts to subject criminals to extraterritorial forms of legislation (Parrish, 2009; Zerk, 2010).

Extraterritorial enforcement, defined broadly as the application and enforcement of national laws to subjects acting beyond the borders of a given country, has been used in various forms (Hock, 2020). For example, the US follows the so-called effects doctrine, which is based on the view that 'each state has the right to regulate conduct abroad which is directly capable of producing serious (or "substantial") effects (usually economic effects) within the territory of the regulating state' (Zerk, 2010, p. 26). Table 11.6 illustrates key modalities of extraterritorial enforcement.

Table 11.6 Extraterritoriality and economic crime

Modality	Example
Wide interpretation of territorial jurisdiction	Only a very minimal presence in the territory of the given state might trigger enforcement. For example, an employee of a Hungarian corporation might send an email to a foreign government official via a server hosted in the US. Similarly, bank transfers from Europe to a developing country can be sent via correspondent accounts in New York, hence triggering US jurisdiction.
Indirect bribery	Organisations can be held liable for economic crimes of other organisations. For example, an organisation can be held liable for its failure to prevent bribery of its associated persons. Similarly, the headquarters can be held liable for acts of its independent foreign subsidiaries.
Complicity	Criminals, both individuals and organisations, often act as an organised group. Extraterritorial laws allow the prosecution of all members of such a group, even if only one member acts in the territory of the enforcing state.
Territorial extension	This is a less expensive form of extraterritorial enforcement, typical for the EU. Scott (2014, p. 90) argues that 'the application of a measure is triggered by a territorial connection but in applying the measure the regulator is required, as a matter of law, to take into account conduct or circumstances abroad'. For example, under EU law, credit ratings issued by an agency established outside the EU can only be relied upon by organisations established in the EU if the credit rating is endorsed by an EU authority, or if a non-EU agency is certified by an EU agency (ibid.).

Extraterritoriality has been widely used in the area of international bribery (see Chapter 4). Historically, policing of international bribery was limited to the jurisdiction of the Foreign Corrupt Practices Act (FCPA). The DOJ and the SEC have enforced the Act against multiple non-US corporations that were not under similar regulatory scrutiny in their home jurisdiction and in the developing countries in which they bribed foreign government officials. For example, French corporations agreed to pay hundreds of millions of US dollars for their bribes in third countries (Hock, 2020). Until the late 2010s, the US transnational enforcement had been dominating the enforcement landscape, with other jurisdictions only complementing the US enforcement.

This way of enforcing national economic crime laws is controversial. Following the adoption of international convention endorsing extraterritorial forms of national jurisdiction in the late 1990s, the academic discussion focused on the question of moral imperialism.[4] Moral imperialism is the imposition of moral values onto a culture that does not share those values, either through force or through cultural criticism (Hock, 2014, pp. 7–8; Spahn, 2012). Some authors argue that anti-corruption moral values are not universal but culturally specific, hence extraterritorial imposition of foreign laws in developing countries leads to numerous unintended consequences (Spalding, 2010). Others, on the other hand, indicate that given devastating impacts of global economic crime, 'stronger' legal regimes of the North should discipline their own organisation's role in corrupt relationships with bribe takers (Spahn, 2012).

Despite the criticism, extraterritorial forms of policing transnational economic crime have been adopted and practised by multiple countries, including the UK. For example, the *Airbus* case (SFO v Airbus SE, 31 January 2020) in which the UK enforcement authorities formed a joint-investigation team with French enforcement authorities to join the US in agreeing a global settlement (see Chapters 3 and 4). Moreover, the UK has recently introduced the Global Anti-Corruption Sanctions Regulations 2021 (SI 2021/488). This new sanctions regime allows the UK authorities to impose asset freezes and travel bans on both individuals and organisations, in cases when the UK authorities have, for example, reasonable grounds to suspect that they are responsible for or engage in serious corruption, facilitate or provide support for serious corruption, or profit financially or obtain any other benefit from serious corruption (Section 6 of the Regulations).

Transnational policing organisations

Extraterritorial enforcement of national laws has proved to be a better alternative than the absence of any enforcement of laws against transnational forms of economic crime. Yet, this form of enforcement rarely results in a sustainable and collaborative response to global problems (Parrish, 2012). Extraterritorial enforcement is usually accompanied by loose multilateral arrangements that can hardly ensure long-term cooperation within a larger group of states. An external organisation is often needed to enhance cooperation between relevant actors.

There is just one international police force with the recognisable characteristics of national police forces. The United Nations Police (n.d.) has 11,000 police officers deployed around the world to support or substitute local police forces in conflict and crisis situations. A permanent contingent of officers is supported by officers seconded from national authorities. Its primary mission is peace-keeping, maintenance of public order and safety. To bring effect to their deployments, UN officers are the same as national police in that they are uniformed, able to use legitimate force, have the power to arrest and investigate crimes. However, they are not involved in policing economic crime.

Table 11.7 is a non-exhaustive list of intergovernmental organisations involved in policing economic crime. Whilst all these contribute to policing,

Table 11.7 Transnational policing organisations

Organisation	Activity	Members
Policy and standards setting		
Organisation for Economic Co-operation and Development (OECD)	Creates policies for combatting economic crime; focus on market competition	37
Financial Action Task Force (FATF)	Creates policies and standards for co; focus on international security	39
Investigation and capacity building		
Aseanapol	Coordinates investigations, law enforcement capacity building for serious organised crime and terrorism	10
Afripol	Coordinates investigations, law enforcement capacity building for serious organised crime and terrorism	54
Ameripol	Coordinate investigations, law enforcement capacity building for serious organised crime and terrorism	35
European Commission	Investigates and sanctions cartel offences; competencies related to the protection of EU's financial interests	27
Europol	Investigates crimes, coordinates investigations, law enforcement capacity building for serious organised crime and terrorism	27
Interpol	Investigates crimes, coordinates investigations, law enforcement capacity building for serious organised crime and terrorism	194
Egmont Group	Group of Financial Intelligence Units (FIUs), e.g. UKFIU and FinCEN, financial intelligence sharing to combat money laundering and terrorism, capacity building	166
EU European Anti-Fraud Office (OLAF)	Investigates fraud and corruption involving EU's financial interests, coordinates investigations by member authorities	27
Capacity building		
Economic Crime and Cooperation Division (ECCD)	Law enforcement and justice capacity building for combatting economic crime	29
European Competition Network (ECN)	Enforcement capacity building for combatting cartels and other violations of competition law	27
Group of States Against Corruption (GRECO)	Supports law enforcement and justice capacity building for fighting corruption	50

(continued)

Table 11.7 Cont.

Organisation	Activity	Members
International Competition Network (ICN)	Law enforcement capacity building for combatting cartels	141
EU MONEYVAL	Capacity building for fighting money laundering and terrorist financing	27
Network of Corruption Prevention Authorities (NCPA)	Enforcement capacity building for combatting corruption	29
Organization for Security and Co-operation in Europe (OSCE)	General law enforcement capacity building	57
UN Office on Drugs and Crime (UNODC)	General law enforcement and justice capacity building	193
World Bank Financial Integrity	Regulator and law enforcement capacity building for fighting money laundering and terrorist financing	189
World Bank International Corruption Hunters Alliance (ICHA)	Capacity building for combatting corruption	100

none have the breadth of peace-keeping, coercive and enforcement powers of national forces or the UN Police. The European Commission is somewhat unique in that it is a transnational regulator with police-like powers to enter premises and obtain evidence in support of cartel investigations anywhere in the EU (Council Regulation (EC) No 1/2003). Yet, it is also very different to the police in that all the accused are corporations not individuals, and it is also the judge of serious cases, handing down orders and substantial fines. The investigative and sanction competencies of the European Commission make it the only agency in the list with actual enforcement powers.

Interpol (International Criminal Police Organization) is perhaps the most recognisable international policing agency. With 1,000 staff, it bears many of the characteristics of police forces: it is uniformed, it conducts CIs and a quarter of its staff are police officers seconded from member states (Interpol, 2020). It is far more global than the UN Police, conducting operations in all 194 member states, with a broad remit covering intelligence gathering, coordination and sharing, facilitating and supporting operations, training and development (Bowling et al., 2019). Its intelligence, investigation and capacity building roles are focused terrorism and serious organised crime including people smuggling, cybercrime and environmental crime. It also places significant emphasis on a wide range of organised economic crimes involving bribery, IP crime and illicit trade, fraud and money laundering.

There are four regional agencies that are modelled on Interpol and duplicate its activities: Afripol, Ameripol, Aseanapol and Europol. Europol is the most active and is a similar size to Interpol with a staff of 1,000 permanent employees and police officers seconded from member nations. However, despite their titles, Interpol and the four regional agencies are not police forces. They cannot issue minor sanctions and they are not the gatekeepers to criminal justice systems; they do not have coercive police powers to use force, enter and search premises, make arrests and hold individuals in custody. Interpol and the regional policing agencies rely on and coordinate national police forces to perform these functions.

The European Anti-Fraud Office (OLAF, n.d.) is a European Commission agency that investigates fraud and corruption involving EU finances. It is a unique agency in that its remit is both internal and transnational. It conducts internal investigations into the fraudulent and corrupt misconduct of EU staff within EU institutions. These investigations may lead to disciplinary action against staff within the relevant institutions or prosecutions by national authorities. It also conducts external investigations, or coordinates investigations, outside the EU institutions across the 27 member states that may lead to prosecution by local prosecutors or the European Public Prosecutor's Office (EPPO).

OLAF works with member agencies, Interpol, Europol, Eurojust and the EPPO. Eurojust is a regional intergovernmental agency within the European Union. It is an administrative body that coordinates the legal processes in cross-border cases of serious and organised crime, such as court orders, the European Arrest Warrant and the European Investigation Order. The EPPO was formed in 2021 with the remit of prosecuting serious cases of fraud and corruption involving EU finances. However, the EPPO very much relies on the EU Member States as it can only bring prosecutions in national courts.

The rest of the intergovernmental organisations in the list consist of cooperative networks of government agencies that create policies and standards (FATF, OECD), share intelligence (Egmont Group) and support capacity building across the world. All these networks espouse high value mission statements to make the world safer and better for everyone. However, as Schütte (2020) noted, it is difficult to determine exactly what they do. Capacity building is the most common feature, which involves training, sharing good practice and advising on the best way to strengthen the national institutions of enforcement and justice. Although these are valuable activities, the architecture of transnational policing does resemble the UK structure: highly duplicated and fractured with many people doing important things, but very few actually enforcing the law.

Conclusions

The policing of economic crime in the UK and transnationally is fractured and inadequate to the task. Public policies that seek to plaster over the inadequacies are based on several exemplary extraterritorial enforcement actions and increasing cooperation and coordination between policing entities.

However, these policies do not address the core issues of inadequate, competing resources and incoherent structures. With some minor exceptions, such as the NCA, ROCUs and the specialist units in the CoLP, the police service is organised to deal with local issues, most of which are not economic crime related. There is little appetite for reorganising the police for two principal reasons. Firstly, the criminal justice system in the UK is a dysfunctional institution for prosecuting economic crime. One of its primary purposes is to deter people from committing these crimes, but it is more successful in deterring the police and other agencies from considering prosecutions. Secondly, the priority the policy makers and police place on economic crime reflects the public's view that it is a low priority crime. The public is far more concerned with crimes of violence, physical theft and antisocial behaviour.

The public's priorities explain the economic crime paradox: despite the scale of the economic crime problem and its attendant harms, it is low on the police agenda because it is low on the public's agenda, and often not regarded as a real crime. Consequently, attempting to overcome the inefficiencies of the prosecution process by ploughing more resources into policing economic crime instead of local crime and social problems would be democratically unsustainable. The increasingly regulatory approach to economic crime is thus not only pragmatic, it is also justified by the public's priorities. The problem is distinctly different and far worse in some countries where, despite the demands of agitated citizens, political elites are the blockage to effective enforcement because they are the most egregious offenders. Although this accountability problem in developing nations explains why much of the transnational policing effort is directed towards capacity building, it is not clear how effective it can be without the commitment of their political leaders.

Notes

1 The Procurator Fiscal in Scotland does have an investigative role, particularly in serious cases involving sudden, suspicious and unexplained deaths.
2 Cifas is a non-governmental organisation that maintains a fraudster database www.cifas.org.uk/.
3 Transnational policing is not new (Bowling et al., 2019). European colonialism exported policing and established strong links with local police forces (Brogden, 1987). However, the world has substantially changed, particularly with the technological advancements and the globalisation of business.
4 Consider, for example, the OECD Anti-Bribery Convention (see Chapter 4).

References

Adriaenssen, A., Paoli, L., Karstedt, S., Visschers, J., Greenfield, V. A., & Pleysier, S. (2020). Public perceptions of the seriousness of crime: Weighing the harm and the wrong. *European Journal of Criminology, 17*(2), 127–150. https://doi.org/10.1177%2F1477370818772768

Aluko, O. I. (2020). Breaking the cycle of corruption in Nigeria: The myth and reality. *Journal of Co-Operative and Business Studies, 5*(1), 115–125. https://mocu.ac.tz/wp-content/uploads/2020/05/PAPER-10-ALUKO-1-4.pdf

Amundsen, I., & Jackson, D. (2021). *Rethinking anti-corruption in de-democratising regimes. U4 Ant-Corruption Resource Centre.* www.u4.no/publications/rethinking-anti-corruption-in-de-democratising-regimes

Attorney General. (2006). *Fraud review.* https://webarchive.nationalarchives.gov.uk/20070222120000/http://www.lslo.gov.uk/pdf/FraudReview.pdf

Bittner, E. (1980). *The functions of the police in modern society.* Olgeschlager, Gunn and Hain.

Bowling, B., Reiner, R., & Sheptycki, J. (2019). *The politics of the police* (5th ed.). Oxford University Press.

Braithwaite, J. (2002). *Restorative justice & responsive regulation.* Oxford University Press.

Brogden, M. (1987). The emergence of the police: The colonial dimension. *British Journal of Criminology, 27*(1), 4–14. www.jstor.org/stable/23637268?seq=1#metadata_info_tab_contents

Button, M. (2011). Fraud investigation and the flawed architecture of counter fraud entities in the United Kingdom. *International Journal of Law Crime and Justice, 39*(4), 249–265.

Button, M. (2019). *Private policing* (2nd ed.). Routledge.

Button, M. (2021). Hiding behind the veil of Action Fraud: The police response to economic crime in England and Wales and evaluating the case for regionalization or a National Economic Crime Agency. *Policing: A Journal of Policy and Practice.* https://doi.org/10.1093/police/paab022

Button, M., Johnston, L., & Frimpong, K. (2008). The fraud review and the policing of fraud: Laying the foundations for a centralised fraud police or a counter-fraud executive? *Policing, 2*(2), 241–250. https://doi.org/10.1093/police/pan027

Button, M., Shepherd, D., & Blackbourn, D. (2018). 'The iceberg beneath the sea', fraudsters and their punishment through non-criminal justice in the 'Fraud Justice Network' in England and Wales. *International Journal of Law, Crime and Justice, 53*(1), 56–66. https://doi.org/10.1016/j.ijlcj.2018.03.001

Button, M., Tapley, J., & Lewis, C. (2013). The 'fraud justice network' and the infrastructure of support for individual fraud victims in England and Wales. *Criminology and Criminal Justice, 13*(1), 37–61. https://doi.org/10.1177%2F1748895812448085

Button, M., Wakefield, A., Brooks, G., Lewis, C., & Shepherd, D. (2015). Confronting the "fraud bottleneck": Private sanctions for fraud and their implications for justice. *Journal of Criminological Research, Policy and Practice, 1*(3), 159–274. https://doi.org/10.1108/JCRPP-04-2015-0006

Cohen, H., & Feldberg, M. (1991). A social contract perspective on the police role. In H. Cohen & M. Feldberg (Eds.), *Power and restraint: The moral dimension of policework* (pp. 23–38). Praeger.

de Grazia, J. (2008). *Review of the Serious Fraud Office, final report.* Serious Fraud Office. Retrieved from the Inner Temple website www.innertemplelibrary.com/2008/06/jessica-de-grazia-full-report-into-the-serious-fraud-office-attorney-generals-office/

Doig, A., Johnson, S., & Levi, M. (2001). New public management, old populism and the policing of fraud. *Public Policy and Administration, 16*(1), 91–113. https://doi.org/10.1177%2F095207670101600106

DWP. (2020). *Department for Work and Pensions annual report and accounts 2019-20*. www.gov.uk/government/publications/dwp-annual-report-and-accounts-2019-to-2020

Fisher, J. (2010) *Fighting fraud and financial crime*. Policy Exchange. www.policyexchange. org.uk/wp-content/uploads/2016/09/fighting-fraud-and-financial-crime-mar-10.pdf

Fraud Advisory Panel. (2010). *Roskill revisited: Is there a case for a unified prosecution office?* www.fraudadvisorypanel.org/wp-content/uploads/2015/04/Roskill-Revisited-Final-24-Mar10.pdf

Goldman, H. (2008). Between ROC and hard place: The Republic of Congo's illicit trade in diamonds and efforts to break the cycle of corruption. *University of Pennsylvania Journal of International Law, 30*(1), 359–396. https://heinonline. org/HOL/Page?handle=hein.journals/upjiel30&div=8&g_sent=1&casa_token= &collection=journals

HMG. (n.d.). *Counter-fraud standards and profession*. www.gov.uk/government/groups/counter-fraud-standards-and-profession

HMICFRS. (2019). *Fraud: Time to choose: An inspection of the police response to fraud*. www.justiceinspectorates.gov.uk/hmicfrs/wp-content/uploads/fraud-time-to-choose-an-inspection-of-the-police-response-to-fraud.pdf

HMRC. (2021). *Quarterly performance indicators 2020-21*. https://data.gov.uk/dataset/3570aac7-5345-4bcd-94bd-a3136e76657e/hmrc-business-plan-indicator-and-quarterly-data-summary

HM Treasury and Home Office. (2019). *Economic crime plan 2019-22*. www.gov.uk/government/publications/economic-crime-plan-2019-to-2022

Hock, B. (2014) Intimations of global anti-bribery regime and the effectiveness of extraterritorial enforcement: From free-riders to protectionism? TILEC *discussion paper no. 2014-009*. https://ssrn.com/abstract=2395156 or http://dx.doi.org/10.2139/ssrn.2395156

Hock, B. (2020). *Extraterritoriality and international bribery: A collective action perspective*. Routledge

Home Office. (2020a). *Crime outcomes in England and Wales 2019 to 2020*. www.gov.uk/government/statistics/crime-outcomes-in-england-and-wales-2019-to-2020

Home Office. (2020b). *Police workforce, England and Wales: 31 March 2020 third edition*. www.gov.uk/government/statistics/police-workforce-england-and-wales-31-march-2020

Hough, M., & Roberts, J. (2017). Public opinion, crime, and criminal justice. In A. Liebling, S. Maruna & L. McAra (Eds.), *The Oxford handbook of criminology* (6th ed.). Oxford University Press.

Interpol. (2020). *Annual report*. www.interpol.int/en/Who-we-are/What-is-INTERPOL

Ipsos MORI. (2017). *Public perceptions of policing in England and Wales 2017: Report for Her Majesty's Inspectorate of Constabulary and Fire & Rescue Services*. www.ipsos.com/ipsos-mori/en-uk/public-perceptions-policing-england-and-wales-2017

IRS:CI. (2020). *Annual report*. www.irs.gov/pub/irs-pdf/p3583.pdf

Jolly, J. (2021, April 26). *Trial of former Serco executives collapses as SFO fails to disclose evidence*. The Guardian. www.theguardian.com/business/2021/apr/26/serco-trial-collapses-as-serious-office-fails-to-disclose-evidence

Kent Police. (2021). *Safer in Kent*. www.kent-pcc.gov.uk/SysSiteAssets/media/downloads/plan-annualreports-hmic/safer-in-kent-plan-202122_wsite.pdf

Levi, M. (1986a). Fraud in the Courts-Roskill in context. *British Journal of Criminology, 26*(4), 394–401. https://heinonline.org/HOL/Page?handle=hein. journals/bjcrim26&div=41&g_sent=1&casa_token=&collection=journals

Levi, M. (1986b). Investigating fraud. *Policing, 2*(3), 196–211.

Levi, M. (2010). Hitting the suite spot: Sentencing frauds. *Journal of Financial Crime, 17*(1), 116–132. https://doi.org/10.1108/13590791011009400

Levi, M. (2013). *Regulating fraud: White-collar crime and the criminal process.* Routledge.

Loader, I. (2000). Plural policing and democratic governance. *Social and Legal Studies, 9*(3), 323–345. https://doi.org/10.1177%2F096466390000900301

Mawby, R. C. (2008). Models of policing. In T. Newburn (Ed.), *Handbook of policing* (2nd ed.). Routledge.

Mayor of London. (2017). *A safer city for all London.* Greater London Authority. www.met.police.uk/police-forces/metropolitan-police/areas/about-us/about-the-met/police-and-crime-plan/

MoJ. (2020). *Criminal court statistics quarterly: January to March 2020.* www.gov.uk/government/statistics/criminal-court-statistics-quarterly-january-to-march-2020

National Audit Office. (2018). *Financial sustainability of police forces in England and Wales 2018.* www.nao.org.uk/wp-content/uploads/2018/09/Financial-sustainability-of-police-forces-in-England-and-Wales-2018.pdf

NPCC. (n.d.). *Reform and transformation.* www.npcc.police.uk/NPCCBusinessAreas/ReformandTransformation/Reformandtransformation.aspx

Nussbaum, B., & Doherty, J. E. (2021). Italy's Guardia di Finanza: Policing financial crime and domestic security in a changing world. *Journal of Financial Crime.* https://doi.org/10.1108/JFC-10-2020-0207

OLAF. (n.d.). *What we do.* https://ec.europa.eu/anti-fraud/about-us/mission_en

ONS. (2020). *Crime in England and Wales: Year ending March 2020.* www.ons.gov.uk/peoplepopulationandcommunity/crimeandjustice/bulletins/crimeinenglandandwales/yearendingmarch2020#fraud

Parrish, A. L. (2009). Reclaiming international law from extraterritoriality. *Minnesota Law Review, 93*, 815–874.

Parrish, A. L. (2012). Domestic responses to transnational crime: The limits of national law. *Criminal Law Forum, 23*, 275–293.

Reiner, R. (2010). *The politics of the police* (4th ed.). Oxford University Press.

Schalchi, A. (2021). *Unexplained wealth orders.* House of Commons Library. https://commonslibrary.parliament.uk/research-briefings/cbp-9098/

Schütte, S. (2020). *Networks of anti-corruption authorities.* U4 Anti-Corruption Resource Centre. www.u4.no/publications/networks-of-anti-corruption-authorities

Scott, J. (2014). Extraterritoriality and territorial extension in EU law. *American Journal of Comparative Law, 62*, 87–126. http://dx.doi.org/10.5131/AJCL.2013.0009

SFO. (2020). *Annual report.* www.sfo.gov.uk/2019/07/22/sfo-annual-report-and-accounts-2018-2019/

SFO. (2021). *Annual report.* www.sfo.gov.uk/download/annual-report-2019-2020/

Shepherd, D. (2020). DIY fraud investigation and access to justice: A case study. *Policing: A Journal of Policy and Practice.* https://doi-org.eres.qnl.qa/10.1093/police/paaa002

Skidmore, M., Ramm, J., Goldstraw-White, J., Barrett, C., Braleaza, S., Muir, R., & Gill, M. (2018). *Improving the police response to fraud*. The Police Foundation. www.police-foundation.org.uk/project/improving-the-police-response-to-fraud-2/

Smith, I., & Shepherd, D. (2019). *Commercial fraud and cyber fraud: A legal guide to justice for businesses*. Bloomsbury.

Spahn, E. K. (2012). Multijurisdictional bribery law enforcement: The OECD anti-bribery convention. *Virginia Journal of International Law, 53*(1), 1–49.

Spalding, A. B. (2010). Unwitting sanctions: Understanding anti-bribery legislation as economic sanctions against emerging markets. *Florida Law Review, 62*, 350–408.

Stapenhurst, F., Karakas, F., Sarigöllü, E., Jo, M. S., & Draman, R. (2017). The supply and demand sides of corruption: Canadian extractive companies in Africa. *Canadian Foreign Policy Journal, 23*(1), 60–76. https://doi.org/10.1080/11926422.2016.1250655

Sutherland, E. (1949). *White collar crime*. Dryden.

United Nations Police. (n.d.). *UN Police Services*. https://police.un.org/en

West Midlands Police. (n.d.). *Police and crime plan 2016-20*. www.westmidlands-pcc.gov.uk/your-commissioner/police-crime-plan/police-and-crime-plan-2016-20/

Wright, R. (2003). Fraud after Roskill. *Journal of Financial Crime, 11*(1), 10–16. https://doi.org/10.1108/13590790410808997

Zerk, J. A. (2010). *Extraterritorial jurisdiction: Lessons for the business and human rights sphere from six regulatory areas*. Harvard University, John F. Kennedy School of Government. www.hks.harvard.edu/sites/default/files/centers/mrcbg/programs/cri/files/workingpaper_59_zerk.pdf

Chapter 12

Private policing of economic crime

Introduction

One of the most striking themes that emerges from the consideration of the policing of economic crime is the dominance of private actors. Organisations with their own private capacity protecting themselves from economic crime, commercial organisations charging fees to clients to do such work and volunteers offering their time to frustrate scammers are just snippets of the significant contribution they make. Indeed, there are many serious economic crimes where the state plays no role. For economic crime, the private contribution is the largest, but this is not to dismiss state involvement; they play an important role as the previous chapter illustrated. State structures in policing are also often important as the gatekeepers to prosecution and access to special powers of search. This chapter will begin to reveal the extensive involvement of the private sector in policing economic crime.

This chapter will begin by exploring the concept of 'private' and 'privateness'. It will then move on to explore first, the private 'in-house' capacity of organisations combatting economic crime, before examining the many firms which charge fees to organisations for the provision of services to combat economic crime. The chapter then moves on to consider the very important role played by non-governmental organisations (NGOs) fighting economic crime, before considering the extensive voluntary capacity. It will end by considering some of the issues that emerge from large-scale private involvement.

The 'privateness' of policing

The previous chapter defined policing and focused on public services. Adding the adjective 'private' to policing adds a new layer of complexity (Button, 2019). Simply defining the private in its simplest form of commercial profit-making organisations offering services for fees ignores the breadth of private involvement in policing. Drawing upon several writers in this area, Button (2019) identifies the following important dimensions:

DOI: 10.4324/9781003081753-12

- Location: is the body a government organisation, charity or company?
- Funding: how does the organisation get its funding, from state taxation to private fees?
- Nature of relationship: does the organisation serve the public or specific clients?
- Spatial context: where does the organisation principally perform its functions, in public, quasi-public or private space?
- Status of staff: do the staff have special statutory powers or are they 'ordinary citizens'?

Button (2019) argues these dimensions can be used to distinguish between degrees of privateness and publicness. Thus, at one extreme, an organisation like the Metropolitan Police Service (MPS) in London is a public organisation, funded principally by taxation, serves the public, operates largely on public space and whose police officers (and some staff) have special powers. It therefore exhibits a high degree of publicness. At the other extreme, an organisation like Kroll offering commercial investigation services is a private company, funded by fees from clients, serves those clients, operates largely on private space and whose staff are ordinary citizens with no special powers. Kroll therefore exhibits a high degree of privateness.

However, there is a blurred region of privateness between these two extremes. Take for instance the Counter Fraud, Compliance and Debt (CFCD) group which deals with social security fraud within the Department for Work and Pensions (DWP) in the UK (see Chapter 2). The CFCD is located in a government department, funded from taxation, operating on a mix of space, with some staff with some special powers (related to access to information), but which serves one client, the DWP. It is essentially the DWP's own private fraud police. One could properly argue that the CFCD is a public body performing a public function in protecting taxpayers' money; nonetheless, it exhibits a level of privateness. Such bodies were considered in the previous chapter, as they are largely public bodies.

Other bodies exhibit more privateness than the DWP, but not to the same extent as Kroll. For example, consider an industry body like the Federation Against Copyright Theft (FACT), which conducts surveillance, disrupts offenders and undertakes criminal investigations in relation to copyright breaches (see Chapter 6). This is a not-for-profit organisation funded by industry to police copyright legislation for its members (largely the movie industry), operating on largely private space and employing staff with no special status. There are also not-for-profit vigilante groups like 419eater which seeks to frustrate, expose and punish (in a shaming context) scammers. It is a private association, funded by members, but arguably serving the public using volunteers with no special powers or status.

There are therefore a wide range of organisations and individuals involved in the policing of economic crime that exhibit varying degrees of privateness. The next section will explore some of this private capacity.

Private policing capacity of organisations

The scale of economic crime risks for many organisations leads them to create their own policing capacity to prevent, detect and investigate economic crimes. This private capacity exists in public, private and charitable organisations. Central government in the UK employs a substantial resource to protect its revenues and expenditure and, as illustrated above, cannot be considered as completely public. Such bodies, however, were considered in the previous chapter and this section will focus more upon the capacity of private organisations. It is an area which has been largely neglected by criminological researchers (Gottschalk, 2017).

For many organisations, the economic crime risks they face lead them to employ their own staff to protect them from such risks. The scope and nature of such risks, combined with the size of the organisation, leads to different shapes of the private structures that emerge. For example, banks and insurance companies with high-volume transactions associated with fraud and money laundering risks often employ significant investigative capacity to deal with this and ensure compliance with regulations related to these. A large manufacturer of defence equipment by contrast might experience a much smaller risk in this area and have a smaller investigative/compliance capacity, if any. Most large organisations will have a security function which will cover the protection of assets: physical security and cybersecurity. It might also deal with the prevention and investigation of economic crimes. Many organisations, particularly those in the financial sector, which deal with high volumes of transactions, usually have dedicated compliance staff to ensure compliance with money laundering regulations and other related controls. Indeed, many organisations have several departments dealing with different economic crimes.

Private entities do not have to publicise their structures for dealing with economic crime, so it is much harder, compared with the public sector, to find published organisational structures with departmental names, roles, staff numbers etc. Resources dealing with economic crimes may therefore be found distributed across: security, cybersecurity, information services, risk, audit, compliance and investigations. Some of these have much wider remits than economic crimes. For example, many organisations possess security functions which develop and implement strategies to protect organisations from a wide range of risks, such as burglary, theft, robbery, terrorists, safety threats and often focused upon physical security (fences, barriers, security staff), but they may also cover economic crimes such as industrial espionage, staff frauds and bribery.

Shepherd (2016) provides an example of a department in a company concerned with protecting it from economic crimes. 'DEF Group', a large European company with 12,000 employees and sales of £1.2 billion, is based on the distribution of low-value products via over 1,000 branches. The biggest security concerns of the organisation were shrinkage through theft, fraud and related acts. The corporate security function was situated in the Security and Compliance Department (SCD) which had 41 staff based in its head office. There were four parts to the department: physical security, business support (training, advice, data analysis), compliance control (health and safety, detection, business procedures) and enforcement (criminal and civil investigations). The department was headed by a 'Business Controls and Procedures Manager' who reported to the Finance Director. The department invested a great deal in the prevention through the creation of appropriate procedures and deployment of appropriate security strategies. During 2012, it reported over 1,165 security incidents, including almost 300 frauds and almost 250 thefts. The work of the department culminated in 18 external arrests, 182 staff disciplinaries and 42 staff dismissals (Shepherd, 2016, p 118).

Another way of looking at the private capacity of organisations is to consider some of the principal occupations or roles that often have economic crime responsibilities. Below in Table 12.1 are some of the key functions and their broad responsibilities. It is important to note some of these functions attract different names/titles in certain organisations and the list below does not cover all relevant functions, just some of the most common. For example, loss prevention manager is the title used to describe some security managers, the latter are sometimes called chief security officers and the latter part of the title might be used alongside manager, analyst to name some (Button, 2019). Those dealing with cybercrime involve a wide range of specialist functions from security architects, security software developers and chief information security officers to name some, but most report to the latter; so they have been the sole common name listed (Rashid et al., 2017). Others vary in how much economic crime they deal with, some auditors, for example, much more orientated to fraud than others (Tickner, 2012).

Private policing capacity offering services for fees – 'the new private security industry'

Many victims and potential victims of economic crimes have to purchase the services of firms with expertise in dealing with such crimes to protect themselves or secure a response. Standing out are the variety of organisations that offer investigative services, to discover what has happened after an incident for the purposes of information, internal sanction through to criminal prosecution. Such bodies also offer other services from intelligence, preventative advice to due diligence to name a few. The provision of these services is largely supplied by firms of specialist private investigators, professional service companies in firms of accountants and lawyers through to generic security companies (Button, 2019). These will shortly be explored. There are also specialist companies offering very unique services that help organisations deal with economic crimes such as those offering data analytics services, cyber-related services too. These will also be explored in this section.

Table 12.1 Job functions combatting economic crimes

Job function	Responsibilities	Common economic crimes
Security managers/chief security officers	The protection of assets of an organisation from crimes, negative acts/behaviours and ultimately from loss	Fraud, corruption, industrial espionage, economic cybercrime
Fraud investigators/specialists/examiners	The prevention, detection and investigation of economic crimes such as fraud, corruption and money laundering	Fraud and corruption
Internal auditors	The internal independent assessments of an organisations systems, finances and activities	Fraud and corruption
Compliance officers/managers	Ensuring compliance with regulation/law and company policies	Money laundering, terrorist financing, bribery
Chief information security officers (and other cyber-security functions)	The protection of data/computer systems of an organisation	Economic cybercrime, industrial espionage
Brand protection officer/manager	The protection of unauthorised use of a company's brand, intellectual property	Intellectual property crime, industrial espionage

Sources: Button (2019), Chen et al. (2013), Rashid et al, (2017), Miller (2015), Tickner (2012).

Private investigators offer a wide range of services and some of these are not related to economic crime, such as searching for missing persons, infidelity investigations related to divorce to name some (Gill & Hart, 1997). However, there are a wide range of services such firms offer that relate to economic crime. These include:

- fraud investigations;
- corruption investigations;
- espionage and intellectual property-related investigations;
- financial investigations (money laundering);
- cyber investigations;
- asset-tracing investigations (finding assets lost to economic crimes);
- due diligence investigations (checking individuals and organisations' statements and credentials is credible); and
- vetting (checking the credentials of potential and existing staff).

An example of a firm of private investigators is Kroll, which has a long history of offering investigative services from when it was founded in 1972.

It has grown into a global firm offering a wider range of services beyond investigation including risk, security and cybersecurity consultancy (Duff & Phelps, n.d.). Another example is Pinkerton, which can also claim to be one of the, if not oldest, private investigation agencies, which has a global reach employing 1,500 staff with an additional network of 10,000 contractors to draw on (Pinkerton, n.d.). Pinkerton was acquired by Swedish firm Securitas in 1999 (Pinkerton, n.d.). It is also important to note, however, there are some specialist firms which concentrate on offering specific services, such as surveillance, counter espionage or cyber investigations. For example, the UK firm Esoteric offers specialist services such as surveillance, counter surveillance and bug detection amongst many others (Esoteric, n.d.). One of the biggest investigator firms in the UK is the 'Cotswold Group' which was bought by G4S, but trades under its original name. It was founded in 1990 and has over 280 staff offering a range of investigative services to clients such as intelligence, fraud and litigation-related investigations (Cotswold Group, n.d.). It also illustrates the blurring of security companies also offering investigative services, something which a significant number do.

The biggest blur, however, is the involvement of the professional services sector in the provision of investigation services (Gottschalk, 2016 & 2020). This includes the audit firms offering 'forensic' services and firms of lawyers who rather than contracting out investigation to a firm (which is common) offer a full service of investigation and legal services. The audit firms use a mixture of specialist forensic accountants as well as investigators, and for some, because of offices across the world, offer a global reach too. For example, EY claims 4,500 fraud investigation and dispute professionals around the world offering the services of investigations, disputes, business integrity and corporate compliance, forensic technology and discovery services (EY, n.d.). Some firms of lawyers also offer a wide range of services that include investigations and use their own staff, rather than contracting to private investigators. For example, firms such as Keoghs have built up expertise in fraud investigations in the insurance and related sectors (Keoghs, n.d.).

Economic crimes have also spawned a variety of companies offering specialist services to prevent and detect economic crimes. One of the most significant areas is data analytics. Firms use data-matching and data-mining techniques linked to artificial intelligence and machine learning to assess large datasets on an industrial scale. Fraud prevention is one of the most common areas where financial institutions and retailers purchase the services of such companies to determine in a millisecond whether a transaction is high risk for fraud. For example, in one quarter, the company ThreatMetrix assessed over 8.3 billion transactions for their legitimacy based on hundreds of attributes. They found over 151 million attacks and 1.6 billion bot attacks (ThreatMetrix, 2019). Many of the prevented attacks will involve the effective designation of the customer as a fraudster, without reference to formal criminal justice structures. There are many other data companies offering such services around the world, such as companies Experian and Synectics Solutions designating individuals and data associated with them as potential fraudsters (see, Christl, 2017).

Companies seeking to protect their intellectual property also have access to a wide range of specialist companies offering a variety of services. Some monitor the internet with specialist software to identify sellers of counterfeit goods and then send removal requests to online marketplaces such as Amazon and delisting requests to search engines (see above). Firms specialising in disrupting IP crime in this area include Digital Millennium Copyright Act (DMCA) Services, Red Points, Remove Your Media, SnapDragon, Copytrack and Pixsy. Betting companies face risks from corrupt sportsmen and women engaging in behaviours which enable those 'in the know' to profit from it. There are companies offering specialist betting monitoring services, which enables them to identify unusual patterns in betting and therefore detect potential corruption, such as the company, such as Genius Sports. The above are just a snapshot of many companies that offer services to organisations to specifically protect them from economic crime.

The needs for organisations and individuals to deal with the growing cybersecurity problems have spawned a wide range of new companies to offer such services as well as some traditional security companies and others moving into this area too (Button, 2019). Some of the companies that have emerged from the 'old' security industry, offering the full range of services, include G4S, which has a Risk Consulting arm that offers these services. There have been companies from other sectors that have moved into this area, such as the traditional consultants. For example, PWC offers cybersecurity services amongst all the other extensive services offered. BAE Systems has also developed such services coming from a largely defence manufacturing background and mainstream IT services providers like IBM. Others are new and like the tech giants have grown rapidly, for example, Checkpoint Security Technologies, Symantec, RSA and Kaspersky.

Button (2020) has argued this constitutes a 'new private security industry', which is new and expanding sector, very dynamic as technology evolves and threats change, and there has been very little research on this sector from a criminological perspective. Table 12.2 is a list of some of the key segments of the 'new' private security industry.

Non-governmental organisations (NGOs)

NGOs are not-for-profit private organisations that are independent of government. There are a very wide range of such bodies engaged in the policing of economic crime. In fact, there are so many it would not be possible to cover them all in this section; so a snapshot of examples will be provided to illustrate the important role they play in countering economic crime.

Table 12.2 Activities of the 'new' private security industry related to economic cybercrime

---

Outsourced cybersecurity solutions (some organisations completely outsource this function to specialist providers)

Design, build and maintenance of security systems (organisations offering services to others to do all or some of these functions)

Threat intelligence, analytics, monitoring and moderating (monitoring for emerging threats and putting in place measures to deal with such risks as they emerge)

Penetration/vulnerability testing (ethically penetrating systems to check for vulnerabilities)

Phishing awareness (raising awareness of phishing scams)

Incident response (responding to attacks and incidents)

Digital investigation services (conducting investigations relating to digital services)

Disaster recovery (dealing with recovery following major attack)

Data compliance and protection (ensuring systems comply with data regulations and are suitably protected)

Data (mining and matching) systems for the prevention of crimes (largely fraud)

Cyber security software products (anti-virus, malware detection etc.)

Moderating websites

In the sporting world, there are a variety of enforcement bodies at national and the international level that have been created to deal with these types of behaviours. They often have their own rules which overlay national and international regulations, alongside their own investigative capacity not to mention systems of justice. In the UK, horse racing is policed by the British Horse Racing Authority (BHRA) formerly the Jockey Club. There are significant risks in horse racing of corrupt acts by those 'under the rules' of racing, such as jockeys, trainers and owners. In addition to corruption-related risks, there are also risks related to the treatment of animals, conduct in races, drugs to name some. Some of the issues it deals with are purely racing rules-related issues, such as breaching the ban on betting by jockeys. Others could potentially also be issues for the police, such as a jockey taking a bribe to not perform in a race. In 2011, 11 persons were banned from racing, including 4 jockeys for a variety of offences by the BHRA. These offences included not riding horses to their full potential, betting on races and passing information, which fall under the BHRA's corrupt offences (BBC News, 2011).

The BHRA has a staff who utilise a range of policing strategies. Central to them is an intelligence database, betting monitoring systems, surveillance at race courses to name some. Despite having no special statutory status, they assume an impressive range of powers through the rules of horse racing. Controversially, the Security Department has powers to demand access to jockeys and trainers' personal documents, such as telephone bills and betting accounts. Failure of a jockey or trainer to agree could result in a fine or even a ban (Wood, 2000).

Some sports have strong capacity at an international level dedicated to economic crimes, as well as other behaviours. Tennis has suffered from a number of scandals associated with corrupt behaviours by players. To address this, the governing bodies of tennis created the Tennis Integrity Unit (TIU) in 2008 to counter corruption amongst all 'covered persons' (players, trainers, officials etc.) globally. The TIU pursues a number of preventative strategies, which includes an education programme, preventing access to 'covered persons' by corrupt persons, betting monitoring to name some. It also investigates breaches of the 'uniform anti-corruption tennis program' rules and the investigators have the right (with consent) to interview, obtain access to laptops, phones and financial records to name some. They have had a number of notable successes, such as the player, Sergei Krotiouk, who was found to have engaged in a number of corrupt practices (not playing to best etc.) and was banned for life and fined $60,000 (TIU, 2013). Most other popular global sports have similar units, although often they are part of the broader global governing body. For instance, in cricket, the world governing body, the International Cricket Council has an Anti-Corruption Unit, which undertakes preventative and investigative work among other responsibilities (ICCACU, n.d.).

There are also a wide range of professional bodies classed as NGOs which regulate or police their professions. Some of the issues they deal with are very specific to the profession, but many involve conduct which could be considered as criminal and dealt with by the public police and sometimes are (see Button et al., 2018). Most commonly, there are integrity, fraud and corruption-related behaviours which are policed. For example, in one case dealt with by a professional accounting body, a Finance Director abused his position to defraud his employer of £250,000 using carefully planned purchasing and asset sale frauds. He was not reported to the police but was referred to the accountancy regulator, the Institute of Chartered Accountants in England and Wales, struck off, fined £25,000 and ordered to pay £33,846 in costs for the case hearing (Eastbourne Herald, 2010).

There are a wide range of NGOs that have been created to protect the revenue of certain industries and sectors of commerce. These have emerged both because of a lack of interest from the police and the need for highly specialised skills to undertake this kind of policing. One of the most prominent examples is protecting the intellectual property of organisations, where a number of NGOs have been created to help police this type of crime.

The FACT is a privately funded body with a budget of around £4 million, staff of around 50 which operates and acts very much like a private police force. Its role originated from the protection of the intellectual property of the movie sector relating to counterfeit DVDs, unlawful streaming of such content. It conducts investigations, gathers intelligence, pursues surveillance and works with the police, National Crime Agency (NCA) and trading standards officers to name most. It will work with state bodies to secure prosecutions but has also used private prosecutions. At any time, it claims to have 50 active criminal investigations on the go. The private prosecution angle will be explored further later (Button et al., 2012). As with the sporting bodies, there are also a number of global bodies operating in this area too, providing varying degrees of policing type function. Some of these include:

- International Anti-counterfeiting Coalition (a global body dedicated to fighting counterfeiting of products);
- Global Anti-Counterfeiting Network (a global body of relevant organisations created to share and work together to deal with counterfeiting);
- Audiovisual Anti-Piracy Alliance (an international trade body focused on promoting the fight against piracy in audiovisual and related areas);
- Business Software Association (an international body for the software industry, which also promotes fight against piracy).

There are also a variety of NGOs more focused upon campaigning in the economic crime area. Some organisations focused upon anti-corruption also engage in investigations and preventative work, such as Transparency International, Public Concern at Work and Corruption Watch.

Voluntary private policing capacity

Voluntary action in policing is very common through formal schemes such as the special constabulary through to individuals doing acts of policing in their own time or as a consequence of activities they are paid for (Button & Whittaker, 2021). For example, journalists are paid to write stories, but in the process, some uncover crimes which they expose lead to action. This section will show the wide diversity of voluntary contributions to fighting economic crime. Some of this contribution is more controversial and generally not supported by the state, what Johnston (1992) describes as 'autonomous citizenship', some is, 'responsible citizenship'.

Responsible citizenship

Encouraging tip-offs for economic crime is a very important part of strategies to tackle it. Many organisations have tip-off lines and some sectors have them too, as well as national level initiatives. Crimestoppers is one of the most famous examples, which encourages tip-offs and another example is the UK insurance industry, which funds the 'cheatline', through its NGO the Insurance Fraud Bureau, where people can report frauds. Some initiatives are more controversial such as the Indian 'I Paid a Bribe' website (www.ipaidabribe.com/) where victims of bribe-seeking officials can not only report them, but they are also named on the website.

In some countries, law enforcement agencies have sought to engage volunteer capacity to help counter economic crime in more formal ways. The NCA – in the UK – has sought to utilise volunteers in a much wider range of specialisms, related to some of the niche areas in which they operate. On their website, they list specials contributing in:

- cybersecurity;
- financial markets;
- specialist forensic accountancy;
- academia;
- language skills; and
- in-depth cultural awareness (NCA, n.d.).

The problem of fraud and cybercrime, however, has spawned more official initiatives to draw in volunteer action to support the state. For example, in January 2016, Hampshire Constabulary launched an initiative to recruit Cyber Special Constables and Cyber Volunteers. Volunteers were expected to contribute 16 hours per month and advise on and support digital investigations (Hampshire Constabulary, 2016).

Some groups which are outside the formal control of the state, but are supported by it, have solicited volunteers to combat economic crimes. For example, https://petscams.com/ is run by volunteers and seeks information on suspected pet scam websites, which when confirmed it uses to report to relevant authorities to close down (Whittaker & Button, 2020).

The media, through investigative journalism, has been involved in exposing a wide range of economic crime, some of which have led to successful criminal prosecutions (Andresen & Button, 2019). A wide range of television programmes and journalists pursue investigations into criminal behaviour. One of the most prominent in the UK was the so-called fake Sheikh, Mazheer Mahmood, whose investigative reporting for the newspapers the *Sunday Times* and *News of the World* led to almost 100 convictions and included notable high-profile cases such as the involvement of members of the Pakistan cricket team in corruption (Independent, 2012). Mahmood was, however, later exposed as using dubious methods and was convicted himself of conspiracy to pervert the course of justice in 2016. There have, however, been many significant examples of journalists exposing crime, some of which have led to criminal prosecutions or other sanctions by the 'public policing infra-structure'. For instance, Woodward and Bernstein and the 'Watergate' scandal in 1972 ending the Presidency of Nixon, and the 2009 *Telegraph* expose of British Member of Parliament's unethical, and in some cases, fraudulent expense claims, led to numerous resignations and a handful of successful criminal prosecutions (Button, 2019). These are just a few examples of many cases that have been investigated by journalists, which have led to police interest and prosecutions.

Some victims also investigate their own case. Shepherd (2020) describes the case where he was the victim of a significant fraud and used his own skills and time to investigate the case eventually triggering the Serious Fraud Office (SFO) to be interested and resulting in a successful prosecution and civil case which followed.

Autonomous citizenship

The other side of the voluntary contribution according to Johnston (1992) is autonomous citizenship, which covers initiatives the state is generally hostile to or finds very suspicious: governments generally frown on vigilantes taking the law into their own hands. It is important to note, however, this dichotomy has been developed from a Western Anglo-centric perspective and some of the 'responsible citizenship' initiatives above, such as media exposes of corruption, are considered as rogue vigilantism in some regimes.

The growth of the internet has hatched an assortment of organised responses to a variety of different crimes. It has even spawned new names derived from vigilantism, such as 'netilantism' and 'digilantism' (Byrne, 2013; Chang & Poon, 2017). In China, there has been growing use of the internet to expose corrupt government officials (Cheong & Gong, 2010). Such netilantism is increasingly common in China (Chang & Poon, 2017). The world of scams and particularly cyber-frauds has also spawned a variety of more organised online vigilante activists who use their websites to publicise their investigations. Some of these netilante (or digilante) groups focus on specific countries, others are more global. One prominent group, '419eater', engages in 'scambaiting', which it defines as:

> ... put simply, you enter into a dialogue with scammers, simply to waste their time and resources. Whilst you are doing this, you will be helping to keep the scammers away from real potential victims and screwing around with the minds of deserving thieves.
>
> (419eater, n.d.)

The 419eater group focuses on 419 scams but encourages action against other scam types too. The site provides news on scams and tips on how to waste the scammers' time. There are other similar groups, such as and 'RomanceScamBaiter'[1] and 'Scamorama',[2] which focus more on showcasing the variety and comedy value of some attempted scams, rather than baiting them. YouTube also provides a powerful resource for scambaiters, where many examples of scammers are placed on this website by activists.

Some scambaiters have not only wasted the time of the scammers and exposed them but also effectively implemented amusing and shaming punishments. There is often a focus on getting the scammers to display themselves naked in demeaning situations (Byrne, 2013). One article examining the practice noted how one group had convinced a scammer they were a member of the 'Church of the Painted Beast' and tricked the scammer into joining in their initiation rites, which included painting over their chests. In other cases, scammers were persuaded to draw elaborate maps of British towns by hand, tattoo themselves, and rewrite Harry Potter books by hand (Huffington Post, 2011). Inherent in some of the activities of these digilantes is racism, as Byrne (2013, p. 78) notes such activists:

> ... are indelibly bound to the binary of "white power and black deg-
> radation, of white unity and black criminality." So entrenched is this
> binary that when confronted with the opportunity to address Nigerian
> criminality, they invoke more traditional antiblack vigilante aesthetics.
> A companion to this practice is the prevalence of long-standing tropes
> as evidenced by the overwhelming appetite for trophies featuring exposed
> genitalia or references to sexual deviance or group perversion.

These types of vigilante actions tend to be facilitated online and open to the global (English speaking) community, although there may be a bias to particular countries. Such vigilante action, however, is rarely officially supported by the state police and is often viewed negatively. As little research has been conducted into these vigilante activities, further research is required to understand their contribution to private policing.

Evaluating the private contribution to policing economic crime

Earlier in this book, it was noted that around 820 police officers and 798 police staff in the UK are dedicated to economic crime (Chapter 11). Research commissioned by the Security Industry Authority estimated that there are 2,968 private investigator firms which specialise in economic crime, employing between 4,400 and 17,000 investigators (Judes, 2010). This excludes the forensic accounting capacity in accountancy firms. KPMG Forensic alone claims to employ 3,000 staff with accounting, investigation, intelligence and technology skills (KPMG, n.d.) and EY (n.d.) has 4,500 of these specialists. The Tech Partnership (2017) estimated there were 58,000 cybersecurity specialists working in the UK in 2017.

Earlier in this chapter, internally employed staff were considered. It has been estimated there could be at least 10,000 staff employed with counter fraud–related functions within the central UK government alone (Cabinet Office, 2017). Given the private sector accounts for a much bigger slice of the economy than the public sector, a figure in excess of this would seem very plausible for those dealing with fraud in the private sector. There are inherent challenges to estimating the employment of those dedicated to fighting economic crime, such as title, percentage of role relevant to economic crime, and finding accurate numbers of personnel. The brief discussion in this section does not seek to offer a definitive picture of the size of the private economic crime sector. However, the purpose is to illustrate that some individual organisations, such as KMPG and EY, can draw on more staff globally than are employed by the entire UK police to tackle economic crime. The public police thus represent the thin end of the wedge when it comes to policing economic crime. The private sector is the dominant contributor.

The size and the plurality of organisations and agents involved stresses the need for strong partnerships to tackle economic crimes. Assuming the UK is typical, there is a mixed picture when it comes to partnerships. The intellectual property crime sector has developed some very strong partnerships led by some of the organisations noted earlier. These partnerships, however, tend to be of private organisations with little or minimal state contributions. There are some niche areas of economic crime such as insurance fraud and banking fraud where the private sector funds state police, such as the Insurance Fraud Enforcement Department and the Dedicated Card and Payment Crime Unit within the City of London Police (Button, 2019). The private sector is also involved with the police and public sector bodies in intelligence-sharing initiatives. The Joint Money Laundering Intelligence Taskforce (JMLIT) run by the NCA includes 40 financial firms, regulators and the police (see Chapter 11).

At a strategic policy level, the National Fraud Authority (NFA) and then the Home Office led the 'Fighting Fraud Together' initiative which has brought together a large number of state and largely trade associations, such as the City of London Police, Cabinet Office, British Retail Consortium, Association of British Insurers and Victim Support. It produced a strategic plan with aspirational objectives which all participants signed up to (Home Office, 2011). But it fairly quickly ran out of steam and disappeared off the radar shortly after the demise of the NFA. More recently, leaders of local authorities in the UK have developed the third iteration of a strategy for 'Fighting Fraud and Corruption Locally' (Cifas, 2020). It focuses on collaboration but is still mainly consumed with setting up lots of working parties to investigate economic crime issues that impact on local authorities. The Joint Fraud Taskforce was set up by the UK government in 2016 to consider the fraud problem. It includes public sector, law enforcement and private sector representatives. Four years later, its members were still grappling with its purpose, structure and future (Home Office, 2020).The Home Office also leads an Economic Crime Board, which is similar to the Joint Fraud Taskforce in that it discusses plans to deal with economic crime, but it includes more senior people from the public and private sectors (Home Office, 2021). These initiatives are laudable, but other than raising awareness amongst civil servants and politicians, their purpose and value remains unclear.

More promising within central government in the UK, the Cabinet Office has facilitated a partnership of dozens of public bodies based upon common standards of competence, operation, sharing information and data and training (Cabinet Office, 2017). This initiative has led to the creation of the 'counter-fraud profession' within the public sector with over 10,000 members (HMG, n.d.). Though at the early stages of development, the programme provides a model for the private sector to build a coherent, participative and collaborative economic crime profession.

The initiatives described above are laudable, but ultimately partnerships are either non-existent, patchy and light in their objectives. Central to any strong partnership in countering economic crime is information sharing. The Serious Crime Act 2007 Section 68 created provisions for the public sector to share with Specified Anti-Fraud Organisations. The National Fraud Authority (2010) and Information Commissioners Office (2015) noted that there were still barriers in the public sector sharing with the private sector. Practical barriers related to how the data was held and a reluctance of private sector bodies to become involved. Private organisations do share data with one another for the purposes of preventing fraud, usually through bodies such as Cifas, the Insurance Fraud Bureau or companies such as Synectics Solutions (Button et al. 2016). Most of the sharing is legitimised by the terms and conditions that consumers agree to in, for example, insurance, banking and telecoms contracts. This enables effective sharing within the financial services sector in banking and insurance. But these areas only represent part of the economy and there is some evidence of challenges even within this sector. For example, Skidmore (2020) identified the lack of information sharing in a variety of areas, hindering the effective combatting of pension scams. Wood et al. (2021) also noted gaps in sharing information on the organised crime threat to the counter fraud community. The sharing of information is just one aspect of an effective partnership to counter economic crime. Below are some of the key ingredients, which are largely lacking, but which should form the basis of more effective partnerships across the whole economy:

- Common standards of training/character for operatives investigating economic crime: ensuring staff have appropriate character, meet minimum standards and can produce cases to the appropriate evidential requirements where sanctions are the aim.
- Forums for such staff to work together and share information, intelligence and best practice at local, sectoral and national levels.
- Strong networks to facilitate access to state agent's special powers/privileges when required.
- Partnerships built upon the totality of public, private and voluntary sectors, not just selected sectors.
- Provisions to share data ethically and legally to counter economic crimes.

- Direct links to key government/policing bodies to facilitate timely actions, regulatory and legal changes in order to respond to emerging economic crime threats.

Partnerships that exhibit some of these hallmarks have emerged within the public sector in the UK: professionalisation of counter fraud, sharing best practice, information sharing and inter-agency cooperation in investigations. However, effective partnerships within the private sector and between the private sector and the public sector are rare.

The final issue to explore regarding the private policing of economic crime is the lack of scrutiny by both academics and policymakers. In 2012, in the UK, a media storm emerged surrounding a proposal by West Midlands Police and Surrey Police for a £1.5 billion contract which was purported to cover politically sensitive services such as 'investigating crimes' and 'patrolling neighbourhoods' (Guardian, 2012). Politicians, media commentators and trade unions were united in outrage at the proposals, particularly the potential for the private sector to investigate crimes, culminating in the withdrawal of the plan. However, as this chapter and others have illustrated this is the norm for economic crimes and occurs with little outrage, controversy and scrutiny. Very few academics have ventured into critically studying the private contribution to this area (see, for example, Button, 2020; Button and Brooks, 2016; Byrne, 2013; Chang & Poon, 2017; Gottschalk, 2020). The activities of private actors deserve much greater attention, not for the sake of criticism, but for effective scrutiny and to offer perspectives on how the capacity of this substantial sector can be better harnessed to protect society from economic crime.

Conclusion

This chapter has considered the substantial involvement of the private sector in the policing of economic crime. It began by considering the concept of 'privateness' before examining some of the in-house capacity organisations create to deal with these challenges, such as internal investigators, compliance functions and brand protection to name some. The chapter then moved on to explore some of the many private actors who charge fees for offering services to deal with economic crimes from investigators to companies analysing data. NGOs were considered followed by the voluntary contribution to policing. The chapter ended with a consideration of some cross-cutting issues, such as the substantial size, partnerships and ended with a call for more academic interest in this very important area.

Notes

1 www.romancescambaiter.com.
2 www.scamorama.com.

References

Andresen, M. S., & Button, M. (2019). The profile and detection of bribery in Norway and England & Wales: A comparative study. *European Journal of Criminology*, *16*(1), 18–40.

BBC News. (2011). Four jockeys banned for corruption by BHA. www.bbc.co.uk/sport/horse-racing/16186624.

Button, M. (2019). *Private policing* (2nd ed.). Routledge.

Button, M. (2020). The "new" private security industry, the private policing of cyber-space and the regulatory questions. *Journal of Contemporary Criminal Justice*, *36*(1), 39–55.

Button, M., Blackbourn, D., & Shepherd, D. (2016). *The fraud 'justice systems': A scoping study on the civil, regulatory and private paths to 'justice' for fraudsters*. https://pure.port.ac.uk/ws/portalfiles/portal/5069284/Fraud_Justice_Systems_2016_Final_Report_1_.pdf.

Button, M., & Brooks, G. (2016). From 'shallow' to 'deep' policing: 'crash-for-cash' insurance fraud investigation in England and Wales and the need for greater regulation. *Policing and Society*, *26*(2), 210–229.

Button, M., Lewis, C., Shepherd, D., Brooks, G., & Wakefield, A. (2012). *Fraud and punishment: Enhancing deterrence through more effective sanctions - main report*. Centre for Counter Fraud Studies. https://pure.port.ac.uk/ws/portalfiles/portal/1925554/filetodownload%2C161060%2Cen.tmp.pdf.

Button, M., Shepherd, D., & Blackbourn, D. (2018). 'The iceberg beneath the sea', fraudsters and their punishment through non-criminal justice in the 'fraud justice network' in England and Wales. *International Journal of Law, Crime and Justice*, *53*(1), 56–66.

Button, M., & Whittaker, J. (2021). Exploring the voluntary response to cyber-fraud: From vigilantism to responsibilisation. *International Journal of Law, Crime and Justice*, *66*, 100482. https://doi.org/10.1016/j.ijlcj.2021.100482.

Byrne, D. N. (2013). 419 digilantes and the frontier of radical justice online. *Radical History Review*, *117*, 70–82.

Cabinet Office. (2017). *The government counter fraud profession*. Cabinet Office.

Chang, L. Y., & Poon, R. (2017). Internet vigilantism: Attitudes and experiences of university students toward cyber crowdsourcing in Hong Kong. *International Journal of Offender Therapy and Comparative Criminology*, *61*(16), 1912–1932.

Chen, Z., Yu, L., & Murray, R. (2013). Brand protection and counterfeiting in the United Kingdom and China. *International Journal of Management Cases*, *15*(4), 373–385.

Cheong, P. H., & Gong, J. (2010). Cyber vigilantism, transmedia collective intelligence, and civic participation. *Chinese Journal of Communication*, *3*(4), 471–487.

Christl, W. (2017). *Corporate surveillance in everyday life*. Cracked Labs.

Cifas. (2020). *Fighting fraud corruption locally strategy 2020*. www.cifas.org.uk/insight/public-affairs-policy/fighting-fraud-corruption-local-authorities/ffcl-strategy-2020.

Cotswold Group. (n.d.). *About us*. www.thecotswoldgroup.co.uk/about-us/.

Duff and Phelps. (n.d.). *About Duff and Phelps*. www.duffandphelps.com/about-us.

Eastbourne Herald. (2010). *Former Eastbourne boss fined £25,000*. www.eastbourneherald.co.uk/news/former-eastbourne-boss-fined-163-25-000-1-1433071.

Esoteric. (n.d.). *Services*. www.esotericltd.com/counter-surveillance-services/.

EY. (n.d.) *Assurance services.* www.ey.com/uk/en/services/assurance/fraud-investi
gation---dispute-services.

Gill, M., & Hart, J. (1997). Exploring investigative policing: A study of private
detectives in Britain. *British Journal of Criminology, 37*(4), 549–567.

Gottschalk, P. (2016). Private policing of financial crime: Fraud examiners in white-
collar crime investigations. *International Journal of Police Science & Management,
18*(3), 173–183.

Gottschalk, P. (2017). *Investigating white-collar crime.* Springer.

Gottschalk, P. (2020). Private policing of white-collar crime: Case studies of internal
investigations by fraud examiners. *Police Practice and Research, 21*(6), 717–738.

Guardian (2012) Revealed: Government plans for police privatisation. www.
theguardian.com/uk/2012/mar/02/police-privatisation-security-firms-crime.

Hampshire Constabulary. (2016). *Project recruits specialist volunteers to support fight
against cyber crime.* www.hampshire.police.uk/internet/news-and-appeals/2016/
january/200115-cyber-volunteers.

HMG. (n.d.). *Counter-fraud standards and profession.* www.gov.uk/government/
groups/counter-fraud-standards-and-profession.

Home Office. (2011). *Fighting fraud together.* https://assets.publishing.service.gov.uk/
government/uploads/system/uploads/attachment_data/file/118501/fighting-fraud-
together.pdf.

Home Office. (2020). *Joint Fraud Taskforce board minutes: 18 November 2020.* www.
gov.uk/government/publications/joint-fraud-taskforce-management-board-
minutes-2020/joint-fraud-taskforce-board-minutes-18-november-2020.

Home Office. (2021). *Economic Crime Strategic Board 17 February 2021 agenda and
minutes.* www.gov.uk/government/publications/economic-crime-strategic-board-
minutes-and-agenda-17-february-2021/economic-crime-strategic-board-17-
february-2021-agenda-and-minutes.

Huffington Post. (2011). *Nigerian email fraudsters, humbled by vigilante justice.* www.
huffingtonpost.com/jonathan-ezer/nigerian-email-fraudsters_b_544362.html.

ICCACU. (n.d.). *ICC ACU – overview.* www.icc-cricket.com/about/integrity/anti-
corruption/about-us.

Independent. (2012). *Fake Sheikh's editor fails to find evidence for his grand claim to
Leveson.* www.independent.co.uk/news/media/press/fake-sheikhs-editor-fails-to-
find-evidence-for-his-grand-claim-to-leveson-8063485.html.

Information Commissioners Office. (2015). *ICO review: Data sharing between the public
and private sector to prevent fraud.* https://ico.org.uk/media/action-weve-taken/aud
its-and-advisory-visits/1043719/ico-review-data-sharing-to-prevent-fraud.pdf.

Johnston, L. (1992). *The rebirth of private policing.* Routledge.

Judes, L. (2010) *Scoping the private investigation market: Stakeholder interviews summary.* Central Office of Information.

KPMG. (n.d.). *Forensic.* https://home.kpmg/xx/en/home/services/advisory/risk-con
sulting/forensic.html.

National Fraud Authority. (2010). *Information sharing project report on data sharing
for the prevention of fraud under section 68 of The Serious Crime Act 2007.* https://
assets.publishing.service.gov.uk/government/uploads/system/uploads/attachment_
data/file/118464/info-sharing-serious-crime-act.pdf.

NCA. (n.d.). *NCA Specials.* www.nationalcrimeagency.gov.uk/careers/specials.

Pinkerton. (n.d.). *Our history.* https://pinkerton.com/our-story/history.

Rashid, A., Danezis, G., Chivers, H., Lupu, E., & Martin, A. (2017). *Scope for the cyber security body of knowledge.* www.cybok.org/media/downloads/CyBOKScopeV2. pdf.

Shepherd, D. (2016). Complicit silence: organisations and their response to occupational fraud. PhD Thesis, University of Portsmouth.

Shepherd, D. (2020). DIY fraud investigation and access to justice: A case study. *Policing: A Journal of Policy and Practice.* https://doi-org.eres.qnl.qa/10.1093/pol ice/paaa002.

Skidmore, M. (2020). *Protecting people's pensions: Understanding and preventing scams.* Police Foundation. www.police-foundation.org.uk/2017/wp-content/uploads/2010/ 10/preventing-pension-scams-sep20.pdf.

Tech Partnership. (2017). *Factsheet: Cyber security specialists in the UK.* www.thetechpartnership.com/globalassets/pdfs/research-2017/factsheet_ cybersecurityspecialists_feb17.pdf.

Tennis Integrity Unit. (2013). *Sergei Krotiouk anti-corruption disciplinary hearing.* Tennis Integrity Unit. www.tennisintegrityunit.com/media-releases/sergei-krotiouk-anti-corruption-disciplinary-hearing.

ThreatMetrix. (2019). *Q2 2018 cybercrime report.* www.threatmetrix.com/digital-identity-insight/cybercrime-report/q2-2018-cybercrime-report/.

Tickner, P. (2012). *How to be a successful frauditor: A practical guide to investigating fraud in the workplace for internal auditors and managers.* John Wiley & Sons.

Whittaker, J. M., & Button, M. (2020). Understanding pet scams: A case study of advance fee and non-delivery fraud using victims' accounts. *Australian & New Zealand Journal of Criminology, 53*(4), 497–514.

Wood, G. (2000) Jockeys leader hits out at security purge. *The Independent,* 8 December 2000.

Wood, H., Keatinge, T., Ditcham, K., & Janjeva, A. (2021). *The silent threat: The impact of fraud on UK national security.* RUSI. www.tomkeatinge.net/uploads/1/7/8/ 4/17845871/the_silent_threat_web_version.pdf.

Conclusion

An agenda for economic criminologists and economic crime practitioners

Introduction

This final chapter provides a brief precis of the book. The chapter then sets out an agenda for practitioners and economic criminologists to better combat and understand economic crime. It starts by emphasising the importance of measurement and then looks at the importance of prevention. The focus then turns to the policing structures at a state level for the public and private sectors before considering the international dimension.

Key summary

Economic Crime: From Conception to Response has charted the origins, scope as well as the policing and regulation of economic crime. Most importantly, it has highlighted the scale, breadth and impact of economic crime. Chapter 1 began by introducing the term, defining it, exploring the origins and noting the potential scale of the problem and how – with a conservative estimate – it costs society at least 16 times more in value lost than all other traditional acquisitive crime. The chapter also made the case for greater research and for a new paradigm in criminology labelled 'economic criminology'.

Chapters 2–8 then explored each of the main categories of economic crime in depth: fraud, bribery and corruption, cartel and antitrust offences, economic cybercrime, intellectual property crime and illicit trade, industrial and economic espionage and money laundering. Each chapter illustrated in depth the nature of these crimes, the extent, the impact and the types of offenders. Chapter 9 sought to integrate various theories and research to explain why economic crime occurs. Chapter 10 then considered the law and regulation of economic crime, covering the important mix of international and national laws as well as self-regulation and collective action approaches to tackling economic crime. Two chapters then provided an overview of the policing of economic crime. Chapter 11 introduced policing by the state, drawing on examples from several countries, and international policing. Finally, the very important contribution of the private sector to the policing of economic crime

DOI: 10.4324/9781003081753-13

was examined in Chapter 12. Each of the chapters have raised a range of issues and ideas. The next section draws together the most important themes.

An agenda for economic criminologists and practitioners

Drawing together the major themes from the book, this section sets out an agenda for research and action for economic criminologists, practitioners, governments and organisations to better understand and combat economic crime.

Accurate and regular measurement of economic crime

Coherent strategies for addressing a problem are grounded on a thorough understanding of the nature and scale of the problem. As Chapter 1 illustrated, there are significant gaps in the accurate measurement of economic crime, which leads to deviancy attenuation and apathy (Button & Tunley, 2015). Accurate measurement, however, is built upon more than detected levels of economic crime. As a largely invisible crime that relies on activity to uncover, detection only reflects the effort to tackle a problem, not the size of it (Button & Gee, 2013). More innovative approaches are necessary to gauge the scale of it.

England and Wales has recently led the way by introducing fraud and computer misuse into the Crime Survey for England and Wales, thus exposing the very high crime rates against individual victims (ONS, 2021). The UK has also led the way in developing surveys of organisations, with the introduction of the annual cyber-security breaches survey and a nascent economic crime survey (yet to be published) (Department for Culture, Media and Sport & Ipsos MORI, 2021). Techniques built upon more sophisticated methods are also required such as loss measurement exercises, which have proved effective for fraud; public expenditure tracking surveys, which have been useful in corruption; and economic modelling methods, which have been used in intellectual property crime (see Button et al., 2015; Tunley, 2014). Measurement needs to focus on *all* economic crimes and cover both individuals and organisations on a *regular* basis. Only this will address the attenuating instincts of leaders that leads to apathy and immoral phlegmatism. Measurement is not just an activity to be pursued at a national level, but it is also a strategy organisations should embrace, using innovative techniques that go beyond basic detection. This will aid the macro understanding of the extent and cost of economic crime.

Focus on the prevention of economic crime and what works

The opportunity and situational characteristics of many economic crimes suggest that situational crime prevention is a useful analytical tool (Clarke,

1980). Unfortunately, there is limited research to show what works in economic crime (Prenzler, 2019). There have been attempts to apply situational crime prevention to fraud (see Graycar & Prenzler, 2013; Suh et al., 2019; Tunley et al., 2018). Many strategies are developed using techniques of situational crime prevention, but without proper evaluation of their effectiveness. It is therefore important that organisations and agencies evaluate different prevention methods and disseminate the findings. This would build a body of knowledge which can be used by practitioners to tailor the most effective response to the crime problems they face. This kind of approach is being used for traditional volume crimes – see Center for Problem-Orientated Policing – https://popcenter.asu.edu/.

Develop effective well-resourced state bodies to combat economic crime

Chapter 11 illustrated how the structure of state policing is not optimised to meet the challenges of economic crime. Policing economic crime is typically characterised by low priority, under-resourced and fractured structures (Levi, 2013). More research and debate is required to understand what the most effective structure should be (see, Button, 2021; Ryder, 2011; Skidmore et al., 2018). It is clear, however, that given the scale of economic crime, law enforcement agencies need more effective coordination as much as they need substantially more resources, to tackle what is now becoming clear as a 'national security concern' (Wood et al., 2021). Considering economic crimes have common characteristics and demand similar investigative approaches, there would be clear advantages in rationalising the number of agencies involved.

Develop strong public–private partnerships

Chapter 12 illustrated the important contribution of the private sector to combatting economic crime. There are substantial resources locked up in the private sector which could be better utilised in the fight against economic crime. Building networks of suitably trained and accredited staff, who can easily work with other private and state agents in investigations. Creating better mechanisms to enable the sharing and analysis of data as well as best practice should also be a priority. Chapter 12 also illustrated how in the UK a strong network is being created for the public sector in tackling fraud and this provides a model for the private sector to develop and to do so focused upon all economic crimes. These also provide inspiration for other countries.

Enable effective cross-border cooperation and coordination

Many economic crimes cross-borders. Some frauds involve offenders in one country, victims in another and money laundering in yet another. Counterfeit products might be manufactured in one country, marketed in another, sold in many others and then the proceeds laundered in another. Some economic crimes such as espionage and economic cybercrime involve state agencies or their surrogates targeting victims in other countries. Many economic crimes are inherently global ventures. Tackling cross-border crimes is challenging with national policing structures focused upon offending in their own countries (Cross, 2020). There are transnational structures as Chapter 11 illustrated, but like the national-level structures economic crimes are often low priority and attract limited resources. It may well be there is a case for a new global agency to lead on economic crime or more defined (and protected) capacity in an existing body (Button, 2012). Clearly, more research and consideration needs to be given to such a radical idea. However, there is clearly a case for more space, resources and priority for economic crime in existing international bodies. Central to their work should be the support of global partnerships and coordination and where they don't already exist and are needed, the creation of new structures. There should also be a focus on international 'hot spots' of economic crime to disrupt activities.

More 'economic criminology'

The ideas above have already alluded to the need for more research. As was noted in Chapter 1, 'economic criminology' draws academics from a much wider base than criminology. More criminologists need to investigate economic crimes and not just cybercrime which is one of the few areas that has been growing. Other disciplines where researchers are exploring economic crime such as business studies, computer studies law to name some need to find ways with criminologists not only to share and influence each other's work, but also to work together. Researchers also need to delve into some of the more difficult areas to research such as investigating offenders and the networks and tools they use to refine their skills, particularly in some of the more difficult geographical locations where they flourish (Gill, 2011; Lazarus, 2018; Shepherd et al., 2019; Zakari & Button, 2021). There are so many areas in economic crime where there are gaps in knowledge that need attention. Funders of research should also encourage more interest in the subject and facilitate the entrance of new contributors to this field.

Conclusion

This chapter has ended the book with a brief precis of it and an agenda for academics and practitioners to pursue to better understand and combat economic crime. The conclusion highlighted the need for accurate and regular measurement. It also suggested there must be more focus on prevention to smother the opportunities that underpin so many acts of economic crime. The agenda set out also called for more resources, for state agencies to lead on

combatting economic crime and for there to be better cooperation and coordination among those involved. It was also argued this needs to be pursued on
a global level too, to address the common cross-border elements of this crime.
Finally, the chapter called for more 'economic criminology', which hopefully
this book will inspire researchers to pursue.

References

Button, M. (2012). Cross-border fraud and the case for an "Interfraud". *Policing: An International Journal of Police Strategies & Management, 35*(2), 285–303. https://doi.org/10.1108/13639511211230057

Button, M. (2021). Hiding behind the veil of Action Fraud: The police response to economic crime in England and Wales and evaluating the case for regionalization or a National Economic Crime Agency. *Policing: A Journal of Policy and Practice.* https://doi:10.1093/police/paab022

Button, M., & Gee, J. (2013). *Countering fraud for competitive advantage: The professional approach to reducing the last great hidden cost.* John Wiley & Sons.

Button, M., Lewis, C., Shepherd, D., & Brooks, G. (2015). Fraud in overseas aid and the challenge of measurement. *Journal of Financial Crime, 22,* 184–198. https://doi.org/10.1108/JFC-02-2014-0006

Button, M., & Tunley, M. (2015). Explaining fraud deviancy attenuation in the United Kingdom. *Crime, Law and Social Change, 63*(1–2), 49–64.

Clarke, R. (1980). Situational crime prevention: Theory and practice. *British Journal of Criminology, 20*(2), 136–147.

Cross, C. (2020). 'Oh we can't actually do anything about that': The problematic nature of jurisdiction for online fraud victims. *Criminology & Criminal Justice, 20*(3), 358–375.

Department for Culture, Media and Sport & Ipsos MORI. (2021). *Cyber security breaches survey 2021.* https://assets.publishing.service.gov.uk/government/uploads/system/uploads/attachment_data/file/972399/Cyber_Security_Breaches_Survey_2021_Statistical_Release.pdf

Gill, M. (2011). Fraud and recessions: Views from fraudsters and fraud managers. *International Journal of Law, Crime & Justice, 39*(3), 204–214.

Graycar, A., & Prenzler, T. (2013). *Understanding and preventing corruption.* Palgrave MacMillan.

Lazarus, S. (2018). Birds of a feather flock together: The Nigerian cyber fraudsters (yahoo boys) and hip hop artists. *Criminology, Criminal Justice, Law & Society, 19*(2), 63–80.

Levi, M. (2013). *Regulating fraud: White-collar crime and the criminal process (Routledge revivals).* Routledge.

ONS. (2021). *Crime in England and Wales: Year ending March 2021.* ONS. www.ons.gov.uk/peoplepopulationandcommunity/crimeandjustice/bulletins/crimeinenglandandwales/yearendingmarch2021#computer-misuse

Prenzler, T. (2019). What works in fraud prevention: A review of real-world intervention projects. *Journal of Criminological Research, Policy & Practice, 6*(1), 83–96. https://doi.org/10.1108/JCRPP-04-2019-0026

Ryder, N. (2011). The fight against illicit finance: A critical review of the Labour government's policy. *Journal of Banking Regulation, 12*(3), 252–275.

Shepherd, D., Beatty, E., Button, M., & Blackbourn, D. (2019). The media, personal digital criminal legacies and the experience of offenders convicted of occupational fraud and corruption. *Journal of Criminological Research, Policy & Practice, 6*(1), 3–16. https://doi.org/10.1108/JCRPP-05-2019-0033

Skidmore, M., Ramm, J., Goldstraw-White, J., Barrett, C., Braleaza, S., Muir, R., & Gill, M. (2018). *Improving the police response to fraud.* The Police Foundation. www.police-foundation.org.uk/project/improving-the-police-response-to-fraud-2/

Suh, J. B., Nicolaides, R., & Trafford, R. (2019). The effects of reducing opportunity and fraud risk factors on the occurrence of occupational fraud in financial institutions. *International Journal of Law, Crime & Justice, 56*(1), 79–88.

Tunley, M. (2014). Mandating the measurement of fraud: legislating against loss. Springer.

Tunley, M., Button, M., Shepherd, D., & Blackbourn, D. (2018). Preventing occupational corruption: Utilising situational crime prevention techniques and theory to enhance organisational resilience. *Security Journal, 31*(1), 21–52.

Wood, H., Keatinge, T., Ditcham, K., & Janjeva, A. (2021). *The silent threat: The impact of fraud on UK national security.* RUSI. www.tomkeatinge.net/uploads/1/7/8/4/17845871/the_silent_threat_web_version.pdf

Zakari, M. B., & Button, M. (2021). Confronting the monolith: Insider accounts of the nature and techniques of corruption in Nigeria. *Journal of White Collar and Corporate Crime.* https://doi.org/10.1177/2631309X211004567

Index

Printed in the United States
by Baker & Taylor Publisher Services